Portraits from the Quattrocento

Portraits from the Quattrocento

by

EUGENIO GARIN

Translated by
Victor A. and Elizabeth Velen

Harper & Row, Publishers
New York, Evanston, San Francisco, London

These essays were originally published separately as follows:

"The Humanist Chancellors of the Florentine Republic," "Aeneas Sylvius Piccolomini," "Paolo Toscanelli," "The Cultural Background of Politian," and "Girolamo Savonarola" in "La Cultura Filosofica del Rinascimento Italiano," G. C. Sansone Editore, Florence, Italy, 1961.

"Donato Acciaiuolo, Citizen of Florence," "Images and Symbols in Marsilio Ficino," and "Florentine Culture at the Time of Leonardo" in "Medioevo e Rinascimento," Gius. Laterza & Figli, S.p.A., Bari, Italy, 1961.

"Giovanni Pico della Mirandola," Comitato per le celebrazioni centenare in onore di Giovanni Pico, Parma, Italy, 1963.

The following two essays were later republished in "Scienza e Vita Civile nel Rinascimento Italiano," Gius. Laterza & Figli, S.p.A., Bari, Italy, 1965: "The Humanist Chancellors of the Florentine Republic" and "Florentine Culture at the Time of Leonardo."

PORTRAITS FROM THE QUATTROCENTO

 For information address Harper & Row, Publishers, 49 East 33rd St., New York, N.Y. 10016. Published simultaneously in Canada by Fitzhenry & Whiteside Limited, Toronto.

First HARPER & ROW edition published 1972.

LIBRARY OF CONGRESS CATALOG CARD NUMBER: 73–159636

STANDARD BOOK NUMBER: 06–138629–4

CONTENTS

Introduction

The nine "portraits" brought together here were written within a period of little more than a decade (the major depart between 1950 and 1960), and nearly all were originally conceived as lectures or commemorative speeches. They were written, in short, for special occasions and conform to a style answering the needs of a public address. My purpose in each case was to present a major figure by correlating his life and work with the events and character of an extraordinary moment in history. Clearly, compositions of this type are necessarily limited: not all that is said is adequately discussed or documented, nor is every perspective fully developed. Further, not all of these essays express the same interpretative point of view, since they were not written consecutively, and some explanations may at times appear at odds with one another. Moreover, the fact that the various portraits were composed for diverse occasions has led to repetitions of themes, although the persistent recurrence of certain observations may perhaps serve to accentuate the constants of a period.

However, the notes, especially those that indicate primary sources and the critical literature, should obviate some of these inconveniences. In this regard, it should be borne in mind that these are sources and critical literature that were used specifically in the writing; that is, it seemed out of place to bring the citations up to date (this would not have been difficult) at the risk of contradictions arising between the text and the footnotes. Obviously the text as a whole has at no time appeared outdated in its substance and conclusions. But in a field in which the research is most active and well-nourished by historical-critical production, in the course of the years that have passed—in some instances two decades—new documents have come to light, new studies have discussed these same pages and, taking them as premises, have gone beyond them. Some examples will help to illustrate this as well as offer the possibility of adding new documentary evidence.

The discovery, which I made myself, of a remarkable collection of

Latin dialogues by Leon Battista Alberti, which had been assumed lost and which proved to be especially important, would enable one today to expand considerably one of these representations, although it supports with exceptional documentation, it seems to me, certain of my more controversial theses. The unexpected discovery of a direct dependence of some of the most unusual passages of Ariosto on the Latin writings of the more original and bizarre Alberti could not be without weight in the evaluation of various cultural phenomena. The relations between Erasmus and Machiavelli are revealed to be ever more complex and others unsuspected up to now appear and take on documentary consistency, such as, for example, some of the Italian dialogues of Giordano Bruno. Alberti, along with Erasmus, Machiavelli, Ariosto, and Bruno, shed new light on the entire Quattrocento, and certain broad interpretations that stress divisions and irreconcilable contrasts appear ever less convincing.

The enticing morsels that Vittore Branca offers of the second *Centuria* of Politian's *Miscellanea* enriches in more than one place what is written here, while the material that is being accumulated under the expert guidance of Alessandro Perosa, in the deciphering and study of the comments and notes of the great master of the Florentine Studio, now offers the basis for a well-articulated discussion of his methods, his culture, and his history.

Quite accurate research on the documents of the Studios of Florence and Pisa in the decisive years of the cultural life of the Quattrocento provides, along with a wealth of information, still more important revelations of the internal tensions and the complex variety of relationships with nonuniversity circles. The studies on Alamanno Rinuccini of Vito R. Giustiniani, and on Giannozzo Manetti of Heinz Willi Wittschier and G. M. Cagni, add new aspects to the ambience of Donato Acciaiuoli; the writings of Ermolao Barbaro, edited by Branca, give a more rounded picture of the setting in which Pico moved.[1]

This list should be extended, but just a summary mention of the continuously growing number of sources in recent years shows a rapid shift in the front of the research, so that not even a complete numerical accounting would be possible here. However, at least one other acquisition deserves mention; that is again a discovery of texts, and a sensational one: the uncovering of the manuscripts of Leonardo da Vinci by the Biblioteca Nacional of Madrid. The only "record of the works . . . locked in the chest," which is written on folio 2 *verso* of codice 8936, would now permit one to write the most ample discourse on the reading and knowledge of Leonardo, even though its conclusions might not be different.

Finally, there now exists a precious tool that is not only an exceptional aid in this type of study, but also broadens its range: the two volumes issued up to now of the *Iter Italicum* of Paul Oscar Kristeller, which encompass the Italian libraries, and whose data alone, not to speak of their indications, expand our horizon by not a little.

If one passed from the sources to the critical literature, the discussion should be longer still. On Aeneas Sylvius Piccolomini alone, since the essay included here was first written and published, a mass of material has been accumulated, stimulated among other things by the celebration of the five hundredth anniversary of his death. The study of the Florentine chancellors, variously dealt with, has been involved for reasons of its own in the recently aroused criticism of the well-known thesis of Hans Baron; noteworthy contributions have appeared on Leonardo Bruni, especially on his activity as a historiographer.[2] Works such as those of Lauro Martines on the one hand, of Christian Bec on the other, or the research of Myron P. Gilmore on *Humanists and Jurists* would have had an incisive influence on not a few of the essays gathered here. After reading the most recent work of Charles Trinkaus, I would change at least the emphasis of certain parts of this book.[3]

Some of the works mentioned have made use of or discussed the material included here, accepting or rejecting its conclusions. The author flatters himself that he is not a mute participant in such a lively dialogue nor an uninvolved spectator in the work of groundbreaking that has become ever more substantial and persistent. The essays presented here were intended to be inserted gradually into the research in progress. They are based on a constant recourse to primary sources, still unexploited in more than one case. Through an acquaintance with some of the protagonists of an especially noteworthy century, in their constant referral to a city rich in ferment, I have sought to bring to light the dominant aspects of a culture characterized by profound contrasts and dramatic scissions rather than by harmonious conclusions—but contrasts and tensions presented, without the abstract separation of "ideas," but in their living relationships, as they are condensed and take on consistency within the thoughts and feelings of men.

Current historiographical tendencies frequently make use of opposing abstractions: humanism versus science, letters versus philosophy, piety versus impiety, man against nature, renaissance and counter-renaissance. In concrete historical experience, where ideas move in the heads of men, one encounters a different reality. A notary of the *Riformagioni*, Ser Filippo Pieruzzi, who for political reasons ended up a master of Latin, compiled a scientific library of the first magnitude in Florence in the early decades of the Quattrocento. Leon Battista Alberti was a mathematician and a great humanist. Politian concerned himself, and not formally, with medicine and law, logic and metaphysics. Ficino started out with Lucretius and finished with magic and astrology. Savonarola, who was certainly not a "humanist," abandoned worldly life quoting verses of the *Aeneid* and annotated texts of Plato and Aristotle for his sermons (in a collection believed lost but which I have retraced).[4]

At closer range we see the teeming exchanges of ideas between Brunelleschi and Toscanelli and between Toscanelli and Nicholas of Cusa, and the friendship between Alberti and Toscanelli fed by convergences of interests. The positions interweave in a close dialogue in which fictitious separations do not exist. The humanist in more than one case was also a scientist and combined his ability in "letters" with the science of matter. On the other hand, in more than one case, the man of culture was dramatically divided within himself. If the image of contraposed fronts—on the one hand "grammarians," on the other, "philosophers"; here "renaissance" and there "counter-renaissance"—is only historiographical ingenuity, the reality instead is the experience of an unremitting conflict. One continues to speak of Alberti as a personality who in himself harmonized science, literature, and the arts: "the image of perfection at rest with itself," as Wölfflin has quoted Joan Gadol, the most recent student of the "universal man of the early renaissance." Whoever confronts Alberti's work in its entirety, however, gets a very different picture.[5] The anonym or the pseudonym already indicates a subtle taste for mystification, culminating in Lepidus, the false man of letters, the antique mask with which Alberti loved to conceal his own face. And everywhere a dark sense of the tragedy of life circulated, of the implacable attrition of things, of an obscure and invincible end of reality, of tranquility gained through hard work and pain as resignation in the face of the ineluctable. "Virtue" was the extreme will to struggle, destined to final defeat. A bitter memory of unhealable wounds, a childhood humiliated and endured, lent scant comfort to a life devoid of faith, redeemed only through the construction of works whose perfection and strength were a rampart vainly opposed to decadence. Time, the inexorable destroyer of things (*pervicax rerum prosternator*), would fatally reduce to dust the best-designed building, while above in the heavens a race of lighthearted and corrupt gods appeared to make merry under the reign of a distracted and silly Jove.

This is said of Alberti because he often assumed the character of almost a symbol of serene harmony. One could insist that Piccolomini (Pius II) and still earlier Salutati, or Pico with his tormented religion and his scientific anxiety, are difficult to enclose within a scheme. The truth is that these men—and not virgin ideas—lived in a period of struggle and crisis, in the Italian cities overwhelmed by dramatic conflicts, in a universe that transformed its own aspect, translating into cultural terms the harshness of an experience suffered. In this situation "letters" were utilized in the daily battle: the ancient Romans and the classic Greeks were taken up in the service of propaganda; adapted to the construction of ideologies in the field of political combat, they proved themselves no less efficacious than formations of armed knights. Certainly *libertas* and *justitia* often changed content, nor could they be translated simply as *liberty* and *justice* in the modern sense. (But even today, do they have a univocal sense; don't they vary from place to place, and in the same place from time to time, and even under the pen of the same author from moment to moment?) The fact remains—and this cannot be avoided—that those orations and letters were not schoolbook exercises, or not *only* schoolbook exercises. The speeches were pronounced from the *ringhiera* amid the tumult of the square and in the assemblies of the signori of the city; the letters were written to enemy chiefs of state. Having spoken or written, one could be banished or murdered or executed if one did not recant or be false to oneself. Machiavelli, who was no stranger to politics and arms, was to write at one time: "To persuade or dissuade a few from something is easy, because if words are not enough, you can use authority and force. But the real difficulty is to dissuade a multitude from a dangerous opinion and one that is contrary to the common good or to your opinion. Where one can use but words, these should be heard by all with the aim of persuading all. For this it is well that outstanding captains be orators, because, without knowing how to address the whole army, one can effect a good thing with difficulty."[6] "Rhetoric," without doubt; but it is exactly on the value of this rhetoric that it would be well to be more precise: for Cicero was not Quintilian, nor are the double-faced speeches of Salutati those *Dialoghi* of Bruni, nor should Guarino be confused with Valla.

To speak of "rhetoric" in reference to Salutati is easy. His speeches on the one hand for the hereditary, on the other for the elective, magistratures were obviously dialectical exercises. His official letters on "the liberty of Florence," opposed to the tyranny of the Visconti, were certainly effective pieces of rhetoric. But what does this signify? The real aims of Salutati's "rhetoric"—which form the core of his attitudes on the active or the contemplative life, on laws or medicine—were to enlist in the service of his own city all the most refined "techniques" of propaganda, to transform the myth of antiquity into an ideological function at the service of a political purpose, and to proclaim the value of "liberty" in a serious historical crisis. His positions were often antitheses which are not explained by speculations about his maturation or by changes in the times. Attitudes of dark bitterness and of calm resignation coexisted in Salutati as they coexisted in Alberti. But in what way did Chancellor Salutati utilize dialectical techniques and those of persuasion in his real activity? Was he an indifferent polemicist, or with all the passion of a *civis Florentinus* did he fashion weapons for his city, to uphold its *libertas?* Salutati himself harshly attacked in famous words the logic of the "*barbari Britanni,*" that is, the logic then dominant in the schools. And it is from that criticism, from its significance, from the contraposition of the new "rhetoric," that one should proceed as a point of departure in order to understand what the new use of tools that were otherwise not new really meant. Salutati, moreover, never intended to probe deeply a theoretical problem of great moment—precisely that of "rhetoric"—to explain the entire humanist culture. If we do not understand the significance and sense of this, too many aspects of the renaissance and of its "philosophy" escape our notice.

The truth is that the quest had by that time reached a point of crisis. Opposing the sterility of the scholastic logicians (the "nominalists" or their adversaries) was mathematics, which was emerging as the valid key to the natural sciences, precisely because numbers regulated things and the reality was constructed according to the number. On this point both the physics and the syllogistics of Aristotle were superseded, Leon Battista Alberti and Leonardo da Vinci taught. While his friend Toscanelli meditated on Archimedes, Alberti spoke of the "infinite reasons" with which nature is *inseminated* and wrote works that were to serve Leonardo. The latter, in his turn, pronounced: "There is no certainty where you cannot apply one of the mathematical sciences. . . . No one who is not a mathematician should read me. . . . Whoever deprecates the certainty of mathematics spreads confusion. . . . Proportion may be rediscovered not only in numbers and measures, but also in sounds, weights, time, and place. . . . Mechanics is the paradise of the mathematical sciences. . . ." These are famous words, but words upon which we have not perhaps reflected enough. In his lapidary style Leonardo confronted the "eternal clamor" of the discussions in which diverse opinions clashed with the "silence" that the mathematical sciences imposed on vain disputes. On the one hand was the rigor of mathematical demonstration; on the other, the flow of opinions within the forum of everyday life, in which men examined ideals and beliefs, in which fantasy jousted with sentiment and passions, in which one could convince with persuasive techniques (renouncing authority and force, thus opening the way to free choice), in which calculated necessity no longer ruled and a margin was always open to the possible. Faith and action, a world of active participation and not of pure contemplation: that active life to which the humanists pointed from Salutati on as the arena in which man gives the measure of himself.

This, then, is the field of "rhetoric." Hence, we should not speak of it generically, but as that totality of methods that the humanists specified and defined in their study of the human dialogue, with special reference to a life of action. And we should distinguish the influence of Cicero from that of Quintilian, which Valla was to choose as the invincible armor of Achilles (*tamquam Achillis armaturam*) in order to fashion from it an instrument of the "new" theology that he intended to contrapose to scholastic Aristotelianism. But only a careful examination of his "Dialectics" (especially in the first, as yet unpublished, draft[7]) gives an idea of the importance he assigned to the "new rhetoric" for a renewal of all the "moral" disciplines; only in this way, and through a very comprehensive example, will a first serious understanding of the relationship between philosophy and rhetoric be possible.

Beyond any doubt the cultural revolution of the age of humanism has especially wide manifestations in the field of education. As I have sought to demonstrate elsewhere, in a brief span of years methods, books, and schools changed. To use a well-known allusion of Ramus, in one century the world of culture became unrecognizable. Can one therefore truly believe that such a radical transformation of educational ideals and methods could come about independently of an equally fundamental modification of the conception of reality and of man's fate?[8]

This profound renewal—in all the dramatic reality of its difficult birth—found its conscious expression precisely in these men. In this lies their fascination and their greatness when, once the easy counterpositions and comfortable classifications have been abandoned, a constant dialectical tension is discovered in the place of Manichean separations. An obvious example: magic and astrology by then figured as a part both of the science of nature and of the philosophy of history, although belaboredly and not without uncertainty and regressions. The great debate defined by Pico, and on which the century closes, encompasses the entire problem of medicine and its methods, the entire relationship of man and nature, the entire question of the regularity of phenomena and of natural laws. Involved together in this were Ficino, Pico, Savonarola, and Pomponazzi. In the seventeenth century Kepler was still to feel the urgency of returning to this problem.

To discuss, not the individual horoscope of astrology, but the theory of the great conjunctions—that is, the rhythm of major events in the world, meant at the same time to elaborate a new philosophy of history. The polemic raised by Pico against the conjunctions meant to question the origin of religions, extraordinary events, the cyclic nature of historical evolution—and hence the theme itself of the *rebirth* of civilization from Albumasar to the famous *summa* of John of Eschenden. The alternate motions of Machiavelli and the historical recurrences of Vico are glimpsed in the background, but dimly, through the pathos of searing conflicts and unresolved problems.

Perhaps then the true flavor of the Quattrocento is rediscovered in the dramas of men rather than in the movement of ideas. The accent then placed on man was not rhetoric: it was a great experience. Nearly two centuries later, at the time of Newton, an English "metaphysical" poet, Thomas Traherne, was to write: "for which cause Picus Mirandula admirably saith, . . . I have read in the Monuments of Arabia, that Abdala, the Saracen, being Asked . . . What in this World was most Admirable? Answered, MAN."

Florence, April 1970 Eugenio Garin

Notes

1. L. B. Alberti, *Intercenali inedite* (Florence, 1964); C. Segre, *Esperienze ariostesche* (Pisa, 1966), pp. 85–95; V. Branca, "La seconda incompiuta Centuria dei *Miscellanea* di Angelo Poliziano." *Lettere Italiane* 13(1961): 137–77. See also I. Maïer, *Les Manuscrits d'Ange Politien* (Geneva, 1965); I. Maïer, *Ange Politien: La Formation d'un poète humaniste, 1469–1480* (Geneva, 1966); V. R. Gustiniani, *Alamanno Rinuccini, 1426–1499: Zur Geschichte des florentinischen Humanismus* (Köln-Graz, 1965); H. W. Wittschier, *Giannozzo Manetti: Das corpus der Orationes* (Köln-Graz, 1968); E. Barbaro, *De coelibatu-De officio legati*, ed. V. Branca (Florence, 1969); and G. M. Cagni, *Vespasiano de Bisticci e il suo epistolario* (Rome, 1969).

2. P. Herde, "Politik und Rhetorik in Florenz am Vorabend der Renaissance," *Archiv für Kulturgeschichte* 47(1965): 141–220; J. E. Seigel, "Civic Humanism or Ciceronian Rhetoric," *Past and Present* 34(1966): 3–48; H. Baron, "Leonardo Bruni: Professional Rhetorician or Civic Humanist?" *Past and Present* 36(1967): 21–37; J. E. Seigel, *Rhetoric and Philosophy in Renaissance Humanism* (Princeton, 1968); H. Baron, *From Petrarch to Leonardo Bruni* (Chicago and London, 1968). The appendix to this work contains the first edition of Bruni's *Laudatio Florentinae Urbis.* With particular reference to Bruni as a historian, see J. D. Wilcox, *The Development of Florentine Humanist Historiography in the Fifteenth Century* (Cambridge, Mass., 1969). For the edition of *De militia* see also C. Bayley, *War and Society in Renaissance Florence* (Toronto, 1961). On Florence, see G. Holmes, *The Florentine Enlightenment, 1400–50* (London, 1969) and G. A. Brucker, *Renaissance Florence* (New York, 1969). On Pius II, see *Enea Silvio Piccolomini-Papa Pio II*, "Atti del Convegno per il quinto centenario della morte e altri scritti raccolti da Domenico Maffei" (Siena, 1968).

3. M. Gilmore, *Humanists and Jurists* (Cambridge, Mass., 1963); L. Martines, *The Social World of the Florentine Humanists* (Princeton, 1963); Christian Bec, *Les marchands Florentins. Affaires et humanisme a Florence, 1375–1434* (Paris-The Hague, 1967); L. Martines, *Lawyers and Statecraft in Renaissance Florence* (Princeton, 1968); Charles Trinkaus, *In Our Image and Likeness: Humanity and Divinity in Italian Humanist Thought*, 2 vols. (London, 1970). See also H. A. Enno Van Gelder, *The Two Reformations in the 16th Century* (The Hague, 1964).

4. In the manuscript collection of the National Library of Florence, Conv. Soppr. D.8.985.

5. Joan Gadol, *Leon Battista Alberti: Universal Man of the Early Renaissance* (Chicago and London, 1969).

6. The text is also referred to by Hanna H. Gray, "Renaissance Humanism: The Pursuit of Eloquence," originally published in the *Journal of the History of Ideas* 24(1963), and later included in P. O. Kristeller and Philip P. Wiener, eds., *Renaissance Essays* (New York, 1968), p. 207.

7. See the manuscript of Perugia, Badia di S. Pietro, CM 53,ff. 1–87*v*.

8. *L'educazione in Europa, 1400–1600* (Bari, 1966); *L'età nuova* (Naples, 1969).

Portraits from the Quattrocento

I

The Humanist Chancellors of the Florentine Republic from Coluccio Salutati to Bartolomeo Scala*

In this illustrious city, flower of Tuscany and mirror of Italy, rival of that most glorious Rome from whom its descends, and in whose ancient footsteps it follows, fighting for the salvation of Italy and the liberty of all, here in Florence I am committed to uninterrupted but most welcome work. This is no ordinary city. I am not limited to communicating the decisions of a great people to neighboring countries: I must keep the sovereigns and the princes of the whole world informed of events.

These are the opening comments in a letter from Coluccio Salutati to Gaspare Squaro de' Broaspini, written on 17 November 1377. Broaspini was calmly pursuing his studies in Verona. Salutati, charged with a very high office in Florence, surrounded by the din of battle and factional strife at a time between the war with Gregory XI and the outbreak of the Ciompi riots,† evidently enjoyed contrasting his own feverish activity with the tranquil life of his friend: the *perpetuum negocium* of Athens in arms with the sacred idleness of the Muses.[1]‡

On April 15, 1375, the Council of the People of Florence had approved his nomination as Chancellor Secretary of the Commune,

* [Symbols indicate translator's notes.] Reference is made here to a definitive work by Demetrio Marzi, *La Cancelleria della Repubblica Fiorentina* (Rocca San Casciano, 1910), which will hereafter be referred to simply as Marzi, followed by the page number. The archives consulted were primarily the Registers of Letters of the First Chancellery, State Archives of Florence. These are indicated as follows: ASF Sig.[nori], I Cancell.[eria], Reg. (number of the Registry, followed by the page number). See also Nicolai Rubinstein, *The Government of Florence under the Medici, 1434–1494* (Oxford: Clarendon Press, 1966).

† The famous uprising of the wool carders in Florence, 1378.

‡ The author's footnotes (of which this is the first) are gathered at the end of the chapter.

replacing Ser Niccolò di Ser Ventura Monachi, who had fallen from favor. The man called to this high post was neither young nor unknown. Born forty-three years earlier at Stignano in the Val di Nievole, he had led an active life. At the Bologna school of Pietro da Muglio he had learned to esteem the great men of the century. He had always had an unreserved admiration for the poetry of Dante, and he defended the "divine" Dante against the envy of Cecco d'Ascoli. He was a friend and correspondent of Petrarch and Boccaccio. He regarded Petrarch as an unexcelled model of a man of culture, an authority on everything, including political life, capable of commanding the attention of popular tribunes, sovereigns, popes, and emperors.

Ser Coluccio's career as a notary had been arduous. In Rome, in the services of Chancellor Francesco Bruni during the Italian interval of Urban V, he established his reputation as an "intellectual" but not as a man of practical affairs. In Lucca, after 1370, he experienced the duplicities of popular regimes. He was appointed *Notaio delle Tratte** in Florence in 1374. With the chancellorship, in 1375, he finally attained an office—as he himself wrote—*magni splendoris et nominis*. It was certainly a difficult post, but not an impossible one for a man endowed with his quiet enthusiasm; its reward was that it brought him fame in his own country. "I hope," he once wrote to Benvenuto da Imola, "that one day it will be inscribed on my tomb that I had been Chancellor of Florence."[2]

In Florence he was called chancellor rather than secretary—that is, a notary inscribed in the guild of Judges and Notaries with the specific function of maintaining the records of foreign political affairs: "a chancellor who is always at his desk in the palace, writing all of the letters and notes dispatched to the world's princes or to any authority or private individual in the name of the Commune."[3] To write letters abroad was the task of a notary and rector only in appearance; in reality, according to the personality and prestige of the chancellor, it could be the most delicate function of a permanent secretary of state for foreign affairs. The form of official relations with foreign powers, including the Church, could take on decisive weight. Not only did legal science, political judgment, and diplomatic

* A notary who controlled elections and voting. See Marzi, pp. 106ff.

skill enter into play, but so did psychological insight, literary talent, and an ability to persuade.

Salutati's letters were at times careful instructions to ambassadors, at times precise directions to army officers for the disposition of troops; or then again they might assume the character of manifestos, of "white, yellow, or green papers," cleverly conceived and designed to throw light on the attitudes of the parties concerned. When Aeneas Sylvius Piccolomini praised Florentine democracy for having always chosen great chancellors, he particularly stressed the care with which sensitive posts were entrusted to specialists who were at the same time persons of great prestige. Notaries—specialists in legal science and rhetoric, as well as in the techniques of persuasive oratory and human relations—and the Florentine chancellors, whose position remained stable throughout the rapid upsets in the supreme magistrature of the Republic, represented an element of political continuity, of wisdom sustained by a specific doctrine, by personal experiences and contacts, and by friendships with officials drawn to the magic of a great name. Coluccio Salutati remained in office for over thirty years, until his death, and all evidence attests to the fact that he retained his authority with all governments, even during the gravest moments of the Ciompi crisis. The word of the chancellor, pronounced from the ringhiera, was as solemn as that of an oracle.

In another way, his political role with respect to the Commune of Florence was probably of decisive importance in the reawakening of knowledge to which Petrarch had given so profound an impetus. The first expression of humanism appeared in oratory, logic, and rhetoric, and, in conjunction with these, in morals and politics. The fact that an admirer of Petrarch, steeped in classical culture, an ardent and successful collector of ancient manuscripts, should become the chancellor of a great republic, gave an original stamp to the outward forms and, through the forms, to the entire style of the political life of a great country, At the same time it inspired a profoundly innovating cultural orientation toward a precise "civic" bent.

Whoever studies Florentine culture between the end of the Trecento and the beginning of the Quattrocento cannot but be struck by its political commitment. The "literature" of the period is imbued with a concept of the world at large, with a vision of the duties of man as a citizen. It is no coincidence that precisely in these decades Florentine culture exercised a kind of hegemony in Italy, and not only in Italy. And it is noteworthy that its influence was marked by a dedication to political values. In the war against Gregory XI, as in the life-and-death struggle against Gian Galeazzo, Salutati established the image of Florence as the heir of ancient republican Rome, the bulwark of liberty for all peoples, master and inspirer of modern Rome itself. At times, in his official letters, Salutati seems to echo the stirring tone of Cola, with the difference that the mission of Rome was now assigned to Florence.[4] In the name of liberty—that is, the value that alone makes life worth living—Florence became the ideal fatherland of men. Another chancellor, Leonardo Bruni, a pupil of Salutati, evoking a classical eulogy to Athens, aptly commented that every Italian has two fatherlands: his birthplace and Florence, the most humane city because of its humane calling. He stated further that every oppressed man, every exile, every fighter for a just cause was ideally a Florentine.[5]

The elaboration of this vision of Florence was Salutati's last great act in the life of the republic, when it still dealt as an equal with great powers. The fact that he stressed it insistently in hundreds of letters dispatched all over Europe, that this image inspired the diffusion of the new studies, that it imposed itself on magistrates and chancellors of enemy states as well, that it was proclaimed by scholars and admirers of Salutati other than Bruni, Loschi, or Uberto Decembrio, was decisive in the history of the rebirth of antique knowledge.[6] Humanism emerged stamped by this seal; its teaching was not handed down from university chairs nor disseminated abroad by the rhetoricians of refined court circles. Born with Petrarch, its highest chair was the Palazzo dei Signori of Florence; its masters were the chancellors of the republic: Coluccio Salutati, Leonardo Bruni, Carlo Marsuppini, Poggio Bracciolini, Benedetto Accolti, and Bartolomeo Scala.

Petrarch had died in 1374. From 1375 to 1406 Salutati took his place as the mentor of the most open-minded intelligentsia. Patron of wisdom and taste, researcher and interpreter of Latin learning, publicizer of Greek philosophy and poetry, he was at the same time one of the architects of the foreign policy of Florence, then still a great power. It was a dramatic moment. The Hundred Years War had reached a critical phase; the English had been driven back almost to the sea. Charles IV was dying, leaving Wenceslas in the midst of difficulties. The Church was torn between Avignon and the schism. Bernabo Visconti watched as the power of the traitorous Gian Galeazzo grew. Joan I was approaching her end. And the rivalry between Venice and Genoa was intensifying. Florence was about to enter a war against Gregory XI and was appealing for help to Pisa, Siena, Lucca, the Visconti, and Hungary. The city was to fall under interdict, and the end of the war was to witness bloody fighting in the streets and the palace put to flame by the rebellious Ciompi. Then came the mortal duel with Milan, and the relentless advance of the Count of Virtue.* "Never absent from the palace," the chancellor was on hand to advise, to persuade, to write thousands of letters. The rough drafts, frequently signed, are contained in twelve registers of the Florentine archives and are stirring documents of style, political wisdom, and humanity.[7] It is an arresting experience to read through them, to pause at the most dramatic and high-minded ones, to note the deletions, additions, and corrections, and to find in the modified, worried sentences and finally in the writing itself a mirror of his emotions. The so-called imitation of antiquity, or humanist rhetoric, about which so much nonsense has been written, loses all literary flavor when we discover a quote from a text of Cicero or Livy, a verse by Virgil or a phrase from Seneca in a moving letter to a soldier of fortune or a sovereign.

At night, at home, Salutati wrote private letters. His huge correspondence rivaled that of Petrarch, but it is impossible to distinguish private letters from official communications, dispatches from treatises. And it is astonishing that historians persist in neglecting, in the reconstruction of this important moment of humanism, one of the greatest memorials of Florentine history, until now exploited only for occasional fragmentary information. His daytime work at the palace and his work in the evening at home in his study were woven together in the activity of the great chancellor. In the files of letters of the Signori it is possible to read drafts of letters referring to ancient codices, while many private letters to princes and chancellors continue the political debate.[8] Works such as the *Invettiva* against Loschi or treatises such as the *Tiranno* are bound inextricably to the letters dispatched in the struggle against the Visconti. The same

* Gian Galleazzo Visconti derived the title "Conte de la Vertu" from his first wife, Isabella de Valois.

sentences and arguments recur. The treatises are based on experience, and experiences are articulated in an unbroken line of thought. And if in the official letters on the nomination of Luigi Marsili to the bishopric we note a tone of warm friendship, we cannot disregard the emphasis the writer places on the friar's Parisian studies, on theological doctrine consecrated by a title that is merited and not owed to privilege. Certain attacks against ecclesiastical corruption and prepotence not only recall the letters of the great Augustinian to Guido del Palagio, but also remind us that it was precisely in Florence, in 1363, that the *Defensor Pacis* by Marsilius of Padua was translated.[9]

Salutati and the hidden meaning of that great cultural movement that was at the origin of our civilization cannot be found in books that are divorced from the documentary record of an absorbing practical activity. They are constantly linked, and this constitutes their incontrovertible stamp. Here, at this meeting point, the return to the ancients is no longer mere rhetoric. And until we read the texts of these creators of the Renaissance, and the footnotes that constantly refer to their official writings—that is, to their entire active lives—we will never grasp its flavor. This is a reading that unfortunately has not yet begun.

At the time of the war of the Otto Santi,* when the chancellor addressed himself to the Romans, his evocation of an age-old history of struggle for the freedom and the unification of Italy, his appeal to the legendary ties between Rome and Florence, and his recall of the wars against the Gauls, are far from rhetorical passages. If these letters—and there are many of them—approach the finest prose of Cola and Petrarch, they always have the ring of well-conceived, effective propaganda based on a clear and conscious vision of the Italian situation. Beyond the Gauls there was the Avignon papacy and French policy to consider. The myth of Rome and the myth of Florence, its daughter and heir and the new leading state of the peninsula, have a precise significance and awaken echos that cannot be ignored, while the call to Roman history as a model event in itself constitutes a scientific basis for a theory of political action: "If we ever want to revive the ancient vigor of Italic blood in our breast, now is the time, now with a holy cause spurring us on is the moment

* The eight Florentine officials responsible for conducting the war against the Pope in 1378.

to try. Who among Italians, who among Romans, who have inherited human virtue and the love of freedom, could bear to see so many noble cities, so many castles subjected to the barbaric devastations of the French sent by the dignitaries of the Church to despoil all of Italy, to enrich themselves with our possessions and to get drunk on our blood? More cruel than the Gauls, more terrible than the Thessalians, more perfidious than the Libyans, more barbarian than the Cimbri, they have invaded Italy in the name of the Church; they are men devoid of faith, without pity, without charity; when they lack sufficient strength they rely on our discords, and incite, revive and nourish them in order to oppress us."[10]

It was a tragic moment for Salutati. He was religious, with an austere and profound faith, which he felt with all his being. In serving his city, he brought on himself the most severe condemnation of the Church, which placed him outside the communion of the faithful. But if his loyalty to the Church of Christ did not waver, this did not soften his violent accusations, among the most memorable of which was the letter to all the kings and princes denouncing the massacres of Cesena. On the one hand were the atrocities of the Breton militia of Robert of Geneva; on the other, the insistent demands of the Florentine political program: "What can we not do for liberty? It alone, in our view, makes even war legitimate." And, in contrast, was his sarcastic attitude toward the well-meaning naïveté of the Romans:

Will you wait forever for the Messiah to save Ishmael? Do you not recognize the Pope's stratagem, that while he makes you hope for his return he seeks instead to overwhelm the people in war? . . . O devout and credulous Roman souls, O admirable and pious simplicity of all Italians, in the most holy name of the Church, Italy has succumbed to a heavy and abominable yoke; oppressed and overrun by the war, facing nothing but abject ruin, it has rediscovered freedom. We ourselves, who were the first to oppose this barbarian insolence, were at the point of losing our liberty because of our devotion and our simplicity, if the cunning and perfidy of evil men had not awakened us from a deep sleep through hunger, chains, deceit and betrayal. . . . Revered brothers, we who are your flesh and blood urge you to avoid a terrible war; let us unite our forces for the common salvation of Italy; together we will redeem Latin lands without difficulty. If the Supreme Pontiff returns, he will be compelled to concede to all Italy the peace that he now denies it; if he does not come, the appeal will be made to him as well to return to a liberated and pacified Italy.[11]

In the copious and articulate letters of these years between 1375 and 1378, the chancellor set forth what were to become the main themes of his political theory: the characteristics of the tyrannical state, the foundations of civic life. He wrote to the Romans: "Every regime that does not sincerely aim to benefit the governed is necessarily transformed into a tyranny," and to the Emperor: "Nothing is so great, so noble nor so stable that it would not fall in ruins if the foundation of justice were to be weakened." In a solemn admonition to the people of Perugia, on 19 August 1384, he outlined the principles of good government: that it be in the hands of unbiased magistrates, impervious to vengeance and wrath, temperate and peaceful, who express the will of the citizens. "It is a great wrong to put at the head of the state one who displeases the people and who is not desired by the majority. It results in great harm for one to assume the functions of government who is unfit for it, who does not know how to advise his country. It is fatal to elevate to power agitators, those who tend to violence, who would be feared by the citizens for whose common welfare they should provide."[12]

At the time of the Ciompi uprising, Salultati survived the storm unharmed and maintained his position and salary as they had been before and after 1382. His attitude was the subject of a great deal of discussion. A private letter, written to Domenico di Bandino in 1378, speaks of the riots but also of *benignissimi homines quos michi videtur divine potentie digitus elegisse.** A letter to the pope on 3 February 1380 contains a long passage, later almost entirely deleted, that corresponds verbatim to the letter to Bandino; it is a eulogy to the guilds, *per quas sumus quod sumus,*† which if taken away, Salutati said, would put an end to the greatness of Florence. The excesses of the Guelf Party were contrasted to the considerable moderation of the revolutionary government, to the small number of executions and condemnations, and to the hope left even for those most guilty.[13] Coluccio forcefully upheld the idea that in free cities the people are sovereign. In Florence, a city of artisans and *mercatores* rather than knights and soldiers, a peaceful, industrious city, the guilds were governing and tyranny had to be banished. Coluccio

* "the most excellent men [the artisans], whom I would say were pointed out by the finger of God himself."

† "thanks to whom we are what we are."

constantly praised the *mercatores:* "a race of men essential to human society, without whom we could not live," he wrote to the people of Perugia in 1381. Then, nearing the end of his life, on 23 April 1405, he wrote to the members of the town council and the burgomasters of Bruges, extolling those whom he called the fathers of commerce, which he believed necessary to the world and which must be defended "*velut pupilla oculi.*"[14]

But this peace-loving people were prepared for war. Salutati defined his political ideal in 1389 in his clash with the Visconti: "We the city of the common people, dedicated solely to trade, but free, and for this reason most hated; we, who are not only loyal to liberty in our fatherland but the defenders as well of freedom beyond our borders, we want the peace necessary to conserve our sweet liberty." Thus he wrote in the manifesto to the Italians, on 25 May 1390, attacking the Milanese viper which had risen through cunning out of obscurity.[15] Gian Galeazzo had dispatched his famous ultimatum to the Florentines on 19 April 1390: "We have always sought the peace of Italy with all our strength." To which Coluccio immediately replied:

> That word, peace, which is the most important word of the letter is an impudent lie; and he declares it while invading our land. . . . Are these peaceful deeds? . . . We will declare war on the Lombard tyrant, who aspires to be anointed king, in defense of our liberty, and we take up arms to free people oppressed by such a terrible yoke. We trust in the eternal, ineffable justice of the supreme God that he may protect our city, that he may behold the misery of the Lombards, and not place the ambition of one mortal man above the liberty of the people who are immortal and the salvation of so many countries.[16]

More than ten years later, on 20 August 1401, when the threat of the Visconti was finally nearing an end, it was again Coluccio who wrote a missive to the emperor of Constantinople, who had sent Demetrios Paleologos to Florence to ask for aid against Bajazet: "We are also menaced by an Italian Bajazet, a friend and supporter of your persecutor; he aims to subject us and all of Italy to his tyranny, resorting not only to the barbarism of war but also to the deceptive stratagems of peace."

This was perhaps Coluccio's greatest moment. Political doctrines and moral ideals translated a daily experience into concrete terms and served to define and orient it. He collected the classics and put together a remarkable library. He invited the first great teacher of Greek, Manuel Chrysoloras, to come from Byzantium. His house and his city were a sanctuary for study; young people looked upon him and venerated him as a father and teacher; studies came alive in his activities as a statesman; he was not only crowned with an aura of wisdom but also renowned for unmatched competence. While Italy, Europe, and the Near East moved rapidly toward war, Florence was not only building those churches and palaces described in the prose of the chancellor in delicate and honeyed words, but was also assisting in a resurgence of culture and art that could not be explained apart from its solid connection with civic obligation. Ancient history was not read in university halls: it resounded solemnly in the communications from the Signoria to the Count of Virtue: "Please read again the history of the Romans, from whom we descend; examine their annals and think of the centuries of consular rule after the expulsion of the kings, . . . and remember Brennus, Pyrrhus, Hannibal, and Mithridates." If the power of Caesar was made legitimate by the investiture of a sovereign people, he said, the execution of a tyrant is a holy deed.[17] And Virgil is invoked in a letter to Benedetto Gambacorti: "Impending over all mortals is that fearsome crisis wherein what is immortal in us abandons what is subject to death. There is no age protected from death, nor does death pardon anyone: as the poet says, this day awaits everyone. . . . Man is like a bubble."[18]

Writing to John Hawkwood, who had embarked on a war, the chancellor transforms the history of the Signoria into a solemn chapter on virtue and success and on the folly of trusting in the superiority of arms: "Of all mortal things none is more uncertain than the outcome of wars, nothing is more unpredictable, nothing goes further beyond the thoughts of men. Victory depends neither on numbers nor on strength. . . . War will never be declared and will never be started unless implacable necessity compels us to it."[19] And for Coluccio there was only one truly compelling necessity: defense of the people's freedom. Hence his continued castigation of the mercenary militia, the plague and torment of Italy; hence, amid the clash of arms and in instructions to military leaders one recognizes his great desire for peace.

If the letters to his friends are fascinating to read, it is even more difficult to tear oneself away from the volumes of his official letters. In these Coluccio lives in his city; Florence comes alive and Florentine culture is one with its history: here the classics are educators of the people and nourish a new political practice. If in Petrarch the revival of the *humanae litterae* finds its most arresting expression and guide in discovering the unexplored regions of the soul, with Salutati it is strengthened. It becomes elaborated into a vision of life endowed with dynamic force. Florentine civilization develops harmoniously within the unity of an exemplary city. His voice, which resounds in Poland, Hungary, on the Bosporus, along the shores of Africa, in Spain, France, and England, heralds a new season of human existence.

When the entire populace accompanied their chancellor to his final resting place, on 5 May 1406, the epitaph that Coluccio had dreamed of thirty years earlier was sculptured on his tomb at Santa Maria del Fiore; but in Florence he had raised quite another monument. Although he had not produced works comparable to those of the great Trecento writers whom he admired so much, he had linked the name of Florence and its people *pene immortalis* to the diffusion of humanistic culture. The thanks given Florence in the following century by a great German university in the name of scholars all over the world was intended in large part for Chancellor Salutati.

With him the heroic age of Florentine humanism is in a certain sense concluded; after him the very close tie between politics and culture was to break. When Salutati died scores of friends and disciples could find the words to pronounce a lofty funeral oration, but finding a successor to him was another matter. Nor were Benedetto Fortini or Piero di Ser Mino da Montevarchi or Paolo Fortini certainly his peers. His only continuator, though on a different level, was Leonardo Bruni of Arezzo, who held office between 1410 and 1411 and then uninterruptedly from 1427 until his death on 8 March 1444. Under his leadership the chancellery was reformed and organized into two offices, which were then reunited under Marsuppini and again separated under Bartolomeo Scala. If the personnel as well as the work increased, this was due more to an increase in bureaucratic specialization than to political expansion. Relations with the small local centers of the state were becoming better defined, whereas relations with the great powers were falling off or changing.

Salutati was something more to Bruni than a teacher: "If I have learned Greek, Coluccio is responsible. If I have a deeper knowledge of Latin literature, it is thanks to Coluccio. If I have read, studied, known poets, orators, writers of every sort, it is due to Coluccio." The revered Coluccio was an inspiration and a father to him; from him he learned the ideals of freedom that are contained in the outline draft of the Florentine constitution addressed *ad magnum principem imperatorem:*

Popular government, which the Greeks call democracy . . . finds its likeness in the fraternal relationship. Brothers are each other's peers and equals. The basis of our government is the parity and equality of the citizens. . . . All our laws have only this aim, that the citizens be equal, because only in equality does true liberty have its roots. We therefore exclude the most powerful families from the government of the state, in order that they do not become too formidable through the possession of public power. For this reason we have established that sanctions against the nobility should be heavier and more grave.[20]

Leonardo Bruni apparently wrote these words in 1413. For him too Florence was the model city. In Florence what was of value in life was revealed to him. Here with Manuel Chrysoloras he learned Greek well enough to be able to write in Greek the treatise on the Florentine constitution, which in the only copy still extant (in the Marciana Library among the papers of Cardinal Bessarion) contains a postscript in the hand of the venerable Georgius Gemistus Pletho. In the *Laudatio* Bruni, besides describing the landscape and the art, extols the Florentine system of government: "There is no place on earth in which greater justice can be found, nor does there appear to be more liberty anywhere else, nor between the great and the small such equal conditions." The great wisdom of the republic, in his view, consisted in the greater punishment meted out to the more powerful: "Since human conditions are unequal, so too the punishments should not be equal; and [the republic] is most prudent and just that gives more aid to those in greater need." The palace [of the Signori] is the moral center of the city, "just as the ship of the commander of a fleet." At the palace the chancellor lives his great moments.[21]

Vespasiano da Bisticci relates how Leonardo Bruni, then in his eighties, during a violent debate on the exceptional decision as to whether Pope Eugene IV ought to be detained by force, mounted the ringhiera and persuaded the assembly, which had already voted to arrest the Pope, not to do so. At midnight the aged chancellor, exhausted after having spoken at length and the last to speak by right, was forced to retire. His counsel was adopted, but a citizen, profiting by his absence, spoke after him and against him. The following morning, before the decision had been ratified, "Messer Lionardo, . . . who was a man of liberal spirit, gained a foot of the stairs and made known his wish to speak to the Signoria, in the presence of this citizen." Although born in Arezzo, he said, he had made Florence his fatherland, and "he had advised it without hate or passion, as the advice of good citizens ought to be." His counsel had been given "for the benefit and ennoblement of his city, whose honor he valued as much as his own life, and he had not acted out of passion and inconsiderately, that in giving such advice one must be motivated by respect for the common good and not by private passion." "All my counsel," he continued, "in the course of so many years, I have given with that faith and love that a good citizen must have. And not only have I advised it [the city] . . . but I have honored and exalted it to the best of my feeble strength, describing its history, immortalizing it in literature and rendering it eternal. . . . But at present I address myself to . . . the person who has reproved me. . . . What advice has he given to the fatherland? What fruit has it borne? Where has he gone as ambassador?"[22]

Whether the account of Vespasiano is accurate or not, it shows clearly not only the political influence of the chancellor, but also his ideal of life. He affirmed it solemnly in his *Vita di Dante:*

> I must critize the error of many ignorant people who believe that no one is serious unless he isolates himself in solitude and contemplation; but I have never seen anyone among those removed and protected from the conversation of men who knew three words. Real intelligence does not require such subterfuges; in fact, the conclusion is certain that what is not clear at the very beginning will never become clear; so that not to take part in the exchange, to divorce oneself from it, is typical of those who have such a low degree of intelligence that they are unable to undertake anything.

For him Minerva was also armed: "The greatest philosopher cedes his place to the highest captain," he exclaimed in a speech given in the presence of the "excellent Signoria and the entire people," on the festival of St. John the Baptist in 1433.

As a philosopher he translated Aristotle and Plato, inquiring into their moral and political doctrines. He delineated in the most edifying way the new ideal of human culture and demonstrated, with the texts of the Fathers in hand, how it was not in contradiction with the word of Christ. A remarkable historian, he celebrated in the history of Florence the glory of a free people:

> I myself have pondered a long time . . . whether the deeds done or the battles fought abroad and within the city by the people of Florence, and their glorious works, accomplished in time of war and peace, should be written and immortalized. . . . I was inspired by the greatness of these deeds which this people, first in civil strife among themselves, then against neighbors, and finally in our time, with Florence grown into a major power, against the Duke of Milan and King Ladislas, both very powerful princes, have accomplished in such a way that the clash of arms has filled the length and breadth of Italy from the Alps to Apulia.

He wanted to glorify the people of Florence, but not with rhetorical praise. A *laudatio* is one thing; history is another. "History is truth" (*historia sequi veritatem debet*): "It is . . . easy, if you make a little effort, to compose a libel or a letter; but in undertaking to write a history which gives an order to various, different events, which throws light on the reasons for the positions taken and passes judgment on what has occurred, it [the truth] is as dangerous to swear to as it is difficult to observe." The truth: to this is owned the glory of Florence, "beyond the common and unfounded opinions." Ugo Foscolo said of Bruni's history: "It would bear more fruit than thirty or fifty so-called classics"; and Leonardo he called "a truthful man," who "had access to all the archives and explored them." For Bruni humanism was as the light after seven hundred years of darkness; and yet he recognized the value of the Middle Ages, and he looked for it in the birth of the city. Rome was at an end with the advent of the Caesars. Although Caesar was no ordinary man, we have only to consider the cruelty of Tiberius, the violence of Caligula, the madness of Claudius, the rage of Nero, and "doubtless we would grant that the greatness of the Romans began to decline when the name Caesar, in itself a manifestation of decay, entered the city of Rome. Since liberty gave way to the power of the empire, and following the destruction of liberty, virtue disappeared."

But the empire with its power not only extinguished the virtue of men; it also prevented the flowering of the city: "As great trees when they are close to small plants hinder their growth, so the great power of Rome put all the rest in shadow." Its ruin brought with it the immense tragedy of the invasions, but it liberated stifled energies, the multiple possibilities that had been blocked.

It is here, in his review of the long road to the ascent of Florence, that Leonardo Bruni shows the measure of his greatness as an historian; his critical use of the sources appears ever more rigorous as he approaches the centuries closest to his time. In the last three books on the duel between Florence and Gian Galleazzo he continuously draws on the records of the archives and those *Missives*, drafted in the hand of his Coluccio, which he at times transcribes to the letter. What has mistakenly been called a rhetorical work is constructed, even to the orations in Livian style, on the basis of original documents, skillfully exploited in a happy montage. Death caught him at work. "If he had lived longer," Donato Acciaiuoli wrote in his dedication for the translation into the vernacular "to the most excellent Signori Priors of Liberty and the Gonfalonier of Justice of the people of Florence," "in order to give greater benefit to the city, he himself would have translated" his work into the Italian language, "so that [the citizens], by considering past events, could better judge the present and the future, and could advise the city wisely on the needs of the republic."[23]

Although engaged in political life and faithful to republican ideals, Leonardo Bruni already belonged to a different age from that of Coluccio. If the anonymous annotator of the Sessorian Codex 1443 of Salutati's *de tyranno* could contrast Coluccio's sympathy for Caesar to Leonardo's rigid republican beliefs, it is nonetheless true that Leonardo not only assisted in the triumph of Cosimo, but also personally drew up the tragic letter to the magistrates of Siena against the exiles—an incitement to violence and persecution.[24] When the city was then thrown into turmoil, Leonardo took refuge in reading Plato and regarded the unruly factions that beat against the walls of the Florentine palaces from the melancholic retreat of already detached thought. He also spoke as an equal with lords and kings; but he was to be known as a man of culture rather than a statesman. If Salutati regarded Caesar as a sovereign recognized by the popular will, he did not have the bitter experience of serving, beyond the Priors of Liberty and the Gonfalonier of Justice, a "tyrant," however noble and great. Bruni lived to see the triumph of Cosimo and the defeat of his friends, and to see republican institutions emptied of significance. Shortly after Bruni's death on 8 May 1444, the *Notaio delle Riformagioni,** Ser Filippo Pieruzzi, was relieved of his post and sent to teach Latin to the novices of the Badia at Settimo, although it was he who had always opposed unjust burdens, and who had asked the popular assembly on 9 September 1433, in the name of the Signori, to nominate a Balía in order "to put the state in order."

Bruni's letters are certainly more elegant than those of Salutati, but they do not have the fiery passion. The negotiations for the transfer of the Council of Basle to Florence to a certain extent form the core of his comments about the city.[25] The letters to lords and remote kingdoms refer again, although in a period of the city's decline, to the untiring industry of the Florentine *mercatores,* who were engaged in commerce from Northern Europe to Pera, from North Africa to Ethiopia, Asia, and the Danubian countries. On the other hand, the elegance and refinement of the man of culture saved the politician. But the break between political and cultural life became accentuated. In a period in which "good and learned men" such as Palla di Nofri Strozzi were being expelled and were dying in exile, the ideal city dissociated itself from the real city. The alternative, which never confronted Coluccio even at the time of the interdict, was by now clearly delineated. And already on the horizon the drama which in the future would take the name of Machiavelli was clearly in evidence—the necessity for the city to lose its soul in order to save itself. The functions of the chancellor were changing; from then on he was to lose all political weight, to become a solemn ornamental figure such as Poggio Bracciolini, or a self-important executive such as Bartolomeo Scala. The second half of the century witnessed a complete change in the life of Florence.

Bruni remained outside the crisis. Giannozzo Manetti delivered the funeral oration at the chancellor's bier; the hands of the deceased held a book, just as Rossellino depicted in the monument in the church of Santa Croce. People and symbols still related to Coluccio's time. And to this moral order also belonged the notary, Ser Filippo Pieruzzi, who was banished a few months later. In some of the notary's codices his name appears alongside that of Salutati, for

* A notary in charge of the formal drafting of laws.

instance on a copy of the treatise on *Prospettiva* by John Peckham, which we can imagine in the hands of Paolo Toscanelli and Filippo Brunelleschi, as later Leonardo da Vinci was to draw his inspiration and concepts from it.

The admirable collection of ancient and medieval scientific codices of the austere *Notaio delle Riformagioni,* a friend of the great humanists and a humanist himself, is a cultural record of great importance, although it is generally neglected. These codices are still in large part among the manuscripts of San Marco that have been transferred to the Laurentian and National Libraries, and constitute a library of the highest level—Euclid, Archimedes, Ptolemy, the great Arab scientists, and medieval scientific thought. The fact that this material was accessible in Florence to learned circles, that it was collected by a notary linked with Manetti, Bruni, and Marsuppini, is not of negligible interest to anyone who wants to understand the thorough preparation of the theoreticians of the *studia humanitatis* and their relations with artists and the cultivators of the mathematical and natural sciences.[26]

It has been said that in some of these codices the signature of the owner, Ser Filippo di Ser Ugolino, follows that of Ser Coluccio, and that in many Ser Filippo's is followed by that of Cosimo. Thus the succession of events in the city is reflected on the covers of manuscripts. Pieruzzi was banished, according to Niccolò Machiavelli, because from that time on "government was by the will of the powerful." Hence, Carlo Marsuppini, a friend of Cosimo and an enemy of Filelfo, was appointed to the first chancellery succeeding Bruni in 1444. It has been rumored that it was he who tried to have Filelfo, the elegant humanist professor at the Studio, assassinated on 18 May 1433. With him in fact the duty of the chancellor became one of translating deliberations and instructions into fine Latin. It is to be hoped that in addition to the few examples extant of Marsuppini's literary activity, some of his unusual and gracious letters of recommendation will soon be added, such as the one given the oculist Christodilos of Thessalonike, whose eyewash was so excellent that it removed even the slightest *nubeculae* from the eyes of the Florentines, and hence it seemed fitting to recommend him to all princes and sovereigns so that, thanks to his cure, they might also be able to see as clearly. Not to speak of Giorgio di Giovanni Teutonico, who for thirty years blew his trumpet so well that he seemed to incorporate

Marsias, the Muses, and Apollo. In praising the good trumpetist, Marsuppini did not hesitate to refer to Pythagoras and Plato and to expound on the value of music, explaining that the soul itself is harmony and that harmony rules the universe.[27]

He was a very learned man, always with an edge of irony, perhaps of cynicism. In official letters to the Sultan, to the King of Tunis, or to other Moslem lords it was customary to use language of the utmost courtesy. Marsuppini's letter to the Sultan of May 11, 1445, is unique in this respect: not only does he extol the virtues, goodness, and wisdom of his sublimity, but adds that one sole desire burns in the breasts of the Florentines: to venerate, love, and serve the Sultan (*diligendum et amandum colendum et observandum*).[28]

Marsuppini was certainly a great intellectual and probably an effective professor. No doubt he was very dear to the Medicis. His funeral on 23 April 1453, according to descriptions, was quite sumptuous indeed; the address by Matteo Palmieri was impressive, and the monument by Desiderio da Settignano, beautiful. Among his contemporaries doubts circulated as to the fate of his soul, but present-day historians consider them unfounded.[29]

Such an air of piety did not surround the works of his successor, Poggio Bracciolini, named chancellor at the age of seventy-three. The Mediceans favored him because of his loyalty to their party; and the Florentines turned to him because of his celebrity and his eminent position in the *curia,* in which he had served for over fifty years. By that time he was more a political institution than a man. He had been a friend of all the leading men of the century. At the time of the Council of Constance he not only freed the classics from their prisons, but he also raised them to the realm of legend in a memorable letter. His travel impressions were written with incomparable elegance and contain passages of rare polemic vigor. His prose had already become the model to be followed, even by one of the most gifted writers in Italy's literary history, Aeneas Sylvius Piccolomini. His history of Florence, a truly rhetorical history, merited at least the passing notice of Machiavelli. But in 1453 Poggio was an old man, detached, somewhat skeptical, who wanted to live quietly in the country, far from the city. Machiavelli recounts an old anecdote that one evening when an important session of the Ten was dragging on, Poggio heard the clock strike. After a loud snort, he said: "I heard the clock strike nine! I want to go and eat." The world had changed.

Cosimo was also present at that session of the Ten; and it was Cosimo who was by then the protagonist of Florentine history. The old chancellor could go to dinner.

Poggio was buried without ceremony on 30 October 1459. He was a private citizen; a year before he had voluntarily stepped down from his post. Benedetto di Michele Accolti, who had been a professor of civil and canonic law in Florence since 1435, succeeded to the office on 17 April 1458. A polished writer, his *De praestantia virorum sui aevi* is a milestone in the history of humanism. He contended vigorously that antiquity was an incomparable model but that modern educators had attained a status equal to this ideal and had surpassed the wealth of antique wisdom. Accolti, who was a worthy, decorous, strict jurist and a capable official, died in 1464. His successor, who held office just prior to the turn of the century, was Bartolomeo di Giovanni Scala. The son of a miller from the Val d'Elsa, Scala was a loyal servant of the Medici. He was defeated in 1494 and then reelected along with his substitute, Pietro Beccanugi. A man of no political personality whatever and of minor stature on the cultural level, he owed his fame to events greater than himself. By that time Lorenzo, the architect of Florentine politics, had appeared on the scene. The famous letter of the Signori to Sixtus IV of 21 July 1478 stated that every risk would be taken by the people to protect Lorenzo, for everyone knew that the salvation and the freedom of the state reposed in him (*in quo publicam salutem et libertatem contineri nemo nostrum dubitare potest*).[30]

The center of Florentine politics had shifted from the Palace of the Signori to the house of the Medici. The chancellor was an official, but he was no longer a great political personality or a leading literary figure. The chancellery was packed with favorites in search of a stipend. Positions changed according to the needs of the court clientele, and the court was at the side of Lorenzo. From that time on the famous intellectuals lived there as courtiers. Scala is probably remembered most for his daughter Alessandra, a Greek and Latin scholar, for whose love Politian and Marullo, who both sang her praise in verse, contended. She married Marullo, a poet-soldier, was prematurely widowed, and while still young shut herself away in a convent. "Why do you send me pale violets?" she once asked Politian in Greek distichs. "Is he not perhaps sufficiently pallid, he whose love has drained all the blood?" But by then pale violets suited Florence.

Salutati's republic, with its clear, unambiguous geometric rationality, had given life to a rigorous and severe human culture. The great *mercatores,* the artisans, although beset by serious difficulties, were a vital, contending force. Knowledge and action converged in a harmonious relationship. The Florence of Lorenzo was tinged with the colors of sunset. Underneath apparent order deep contrasts were stirring and colliding. It was no longer the simple Christianity of Coluccio, but the equivocal Platonism of Marsilio and the orphic mysteries. The planet of the new Athens was Saturn, the symbol of melancholy, of sublime wisdom, but tormented and enigmatic: Leonardo and Michelangelo and, in the chancellery, Machiavelli.

Notes

1. Coluccio Salutati, *Epistolario,* ed. Francesco Novati, 2 vols. (Rome, 1891), 1: 277. Marzagaia, a magistrate from Verona, says of Broaspini: "before devoting himself to the most sacred luxury of the muses . . ." (*De modernis gestis lib. IV*, in C. Cipolla, *Antiche cronache veronesi* [Venice, 1890], 1: 301, in "Monum. storici R. Dep. Veneta di St. Patria," 3: 2). On Salutati as Chancellor, see Marzi, p. 106 sqq. The records of the election were published by Novati in an appendix to the collection of letters (Rome, 1911), 4: 437 sqq. With respect to his cultural formation, see F. Novati, *La Giovinezza di Coluccio Salutati (1331–1353)* (Turin, 1888). For his "policies," see A. Segre, *Alcuni elementi storici del secolo XIV nell' epistolario di Coluccio Salutati* (Turin, 1904) (based on the "private" letters published by Novati). Again for Salutati's letters, see S. Merkle, "Acht unbekannte Briefe von Coluccio Salutati," *Rivista Abruzzese* 12(1894): 558 sqq. (from Vat. Capp. 147), and the polemical reply of Novati, "Di otto inedite lettere di Coluccio Salutati," *Revista Abruzzese* (1895). On Salutati's classical education, see B. L. Ullman, "Coluccio Salutati ed i classici latini," in *Il mondo antico nel Rinascimento, Proceedings of the 5th International Convention of Renaissance Studies* (Florence, 1958), pp. 41–48; R. Weiss "Per gli studi greci di Coluccio Salutati," in *Proceedings,* pp. 49–54; and R. Weiss, "Gli studi greci di Coluccio Salutati," *Miscellanea Cessi* (Rome, 1958), 1: 349–56.

2. Salutati, *Epistolario,* 1: 203. To Benvenuto da Imola, 22 May 1375: "I think you know by this time, since news travels, that in addition to the duties to which I have been destined has also been added the honor and the burden of the Chancellery of Florence. I hope at last to prove myself not too unworthy of it. I am profoundly aware that it is above my capacities, whose limitations and defects I recognize; but I will dedicate myself to the work, as difficult and demanding as it is, with energy and enthusiasm, and I will do my best to make myself worthy of the post."

3. [Goro Dati], *ordine degli Uffici . . . ,* in Ant. Franc. Gori, *La Toscana Illustrata,* etc. (Livorno, 1755), 1: 181–88; F. P. Luiso, "Riforma della Cancelleria fiorentina nel 1437," *Archivio Storico Italiano,* series 5, vol. 21(1898). Referring to Salutati's duties at the Ufficio dell Tratto: "the chancellor is no longer only an expert in dictating letters; he is in charge of the entire dispatch of foreign affairs, and further is concerned with the administration of the commune, supervising and noting down election results, and frequently also overseeing elections to all official posts."

4. See, for example, the letter to the Romans dated 4 January, 1376 (ASF, *Sig. Miss. I Cancell.* Reg. 15, 40 *r* and *v*): "Most merciful God, who guides

events and governs the lives of men according to a scheme of absolute justice unknown to us, have mercy on humble Italy. . . ." (The letter was published by Pastor, *Storia dei Papi,* I [Rome, 1925], 1: 715–16, and it is referred to in *Il Rinascimento Italiano* [Milan, 1941], pp. 37–41, with a translation.) See also Reg. 15, 86 *r* and *v* ("What are you excellent men doing, you who should be leaders not only of Italy but of the whole world?"); Reg. 16, 67 *r* and *v* ("I recall having constantly exhorted you in my earlier letters to uphold liberty, so that you might become not only the champions of your own freedom but liberators of all Italy, for which cause your worthy and valiant forefathers fought against an overwhelming multitude of foreign foes. . . . We who glory in being descendants of the Romans, according to what one reads in our histories, souvenirs of an ancient mother . . ."); and Reg. 17, 100 *v.*

5. Leonardo Bruni, *Laudatio Florentinae urbis:* "There is no one in all of Italy who does not take it for granted that he has two fatherlands; individually, each has his own, but ideally everyone has the city of Florence." The subject is discussed by Elio Aristide; Luiso made a comparison in part in *Le vere lode de la inclita et gloriosa città di Firenze composte in Latino da Leonardo Bruni e tradotte in volgare da Frate Lazaro da Padova* (Florence, 1889), pp. 27–32. The *Laudatio* had been studied earlier in a work by Kirner, *Della "Laudatio urbis Florentinae"* (Livorno, 1889) (for some of the codices, see Luiso, *Le vere lode,* p. 63); an exhaustive study was recently undertaken by Baron, *Humanistic and Political Literature in Florence and Venice at the Beginning of the Quattrocento* (Cambridge, Mass., 1955), pp. 69–113. Baron establishes the date of its composition as the summer of 1403.

6. For the relations between Antonio Loschi and Salutati, see the letters in verse by Loschi, contained in Ms. 3977 of the University of Bologna, a.c. 27 *v;* these are verses filled with tender nostalgia: "Celestial Acquarius has already returned for the sixth time since (as fate intended it) I left that city, flourishing with wealth and proud of its genius, and the sweet soil of your fatherland; still I cannot contain my grief, nor can my eyes hold back the tears. You are always before me; your image lives in my grateful breast." With regard to Uberto Decembrio, see F. Novatti, *Anedotti Viscontei,* "Arch. stor. lomb.," 35 (1908): 192–216, and the letters from Ambros. (B 123 sup.).

7. The first registry that contained his letter is the fifteenth. (For another view, see Marzi, p. 117). A. Gherardi drew from it and includes some of its text in *La guerra dei Fiorentini con Papa Gregorio XI, detta la guerra degli Otto Santi,* a work compiled from documents of the Florentine Archives (Florence, 1868) (taken from "Arch. Stor. It.," series III, vol. 5, sqq.).

8. Reg. 22, 96 *v* contains the letter to the Marquis of Moravia (ed. Novati, 2: 427–31), which enclosed *de viris illustribus,* "[the book] on illustrious men, which our Petrarch has put out in an abbreviated version," and requested in exchange a copy of the "chronicle of the kings of Bohemia." (See Wesselofsky, *Il Paradiso degli Alberti* [Bologna, 1867], 1: 298 sqq.) A letter to the bishop of Florence, which contains a eulogy to the Blind Organist (*ab isto ceco lumen accedit*), begins with a classification of the sciences and arts, then assigns a

place to music and defines its significance (Reg. 16, 21 *r* and *v*): "and, finally, the ancients admired the art of music so much that they believed that Orpheus and Amphion could move rocks, cliffs, and trees, and could stop the flow of rivers with the sound of the lyre." Hence, among the documents concerning the Studio which escaped Gherardi's attention, the letter to the Bolognese is worthy of note (Reg. 20, 109 *r*): "Dearest brothers, since we want to assist indigent students who wish to perfect themselves in their several subjects, in order to round out their education, we have decided to allow them to pursue general studies in all the disciplines [taught] in our city, so that, when they have learned to steer their course here in a shallow bay, as it were, they may gain the courage to sail the high seas of your scholarship, which is as profound as the ocean. Nor do we doubt that, on completion of our modest introductory studies, having tried their mettle, many more [students] than you currently have will ask for admission to your famous city, to acquire there deeper learning still. Indeed, the students who are anxious to complete their studies but who have little experience in shifting for themselves do not dare seek admission to foreign schools, to which they used to flock so happily, once they were certain they could go abroad. For they cannot be assured of continuing their studies, although they can depend on funds to be forthcoming. To rectify this situation, we think that your eminent doctors, Sir Jacob of Saliceto and Master Peter of Tossignano, should be nominated to the Chair of Roman Law and to the Faculty of Medicine, respectively. Thus, with full confidence in your good will, would you be so kind as to grant them free access to Florence, in consideration of the above circumstances, and thereby do us a great favor. Your city would gain even greater renown if foreigners were to be chosen by public authority to instruct your citizens. And, not only is it warranted to compare Bologna with the cities of ancient Greece, but even to exalt it above Sparta, as well as above Athens, whose philosophers were asked to instruct foreigners. We shall rely on the goodness of your heart in considering this matter and shall be waiting for your most gracious reply. Given in Florence, on October 11th, in the VIIIth year of the Indiction, 1385. Finally, it would not merely be avaricious but dishonest to withhold the [wisdom of the] scholars from your brothers or to envy them whatever renown might reflect on them as a result of their studies. It should be added that both of the aforenamed [professors] have agreed to come; it would therefore be most shameful to break our faith with them or to invent some excuse or pretext, especially in view of the fact that you already have an abundance of famous scholars in practically every field. . . ." See F. Novati, "Sul riordinamento dello studio fiorentino nel 1385, Documenti e notizie," *Rassegna bibl. della lett. italiana,* 4(1896): 318–23. Another letter concerning the Studio, not mentioned, apparently, by Gherardi, is contained in Reg. 20. 219 *v*.

9. The official letters written with regard to Marsilius were published in part by Wesselofsky and are listed in full by C. Casari, *Notizie intorno a Luigi Marsili* (Louvain, 1900). On the theological studies undertaken in Paris, with sweat and not for privileges, see the letters dated 3 October 1385 (Reg. 20, 119 *v*–120 *v*) and 3 January 1390 (Reg. 22, 19 *r*): "not by dint of some decree,

but as a result of hard work, profuse sweat of the brow, and sleepless nights." The translation of the *Defensor Pacis* is conserved in the Laur. 44, 26 (see the introduction of Scholz, [Hannover, 1932], p. 24). The beginning was translated by Scholz as follows: "This is called the book of the defender of peace and tranquillity and was translated by franciesco [fio]rentino in the year MCCCLXIII [1363]." Yet some doubt remains, on a closer examination of the codex, concerning the supposed lacuna, and hence about *franciesco* [*in fio*]-*rentino.*

10. ASF, *Sig. Miss. I Canc.*, Reg. 16, 67: "Thus, if ever there was a cause inciting to action, all that is needed is a dispassionate look at our times; if we want to revive the ancient vigor of Italic blood in our breast, now is the time, now with a holy cause spurring us on is the moment to try. Who among Italians, who among Romans, who have inherited human virtue and the love of liberty, could bear to see so many noble cities, so many castles subjected to the barbaric devastations of the French, sent by the dignitaries of the Church to dispoil all of Italy, to enrich themselves with our possessions, and to get drunk on our blood? More cruel than the Gauls, more terrible than the Thessalians, more perfidious than the Libyans, more barbarian than the Cimbri, they have invaded Italy in the name of the Church; they are men devoid of faith, without pity, without charity; when they lack sufficient strength they rely on our discords, and incite, revive and nourish them in order to oppress us. Those again who realize they cannot keep us down through duplicity, encourage us to commit treason and in this way get what they want. They appropriate by whatever means anything of value; they search for all the treasures of Italy and carry them off in their rounds of duty, but, once acquired, they let them rot, contrary to all justice and fairness. What then will you do, you noble men, who should be concerned with the freedom of Italy, and that not only because of the state of the country at this moment, but also because you owe it to the grandeur and glory of its ancient name? Will you allow this tyranny to hold sway over us, will you tolerate barbarians and invaders to become the lords of our Latium? . . ."

11. On the massacre of Cesena, see Reg. 16, 90 sqq., "Arch. Stor. It.," series I, 15: 46; new series 8: 2; Muratori, *Rerum It. Script.*, 16: 764; *La potestà temporale dei Papi giudicata da Francesco Petrarca, de Coluccio Salutati ecc.* (Le Monnier, Florence, 1860). On the theme of freedom as the only reason for a just war, see letter to the Romans, Reg. 17, 100 *v*: "Yet, what chance is not worth taking for the sake of liberty? This, in our view, is indeed the only issue for which mortals may with justice rise up in arms. . . ." Against the Church (Reg. 16, 35 *v*): "With what guile the clergy has deceived us, in order to disrupt the unanimity of the Tuscans . . . ; the malice of the clerics . . . ; they sow dissension and hatred. . . ." On the credulity of the Romans, Reg. 15, 86 *r* and *v*: "What are you going to do, brave men, you who should be leaders not only of Italy but of the whole world? Will you wait forever for the Messiah to save Ishmael? Do you not recognize the Pope's stratagem, that while he makes you hope for his return he seeks instead to overwhelm the people in war? This was evident when, after his voyage, displaying his naval power, he

entered the port of Marseille in order to give the impression that he was taking shelter from the winter storms. Indeed, he gave this as the reason for using this as his port of call; but, soon enough, he left for his paludial Avignon as though to his rightful See. O devout and credulous Roman spirits, O simple and admirable devotion of all Italy; in reality, under the most venerable name of the Church, Italy has supported a heavy and abominable yoke; on the one hand oppressed in peace, and on the other, torn apart by war, if it's not too late, provide for its salvation and think of its freedom! We who were immersed in a sound sleep were awakened by the malice, perfidy, arms, deceptions and betrayals of the priests. Alas, were he to come bringing not peace but grim war, his coming would mean for you nothing but the desolation of his campaigns, which we know with absolute certainty he is plotting. One thing that distresses us and weighs heavier on our minds than we can say is that we don't see how such wars can ever be fought without harm to peril to the Romans. . . . Hence, devout brothers, bone of our bone and flesh of our flesh, let us join forces and unite, to the end that you may be spared the horrors of war and, being safe yourselves, may take to heart the rest of Italy. At the same time, we could set free noble Latium, where nascent liberty should make our task easy. So that, should the Pontiff come, he would be forced to sue for the peace that he now denies all Italy, and this without going to war; or, should he choose not to come, he would then be compelled by the same token to keep his hands off a free and peaceful Italy" (12 October 1376).

12. Reg. 16, 85 *r:* "For all government being but an administration solemnly committed to the welfare of the governed, it may deteriorate into a tyranny if its purpose is forgotten. . . ." Reg. 16, 71 *r:* "Since there is nothing so great, nothing so exalted, nothing so powerful that would not be doomed to perdition and ruin if it were not firmly founded in justice. . . ." Reg. 20, 17 *r:* "Great care should be taken that the power to rule not be conferred on men lacking in firmness of purpose, nor on anyone motivated by revenge, but rather on men of moderation, inclined to peace. There is no greater hazard for a republic than that it be governed by men distrusted by their subjects. It is perilous, indeed, to entrust power to men disliked by the people or to those in disfavor with the masses. It is objectionable, moreover, if a man be put in charge of others if he does not know how to rule, or a man who is incapable of giving the people the benefit of his advice. But, it should prove outright fatal if anyone is given rank or office who is bent on sedition, or someone thirsting for vengeance, or someone who stands in fear of those whom appropriately he should bend to his will. . . ."

13. Reg. 18, 108 sqq: "As for the uprising in our city, God knows. . . . We suffered the misdeeds of our fellow-citizens to be punished rather leniently, incurring thereby a manifest risk. We let off scot-free all those who at the time they ruled this noble city under the Guelfs were wont, in their arrogance, to deprive . . . of title and honor men genuinely loyal to their cause; who conspired to overthrow the government of our city, issuing orders to set it on fire and with terrible ferocity slaying their fellow citizens, all of them men beyond reproach. They also ordered the utterly harmless guilds of the

artisans to be closed down and to disgrace the entire city with the innocent blood of its artisans—although it is thanks to the artisanal guilds that we are what we are, and, should they be done away with, the very name of Florence . . . would no doubt cease to exist. The most gracious, merciful, and holy Lord God, however, has thwarted their evil plot. When this appalling conspiracy was discovered, only a handful of the leaders were made to pay with their heads, while some of the others were sent into exile. We were solemnly enjoined to abstain from making further inquiries of our magistrates as to the handling of the affair, in the belief that those that were guilty would be persuaded to reform through their pardon. . . ."

14. Reg. 19, 203 *r:* "This is the kind of man who is indispensable to the advancement of society, and, except for him, we could not exist. . . ." Reg. 26, 94: "It behooves you to safeguard those enterprises like the pupil of your eye, for they are vitally needed by all the world, while at the same time they are always profitable to yourselves. . . ."

15. Reg. 22, 67 *v* sqq: "*To the Italians:* at least the viper has had to show his fangs. At last, O brethren and dearest friends, that Ligurian serpent, emerging from his hole and hiding place, can no longer conceal his designs. Now it is clear what he was plotting to acquire through threats. Now it is all too obvious what his intentions were. The mystery of how a count is transformed into a Count of Virtue—if it is virtue to deceive, to break agreements, to want to impose tyranny over everyone—is plain for all to see; this great enigma, whose hyprocrisy is shocking, has been revealed to us. . . . Why should anyone be afraid of our republic? We are a democratic state, dedicated solely to trading; but, we are free! And, it is precisely this that is such an abomination that we are regarded as arch enemies. And it is not only that we are jealous of our own freedom at home, but we are also committed to preserve it beyond our borders. Thus it is vital for us, apart from being our normal state, to desire peace, for it is only in peace that we can keep the blessings of liberty."

16. Reg. 22, 58 *v* contains the declaration by Gian Galeazzo of 19 April ("We have sought the peace of Italy up to now with all possible diligence and firmness of purpose, sparing neither effort nor expense. . . . It was our hope that, worn out by strife, Italy in our day would once and for all settle down to peace . . ."). The answer follows (59 *v*–60 *v*): "Today we received a menacing letter through the currier of one Galeazzo Visconti [Gian Galeazzo, 1378–1402], who is called Count of Virtue and of Milan, Imperial Vicar General, etc. It is brimming with lies and distortions, and ends on a note as arrogant as it is perfidious. With respect to the content of the letter itself, he claims to have sought the peace of Italy with all diligence, as he writes, and with firmness of purpose, sparing neither effort nor expense. Although there is, indeed, at the beginning of the letter that word [peace], inserted in impudence and bad faith, he admits publicly to having launched the war against the lord of Verona . . . , and he admits also having entered into a loyal coalition with the lord of Padua. . . . We may conclude thereby that it would

be hardly opportune to engage in a verbal debate after we have been overrun, either by irregulars or in open warfare, all the more so since we put no faith whatever in the high-sounding words contained in that insolent letter of which we speak. Hence, turning the tables, we are declaring war on this Lombard tyrant, who aspires to be anointed king, in defense of our liberty, and we take up arms to free people oppressed by such a terrible yoke. We trust in the eternal, ineffable justice of the supreme God that he may protect our city, that he may behold the misery of the Lombards, and not place the ambition of one mortal man above the liberty of the people, who are immortal, and above the welfare of the towns and castles that he is keeping subjugated by force of arms" (2 May 1390). The letter to the Emperor of Constantinople is contained in Reg. 25, 51 *v*.

17. Reg. 22, 10 *r:* "Please read history again and especially the history of the Romans from whom we descend; examine their annals from the expulsion of the kings for about 560 years until the Caesars succeeded the consuls. . . ."

18. Reg. 20, 207 *v:* "Mortal man is forever faced by the chance moment of that fearful rent when what is immortal in him is severed from what is mortal; nor is there a time of life exempt from the lottery of death. Indeed, not a single man will be spared; each has his appointed day, as Virgil said. At any age, any station in life, the approach of death inspires awe; as one approaches old age one lacks as much life as the years that have transpired. As Varro said: if man is but a bubble, how much more true this is of an old man. . . ."

19. Reg. 19, 87 *r* (letter of 23 December 1380): "Of the events for which man is responsible, there is none whose results are more uncertain than war; nothing is more beclouded by ignorance, and there is nothing that turns out as unexpectedly. Nor is this anything to marvel at, for victory lies neither in the number of troops nor in the valor of the combatants. We read that Scipio Africanus said that one should never engage in hostilities unless there is some assurance of victory, or, again, unless there is some compelling necessity. Indeed, both conditions are well put, but it is truer still that war should never be unleashed at all, nor should anyone go to war unless compelled to do so by inexorable necessity. . . ." On the uncertainty of fortune, see the consoling letter to Antonio della Scala of 22 July 1381 (Reg. 19, 152 *r*). On the paid militia, the letter of 28 September 1385 should be noted (Reg. 20, 107 *r*): "Observer as we and, we are sure, all of Italy observe the way of life of the men who have dedicated themselves to the service of arms. See how many arms' workshops are operated by these unscrupulous scoundrels, and how large they are! How many of them are conspiring to set up ambushes on the highways! It is for the benefit of those very men that we till our land, that we tend our vineyards, that we sow the seed in the fertile earth, that we build our country houses, and—more insufferable than anything else—we are paying them . . . whatever is within our means, either as individuals or as members of corporate bodies, in order to buy ourselves free from duress. If only a tiny whit of that ancestral power and vigor were ours; if only we would bear in mind the example our forebears have set. . . ."

20. The text of the letter *ad magnum principem imperatorem* is published in Baron, *Humanistic and Political Literature,* pp. 181–84.

21. The ms. of the *Constituzione fiorentina* by Bruni, corrected by Pletho, is in Marciano gr. 406 (791). On this, see R. and F. Masai, "L'oeuvre de Georges Gémiste Pléthon, Rapport sur des trouvailles récents: autographes et traités inédits," *Bulletin de l'Académie royale de Belgique,* Classe des Lettres, series 5, 40(1954): 536–55. The texts of the *Laudatio* are taken from the quoted version, p. 14 sqq., p. 57 sqq.

22. Vespasiano da Bisticci, *Vite* (Florence, 1938), p. 456 sqq.

23. For Bruni's history, the translation by Donato Acciaiuoli, in the Florentine reedition (Le Monnier, 1861), was used; the specific comparisons of Santini between Bruni's text and archive documents were most useful (*Leonardo Bruni Aretino e i suoi "Historiarum Florentini populi libri XII,"* [Pisa, 1910], taken from *Annali della Scuola Normale Superiore di Pisa,* vol. 22).

24. For the marginal notes cited to *de tyranno,* see F. Ercole, *Da Bartolo all' Althusio* (Florence, 1932), p. 226 sqq. The letter to the Sienese, referred to in the text, was published by the State Archives of Siena (Concistoro, Lettere, 1436, series 1936), in the appendix to the essay by De Feo Corso, "Il Filelfo in Siena," *Bullettino Senese di Storia Patria,* 47(1940): 306. It may be found in the Panciat. 148 (of the National Library of Florence), which contains 648 official letters by Bruni up to 26 February 1444 (this is the missing registry from the State Archives). With reference to Bruni, who translated Plato while the city was beset by riots, the picture is given by Bruni himself in his dedication to the translation of Plato's letters.

25. Among others, the long letter to the Council of Basle of 15 July 1437 would be well worth studying (Panciat. 148, 68 *r*–70 *r*): "It has come to our attention that certain letters, bearing the signature and title of the Duke of Milan and defaming our republic, have been made public at the Holy Council of Basle. . . ."

26. For an initial orientation on the scientific codices, formerly belonging to the Pieruzzi family and later turned over to the Laurentian and National Libraries of Florence, see A. A. Björnbo, "Die mathematischen S. Marcohandschriften in Florenz," *Biblioteca Mathematica* 4(1903): 238–45; 6(1905): 230–38; and 12(1911–12): 97–132, 194–224.

27. ASF, *Sig. Miss. I Cancell.,* Reg. 36, 109 *v:* "Although all arts practiced by free men should be held in high regard, medicine, above all others, is worthy of our esteem. It will cure disease, heal wounds, promote our well-being; it will help to maintain us and, in fact, it will keep illness away by the use of potions. It is for these reasons that the men who had first discovered and established medicine were immortalized by the ancients. They were aware that the gifts and qualities of the soul were impaired or weakened in some way whenever the physical body was debilitated by illness or infirmity . . ."; from the same source, 165 *v:* "We can assume that everyone knows how high a place of honor the art of music was given by the ancients; in their wisdom, they put it far ahead of all others. And, should we first consider the philosophers,

we would find that Pythagoras and his disciples, who contributed so much to the understanding of music, held the view that every celestial orbit corresponded to a specific tone. It is beyond doubt, however, that the heavens and all the heavenly bodies are conjoined in an ordered, harmonious manner and in a certain numerical relationship. It may be true that the pursuit of such knowledge is reserved only for the loftiest minds, but even children may learn from simple facts of life; Nature itself shows them in earliest infancy how to delight in cradle songs and jingling bells. For this reason some believed that the human soul itself was harmony. Plato, the sage, who was gifted with almost divine wisdom, stated in his laws with utmost precision—and not without good reason—what kind of music should be played in his Republic; it was his contention that no sooner is the style of music modified than the way of life in the commonwealth will undergo changes as well. We mention in passing that Aristotle recommended the art of music as indispensable to a happy life, and also that the Greeks never considered anyone educated if he did not have a certain proficiency in this art. Epaminondas himself, as well as a great many other princes famous for their feats in peace and war, was said to have played the Greek lyre incomparably well."

28. Reg. 36, 102 *v:* "[To the Mighty Sultan] There is nothing more pleasing to God the All-powerful and Eternal, who moves the stars and rules the universe as well as the earth, than that the kingdoms, provinces, and principalities be governed with such justice, such saintliness, and such integrity that all mankind, living under the rule of law, should live in peace and multiply. Since everything taking place in your realm is spread abroad by public fame and rumor, we were inspired even before this time not only to honor and to love your Majesty, but also to venerate and to serve him. Thus, since our Republic is actively engaged in trading, apart from pursuing other goodly arts. . . ." Registry 38 contains this annotation on folio 65 *v: "ultima epistola a Carolo Aretino edita."*

29. P. G. Ricci, "Una consolatoria inedita del Marsuppini," *La Rinascita* 3(1940): 363–433.

30. Reg. 49, 52 *v* sqq. One of the registries of letters of Scala is in Palatino 1103 of the National Library of Florence. (For the *Missive dei Dieci di Balia,* see Palatino 1091.)

II
Aeneas Sylvius Piccolomini

Sum pius Aeneas—fama super aethera notus:† Aeneas Sylvius Piccolomini was thinking of Virgil and his hero and not, as commonly believed, of the saint Pope Pius I, when on 19 August 1458, following a series of dramatic clashes and shocking intrigues, the votes of the cardinals converged upon him and, the choice being made, he was asked what name he intended to take as pope.[1]* The fact is not without significance. By his own admission his adversaries in the conclave had criticized him for his past weakness for poetry. "Do we want to put a poet in the chair of St. Peter? Do we want to govern the Church according to pagan institutions?" were questions raised against him by the cardinal of Rouen, whose aim was to be elected at all costs. Piccolomini, in reply, repeated to whoever invited him to yield to the rival candidates in exchange for money and favors: "You say that [if he succeeds] he will not favor me, he will not give me a penny, he will not aid me; that I will be tormented by misery. Poverty is not hard for one who is accustomed to it. I have lived here in poverty. What evil is it if I die poor? He will not take the Muses from me, and they are sweeter when fortune is adverse."[2]

His insistence was admirable in the record of a man who always maintained that culture—the new culture acquired through the study of the ancients—was of central importance to political life. It was Piccolomini in fact who praised Florence for having chosen learned chancellors, and he recalls forcefully the singular effectiveness of Coluccio Salutati's letters. For him knowledge (understood as "human" knowledge—that is, literary and moral) in the sciences of oratory and leadership was fundamental to any political activity. For him as for Guarino da Verona, whom he knew well, the one who has the responsibility of government must be an expert in the moral disciplines, in those worldly "arts" which, taught according to the

* The author's footnotes (of which this is the first) are gathered at the end of the chapter.

† "I am the pious Aeneas whose fame is known beyond the universe."

new methods inspired by the masters of Greece and Rome, had come to occupy as privileged a position in the encyclopedia of the sciences as in the formation of the ruling classes.

It was precisely in choosing the name Pius II as pope that Piccolomini confirmed a true continuity between his own activity as a scholar and the functions of the head of the Church. Beyond renunciations and retractions, he proclaimed openly that a pupil of the Muses, a humanist, and a poet had risen to the chair of St. Peter. It is not a coincidence that the passages quoted above are taken from the writings of the pope himself—from his memoirs, which are probably his literary masterpiece, and which are certainly among the most disconcerting documents of Italian literature. The *Commentarii*, begun by the pope after his election and kept up until the last days of his life, were not published until 1584, more than a century after his death, when the Archbishop of Siena, Francesco Bandini Piccolomini, issued them under a pseudonym. Not content to present them as the work of Johann Gobelinus,* a German acquaintance of Pius II, the Archbishop mutilated and systematically revised them, expunging the most scandalous parts and carefully modifying the style. If one wants to understand the essence of the close of the Counterreformation, to see in the full light of day the distance between the cultural revolution of the Quattrocento and the post-Tridentine reaction, he has only to compare the original lucid, rigorously unbiased, splendidly effective prose of Pope Pius II with the version of his work which was published at the end of the Cinquecento and which was falsified even to the name of the author.[3]

Among the expurgated passages is naturally also the account of the 1458 cardinals' conclave left us by its protagonist. These are unsparing pages of incredible coarseness. In them the cardinals appear either weak and cowardly or grasping and prepotent. Some are pictured as overweening and arrogant, others as avid for honors and money, all of them prepared to buy and sell "without Christ, Christ's raiment." Piccolomini wrote: "A great number of cardinals congregated in the latrines and there, as in a convenient, secret and secluded place, agreed on the mode of electing William [d'Estouteville], and they pledged themselves in writing and on oath. Confident, William

* A German cleric who was commissioned to make a copy of the *Commentarii* in 1464.

then began immediately to promise posts, magistratures and honors, and to hand out dioceses. The place was worthy of the election of such a pope; where better than in the latrines could base agreements be reached?" Deals, blackmail, threats, human weaknesses are described in plain prose. The Church of Christ transformed into a "den of bandits and a house of prostitution"—to use Pius's words—provided the setting for the conflicts of that dramatic night. Piccolomini exhorted the cardinals: "The Pope of Rome is chosen by God and not by men. You, if you are Christian, will not elect as the vicar of Christ someone whom you know to be the creature of the devil." But more terrible than all the invective was the candid answer of Rodrigo Borgia. Encountering him at the end of the day, Piccolomini asked Borgia if he too had sold himself: "And what do you want me to do?" Borgia answered. "The matter is settled. Many of them have gathered in the latrines, and they have agreed to elect him. I do not intend to remain with a few outside the grace of the new pope. I am on the side of the winner, and I am tending to my own affairs. I don't want to lose the chancellery; I have already received a written promise. If I voted against him, the others would elect him anyway and I would lose the post."

In reality, behind all the intrigues, meanness, and cowardice that prompted these unworthy though highly placed men, the interests and disagreements of the great Italian and European powers weighed heavily at a dramatic moment: the house of Anjou opposed the house of Aragon over the question of Naples; the rivalry with Venice, the unending crisis of the empire; and, above all, the advice of Mohammed II, which was aided by the conflicts between the Christian states who in competing with each other sought to use the Turk to eliminate their own enemies. In this tragic hour it seemed urgent to have an energetic pope, without scruples and prepared for anything. After the election Cardinal Bessarion, the great Giovanni Bessarion, admitted this in the name of all those who had supported d'Estouteville: "The Church needs an active head, capable of moving rapidly anywhere to oppose the Turkish threat." Piccolomini at fifty-three was an old man, a sick old man. Responding to Bessarion, who had alluded to his gout, he declared ironically that he was happy that the only defect his adversaries found in him lay in his feet ("*existimasti, o Nicaene. . . . de nobis longe melius quam nos ipsi, qui nobis pedum defectum tantummodo attribuisti*").[4] Yet, though old, sick, and tired, Pius II as no one else had the firm will to realize the dream of the Nicene Cardinal: to wage war on the Turk and to reconquer the Byzantine Empire. This man—unprejudiced, without illusions about his peers, whether lay or clerical, princes or cardinals, an expert on every land and custom, who had enjoyed life in all of its possibilities and who had satisfied his passions in full—now, in his declining years, was preparing to muster all his strength for a great crusade against Islam.

It was a strange sequel to so many storms. When he was elected pope, Piccolomini had been a cardinal for barely twenty months, following an eventful career. Born on 18 October 1405 at Corsignano in the Val d'Orcia, he left his home town at the age of eighteen for Siena, where he completed his studies and set out on his adventures. It is not difficult to tell who his teachers and friends were, even though it may be difficult to determine the exact date of their meeting and the precise terms of their instruction. But certain names may be indicative: Andrea Biglia, Gregorio da Spoleto, Mariano Sozzini, and probably Francesco Filelfo were among his teachers. Panormita, Poggio, Bruni, Guarino, Aurispa were among his friends. A discussion of his relationship with Filelfo would necessarily be lengthy. There are many doubts as to the nature and location of his instruction. Filelfo later demanded money and favors of him, as was his custom; since these demands were not satisfied he accused Piccolomini of ingratitude after the latter's death. It would be difficult not to stress Piccolomini's encounter with Panormita, perhaps the most licentious writer of the century. Panormita wrote exquisite poetry and was a man of aristocratic taste in everything, including vice. Certainly we think of Panormita when we read the not very chaste *Chrysis* of Aeneas Sylvius and, above all, the history in epistolary form, *de duobus amantibus,* written in 1444, which is wrongly defined as Boccaccesque, pervaded as it is with a constant note of melancholy.

Aeneas Piccolomini did not aspire to the virtue of chastity: "*Plures vidi amavique foeminas,*" he once confessed.* A letter to Andreuccio Petrucci, written in 1432, contains the beautiful description of Genoa, "paradise of women" (*paradisus foeminarum*); while the letter contains a description of the sea that may recall a celebrated Venetian seascape by Petrarch, it also resembles, in its pleasant

* "I have beheld and loved many a woman."

lingering over feminine seductions, the charm of a famous passage by Poggio, less visually sensual but permeated with delicate voluptuousness.[5]

The resemblance to Poggio and, beyond Poggio, to the letter-writing tradition up to Petrarch, is not coincidental. In these his first writings, Piccolomini more than has perhaps been revealed, modeled himself on an illustrious tradition that sought in letters a means of expression better adapted to a new way of living and feeling. The letter was at the same time a page of a diary, a short essay, a moral treatise; it followed the deepening of the inner life in its restless worldly rhythm, but, without becoming detached from material things, it sought a balanced continuity between the horizons of thought and of nature. Petrarch, after a night of meditating over a letter, leaned out over the lagoon at the first light of dawn and saw a ship in sail toward the East, slipping away majestically from the Riva degli Schiavoni. Sentiments and ideas are mingled in his letters with towers, palaces, the colors of the lagoon, the hues of the sky. In the prose of Poggio the world of the north—snow, castles, forests, female nudes, cardinals in council, martyrs at the stake—lives in an unusual harmony which in a new form gives subtle attention to a variety of experience in which everything is caught in its human reflection and every feeling is seen extended to material things in a deliberate appeasement of the world. Nature, curiously rediscovered in all its remote and secret aspects, is as though empowered with a virginal passion to effect a union with everything in an atmosphere of joyfully realized harmony. The letters of Cyriacus of Ancona, which are continued in the diaries, are illustrative of this blending of refined culture and lively sensitivity: now an encounter and philosophical discourse in ancient Sparta when it was on the ascendent and where Hellenic philosophy lives again in Gemistus; now a transcribed epigraph, a stormy sea, an oriental market, the crocodiles of the Nile.

Aeneas Piccolomini certainly had in mind Bracciolini's landscapes: the days at Constance he deliberately compares with those at Basle. But as his political and religious involvement in its polemic vehemence already seems a contrast with the more detached curiosity of a scholarly researcher of codices, so the sense of the temporality of things, of their changeableness and variety, of the chances of fortune, acquires a different depth. Piccolomini, an accomplished man of letters, tends to bring together various components of his own life, translating them into a prose in which the finest mosaic of quotations from the ancients and allusions to contemporaries becomes an original work that goes beyond imitation or learned reminiscence. Perhaps it is precisely this sense of the changeable, of the temporal, in human variation that increasingly constitutes the true character of his work. Where Poggio indulges in abstract reflection, Piccolomini inserts a wealth of images: in a Roman landscape a snake sinuously unwinding among the ruins of an ancient palace lucidly evokes the rooms of the queens of antiquity. What occurs is not placed in a context of moral exhortation; it is lived in its consuming melancholy. Barbaric crudeness is not dwelt upon in invective but is the topic of a letter on the education of a prince, in a description of noblemen at a banquet boorishly stuffing themselves with food and drink. Like the later intrigues of the French cardinals, rather than the subject of fiery words of reproof, they were to be relegated to those nocturnal meetings in which the hidden motive, cloaked in shameful corruption, is implied in that insistence on the comings and goings in shadow-filled corridors and on the base place chosen for the gatherings—and on which the prose of the *Commentarii* dwells obsessively.

Thus in the famous epistolary novel voluptuous moods are related to the evocation of physical decadence, while the beginning and the end frame the most excitable sensuality of old age and death. It is improper for a man of forty to tell love stories to a man of fifty: "You may find enamored old men, never loved old men; mature women and girls flee from old age" (*invenies tamen et aliquos amantes senes, amatum nullum, nam et matronis est et puellis despectum senium*). The moralism is not false, nor is the tone of "playful gallantry," as some have believed.[6] This emphasis on the pains and joys of sensual love which penetrates and overwhelms the mind—this uniting of embraces and tears, intrigues, ingenuity, and cunning—is the happy reflection of a rich and passionate life which permeates Piccolomini's thought and literary expression: "I have described, not imagined; these are true things. You too have loved since you were a man. He who has never experienced the fire of love is either a stone or a beast. Well do we know that the burning flame also coursed through the veins of the gods" (*Scripsi, no finxi. Res acta est. . . . Tu etiam operam amori dedisti. . . . Homo enim fueras. Qui nunquam sensit amoris ignem aut lapis est aut bestia. Isse nanque vel per deorum medullas, non lateat, igneam favillam*).[7]

The man who in 1431, following Cardinal Domenico Capranica, bishop of Fermo, set out for the Council of Basle, where the conflict with Eugene IV was to lead to the schism, is revealed in full in his most studied writings. Piccolomini's work during the period of the Council of Basle, his writings in defense of the conciliar authority against the pope, his attitude toward Felix V, his trips as far away as Scotland would warrant a detailed analysis. On the one hand, he exemplifies the most serious clash within the Church of Rome prior to the Reformation. It is not a coincidence that *de gestis Basiliensis Concilii* of 1440 (later withdrawn in 1450 in the letter to Carvajal, *de rebus Basileae gestis stante vel dissoluto Concilio*)* was included in the antipapal collections of the most inflammatory protestant propaganda.[8] The republican, conciliar thesis found a fervent supporter in Piccolomini. Eugene had attacked the Church *ut ventus arundinem*† and had shaken it to its foundations. The authority of the Council rose in opposition to elect Amedeo of Savoy: "*o integerrimam fraternitatem; o verum orbis terrarum senatum; quam pulchra, quam suavis, quam devota res fuit, hic celebrantes episcopos, illic orantes abbates, alibi vero doctores divinas legentes historias audire, et unum ad lumen candelae scribentem cernere, alium vero grande aliquid meditantem intueri!*"‡

Aeneas Sylvius later sacrificed his republican faith and condemned the conciliar thesis in the famous papal bull, *Execrabilis*, of 19 January 1460. But he never regained the ardent fervor of his youth. He had seen the senate of the world in the schismatic fathers of Basle; after he became a monarchist he amused himself by depicting with Dantesque sarcasm the cardinals of the Holy Roman Church, reunited in the conclave from which he himself was to emerge as the vicar of Christ. His position reversed to one of disenchantment with the princes of the Church. Faith in men had led him as a young man to support the conciliar thesis; his adherence to the monarchical cause was accompanied by a deep distrust that thinly veiled a bitter

* "On matters that were dealt with in Basle during and after the Council."
† "like the wind bending a reed."
‡ "O virtuous fraternity, O true parliament of the world! How beautiful a thing it was, how pleasing, and how devout! Here were bishops celebrating mass, abbots saying their prayers; here you could listen to scholars reading sacred history, you might observe someone writing by candlelight, or come upon another deeply absorbed in meditation!"

irony. One might say that in the face of the general corruption and widespread ineptitude one could only survive through an act of submission to mysterious superhuman designs, to a divine spirit that comes and goes at will through incomprehensible and unknown ways.

The eventful voyage to Scotland took place during the period of the Council of Basle. Following a succession of stormy incidents that took him back to Italy, Aeneas transferred to the service of Cardinal Niccolò Albergati and as a member of his retinue set out for Arras where the peace negotiations between France and England, ending the Hundred Years War, were to take place. On the other side of the Great St. Bernard Pass he stopped at Ripaglia to visit the pleasant hermitage of Amedeo VIII, then passed through Basle, traveled along the Rhine, through Strasbourg, Speyer, Worms, Mainz, and Koblenz to Aachen, Liège, and Louvain, until he reached Arras. From Arras he was sent on a secret mission to the king of Scotland. This was one of the most extraordinary of all Piccolomini's travel adventures. In the combined function of secret agent and ambassador extraordinary in remote, barbarian countries; caught in storms at sea that cast him onto the shores of Norway; subjected to intolerable climates; amid political fluctuations and upheavals in the local situations that from one moment to the next transformed a friendly country into an enemy land; having to assume disguises; in escapes and perils of all sorts, Aeneas Sylvius remained the cultivated man of letters, curious about the ancient codices of London, the strange costumes of the Scotch, natural phenomena, and court customs. His travel notes conserve the grey northern landscapes, the forests, the rocks, the snow, the angry sea, the court scenes, and the usual recollections of women: "pale and beautiful women, ready for love; women's kisses there are as casual as a handshake for us" (*feminas albas, venustas atque in Venerem proclives; basiationes feminarum minoris illic esse quam manus in Italia tractationes*).[9] The chaste Archbishop Bandini was compelled to edit these pages frequently, to delete among other things the episode of the young Scotch girls who accompanied Aeneas to his couch, *dormiturae secum . . . , si rogarentur.** The pope, now that he was Pius II recalling old memories, limited himself to saying that on that particular night he was *in somno gravatum,* and *nullus ei*

* "to sleep with him . . . , if they were asked to do so."

*tunc libidinis stimulus erat,** because he was very much afraid of brigands. So that, with his mind more preoccupied with highwaymen than women, he sent the girls away. They left *murmurantes* (*non tam feminas quam latrones mente volvens, quos iam timebat affore, puellas a se murmurantes reiecit*), and he slept only *inter capras et vaccas.*† Nothing befell him, and he considered his salvation *continentiae praemium.*‡[10]

Piccolomini was a born "geographer" in the fullest sense of the word. He was interested in the conjunction between man and earth, in the link between history and its environment, between towns and their inhabitants, between places and the life that went on in them. From composed and literary descriptions similar to Poggio's (whom he certainly imitated in some of his letters) he went on to his major geographical work—not, however, confining himself to isolating and describing the natural framework of events but, beyond that, describing the works of men. Pliny and Strabo were as dear to him as were his closest friends like Guarino. The earth had been altered through so much history. Peoples, wars, migrations, cities built and destroyed, and customs all converge in a vision of the world in evolution: *historia rerum ubique gestarum locorumque descriptio.*

The work was never written; the design was too ambitious. But chapters of it remain as more or less independent essays, from *Germania* to *Europa* to *Asia,* on which he worked during his pontificate. These are arresting fragments of an imposing structure which accents the time that passes for things as well as for men and which reveals an awareness that seas, rivers, mountains, and forests, rather than providing the background for human work, are in reality woven into the fabric of human relationships and are inextricably linked to their history, which not only changes the faces of cities but is indissolubly tied to the earth. Beyond imitating the great models of antiquity, this historical-scientific research of Aeneas reveals so much new curiosity, so much eagerness to know and to do that it is understandable why, among the books annotated by Christopher Columbus, beside the classical Pliny, we find Columbus's near contemporary, Piccolomini. Thrust in the midst of wars, intrigues, and crusades,

* "overcome by sleep, and there was nothing to arouse his lust."
† "between goats and cows."
‡ "the reward of continence."

between the advancing Moslems and Christians fraternally slaughtering each other, between the disputes of theologians and jurists, Aeneas Sylvius wanted to explain the origins of situations and events, of customs and nature; to weave history out of all that is in nature.

Martin Meyr wrote to him that Germany had been impoverished by the rapacity of Rome. Here is his answer in the *descriptio de situ, ritu, moribus et conditione Germaniae:* "You say that Germany, once very rich and powerful, has been reduced to misery and impotence by the greed of the Roman Curia. We are not completely in agreement. The German nation is neither poor, nor weak, nor enslaved. In order to demonstrate this better, we will first show how things once were and how they are now. It will then be possible to determine that never has Germany had so much power. . . . Let us go back to antiquity. . . ." The proof is then elaborated within the historical development from Roman times, with a description touching upon the ways of life of various peoples, their customs, institutions, cities, and products. From this ensues the conclusion, with all its political implications: "If anyone [of the ancients] could speak, we would certainly hear him refuse to recognize Germany in this happy land; all would deny having been born in a country so full of gentility and culture. . . . All, if by chance they emerged from their tombs and if, raising their eyes and perceiving the Great Bear, the Triones and the Little Bear, could identify the sky and the stars under which they were born; but then, observing the land, the flourishing cities, the peaceful ways, agriculture, the religious rituals, they would say that this was not their fatherland, because they would not recognize its face."[11]

It is still customary to classify a large part of "humanistic" production, and history in particular, under the heading of "rhetoric" and "imitation." The work of one author who was dear to Piccolomini and who was certainly in many ways his model, Bruni's *Storia del popolo fiorentino,* despite the equivocal judgment of Croce, is in reality a great book, not only because of the profound civic spirit that animates it but also because of the reliability of the firsthand documentation, the author's experience and political commitment, and his competence which strikes one at every turn. Aeneas Sylvius is on a par with the Aretine. His great historical-geographical works, the historical monographs, the political discussions are interwoven with actual experiences and with a profound knowledge and are animated with the interest of one in high position who is accustomed to assisting or participating in great events. The combining of history with politics, of culture with action, of the works of antiquity with modern experiences is characteristic of the men who were working out with critical awareness a new technique of governing and who were preoccupied with shaping the leaders of a world that was taking shape at an important historical moment. The treatise on education is nothing other than an articulate manual for the use of whoever will have, in his capacity as a prince, the responsibility of government. And even though models of school texts are included, nothing is further from rhetoric than this work, which had as its aim the "scientific" preparation of leadership cadres for the achievement of the common good of humanity through the conscious elaboration of the moral sciences in their historical dimension.

Basle and the succession of events of the Basle period had considerably matured Aeneas Sylvius. A champion of the conciliar thesis; a supporter, laudator, and chancellor of Felix V; habitually in the company of men like Nicholas of Cusa, his polemic power and his skill in argument were nourished by an extraordinary capacity for speculative thought. The opening of the dialogues *de generalis concilii authoritate,* in which the Cardinal of Cusa himself appears among the speakers, is forceful and full of faith. "A Christian who seriously wishes to be a Christian must hold one thing above all others: to keep unsullied the purity of the religion of the fathers. Therefore, whenever evangelical traditions are attacked, all must rise in a united effort to put out the common fire. Nor does it behoove us to fear that our words will make us hated, nor should we stir up animosities. It is of little importance whether it is Paul or Peter who is drawn from the ways of the Gospel. *Quot Philippicas, quot Verrinas Eugenii scelera possent complere!*"[12]

Dispatched by Felix V to the emperor from Frankfurt to Nurnberg, in the clash between the pope and the antipope, and involved in the attempts of Frederick III at mediation, Aeneas Sylvius was able to observe firsthand the decline of the great protagonists of many centuries of history. But at the end of 1444, when news of the defeat of Varna was spread abroad, the sense of the collapse of the West must have become exceptionally acute. The Church of Christ was shaken to its foundations. Islam was advancing irresistibly from the east. The Christian world was being torn to pieces. The Europe that was the center of Piccolomini's geographical and historical works seemed to be atomized before his eyes. The centrifugal forces were exploding—forces that he himself had nourished. The secret of the conversion to the "monarchy" of a fiery "republican" is perhaps all here: in the Turkish advance and the awareness of the ruin of an ancient tradition. In 1446, in the *de ortu et autoritate Romani Imperii,* he attempted to transform into a political program what was by this time only a utopian dream: the Empire.[13] The man who saw perhaps better than anyone else the weakness of Frederick III's authority sought to revive an outmoded ideal. At the same time the man who had fought so vehemently for conciliar supremacy, after a short period of withdrawal to a neutral position did his utmost in favor of unity under the supremacy of Eugene IV. On 23 February 1447, Eugene was dying. At about this same time Aeneas Sylvius took the holy orders. "I have erred enough and more than enough," he wrote from Vienna in March 1446. "Now is the season of Lent, now the day of salvation, now the hour of grace. Put that girl of yours out of your mind. Imagine her dead. . . . I have had enough, I am fed up, I am disgusted by the thought of love. Then, after all, it's true that my forces are letting me down, that my hair is turning white, that my nerves are frayed, that my bones are drying up, that wrinkles furrow my skin, that no woman would get much pleasure out of me, nor a woman give any pleasure to me."[14]

Nicholas V was elevated to the chair of Saint Peter. Aeneas Sylvius, who was ordained a priest on 4 March 1447, became Bishop of Trieste. Felix V, the antipope, ended his days a cardinal of the Holy Roman Church. Popes, emperors, and bishops were weaving their plots. Piccolomini was named Bishop of Siena. Frederick III married Eleanor of Portugal and was crowned. The Germanic world was trembling. Revolts were multiplying. Everywhere the fire was spreading. On 19 May 1453, Constantinople fell. A shudder of horror ran through Piccolomini's letter to the Cusan. The *res publica christiana* was coming to an end, and it was not being felled by the Turkish scimitar. Germans were killing Germans, Italians were destroying Italians: *inter finitimos viget ubique simultas, immortale odium et male sanabile vulnus.** Aeneas dreamt of and called for the

* "Wherever there are neighbors, feuds will flourish, hatreds will persist, and old wounds will never heal."

crusade, and he sought to spread the new culture in the Germanic world. On 24 March 1455, Nicholas V died and was succeeded by Callixtus III. Aeneas was named cardinal of Santa Sabina and subsequently became involved in the complicated politics of Italy. At the end of 1457 Ladislas Postumus died. He was the young king of Bohemia for whom Piccolomini had written in vain the treatise on education. On 6 August 1458, Callixtus III died. And the poet Aeneas Sylvius was elected head of the Holy Roman Church.

*Europei, aut qui nomine christiano censentur.** In the little over fifty years of his life Pius II had been engaged in political activity at the highest level. He was an expert in the ups and downs of all the Italian states; he was in touch with the sovereigns of England and Scotland, with French affairs, with the emperor, with popes and antipopes, and with the kings and princes of the empire. He was now witness to the end of Christian unity as it had been conceived and realized in the Middle Ages. Behind the religious revolts of Bohemia, the independence aspirations of the curia of England, France, and Germany, the conciliar thesis, the ever more inflammatory polemics against the corruption of the clergy and the debauchery of the men of the curia, and the revolt against Roman demands for money, lurked much more serious threats to Christianity than Muhammad II. The union with the Greek Church, negotiated with extreme reluctance under the pressure of events at Ferrara and Florence, was to coincide paradoxically with an extreme tension within Christianity. Pius knew this very well.

When he drew up the draft program for moral reform in 1460, in the article *de moribus curialium* ("on the morals of the clergy"), his vision was clear and resolute: members of the curia must rid their houses of *scurras, histriones, ioculatores, lusores,* ("fops, actors, gamblers"), male and female concubines; they should be fined if found *cum scorto* ("in the company of harlots") or *per tabernas vinarias* ("in wine taverns") or if surprised blaspheming the Lord and the saints, and so forth.[15] Hostile to friars, with little faith in miracles, aware of the reasons for dissensions, he understood quite well that the same cultural orientation for which he had fought so hard was an expression of the break with medieval unity. The universality of the *humanae litterae*, about which Valla had written a stir-

* "Europeans, or those who go by the name of Christians."

ring chapter, no longer had anything to do with the unity of medieval culture. Pius II launched an attack from Vienna against barbarian and gothic Latin; but at the very moment that he exalted the pure language of Rome he recommended to the princes a full mastery of the vulgar tongues of the people they governed.

The Italian movement toward the *humanae litterae* had been an independence movement to recover the national tradition and the national history from "gothic" domination. The return to antiquity was understood as such, and as such was also systematically theoreticized. The demand for spiritual autonomy ran parallel to the claim of political autonomy. Precisely for this reason the return to the Greco-Latin language and culture was considered, not to conflict with, but to be in accord with the development of Italian culture and the Italian vernacular tongue. On the other hand, emerging as part of a period of extreme refinement and singular perfection, the new cultural orientation appeared from the start to be endowed with a powerful expansionist force and nominated itself to a central role in European reunification.

But the new Europe which was to be reborn out of the ashes of the shattered unity of the Church and Empire was something else entirely. The new Church was to be the *res publica* of learned men, the senate of the wise: those sage men that Piccolomini had dreamed of in Basle, austerely bent over their reading of the codices by candlelight. The cultural and political direction of this Europe reborn was to be achieved through a historical-scientific awareness solemnly defined by Pius II in the preface to the new encyclopedia, which he drafted under the banner of a universal geography: "*prudentia est quae vitam ducit; prudentiam vero multarum et magnarum rerum cognitio parit; quam nemo inter scriptores melius historico parit.*"*[16] The ecclesia, the new Christian republic, the new unity, should be sought beyond the dissolution of the old, just as the decrepit Empire could not aspire to become again the center of convergence of a political world that had broken up into fragments. Piccolomini's dramatic greatness is all here: he concluded his work on a note of contradiction between the ends to which he consciously aspired and

* "It is wisdom that governs life; it takes the knowledge of a great many and sublime things to acquire true wisdom. No writer knows this better than the historian."

the means he used. This Christian Europe, whose cultural unity he felt justified a unity of structures, of natural configuration, of historical traditions, had nothing more to do with the "gothic" institutions which he had attacked. Germany, so changed as to be unrecognizable to its first sons, was by this fact alone woven into a new fabric of relationships, just as the Christianity under whose banner Muhammad II was to have reorganized a new community capable of including the peoples of the Eastern Mediterranean and parts of Asia was entirely original.

The parallel between Muhammad II and Constantine the Great is among the most arresting and illuminating affirmations of Pius II. He did not doubt the superiority of the Sultan over the despots of Morea, who were corrupt, untrustworthy, inept, and contemptible, even though Christians. He knew that the cruelties and infamies committed by Christian and Catholic princes or henchmen in their pay were infinitely worse than those of the Turks. He knew perfectly well that these same Christians were serving the Turks against other Christians. Vlad, the "Voivode of Palo," a relative of Mathias Corvinus with whom Pius sought an alliance and who was continually on the verge of desertion in the struggle against Valachia, had twenty-five thousand people impaled irrespective of sex or age after the Turks had been defeated in the winter of 1461–62; this practice exterminated defenseless populations and reduced a vast Ottoman territory to ashes.[17] Nor did Ferdinand of Aragon, whom the pope recognized and with whom he was allied, have anything to envy the worst of the infidels when it came to cruelty and treachery. How could one forget the atrocious end of Lesbos, described in a letter addressed to Pius II himself by Archbishop Leonard, who had fled from a Moslem jail? While the island was being sacked and the inhabitants massacred or enslaved by the Turks, Vettore Capello, commanding a Venetian fleet of twenty-five galleys which could have destroyed without a battle the unarmed Turkish vessels, was calmly cruising off the coast and refused to give refuge to the inhabitants of conquered Mytilene. And when the victory over Lesbos was celebrated in Istanbul, the Florentines of Galata and Pera, "good friends" of the Sultan, lighted festive fires and organized public manifestations in which the Florentine ships still anchored in the Golden Horn also participated. It was no coincidence that the Florentine orators, dispatched under the leadership of San Antonino for the election of the new pope, demanded first of all that they be able to continue sending their galleys "into the lands of the infidel," even though they were running arms.[18] Pius II knew the truth; he understood the reasons and grasped their force. The crusade against the Turk, which was the program of his pontificate until his death, was an absurd and contradictory means of restoring a unity and peace that could only have been achieved laboriously through other more difficult ways, and with very different relations with the East which was advancing menacingly.

It is certainly not easy today to determine exactly the gravity of the Turkish threat, as it is not easy to reconstitute the frequently tragic atmosphere of crisis in an age which is customarily pictured as serene and harmonious, joyful and abounding in art. When the news of the fall of Constantinople was communicated to the world, there was a distinct feeling that a turning point in history had been reached—not only because a state that was decayed, corrupt, hated, and scorned in the West—a state that in turn despised the West—had disappeared, but also because it had been no less averse to the attempts at Hellenistic renaissance in the Greek lands than to any agreement with the Church of Rome. The fall of Byzantium signified the disappearance of the last trace of the medieval reincarnation of the Greco-Roman tradition. "Thereafter the hereditary enemy of the Christian faith was confined to the border between the two continents, where up to then the successor of Constantine the Great had dominated Eastern Christianity. . . . The year 1453 has been designated with good reason as the end of the Middle Ages."

Surely an historic cycle appears to have ended in an appalling disaster. An Ottoman chronicler, who usually accompanied Muhammad during his walk, relates that after the victory the Sultan climbed to the dome of Hagia Sophia. "The ruler of the world," wrote Tursun Beg, ". . . ascenced above like the spirit of God. . . . From the galleries of the middle levels he observed the undulations of the paved floor. He then mounted to the dome. When he saw that the structures adjacent to the annex of that massive building had fallen and lay in ruins, he thought that the world was transitory and that it would perish in the end." And he commented aphoristically: "The spider serves as doorkeeper at the porticos of the Cupola of Khosrau. The owl plays the music of the guards at the palace of Afrâsijâb." Whoever reads this cannot but think of the words of Pius II, on observing the ruins of the imperial palaces of Rome: "The snakes unwind in the rooms of the queens of antiquity." Of the tragic megaduke Notaras, who, faced one day with proposals for an alliance between Byzantium and the West, declared; "Better the Turkish turban than the Roman mitra in the city," and the restless Sultan, Aeneas Sylvius was probably closer to the Sultan.[19]

Pius II felt the full strength of the advancing Moslem world, and against it—that is, against the Sultan—he proposed to ally the forces of the Christian West. Only a holy war could accomplish the miracle of placating the internal discords, of re-forming with the hatred of a common enemy the moral and political unity which by then had been spent. As soon as he was elected pope, his entire activity was directed toward settling the unresolved disputes between the various states in order to initiate the crusade. His recognition of Ferdinand of Aragon was prompted by one thought: to assemble a congress to proclaim the crusade. And he departed on his journey not yet knowing whether it was to convene in Mantua or Udine. The congress opened on 1 June 1459 in Mantua (the Venetians had refused Udine as a site), but it was deserted and surrounded by distrust and antagonism. The cardinals were annoyed by the bad climate; the reigning princes were absent; their plenipotentiaries lacked authority; the Venetians and Florentines opposed the congress for commercial reasons. The first session took place only on 26 September in an uncomfortable atmosphere, despite the inspiration of the pope, whose oratory was now no longer modeled on the classics but on the psalms:

Ecce inimici tui sonuerunt,
Et qui oderunt te extulerunt caput.
Superbiunt Constantinopolitana victoria hostes tui
Et, manus nostrae, inquiunt, non dominus fecit haec omnia!
Quousque patieris haec, Domine?
Cur taces? cur obdormis?
An non tibi potestas est
Et virtus, qua coerceas inimicos?
Et quis similis tibi in fortibus, Domine?
Magnificus in sanctitate, terribilis et laudabilis et faciens mirabilia,
Adiuva, nos, Deus, salutaris noster,
Et propter gloriam nominis tui, Domine, libera nos! *[20]

* "See how Your enemies rejoice,
And those that despise You hold their heads high.
Your foes glory in their victory at Byzantium

The speech of Pius II was lofty and eloquent: "Not our fathers but we have allowed the Turks to conquer Constantinople, the capital of the Orient. And while we stay at home in useless idleness, the arms of these barbarians are penetrating up to the Danube and the Save. In the city of the Eastern king they have assassinated Constantine's successor together with his people, desecrated the temples of the Lord, torn down altars, thrown the relics of the martyrs to pigs, killed the priests, dishonored wives and daughters and even the virgins consecrated to God; they have murdered the city's noblemen in the course of the Sultan's banquet; they have dragged the image of our crucified Savior through their camp in mockery and scorn to the cry of 'This is the God of the Christians!'; and they have profaned it with mud and spittle. All this has happened before our eyes, but we are prey to a profound sleep. Yet we are capable of fighting among ourselves; we let only the Turks do what they will. Christians take up arms and fight bloody battles for little reason; against the Turks, who blaspheme our God, destroy our churches and seek to extirpate the name of Christian—against them no one wants to raise a finger."[21]

The appeal fell on deaf ears. Many of the delegates appeared to be more opposed to Pope Pius than to the Turk. The Neapolitan question had poisoned minds. The head of the German delegation, Gregory von Heimburg of Schweinfurt, stirred up animosities. The past lapses of Aeneas Sylvius were flung back ironically in the face of Pius II. The Venetians expected to be given the supreme command, all the booty of war, reimbursement for expenses, three thousand men for their own ships, and twenty thousand infantrymen and fifty thousand cavalrymen to place at the Hungarian border.

In January 1460 Pius II left Mantua, sad and ill, after the delegations had taken their leave, having first dined on the fat oxen pre-

---

And they jeer at our expense!
Was it all not the Lord's doing?
How long will You suffer this to go on, O Lord?
Why are You silent? Why do You sleep?
Is not the power Yours
And the virtue, to check Your enemies?
Who then may rival you, O Lord?
Magnificent in Your holiness,
Inspiring awe and devotion,
Performing miracle on miracle,
Help us, Lord God, our redeemer,
And deliver us, for the glory of Your name!"

sented to the pope by the Duke of Milan. Muhammad II, who was probably better informed than the Christians of the events at Mantua, moved to conquer the despotate of Morea. Italian scholars had looked upon Mistra and the group around Pletho as a reborn school of Athens. The philosopher had conceived a neopagan religion and a communistic organization to promote a Hellenic national revival. But the two despots, Tommasos and Demetrios Paleologos, who were involved in a fratricidal war and were ready for any concession provided they retained their apanage and their privileges, came to a miserable end: Demetrios as a monk in Adrianopolis, Tommasos in Italian exile, a pensioner of the pope at the hospital of Santo Spirito in Rome.[22]

The Turks advanced easily against a Christianity divided, discordant, and corrupt, in which the ministers of God were the first to provide a bad example. Such an example, for instance, was the unaccountable Minorite, Fra Lodovico of Bologna, who managed to swindle at least three popes: Nicholas V, Callixtus III, and Pius II. In his eagerness to launch the crusade, Pius II in 1458 had appointed Lodovico his nuncio to the East. At the end of 1460 the friar returned to Rome with a crowd of picturesque Eastern delegates who, recognizing the "nuncio" as their only authorized interpreter, declared in the name of their sovereigns that their armies had crossed the border and were ready to attack Mohammad. To the great amusement of the Roman street urchins, the delegates of the mysterious Eastern kings devoured great chunks of meat in public, spoke briefly and seldom, and sported bizarre hairdos and even more extraordinary hats. Having tricked Pius II, Fra Lodovico went on to fool Florence, Venice, and, to a somewhat lesser extent, the French court, until finally, unmasked, he disappeared from circulation and with him dissolved the famous league of Eastern sovereigns which for months had excited the dreams and hopes of Christianity.

Meanwhile, the Roman revolts and rebellions against papal authority in France and Germany were added to the war in Apulia. If it had been relatively easy to overcome the heresy of Sigismondo Malatesta, it was not quite so simple to prevail over powers for whom logical-rhetorical arguments and spiritual arms were of little value. After the fall of Sinope and Trebizond, Pius II decided to address himself directly to the Sultan in an extraordinary document: an exhortation to follow the example of Constantine the Great by converting to the Christian faith:

An insignificant thing may make you the greatest, the most powerful, the most renowned living mortal. You ask what it is? It is not difficult to find; you need not go far to look for it. You may obtain it everywhere. It is a little water (*aquae pauxillum*) with which you may be baptized, converted to Christianity, and accepted into the faith of the Gospel. If you do this, there will be no prince on the face of the earth who will surpass you in glory nor who could equal you in power. We will name you Emperor of the Greeks and of the East, and whatever lands you now possess by force, and hold unjustly, will then be yours by right. All Christians will honor you and make you the arbiter of their differences. All the oppressed will take refuge with you as their common protector; from nearly every country of the earth they will turn to you. Many will submit to you spontaneously; they will appear before your tribunal and pay you tribute. It will be your task to overcome tyrants, to uphold the just and combat the unjust ones. And the Church of Rome will not oppose you, if you take the right path. The first ecclesiastical seat will embrace you with a love equal to that given other kings—even greater since your position will be more elevated. Under these conditions you can easily conquer many kingdoms without war and bloodshed. . . . We will never lend aid to your enemies, but will turn to your aid against those who sometimes arrogate to themselves the prerogatives of the Church of Rome and slander their own mother.[23]

The text is baffling, and not only because of the properly apologetic part in which Pius refutes the doctrine of the Koran. The doctrinal substance is lifted from the *Cribratio Alchorani,* which Nicholas of Cusa had dedicated explicitly to his papal friend as a means of winning over the infidels. What is unusual is its pessimistic view of the Western political world.[24] The essence of the argument is that if it were possible to resolve the theological quarrel, how much better the Sultan would appear than the various German or Italian princes, who were weak and violent, lacking in faith, greedy and factious! Let the Sultan put aside the sword of Islam and with the sword of Christ cut down the evil weeds that oppress Europe. Pacified, Europe could then return to peace with the unified East. While the pontifical text may be propaganda, it is a manifesto and an act of accusation against the powerful of Christianity. It is certainly curious that Pius

II, "at the very moment when he was thinking seriously of referring the royal crown of Albania on Skanderbeg, and considering restoring the kingdom of Jerusalem to the Duke of Burgundy, should have entertained the idea of installing the Sultan of the Ottoman infidels as the orthodox Emperor of the East and arbiter of the West." The paradoxical nature of the letter, even more than "the unrest of the Christian world," reveals the Pope's obscure awareness that the unity of the crusade, which was tied to the unity of the Church and the Empire, was a waning myth. Unity and peace could only be regained in freedom from the overriding fear of Muhammad II and the splendid pagan temple of the violent Sigismondo Maltesta, in a different world with different relationships, a world that had cast off outdated myths.

No one believed any more in the crusades. When, faced with the subjection of Bosnia, before the irresistible onslaught of the Ottoman forces, Venice was compelled to fight for her own interests and safety, the Florentines did not conceal the fact that their satisfaction over a war against the Turk was due exclusively to the hope of seeing their rival city weakened and bled white. Neither the defense of the Christian faith nor the unity of Europe was of any importance whatsoever to the princes of the Christian cities. Christ and the Church, and the united front against the Turk, could be excellent pretexts for gaining very specific objectives; but the Turk himself, at times, could serve as well as or even better than the successor to Peter.

Faced with so much political realism, Pius II, weak and ill, decided in March 1462 to descend personally into the arena with a touching gesture: the vicar of Christ offered his own person for the salvation of the faith. In a secret consistory on 23 September 1463, he outlined his project, and the majority of the cardinals approved. On 19 October the Pope, Venice, and the Duke of Burgundy concluded a three-year alliance, pledging themselves not to make a separate peace. But if the papal bull commanding the crusade had popular backing, the great powers were not stirred by it. Nor did the fortunes of war favor the Venetian army. On 18 June 1464, Pius left Rome for Ancona, where the crusaders were to embark. He reached Ancona exhausted on 19 July. The Venetian galleys had not yet arrived, and the cardinals meanwhile had already begun to consider the future conclave. When the ships appeared on the scene, the death of Pius II was imminent. He died on 15 August 1464, four days after the Cusan. Venice immediately proceeded to disarm her fleet.[25]

Pius's dream had ended in the face of the sea. At precisely the same time in Morea, the "pagan" Sigismondo Malatesta attacked the fortress of Mistra, and took as his only trophy the ashes of Georgius Gemistus Pletho in order to return them to final repose in the "pagan" temple of Rimini. Rimini and Ancona: the sociopolitical program of the Greek philosopher, the splendid temple of carnal love, and the old pope who died near San Ciriaco, watching powerless the triremes of the crusade—all three are things of symbolic importance. And the humanist Aeneas Sylvius, who facing *eversio Europae* alone entered the battle against the Turks, was from then on more in cadence with the poetry of Ariosto than with the solemn rhythm of the Song of Roland.

Notes

1. *Aeneid,* 1: 378. See G. Voight, *Enea Silvio de' Piccolomini als Papst Pius der Zweite und seine Zeitalter,* III (Berlin: 1863), 3: ii. For the principal literature on Pius II, see the bibliography in the appendix to G. Burck, *Selbstdarstellung und Personenbildnis bei Enea Silvio Piccolomini* (*Pius II*) (Basle and Stuttgart, 1956), pp. 155–60, and primarily Berthe Widmer, *Enea Silvio Piccolomini Papst Pius II. Biographie und ausgewählte Texte aus seinen Schriften* (Basle and Stuttgart, 1960). Among the general works, besides Gregorovius and the second volume of Pastor, *Storia dei Papi* (Rome, 1925), see: A. Weiss, *Aeneas Sylvius als Papst Pius II. Sein Leben und Einfluss auf die literarische Kultur Deutschlands* (Graz, 1897); W. Boulting, *Aeneas Sylvius Orator, Man of Letters, Statesman and Pope* (London, 1908); C. A. Ady, *Pius II the Humanist Pope* (London, 1913); Thea Buyken, *Enea Silvio Piccolomini. Sein Leben und Werden bis zum Episkopat* (Bonn and Cologne, 1931); and G. Paparelli, *Enea Silvio Piccolomini* (*Pio II*) (Bari, 1950). For Piccolomini's works, the quotations are taken from the following editions: *Opera* (Basle, 1551); *Commentarii* (Rome, 1584). The latter work was integrated by Cugnoni, *Opera inedita,* "Atti R. Acc. Lincei," 1882–82, Memorie Class. Sc. Morali Storiche e Filos., Ser. 3, Vol. 8 (Rome, 1883). Other general sources are: G. Lesca, "I 'commentarii rerum memorabilium, quae temporibus suis contigerunt' d'Enea Silvio de' Piccolomini . . . ," *Annali della R. Scuola Normale Superiore di Pisa,* Vol. 10, 1894; R. Wolkan, ed., *Der Briefwechsel,* "Fontes Rerum Austriacarum" (Vienna, 1909–18), pp. 61–62, 67m, 68; A. F. Kollar, *Analecta Monumentorum omnis aevi Vindobonensia* (Vienna, 1762), 2: 691–791; "Historia Friderici III Imperatore," in Kollar, *Analecta,* 2: 1–550; and I. Sanesi, *Chrysis* (Florence, 1941).

2. See *Prosatori latini del Quattrocento* (Milan-Naples, 1952), pp. 688 sq. The text of this work is reproduced according to Cugnoni, but takes into account the variants indicated by Pastor.

3. An important source for information about the preparation of the "castrated" edition is the article by G. B. Picotti, "Di un manoscritto bolognese de' 'Commentarii' di Pio II," *L'Archiginnasio* 9(1915). See also Picotti, "La pubblicazione e i primi effetti della 'Execrabilis' di Pio II," *Arch. della R. Società Romana di Storia Patria* 37(1914). Picotti puts considerable emphasis on Bandini's butchery of the text, his conscious "lie" (p. 244: "servility and fear weakened his spirits"), and his base subservience to the powerful, which led him to make corrections that were "at times ridiculous, at times prejudiced." Among the "ridiculous" changes he cites are references to the "latrines, where the supporters of the cardinal of Rouen gathered," which

became "a strange or a rather more secret place." Picotti's entire essay is exemplary in illustrating the extent to which Quattrocento manuscripts were at times manipulated. The expression "Castratura Commentariorum Aeneae Silvii" is contained in manuscript 1320 of the National Library of Rome (formerly Sessoriano 262), which contains the censored passages.

4. Piccolomini, *Commentarii*, p. 55a.

5. Wolkan, ed. *Briefwechsel*, 1: 7 sqq. The letter of 9 April 1363, in which reference is made (in addition to Petrarch and the *Senili*), to Francesco Bruni, trans. by Fracassetti (Florence, 1892, 1: 104 sqq.). Petrarch's image corresponds to the ships "towering like mountains" of Aeneas Sylvius. "If you saw it, you would not think it a ship, but a mountain floating on the sea"; the marble shores of one correspond to the marble palaces rising from the sea of the other. Piccolomini had Venice in mind and concluded: "How much more noble is Genoa than Venice. . . ." An analysis, in this regard, of the "humanistic" models from Petrarch to Poggio would be fruitful.

6. Paparelli (*Piccolomini*, p. 93) speaks of the "gentle gallantry" and "insinuating allusions" but also correctly points out the "vague sadness."

7. Letter to Kaspar Schlick written in 1444, in Wolkan, ed., *Briefwechsel*, 1: 394–95. This is in agreement with Sanesi's portrait (*Chrysis*, p. 28) describing how "he constantly focused his attention and thought on the observation and the representation of reality and of life." Sanesi is less convincing when he attempts to establish a clear succession of periods between "the frivolous and thoughtless sensuality" of the writer of comedies and novels and his more serious political and religious activity.

8. *Fasciculus rerum expetendarum et fugiendarum (editus ab Orthuino Gratio . . . Coloniae 1535*, republished by Brown, London, 1690).

9. Piccolomini, *Commentarii*, p. 6a.

10. The whole text is contained in Lesca, "I 'commentarii,'" pp. 33–34.

11. From the slightly modified version of Paparelli, (Florence, 1949 [with the text on the facing page]). On the cultural backwardness of Vienna, see Kollar, ed., *Aualecta*, chapter 11: "The students dedicate themselves to the pursuit of pleasure; they are avid for food and wine, and only a paltry few acquire some learning."

12. Kollar, ed., *Analecta*, pp. 691, 783.

13. The writing of Pius II in the form of letters (*Epistola Enee Silvii de Picolominibus de ortu et auctoritate imperii Romani ad serenissimum et invictissimum principem et dominum, dominum Fridericum, Romanorum regem semper augustum*) has been reprinted several times (Wolkan, ed., *Briefwechsel*, 2: 6–24). The imperial thesis is explicit: "The royal power of Rome, which they call the Holy Empire, has its origin in natural human reason, which is an excellent guide in the conduct of life and which it is well to obey. . . . All peoples, nations, princes, and kings should therefore bow to your command. . . ."

14. Letter to Giovanni Vrunt, in Wolkan, ed., *Briefwechsel,* 2: 31. See also Paparelli, *Piccolomini,* p. 123 (in which he translates "*canis aspersus sum*" as "I am but a beaten dog").

15. The text was published in part by Pastor, but the bull was never promulgated. On the life led by the pope, see E. Piccolomini, *Alcuni documenti inediti intorno a Pio II e a Pio III* (Siena, 1871) (taken from "Atti e Memorie della Sezione Letteraria e di Storia Patria della R. Accademia dei Rozzi," n.s., Vol. 1).

16. Piccolomini, *Opera,* pp. 281–82.

17. F. Babinger, *Maometto il Conquistatore e il suo tempo* (Turin, 1957), p. 307.

18. [C. Guasti], *Due legazioni al Sommo Pontefice per il Comune di Firenze presiedute da Sant' Antonino arcivescovo* (Florence, 1857), p. 56.

19. Babinger, *Maometto,* p. 60.

20. G. Burck, *Selbstdarstellung,* p. 60.

21. Piccolomini, *Opera,* pp. 905 sqq. See also Babinger, *Maometto,* p. 261, from which this version is taken, and the letter to the Cusan quoted in *Opera,* p. 707.

22. D. A. Zakythinos, *Le despotat grec de Morée.* Vol. 1 of *Histoire politique* (Paris, 1932), pp. 241–97; F. Masai, *Pléthon et le platonisme de Mistra* (Paris, 1956).

23. From the letter to Muhammad (Babinger, *Maometto,* p. 301). An edition with a translation on facing pages, edited by G. Toffanin, was published in Naples in 1953.

24. The passages of Book 13 of the *Commentarii* (contained in Voigt, *Enea Silvio,* 2: 367) should be reread: "But everything depends on its usefulness, for our age does not value anything unless it sees some profit in it; honor, it is believed, will follow in the wake of power and wealth, much as a man's shadow follows his body."

25. On the subjects of the crusade, the relations with contemporaries, and the policies of Pius II, see also: A. Ratti, "Quarantadue lettere originali di Pio II relative alla guerra di successione nel reame di Napoli," *Archivio Storico Lombardo* 30(1903): 263–93; E. Rigomera, *Papst Pius der II und der Kreuzzug gegan die Türken* (Bucharest, 1938); A. A. Kurou, *Bessarion o Ellen* (Athens, 1947), Vol. 2; and E. Meuthen, *Die Letzten Jahre des Nikolaus von Kues. Biographischen Untersuchungen nach neuen Quellen* (Cologne, 1958).

III

Donato Acciaiuoli, Citizen of Florence

"Donato Acciaiuoli, Florentine citizen . . . in governing the Republic, applied himself to philosophy, and philosophizing, governed the Republic." Thus Angelo Segni briefly summed up his life in a later, very different period.[1] But it was a worthy epigraph for an active career that had been consecrated entirely to uniting thought and action in a conscious effort to incarnate the civic ideal of early Florentine humanism. Alamanno Rinuccini, a close friend of Acciaiuoli, in his funeral tribute to Matteo Palmieri delivered on 15 April 1475, stressed the supreme wisdom that effects a harmonious balance between contemplative asceticism and the everyday activity of civil life (*communes vitae civilis actiones*): "*prudentissimus vir medium quendam inter utramque viam modum sequitur.*"*[2]

A few years later Cristoforo Landino was to say precisely the same thing in polished and elegant phrases on the occasion of Donato's death, although he had not always been well disposed toward him, perhaps having contempt for the dedicated man of letters who cherished a way of life and a city that by then was quite unlike the one that Acciaiuoli and his predecessors had loved and brought into being.[3] For Landino, a reputable schoolmaster, school was sufficient. Acciaiuoli, on the contrary, belonged to that generation and class which could not admit of any separation between culture and civic activities. When political upheavals compelled another learned friend of Rinuccini, Niccolò della Luna, to retire to the cloister of San Marco, "letters" alone were of little comfort to him.[4]

One has the impression that for these men the greatest fault, as well as the greatest punishment, would be an imbalance between the *humanitas* of learning and the state of the citizen, between the care of the soul and engagement in worldly affairs, so that if there were an excess of one or the other, disrupting the necessary harmony, redress

* "A wise man will follow a middle course between the two."

must in some way be done. Thus Vespasiano da Bisticci, in describing the case of Agnolo Acciaiuoli, demonstrated that because he had wanted too much from his own worldly state, he was then compelled for his own salvation to divorce himself entirely from the world: "The middle way in everything is the most secure way there is. To go counter to this greatest of states is to court exile, or death, or other similar fates. . . . In Naples . . . he became detached from the concerns of the age." He reappears the idea of measure which cultivated Florence, in the first part of the Quattrocento, enjoyed rediscovering in the *Nicomachea;* Florence adhered to this idea in the same way it referred to the *Politics* for the most perfect analysis that could be made of the civic organization of men.[5]

It was precisely within the limits of this measure that Donato Acciaiuoli sought to order his public and private activity, which spanned the same years—from Cosimo to Lorenzo—in which the political situation in Florence was changing. Perhaps better than anything else, it helps us understand the cultural life of this transitional period. It was not a coincidence that some of the most eminent scholars of the period, in Florence and abroad, gravitated around him or were in constant contact with him. And when he died in 1478, shortly after the Pazzi conspiracy, it seemed as though with him disappeared the heart of the Quattrocento humanism that had been the ideal heir of Salutati. With the victory of the Medicis, this type of man of culture, who was at the same time a man of action, appeared less often; however, he was in a certain way reincarnated in Lorenzo. In the Medicean circle even the literary man of noble character at best expended his energy in teaching and lamenting, as Politian did, that he did not have adequate means or subsidies to devote himself to pure and simple scholarly research.[6] This is the difference between Acciaiuoli's group and Ficino's, and it is a distance that cannot be bridged. The difference between the Aristotelianism of the former and the Neoplatonism of the latter is not—as Arnaldo della Torre seemed naively to have believed at the time—the difference between the pupils of Argyropulos and those of the faithful disciples of Pletho or Bessarion; nor is it the same as the divergent interpretations of the relationship between the two supreme Greek philosophers. The difference is rather radically different concepts of life which were related to different political and social conditions and to a profound change in the times. Hence the problems that preoccupy the former (logical-rhetorical and ethical-political) are entirely unlike those that interest the latter (metaphysical and theological).

It is essential to clarify Acciaiuoli's position, as well as that of his group of friends, if one wants to understand in depth the relationship between Ficinian "theology" and the "humanistic" culture which from Petrarch through Salutati was continued in Bruni, Poggio, and Manetti.

Donato Acciaiuoli was born on 15 March 1429. His father, Neri di Donato, died at the time of his birth, and the child was brought up under the care of his maternal grandfather, Palla Strozzi, and of his mother Maddalena, who remarried Felice di Michele Brancacci, an exponent of the anti-Medicean party.[7] These facts are not without significance. The Acciaiuoli were one of the greatest families of Florence; their members had been among its secular and religious leaders. How much they preserved their sense of nobility and Donato's own pride may be gathered from a stern letter written to him by Iacopo Ammannati, who had been his teacher and became a fast friend. "It is true that I have complained of you in the words I have written. . . . And I repeat that you have erred in your relationship with one who was your greatest friend. . . . Certainly you are noble and learned; and for that reason you are behaving in an unbecoming way toward one who is much below your station, who laid the foundation on which your doctrine has matured. . . . Much too often you incur the fault common to all noblemen. It is precisely this that has already once ruined your family, and will ruin it again, if you do not hold in greater regard the standard of those of noble birth."[8]

Donato felt a strong tie to Palla Strozzi, who was far away in exile. When he was twenty he wrote to him with affection, thanking God that, in taking his father from him, He had "conservaret nobis parentem." And he seemed then to be the most worthy heir of Palla's cultural interests, as well as of his attitude. The world to which Donato belonged actively opposed the "tyranny" of the Medicis. In 1448, when the city was harassed on all sides by war and taxes, Donato wrote to Angelo Baldesi, a common friend of Vespasiano da Bisticci and of Giannozzo Manetti, these rather bitter words: "Who is so naive and so stupid as not to have understood by now, and practically grasped with his hands, that these compatriots of ours who rule the state are constantly inciting war after war, nourishing the Florentine people on the false hopes of a future peace?"[9]

His hero at the time was Giannozzo Manetti, who was often discussed and sometimes opposed in his own state, but who was admired and revered in all of Italy, "because if our co-citizens have frequently demonstrated their ingratitude toward Giannozzo, the foreigners are all for him."

To Giannozzo, who had been dispatched to Venice, and to the chancellor Griso Griselli, his loyal friend, Donato sent letters of affectionate support and unbounded admiration which were also, for the twenty-year-old, open professions of a political faith.[10] The dominant theme of these letters was the glorification of a life spent in the service of the city, admiration for the greatness of the man who makes himself respected by all and who through his own prestige enhances that of his fatherland (*enitere quantum in te est patrie tue, cui multum debes, usui esse et glorie*).* He had a profound sense of participation in the *res publica*, together with a lively interest in knowledge, in culture, and in that *humanitas* which constituted the unmistakable fascination of Manetti's own authority and which crowned with a halo of singular light the untiring work of the statesman: "That the salvation of the fatherland remains uppermost in your heart, is worthy of your nobility, and is in conformance with your habit and with the character of your forebears who were so illustrious. As you justly wrote, you have served your country for ten years, confronting dangers openly, evading no effort in order to carry out whatever might succeed to the advantage and honor of the city."[11]

In a draft of a letter to Giovanni, Duke of Calabria, written in 1448, the young Acciaiuoli explicitly describes his cherished ideal of a man. It was not very different from the one he was to describe many years later in dedicating his *Politics* to Federigo da Montefeltro: "I have felt that in you the highest virtues shine brightly: strength, justice, liberality, seriousness, generosity, and a supreme love for that learning to which I myself am also dedicated."[12]

In reality, neither political preoccupations nor private affairs deterred Donato from his studies, as they were not to distract him

* ". . . occupied to the best of your ability in being of aid and glory to your country, to which you owe so much."

later when at an active, mature age he was engaged in the service of his Florence. If we examine the letters written on behalf of Vespasiano da Bisticci, the bibliographical information sent to his teacher Ammannati, or the correspondence with Manetti and Filelfo, we can picture him buried in the midst of codices, of which he speaks at one time in the plain language of a great merchant and at another time with the erudition of an already very learned man. In these letters we find the Greeks, from Demosthenes to Plutarch and Diogenes Laërtius; the Fathers of the Church, from Athanasius to Nazianzus, Tertullian, and Thomas; Statius and Seneca; the treatises of Petrarch; and, copied by his fine hand, that treatise on mnemotechnics by Ravennate which was to be so dear to Giordano Bruno. But beside an ardent love for Cicero or Aristotle we also find the precision of the heir of merchants when he describes for Vespasiano the format of the codices and the type of print, the number of lines and the pay of the copyists, the moods and jealousies of the owners and their prices. The love of culture and civic life are shown united here with unbreakable bonds, as all the practicality of a world of artisans and merchants is also clearly manifest.[13]

Vespasiano da Bisticci, in his *Vita* of Acciaiuoli, which is a collection of tender souvenirs, describes a speech Donato is reputed to have made at the age of fifteen before the officials of the Studio: "He delivered it in a way that astonished everyone, considering his youth. This was his first proof as a man of letters." His autographical papers, in definitive final draft, include a brief speech made at the conclusion of his formal studies ("*peto ut . . . doctorum insignia deferre velis . . .*").* These were customary words for the occasion, recalling his many studies: "*Nam a prima pueritia mihi persuasum est nihil esse in vita magnopere expetendum nisi quod esset cum bonarum artium studio coniunctum.*"† But especially significant are his thanks to two teachers—one, Bartolo, whose science is praised ("*dialectice, phisice et metaphisice, et in omni genere optimarum artium*"), and the other, Alessandro, "*preceptor meus, eximius vir, summus philosophus.*"[14]

Again from Vespasiano we know that as a young boy Donato

* "I submit that . . . you might like to have the title of doctorate."

† "I realized from a very tender age that nothing was worth striving for in life more than something connected with the study of fine arts."

audited courses in logic at San Marco by Angelo da Lecco, "a most learned man," who commented for him on the work of "maestro Pagolo," that is, Paolo Veneto. Later, in 1455, Donato was to address the aging teacher a letter which is a valuable autobiographical document. Acciaiuoli was barely more than a child (*vix e ludo pueritie emersus*) when he began to take an active interest in the study of philosophy, and was to dedicate himself wholly to dialectics, *quamquam laboriosa esset,* under the tutelage of Angelo: "*Sed quedam eo tempore inciderunt que me invitum a tam laudabili tamque liberali studio alienarunt.*"* Obliged to provide for his *saluti et dignitati,* he did not abandon but merely suspended his philosophical studies: (*Ita igitur a philosophia discessi, ut non mihi eius studium deserendum, sed temporibus remittendum, et in aliud tempus differendum.*") †[15]

His literary studies, on the other hand, seem never to have been entirely interrupted; nor did the discussions of moral problems, traces of which appear in many letters to Iacopo Ammannati and Giannozzo Manetti. Iacopo da Lucca, the cardinal of Pavia, had been the tutor in residence of Agnolo Acciaiuoli and had taken care of Donato and his brother Pietro, "and in the shortest time letters were being written that were admirable to behold." From Donato's notes, which in part at least are extant, we may discern the method of study followed under Iacopo's direction: extracts and examples from Cicero, Quintilian, Sallust, Macrobius, Gellius, and Lactantius; lists of sayings, dates, and definitions; stylistic examples and exercises.[16] In January 1449, writing at length to his teacher, Acciaiuoli clearly expresses his own admiration for Cicero: "I have your letters, written as you say effortlessly; they practically compel me to read. Correctly, in fact, you use in your letters that flowing style which Cicero also employed, and which should be observed by everyone. I request therefore that you send me long and frequent letters, so that these may be of use in my studies. In fact I strive to imitate you and to be like you. This, however, does not happen to me with Cicero; when I

* "But, with the many things in which I was involved at that time, I had to forego these commendable and gentlemanly pursuits—very much against my will."

† ("I also had to put aside philosophy; but I did not give up its study altogether. Rather I suspended it for the time being, with the idea of returning to it later.")

read him I forget myself, and I feel that I am unworthy; so that finally instead of inspiring me he fills me with awe."[17]

The letter to Gabriele dei Guicciardini is one of the most eloquent Quattrocento tributes to the *studia humanitatis,* which not only form the man of virtue and make him a model citizen and an excellent father, but also introduce him to a higher city in which time does not vanquish and death does not kill: "What could be more sweet than to experience as though they were contemporary the noteworthy events of past centuries? What could be more pleasing than to listen to the words as they were spoken of the speeches of the wisest scholars long since dead?" The distance is greater between the learned and the unlearned than between man and beast.[18]

Once Donato asked Giannozzo Manetti to give him the *Orator*. But above all he loved to discourse with Manetti on lofty matters, on politics and ethics. The taste for moral problems, savored in the atmosphere of a religion intimately experienced, is characteristic of the production of Florentine humanism of the Quattrocento and mirrors the profound seriousness of the culture, which was preoccupied not so much with sublime or subtle metaphysical and theological disquisitions as with what concerned the life of the man in the street. It was such an atmosphere that ignited the discussion in 1450, in which Vespasiano da Bisticci and Angelo Badesi participated, on children who die without being baptized. Manetti, armed with a solid theological doctrine and enclosed in the most rigid orthodoxy, maintained, in a letter that is a minor treatise, that such children shared the common guilt and hence were damned. Acciaiuoli called upon the authority of the Scriptures: "And yet, when I think," he argued, "that original sin is not that of the children but of the first forebear, I cannot understand why innocent ones must pay the penalty of another's sin; above all when it is written: 'the son shall not pay for the sins of his father.' And also: 'the soul that hath sinned shall die.' I therefore do not see how it could be maintained that God is justice and truth, and at the same time that he punishes justly those who have never sinned. If in fact the transgression of the father is mutually that of the son, why then is the penalty not mutual? Why must the son pay for the guilt of the father any more than the father the guilt of the son? And if everyone must bear his own burden, why should poor children be eternally damned for the guilt of others?"

This concern was to preoccupy Donato, and we see it return in a more subtle, more complex form in another discussion, more than ten years later, which was analogous in its characteristic general formulation and cannot be separated from the first. "It being the year 1463 of the priors of liberty . . . having argued together with you, Giovanni Rucellai, many times about moral questions, it happened that, having raised a doubt, you asked me what was more difficult, to do good or to do evil."

On this occasion Acciaiuoli had maintained that it was more difficult to do good. But his opinion was opposed by a Dominican, Giovanni da Viterbo, who set his thesis down in a brief *quaestio,* a very scholarly exposition although written in the vernacular, which he sent to Rucellai. If one reads Rucellai's own copy, *Oppenione di fra' Giovanni da Viterbo de l'Ordine de' Predicatori sopra una questione, overo dubitazione, di quale sia piu difficile, o bene o male operare,* which Acciaiuoli later read and refuted, one is struck by the attitude concealed beneath the marshalling of texts, ostensibly impartial, in favor of one or the other thesis.[19] In essence the Dominican stressed the idea that man is naturally inclined toward good; having been created by God for virtue, he is directed toward good works by passion and reason in harmonious accord. The impulse to do good is as natural to us as the tendency of a flame to rise or of a stone to fall. Good is a natural goal that beckons man irresistibly to it. How much Pelagian optimism was to live again in Thomistic Aristotelianism is quite evident in Fra Giovanni's unadorned pages. He would have liked to confine himself to a pure and simple *sic et no* ("a libel written by a doubtful author"), but he clearly favors a "naturalness" of doing good, a "natural" tendency of affective, rational man toward virtue.

It was precisely on this point that Acciaiuoli's disagreement was most insistent: man's virtue is "natural" in an entirely different sense from the way the good friar appears to understand it; just as custom or habit take on an entirely different meaning on the moral and on the physical level: "No philosopher or learned writer claims that the tendency of a stone, which naturally falls downward, or of fire, which rises upward, and similar tendencies, should be called customs, or in the order of customs." And it is true, as the "adversary" observes, that sometimes one speaks of natural virtues; but these are interpretations which any serious moralist would take care not to set down as a basis for any kind of pretext to reduce all moral conduct to naturalness—or, vice versa, all naturalness to virtue. It is too easy, Acciaiuoli insisted, to play with the terms of natural inclination to virtue or habit: "We never take moral virtues and then subdivide them, saying that they are due to inclination or habit, and that moral good or evil is due to natural inclination or habit."

His refutation of Fra Giovanni is explicit. The Dominican stated that good is easier because it is more natural, more convenient—because it poses fewer obstacles. But good is, Donato asserted, the one and only correct course to follow among the infinite erroneous possibilities; as it is easier to shoot the arrow to any number of points outside the target, which is solely and uniquely in the center, so it could be said of the good deed. To determine precisely the best solution out of all that has to be taken into account and resolved is anything but the easiest. Who does not see that to choose this middle road, this measure that lies between the extremes, is a difficult and arduous task by comparison with the relative facility of choosing one of the extremes? These latter are clearly evident. All you need do is take them as they are. The ideal goal you must determine laboriously, as the artist labors over the work of art ("it is the same for works of art as it is for moral actions"), which is much more difficult to make beautiful—that is, truly successful art, which is not ugly or mediocre. If doing good is so easy, Donato said, it is difficult to explain the great number of evil people compared with the scarcity of good people. The worst situation Donato judged to be the need of divine help: "What we cannot do by ourselves, unless aided by God and divine grace, is more difficult than what we can do on our own, without such aid."

Acciaiuoli, appealing on the one hand to Augustine and on the other to Egidius Romanus, affirmed that the emotional element in fact drives man, not toward moral good, but often toward things that only appear to be good. "Egidius adds . . . remarkable doctor . . .: desire always stirs under the banner of good. But this good is sometimes genuine and living good, and sometimes only apparent."[20] This is not all: the sensory is, precisely because it tends toward the immoderate, a constant element of sin. While even though the impulse toward real good may be natural, between the impulse and the perfect, virtuous deed lies the whole tiresome effort to achieve perfection. Acciaiuoli observed that the ardent love of knowledge that moved him, that was precisely the manifestation of man's natural thirst for knowledge, was something quite different from acquired knowledge, which requires a difficult and tireless effort, the engagement of reason, ability, and calculation.

In contrast to the too simple answer of Fra Giovanni da Viterbo, Acciaiuoli presented an entire awareness of a morality born out of daily activity, for which temptation and sin are always present. "Who is he who does not understand that to abstain from pleasure and immoral lust . . . is more difficult than to give in and pursue them . . . ? And, likewise, that to make a gift of one's own goods and money, and as much as needed, for the specific aim of doing a generous act is more difficult than to keep one's money at home in the chest, or not to give, or to exceed in taking money beyond what is proper. And . . . it is a difficult and sublime thing to conquer one's own soul. . . ." Virtue is this hard discipline, this continuous trial through which one maintains austere control of oneself; it is a habit which strengthens that measure whose achievement represents the convergence of consummate wisdom and courageous resolution. Compared with the overly optimistic Dominican, Acciaiuoli displays a moral seriousness, an awareness of the ever-present flaws in man's nature, in tones that would be dear to Savonarolian preachment. To complacent calm, to claustral *otium,* the statesman and merchant counterposes an experience capable of giving a very different color to Greek ethics as well as to Christian teaching. The composure of Aristotelian measure is dramatically conceived as the ideal resolution of a continuous and arduous inner struggle, whose goal is not—even for Acciaiuoli the Manichean—rejection of one-half of our lives, but a restitution of nature within the harmony of the law.

"Give my regards to my opponent," Giovanni da Viterbo noted at the end of the answer to Donato, "whom I love all the more for his pious defense of himself, and I also offer him all that pleases him in each of my works, for he is so virtuous."[21]

We have described Donato's political attitude, his preoccupations, his abandonment—at least in part—of his philosophical studies, his serious words on the fate of the city and on the ineptitude of its rulers. His position was unwavering until the end of 1451. If, however, we consider the fine letter sent to Banco di Casavecchia, dated 21 September 1453 and obviously pessimistic about the situation, we are led to suppose a change of mind:

I see that the news brought to you by men who listen to common gossip has upset you. I beg you not to be one of those who always think the worst of city affairs, and not to follow the example of those who, too trusting, judge affairs of state more according to their feelings than on the basis of changing events. Resist the extremes, and maintain with the most wise a just measure. When I consider the condition of our city, I recognize that unquestionably it is agitated by the gravest troubles, that its citizens are subjected to many serious and annoying harassments. Financial difficulties impend over all, and this is highly important, for the nerve of war is money. But as terrible as our difficulties may be, if we compare them with those of our enemies, they are nothing and vanish in the face of the magnitude of those already suffered by our adversaries, and justifiably, as all of Italy knows.

A note of pride in the successes of Florence is detectable in Donato's altered judgment of Cosimo's policies. Acciaiuoli never disavowed his friends; in the most trying moments he remained loyal, in accord with what he considered to be the cause of his city, to those who were united with him by ties of kinship or personal affection. The city had faith in the grandchild of the banished Angelo Acciaiuoli, even in 1478, despite his many connections with the Pazzi. "*Ego vero,*" he wrote to Banco, "*de republica mea semper bene opinabor, et his rebus letabor quas aut ei, aut eius fautoribus salutares esse intelligam.*"*[22]

Peace was near, the peace that Donato warmly welcomed. With the peace he resumed his studies with greater alacrity. In 1451 he expressed the hope of Ammannati of improving his knowledge of Latin and Greek under the tutelage of Marsuppini. In 1453, writing again to Iacopo, he expressed his sorrow over the death of the great humanist in whom he had placed all his hopes: "Carlo Marsuppini revived the Latin language, which for a long time had remained nearly dormant, and almost brought it again to life. . . . What hope now remains for the young lovers of letters, I do not see." And of himself in particular, he added: "My studies had been encouraged by this very learned man. His death will either retard them considerably, or it may even force me to forget them altogether."[23] But we have

* "Most definitely, I have always held our republic in high esteem, and I have rejoiced whenever anything happened that in my estimation was of benefit either to the common welfare or to our leaders."

the very clear impression that an intense fervor for learning possessed Donato, that his grief was comparable to his complaint about the situation and difficulties of Florence—which however sincere and strong, it did not prevent him from active and loyal participation in city affairs.

Between 1453 and 1456 Acciaiuoli felt a new sense of urgency. "*Sompno et otio*," he wrote to Domenico Pandolfini, "*et vanis confabulationibus dediti, inanem vitam ducimus, bellumque gerimus iis artibus que sole sunt, que in secundis rebus ornare, in adversis vero et in omni gravissimo casu et consolari et iuvare nos possint.*"*[24]

One would say that wars and disasters had strengthened the need for meditation ("*incredibili desiderio litterarum afficior*").† To his dearest friends, Alamanno Rinuccini, Marco Parenti, and Antonio Rossi, he wrote insistently that the revival to which Leonardo Bruni and Carlo Marsuppini had given so much impetus should not come to nought: "*Latine littere, et omnes artes libero homine digne . . . , eo vehementius a vobis excitande sunt et in lucem revocande.*"‡[25]

His dedication and research were now aided by Filelfo in Milan, who urged him to continue learning Greek, and, more intimately, by Poggio. His first meeting with Poggio in 1455 moved him profoundly: "I went away from you inspired by a love of letters and by an almost unbelievable longing for knowledge; it seemed to me that there was nothing worthy of being desired in life that was not linked with the knowledge of the highest truth." Poggio was to be his ideal model: "I have selected you alone, among many scholars, and you alone I have chosen as an example to follow." In recounting his excitement to Rinuccini, he was almost afraid of arousing envy. To Ammannati: "What more can I say? I have offered him and dedicated to him all my activity, my work, myself."[26]

His study of Greek is attested to, besides the letters to Filelfo, by his relations with Lianoro de' Lianori of Bologna, a pupil of

* "Dedicated as we are to inertia, sloth, and idle talk, we live frivolously and are bent on destroying precisely those arts that in times of leisure could lend grace to our life and, in periods of adversity and misfortune, could console and comfort us."

† ("I am overcome by a boundless desire for learning.")

‡ "Latin letters and all other arts worthy of a gentleman . . . should be encouraged and stressed all the more strongly by you."

Guarino, whose relations with Tortelli are known.[27] Much could be said about his relations with Antonio Rossi, a man of difficult character, great conceit, and (it appears) arrogance. The letters that reflect his relations with the group of Florentine scholars are rather curious, even if one takes into account the fact that polemics and invective were a fashionable literary genre. No doubt very cultivated, Rossi does not give us the impression that he possessed any particular originality, judging by one of his pompous orations, *de laudibus scientie ed Rev. Dom. Cardinalem Spoletanum.*[28]

Acciaiuoli and Rossi clashed violently, and at one time there was considerable coldness between them. In May 1455 Donato wrote to him cordially, although perhaps somewhat ironically, proposing the resumption of their former relations: "*Posteaquam a facetiis et urbanitate illa discessimus, qua sumus inter nos familiarius usi fortasse quam decuit, numquam ego tuas neque tu meas habuisti litteras.*"* Rossi had by then adopted an oratorical style. "I too," Acciaiuoli added,

> would do the same, if I had the talent equal to the desire. But limited people should not aspire to undertake too much; they should be content with little and not tackle anything beyond their ability. Therefore I write short, rather simple personal letters. I am content with a popular way of expression and I leave the ample, abundant and impetuous talk to you. And I beg of you, if you do not like this humble epistolary style, answer me with orations. I promise you two letters from me in exchange for one of your speeches.[29]

In reality, in his "modest" letters Acciaiuoli delved into some of the most pressing problems that were being discussed in the period. In a letter to Marco Parenti, he invited him to exchange opinions on the relationship between contemplative and active virtue—a question which for Donato was not merely an academic exercise but a truly vital matter.[30]

However, the decisive incentive to complete his own "human" culture and to formulate his viewpoint lay in the teaching of Argyropulos. Donato became actively involved in the teacher's move to Florence, taking sides against Landino as well as against the other

* "Apart from the usual pleasantries and conventional courtesies that we are in the habit of exchanging—perhaps more readily than we should—I have never really received a letter from you, nor you from me."

candidates for the succession to Marsuppini's chair, and disputing also with Angelo Acciaiuoli, who was at the time a very influential citizen. In a letter written on 1 October 1454 to Lianoro de' Lianori, he complained of the scanty knowledge of Greek in Italy, adding, "Illustrious Greece as well, which once was the pride and light of the entire world, has since fallen into the greatest ignorance of letters and of all the noble arts. Now that Byzantium, which alone had conserved some vestiges of ancient Hellas, has also collapsed along with Greece, almost the whole of Greek science has died." A short time earlier, on 5 August he had written to Ammannati about the great impression made on him by Argyropulos, who had just arrived in Florence; although he already knew Argyropulos by reputation, Donato found him superior still to his own fame: "*vir enim mihi visus est, non solum eruditus, ut fama audieram, sed etiam sapiens gravis et vetere illa Grecia dignus.*"*[31]

The events in which Donato and his friends were involved finally led, in 1456, to the successful nomination of Argyropulos to the Studio of Florence. He began teaching officially in February 1457—an event that had been awaited with impatience and that had been deferred to the great annoyance of some. In fact, Alamanno Rinuccini, writing to Acciaiuoli from Florence on 9 November 1456, observed:

> As for our Argyropulos who had raised so much anticipation for his lectures, and to whom we have wanted to listen so avidly, not a word is known. I am more than surprised at his negligence and inconstancy, and I don't want to mention, subtle and deceptive cunning. He has, in fact, not even bothered to send a line since his departure, and it seems that he has also forgotten completely his son, whom he claimed was so dear to him. I intended to point this out to you. Recently, the woman to whom the child was entrusted has complained with great discretion and moderation about those who are to care for him and who lack many necessary things. And she has asked me to write to you of it. Therefore make sure that all that is necessary be done.

Intentionally, Rinuccini inserted a note on how well Landino had begun his courses: "It might interest you to know that our Landino has begun his lessons before a huge gathering of listeners; and, I

* "He made the impression of being not only erudite, as he was known to be, but also eminently wise and a match for [the men] of ancient Greece."

hear, with a rich and elegant mastery of words. I was in the country and was unable to attend."[32]

A short time later the learned Byzantine returned from his European travels. He was completely to win over his pupils, perhaps with less rhetorical effectiveness, but certainly with a rare breadth of understanding and an admirable mastery of the history of Greek thought, which was all present in his comments on Greek philosophers from the pre-Socratics to the Alexandrians. From his lectures, which have been conserved for us primarily by Acciaiuoli and which were also in part re-elaborated by him, it is possible still to hear the echo of Argyropulos's teaching, in terms perhaps somewhat different from those commonly accepted.

The Teaching of Argyropulos

In a letter written from Florence on 24 September 1463, "*nomine Vespasiani librarii ad Alfonsum Palentinum,*" Donato praises Argyropulos's teaching and credits the resumption of his own studies in Florence directly to his influence. Young people were not only learning Greek and Latin as never before, he said, but their knowledge of Plato and Aristotle was so expert that they might have graduated from the Academy of Athens.

> The Byzantine Argyropulos arrived in the city in fact shortly after the death of Pope Nicholas. He is a man of great intellect and erudition worthy of ancient Greece, who for many years has instructed the young people of Florence not only in Greek but also in all the arts related to human excellence and happiness. Thus he has taught and still teaches both moral and natural philosophy with supreme elegance, according to the antique method. He has translated many of Aristotle's works into Latin, and to the stupefied admiration of his listeners, has explained Plato's philosophic doctrines and that arcane and secret knowledge.

The Florentine youth, who had become quite learned, were composing works worthy of wide recognition. The city was blossoming with many new monuments, due especially to the influence of Cosimo, who was engaged in collecting a splendid library. There was an entirely new fervor in library acquisition; manuscripts were being sought everywhere, not only to enhance the city but for the public use of scholars. "Now, as never before, Florence flourishes, and not only in letters and in the noblest disciplines, but in painting, sculpture and in many other fields."[33]

Especially noteworthy in this record from the learned pen of Acciaiuoli are not only some of the expressions typical of the vernacular prose of Vespasiano (such as the "murare" ["wall building"] of Cosimo, which Cavalcanti attacked with such biting sarcasm[34]), but also and primarily the connection established between the rebirth of philosophical culture, attributed to Argyropulos, and the entirely fresh vigor in the sciences and the figurative arts. This kind of representation, which was much in vogue, should be viewed with extreme reserve, however, and should be considered in large part (as in effect it was) an exaggerated piece of publicity writing similar to an advertising flyer accompanying the catalogue of an unusual "book seller." Similar references may be found in manuscripts written a few decades earlier concerning the arrival of Chrysoloras or the group of Salutati's pupils. If one were to take literally all these hymns to the "renaissance" of classical culture in Florence alone, to the renewed interest in the sciences and arts, in libraries, in the ancients, and rediscovered codices, he would soon discover that they are scarcely original if he reexamined the periodical accounts from the last decades of the Trecento. Praise of Petrarch and Boccaccio was recurrent after Salutati in the writings of Bruni and his followers. The Aretine was to describe Chrysoloras in no less glowing and not very different terms from those Acciaiuoli used to describe Argyropulos. This was by then in fact a fashionable panegyric style which served the dual purpose of exalting both the learned foreigner of high reputation, called to the city at an unusual stipend, and his most zealous disciples and supporters.[35]

But beyond academic custom and the merchant's inclination to prize his own acquisitions, it is certain that, just as the teaching of Chrysoloras favored the activity of Bruni and his group, that of Argyropulos gave new impetus and character to Florentine culture after 1450. In the words of Acciaiuoli, who was closest of all to the learned Greek (words confirmed by other authoritative sources), we see clearly not only the importance of the peripatetic teaching conducted according to the classical method, but also the significant effect of this "antique" method. The scant attention which has been paid up to now to the courses of Argyropulos, conserved in the notes (I would like to say "lecture notes") of Donato, has denied us a clear idea about how the Byzantine, an expert in scholastic literature from Thomas to Egidius (we should not forget that he had attended the university of Padua) was consciously and critically detached from it. He reverted to a custom characteristic of Greek commentary in viewing the entire development of classical thought—in particular from Plato to Proclus and the late commentators of Aristotle—as something unitarian, as thought that was to be analyzed in depth, integrated and completed, but that did not represent contrasting or, worse still, irreconcilable schools or positions. Thus, if criticism sometimes echoes in his words, it is directed against Aristotle's polemical excesses that *detorquet* (distort) Plato's meaning.

In his opening lecture, in 1460, of a course on "psychology," Argyropulos set forth his idea of continuity: from Zoroaster and the pre-Socratics, authors of an "obscure and poetic" philosophy; to Socrates who "prodded men to the sciences through moral philosophy"; to Plato "who was divine, the most versed in all branches of knowledge, a supreme poet, the most eloquent of all, a moral, natural, mathematical and above all speculative philosopher, who however did not, like Socrates, systematize learning"; to Aristotle, "for twenty-one years the pupil of Plato, who worked out a perfect order of the sciences." Argyropulos did not set Plato against Aristotle, but viewed their work as different treatments according to the diversity of the sciences and within the unity of knowledge and of research. The divergences—and he recognized them with respect to the *anima* (soul), for example between an Alexander of Aphrodisias and a Themistius—depended upon the development of various possibilities in considering equivocal questions which had been left unsolved by the thinker confronting them for the first time.[36]

Bessarion, a little later, was to continue on a similar plane, although with quite different apologetic preoccupations. For Argyropulos the important thing was precisely the kind of teaching in which Plato, Aristotle, Plotinus, and even Proclus converge and are harmonized. This was the "novelty" at the Studio of Florence, and it was an important one. Perhaps it was not even a radical innovation if Bruni, who translated both Plato and Aristotle, graduated from the school of Chrysoloras, the translator of the *Republic*. Nevertheless, it should be stressed that Chrysoloras and Bruni were still tied to the prevailing interest in practical political and moral matters. Argyropulos was known to have an interest not only in physics, but also in the metaphysical problematics of a type much more than non-Aristotelian —that was Platonic-Neoplatonic (*arcanam illam et reconditam disciplinam*).*

Along with the official courses given regularly on the texts of Aristotle, the learned Byzantine held "private" courses on Plato's Dialogues and read the *Meno* which, despite the existence of an ancient version by Enrico Aristippo, had never been especially well known. He even included, in his courses on Aristotle, arresting fragments of Platonic "theology." Pier Filippo Pandolfini could write with justification to Santo Vireto that Aristotle's works on physics had finally been translated and annotated in such a way that he could now understand the "philosopher" (*tot et tanta audiuntur divina, ut nunc primo Aristotelem philosophorum principem admirari incipiam*).† There is possibly more: Argyropulos tried to combine classical philosophy and poetry in one total view; and for this reason he read and commented on Sophocles, along with Aristotle's *Politics* (*grece vero tragicum illum Atheniensem Sophoclem mira quadam venustate ac elegantia legit. . . . Accedunt et* Politicorum *libri, quos quidem diebus festis sibi declarandos absunsit*).‡[37]

Argyropulos's image in Florence, and his teaching from 1457 on, have too often been distorted as allegedly Aristotelian—in antithesis to the rise of Ficino's Platonism and even to Landino's teaching, so that by now an exact reconstruction is not easy. In reality, it was precisely Argyropulos's commentary that brought to the fore the entire Academy, Plotinus and Proclus along with the later Greek commentators of Aristotle.

We should mention not only his edition of the complete text of the *Aenead*, but also the use he made of Neoplatonic "theology" in his official courses on Aristotle. It was, specifically, in his great lecture on the *Nicomachea* with which he began his teaching at the Florence Studio (almost as though he wanted to measure himself with Bruni or ideally to join with him) that he had to discuss the passages in which Aristotle polemicizes against the *Ideas:* "In a very broad way he

* ("that arcane and profound discipline").

† ("So many divine matters have been discussed for so long that now for the first time I am beginning to appreciate Aristotle, the prince of philosophers.")

‡ ("With inimitable charm and elegence, he reads in Greek Sophocles, the Athenian writer of tragedies. . . . Further, he took up the books on *Politics*, but has set them aside for comment on holidays.")

explained Platonic doctrine. Plato maintained that there was a God, the supreme being and king over all, whose intelligence encompassed all lesser species, but only as causes, not as essences. This God, understanding himself, eternally generates a second God, and that second God has all in his mind, that is, the formal causes of all the species which are essentially in him and are of his substance. And he possesses, in the first place, the species of the universal world, and finally the species of all other things. Regarding them thus, that is, understanding himself, he generates all other species of all lesser created things; and he produces third and fourth gods."[38]

There is no reason to go further. It is important, however, to emphasize that it was Acciaiuoli himself who, in noting the commentary on the *Nicomachea* which gives us in polished form nothing more than Argyropulos's lessons, suppressed (and not unwittingly) this concise digression into Platonic theology. Still, the echoes and reverberations of such teaching were certainly significant in the cultivated Florentine world. The influence of the learned Greek—I would even say of his "Neoplatonism"—may be found nearly everywhere, even with Tignosi, who was a physician by profession but who entered the lists against the "conservatives" specifically in defense of Argyropulos's "moral" commentaries, relating them to the new tendencies and discussing at length Argyropulos's theses on the doctrine of ideas.[39]

The conflict between tradition and innovation, as it so often does, was to revolve most of the time around formal questions of expression and language. In this as in many other arguments, certain manifestations have frequently and mistakenly been pointed to as exemplary because of their forceful eloquence and lucidity. The discussion between Barbaro and Pico on the language of the philosophers—which Melanchthon carried over into Protestant countries and which in Catholic countries was to be touched upon again in a valid way in the treatise on the style of Cardinal Sforza Pallavicino—far from being the original point of view of two prominent personalities, merely resumed, without concluding, a dispute that was everywhere present in innumerable documents.[40] It was, in fact, Tignosi, a source one would certainly not suspect of being a good Aristotelian, a famous physician and hence dedicated to research on nature, who had to defend himself energetically against the criticism of the conservatives and who upheld the method taught by the "philologists" used in translating and commenting on Aristotle and other major philosophers. Though it later became a question of elegance, even of ornamentation, the issue was originally, and basically remained, a question of clarity: a need for clearness of expression corresponding to a clarity of mind. The form, the language, the speech was to be *expressior et elegantior*, but above all more clear, more concise.

Those (and there are many) who cannot recognize the tie between what we call "philological" criticism and the subsequent scientific revival err at the outset when they do not pay attention to the common denominator of the anti-Aristotelian argument, which was then in more than one case primarily a formal argument. The "philologist" criticized a certain mode of expression as being barbaric, "gothic," and therefore unsuitable and inadequate for use in written expression. The translator or the commentator on Aristotle did not render, that is, clarify or express, the author; instead of making the work accessible, he barred the way to an understanding of its sense, its direction, its meaning. The new method advocated by "philology" represented the critical awareness of a period which rejected a language no longer adequate in itself. Tignosi accused the scholastic barbarians and certain "friars" of obfuscation. Politian was to insist on the point again in his lessons on Aristotelian logic, charging the "barbarian" logicians with not understanding Aristotle and therefore of obscuring rather than clarifying his work.[41]

These were frequently rhetorical discourses, not themselves devoid of ambiguity and a tendency toward elegance and ornamentation, not without implicit rhetoric. Although they were perhaps valid arguments in the ethical and political spheres, they were too often wrongly introduced in treating the natural sciences. In his tract attacking Barbaro, which later was to become an authoritative text, Pico was to demonstrate the pitfalls of rhetoric very well. But the unquestionable value of the need for clarity escaped him, and he did not succeed in evading a moralizing tone which in another, detrimental, sense is also rhetorical: better Duns Scotus speaking "barbarously" of God than the most lucid Lucretius speaking of nature.

In essence the great discussion on the *ratio dicendi*—not just as an exercise in argument but also in the basis of its construction—expressed a demand for a more exact language. The attitude was nearly always the same—that of the "philologist" toward texts, whether these were the books of the ancients, the book of God, or the great book of nature, which was also divine law and the living testament of a testator who could not die. It is not a coincidence, I think, that the image of the book was so widespread and persistent, as dear later to Campanella as it was to Galileo.[42]

Above all, then, the actuality of Argyropulos's teaching lay in his rare ability as a Greek scholar, in the precision with which he discussed texts to justify selected subject matter, in his masterly way of moving about in the Greek world while at the same time he was so well schooled in the Latin medieval scholastic tradition. He was "modern" in his clear and polished translations and in his comment, which was not only lucid but articulated with rigorous logic. His chain of reasoning was developed with perfect, unambiguous logic. He esteemed Cicero and admired Aristotle; he was convinced that speech was all the more effective when reason had contributed to constructing it as an organic whole.[43] Sophocles as well as Plato, Aristotle as well as Plotinus, are alive and present in his lectures; so are the great "physicists of antiquity," Simplicius and Philoponus, Alexander and Themistius. As Pandolfini observed, the great fascination in the school of Argyropulos lay in the discovery of Aristotle—of a new, truly vital Aristotle, restored to the world in which he lived and viewed in the current of thought which nourished him and to which he in turn gave so much force.

But the fascination lay also in its encounter with the mysterious and hidden Platonic discipline. It is natural that there was (and still is) much discussion about Renaissance Platonism. Later, when, following on the heels of the great Ficino, the "continuity" of that tradition of "divine" speculation from the ancient Academy to the Court of Lorenzo de' Medici was discovered, it was not difficult to line up names and evidence. Saint Augustine and Scotus Erigena, the school of Chartres and the Franciscans, Avicenna and the Cusan, and later Pletho and Bessarion, all came to take their places in that golden sequence which the wise Marsilio perhaps understood with the help of one of his magic amulets or through the influence of some benign star.

Today the continuity of the Platonic tradition may not seem quite that clear.[44] If one confines his horizon to this Florentine milieu in which the love for the Platonists was most widespread, he may discern quite easily the differences in interests and motives. In the last years of the Trecento the best-known work of Plato's was *Timaeus,* because of the wide dissemination of Calcidius's commentary. Salutati, who for years had tried in vain to procure a copy for himself of *Phaedo,* was also acquainted primarily with *Timaeus.* Pier Paolo Vergerio, who later was to dwell on the *Gorgias* and who read the *Republic,* took down in his own hand extracts of that famous treatise on nature exactly as *Timaeus* appeared to medieval knowledge. Giovanni da Ravenna had studied under William of Conches. Niccoli, who was such a great admirer of all of Plato's works, started out with the teacher Calcidius; Ficino, too, was to start out as a very young man with Calcidius.[45]

The Plato of *Timaeus* is the characteristically medieval Plato, the "physicist," the theoretician of the *naturalis aequitas.* Calcidius chose happy and propitious expressions to define the relationship between Socrates, who, preoccupied with human justice, *induxit effigiem civilis reipublicae,* and the Pythagorean *Timaeus,* who, oriented toward a vision of the cosmos, considered the norm that rules the divine whole and treated the world universe as though he were dealing with the city (*in mundi huius sensilis veluti quadam communi urbe ac republica voluit inquiri*). For the former the consideration of human law was uppermost; for the latter, the rule of the city derived from the cosmic order.[46]

The humanism that had searched for the moral and political Aristotle, that had heard in Cicero the echo of Plato, also asked of Plato the construction of the human world, of civil justice (*Platonis speculemur opus, quo fonte bibisse Tullius asseritur*).[47] On the other hand, the need for rationality which distinguished so many of these writers—the need also to reorganize the world of men according to the laws of reason—gave greater reality to the desire to integrate the consideration of the states as they were historically created with the study of the State as it should be, if a technique dictated by a sovereign intelligence were to preside at its head. It was in fact Cicero (Uberto Decembrio testifies to this) who recognized the urgency of studying Plato's *Republic:* the image of the city as it is, as the experiences of men have slowly constructed it, makes the design of the city as it should be, rational and perfect, more to be desired. Going back again to the roots of the "return" to Plato, we find, not a metaphysical preoccupation, but a political and moral one, specifically in the polemic against a "physical" interest. We suddenly find the need to discover the reason for human behavior in depth. Chrysoloras, Uberto Decembrio, Pier Candido Decembrio, Cassarino: in a few years four versions of the *Republic,* and the translation of the *Laws* by George of Trebizond. Leonardo Bruni, translating the *Epistles* into Latin, expressed well the sense and the direction of these first Platonic letters of the humanists: not only the love of a living and speaking Plato, a man among men (*cum Platone ipso, eumque intueri coram videtur*), but also, for political men, the secret of a great political experience. ("Learn by heart," Cosimo advised, "each of his political maxims.")[48]

Even stripped of all its rhetorical ornamentation and obsequious flattery, Trapezunzio's dedication of the *Laws* to the Venetian Senate bears weight: "it behooves you, who have put into practice the state of reason that Plato outlined, to read Plato."[49] It was certainly fashion that prompted the Duke of Gloucester to solicit a translation of Plato's masterpiece from Decembrio. In the codices one is struck by his note of ownership on the manuscript of the Pier Candido translation, which was completed with so much impassioned haste, and one is impressed as well by his letters, which are so full of enthusiasm and excitement.[50] But after due place is given the rhetoric and the fashion of the time, the important fact remains that the whims of princes and lords centered with so much persistence precisely around Plato's political writings.

And with politics, rhetoric is "reborn." One of the dialogues studied with major attention was the *Gorgias.* Vergerio meditated over it, and Bruni translated it; it was often read and analyzed; it was discussed together with *Phaedrus.*[51] Old Coluccio certainly wanted to read *Phaedo,* so dear to his Petrarch, for so much of the world of antiquity pertained to *Phaedo* as well as to the *Apology* and *Crito,* and his interest was so lively in Socrates. But the *Crito* and the *Apology* also dealt with the problems of the law, of justice, and of unjust condemnation.

Of the great theoretical Dialogues, the *Parmenides* was not translated until about 1450, when it was translated for the Cusan by Trapezunzio, who stressed its very skillful dialectics, its *ornatus verborum,* and its *pompa compositionis.*[52] Among many Platonic readings during the preceding half-century, neither *Meno, Theaetetus,* the *Sophistes, Philebus,* nor even the entire *Timaeus* were to be found. Bruni translated only a small fragment of the *Banquet,* as a piece of supreme beauty; not even the parts of the *Phaedrus* that are essential to speculative thought were made accessible. The *Cratylus,* of which Bruni and Salutati both speak, was considered as a treatise on semantics. It was due to the influence of such thinkers as Argyropulos and Bessarion that interest was stimulated in Plato the "theologist," although the discussion, which was certainly considerable, merely echoed discarded themes without delving deeply into them.

This does not mean, to be sure, that Argyropulos alone inspired the new interest. It we limit ourselves to Florence, we may observe that much changed after the Council, after Cosimo's advent to power, and that there was a considerable change in the orientation of the culture. The appearance of Ficino, a phenomenon that was central to and dominated the last decades of the century—at least until the profound upheaval that marked the rise of Savonarola—ushered in an atmosphere that by now had virtually nothing in common with the early part of the Quattrocento. It is possible that Argyropulos was the focal point, at least on the level of philosophical culture, of the crisis.

Strangely enough, the original and somewhat bizarre figure of Pletho, his personal relations with Cosimo, his ideas on political and religious reform, and the "chaldean oracles" have led to the supposition that his influence was profound. In reality, Pletho is scarcely mentioned by any of the writers of the time, even by those who one would have thought should have had some sympathy for him. Ficino and Pico barely take notice of him, and that only in passing.[53] The animosities and disagreements among the Greeks with regard to his calumny of Aristotle continued with almost no reverberation in refugee circles. As for the Latins, they were confused by all the theological gossip so dear to the Byzantines. Trapezunzio occasionally manifested a momentary interest in Pletho, but he too was little esteemed by his compatriots. Only Bessarion was respected, although not highly, by the cultivators of philosophic disciplines.

The influence of Argyropulos, certainly less apparent, was far greater. His translations and, most important, his university teaching were profoundly felt, especially in Florence, from whence they were introduced surreptitiously everywhere. It is useful to reread a letter written much later (in November 1489) to Roberto Salviati by Alamanno Rinuccini, whose writer recalls and comments on the work of the learned Byzantine.[54] In the Florence before his time, Rinuccini says, ignorance was widespread due to the inadequacy of the teachers, who forced people to study up to their old age what children could have done without: "Philosophy, which comprises the knowledge of nature and thus also of the supernatural, few savored, believing that they had accomplished more than enough when they had learned Aristotle's books on morals. The friars were philosophizing, and those preparing to devote themselves to medicine were cultivating the *studia humanitatis,* as the writings of many long before our time show; but among them, with the exception of Giannozzo Manetti, I would say there were very few scholars who were learned in philosophy." It was to Acciaiuoli's credit, Rinuccini continues, *me socio et comite,* that he understood immediately after their first meeting the worth of Argyropulos, who was passing through the city, and that he induced Cosimo "*ut publice ad philosophiam edocendam publica mercede conduceret.*"* Thus Argyropulos, "*peragrata Gallia, Germania et Britannia,*" decided to accept the Florentine chair, and taught philosophy systematically, not *praepostere et interrupte,* following the plan of Aristotle himself, "beginning with dialectics, to arrive at metaphysics through physics, commenting on the twelve books in a two-year course." It was due to his impetus that many studied philosophy, even though, as Rinuccini leaves us to understand, the results were inferior to those one might have expected. This, however, was not the fault of the master, "*in docendo diligentissimus et in respondendo facillimus ac liberalissimus,*"† but due to the incapacity or indolence of the pupils, many of whom returned to active life, "*curis aut publicis aut familiaribus impliciti,*"‡ considering that they had learned enough. The letter ends with an ambiguous judgment of Pico and his *Heptaplus.*

In fact, Rinuccini was not quite exact. Perhaps his memory, certainly his enthusiasm was deceiving him in reconstructing the event leading to Argyropulos's invitation to Florence, in indicating the order of his courses, and in describing the tone of his teaching, which had started specifically with morals. But Rinuccini, in 1489, bore a grudge; and considering his reserved judgment of contempo-

* ". . . to appoint him, on behalf of the state and at public expense, as a teacher of philosophy."

† ". . . who was most conscientious in his teaching and ready and willing to advise at very great length."

‡ ". . . committed to pursue their public or private affairs,"

rary philosophy (and there was certainly Ficino), he was probably airing his political beliefs. The rest of the letter is intentionally polemical in its overall condemnation of Florentine culture up to the end of 1456, as well as in its words about Pico. After his praise of Aristotle's "systematic" teaching and his metaphysics, after his implied criticism of all those who let themselves be taken up by family or public preoccupations (was he alluding to and blaming Acciaiuoli as well?), Rinuccini equivocates when it comes to Pico, who could dedicate himself entirely to speculative thought and whose Platonic, cabalistic convictions were obviously distasteful to him.

Rinuccini was celebrating an Argyropulos who, by 1489, had already been considerably distorted by argument. But (and this was important and at least partially correct, as he pointed out to Roberto Salviati who was infatuated with Pico), it was specifically and solely to the Byzantine school that the change in the direction of philosophical studies in Florence owed its origin. No less significant, on the other hand, is the fact that Acciaiuoli, who was the most faithful follower of Argyropulos, not only never rejected the old Florentine "moral" tradition, but even reaffirmed it; if anything, he tended to underrate the "Platonic theology," which made its triumphal entry into the city in the "Aristotelian" courses of the Byzantine professor. The comments that Donato edited are those on morals and politics; the passages that he deleted or toned down are the Neoplatonic. In Acciaiuoli's preface to the *Politics,* written on 3 August 1472 and dedicated to Federigo da Montefeltro, the following comments are well worth noting:

> All men of learning are in common accord that Aristotle of Stagyras has left to posterity a body of philosophical doctrine that is remarkable in every part. Even if one leaves aside the dialectics, physics, metaphysics and similar matters certainly worthy of being known, the elegance and the richness with which he treated questions to do with the life of the individual, of the family and the state are astonishing. In the first place, in fact, he demonstrated by what way of life and conduct everyone can attain happiness, within the limits allowed by the human condition. Then, briefly, he dealt with the family, in order that domestic *societas* might also attain its own state of felicity. Finally, step by step, he arrived at the formation of the state, overlooking nothing: what seemed beneficial to one person alone, then to many, and finally to the city and to the people. I too, following the example of the books on morals . . . , thought it

well to face these public questions, in order not to appear to have neglected, like an inept poet, the final act; nor have I overlooked the part that concerns the family. . . . [55]

A year later, on 27 August 1473, Acciaiuoli finished translating the "most remarkable historian, Leonardo Aretino," "since I consider," he declared, "that every good, the more common it becomes and the more widespread among people, the more perfect and important it is. And there can be no doubt that historical information is most useful, and of the utmost value to those who rule and govern, because by examining past events they can better judge the present and the future, and advise their republic more wisely as to the needs of their city." And precisely "so that it should be common not only to those versed in the Latin language, but also to those who know only the vernacular, has it been necessary to translate this work, which makes me quite certain that Leonardo, had he lived longer, would have translated it himself for the greater benefit of the city."[56]

After Acciaiuoli had completed his work, he had it handsomely copied in order to offer it to his city and his lord, and "this copying plus the finest miniature illustrations cost him a good two hundred gold florins."[57] In his heart he must have felt that he had thus rounded out the system and the order of his works—from the "morals" to "politics," to the "history" of the free people of Florence, for the good of his "city." This too was an Aristotelian "order," in his judgment, which had matured in the school of Argyropulos, even though it was somewhat different from that praised by Rinuccini and by others—from the ascent to divine hierarchies developed at Lorenzo's court by the Ficinian Platonists.

The Teacher and the Student

To give a precise idea of Argyropulos's traits is not easy; such an account cannot be pieced together from the many facts gathered by his last biographer. He was a man of great culture, an authority on Greek literature as well as on Latin writers, and he was well versed in the major scholastics. He was also prone to the characteristic restlessness of many Byzantine refugees, who were rarely able to find a peaceful haven in exile.

Certainly the learned Greek found a congenial enough environment in Italy. He enjoyed almost affectionate relationships with devoted pupils as well as with great lords, even though one may gather, specifically from certain of Acciaiuoli's letters, that there often remained a distance and a reciprocal lack of understanding. He traveled extensively throughout Europe. He had a large family, although it appears that he was not equally fond of all his children. He was something of an eccentric and was not always easy to deal with. It is also evident that he was not impervious to feminine wiles, worldly goods, or the favors of the great, though no one ever likened him to so many of his compatriots who were grasping, quarrelsome, and unreliable.[58]

In Florence he was an outstanding professor and an eminent scholar. He even made an impression on Leonardo da Vinci, who recorded a conversation with him. Unless "modern" translations were available, he retranslated Aristotle for his lectures, and he elucidated his thought in other areas beside ethics, logic, physics, psychology, and metaphysics. Primarily, however, he was the first of the Greeks to familiarize his listeners with the Hellenic world in all its complexity. If we read attentively the comments that have been conserved for us in Acciaiuoli's notes, we readily see that Argyropulos's lectures combined rare philological insight with a superior knowledge of history. He accompanied his explanation of the text and the impressive logical connection always established in the author's exposition with analyses of various interpretations and with references to Arab and Latin commentators. But, above all, we find the explicit and declared intention to establish Aristotle's meaning so that his words might truly reflect his world and his culture.

Among others, his treatment of the question of the soul-entelechy, made famous in the pages that open the first century of Politian's *Miscellanea*,[59] is a fairly good example. Confronted with this text of the *Tusculanae*, in which it is stated that for Aristotle the soul is the *endelechia*—that is, *continuata motio et perennis* (continuous and perpetual motion)—Argyropulos explained that Cicero showed himself to be ignorant of this concept both in Greek and in philosophy ("*nec philosophiam scisse nec literas graecas*"). No one, he added, who was in any way familiar with Aristotle's writings did not know that Aristotle's term *entelechia*, on the contrary, did not mean in fact a continuous and perpetual motion, but rather meant accomplished perfection. Argyropulos considered that Cicero's error resulted from a doctrinal confusion which had led him to attribute to Aristotle the

Platonic thesis of the perpetual and autonomous motion of the soul. This then explained the replacement of the correct term (*entelechia*) by the incorrect though close one (*endelechia*) opposed by all the Greek commentators.

Argyropulos's explicit clarification pleased the Greeks (*plaudente Gaza vetere soldali*) but encountered in the scholar Politian a precise and shrewd refutation which naturally gained favor with the Latins (*placet hoc Hermolao*). In fact Politian believed that "on purpose and with justification, a man of Cicero's culture had made the new term used by Aristotle correspond to the Platonic theory of the *Phaedrus* on the perpetual and divine motion of the soul."

Argyropulos's course of lectures on the soul, of which Rinuccini also speaks and which Acciaiuoli has conserved for us, was however not among his most noteworthy; at least it was not the one that aroused Donato's greatest interest. The student had ended his studies directly with the ethics; as we have noted, Argyropulos purposely had begun his teaching with the ethics, even though this was in conflict with that exact plan of studies which he defined in very explicit terms according to his taste for classifying the structure of the sciences. This structure may not have been foreign later on to such a compilation of writings as the *Panepistemon* by Politian himself: "The order of learning is the following: first, learn the grammar, then rhetoric, and, following this, dialectics, morals, mathematics, physics and, finally, metaphysics."[60]

But in Florence (and not only in Florence), the greatest interest was centered around three aspects of practical philosophy: ethics, politics, and economics; the very groups who had called Argyropulos to the city emphasized that this was their attitude. This interest, moreover, may be traced far back in the history of the city. Brunetto Latini, uniting Cicero's rhetoric with Aristotle's morals, wrote: "Tullio said that the most noble science for governing the city is rhetoric, that is, the science of speaking. However, if speaking were not ordered, the city could have no establishment of justice or of human society."[61]

Dedicating his small treatise on dialectics to Piero de' Medici, Argyropulos later said the same thing in substance. The same theme recurred until it became a commonplace in all the most important oratory of the Florentine Quattrocento, beginning with Salutati. These orations in praise of justice, one of which was repeated every two months "from the office of the gonfalonier" "to the ringhiera" in the presence of the magistrates and the people of Florence, have been conserved in great number in the codices along with the religious orations frequently delivered by the same men before lay societies. If one studies these official speeches—religious or secular—in their entirety and does not limit himself to examining some particular feature, he will be struck by their rhetorical tone and the tired, threadbare clichés. Studied en masse, what seemed happy assertions to be duly stressed get lost in the uniform monotony of the contemporary tone. But we would be wrong to understimate this tone, which perfectly expressed a way of public life and a habit of conscious seriousness.

"It is a praiseworthy habit . . . ," Acciaiuoli was to begin his address on 15 May 1469,[62]

> and one that has been observed for a long time, according to which every two months . . . someone from the office of the gonfalonier of this most worthy place, in the venerable presence of you most excellent and honored magistrates, shows how useful and necessary it is for the republic to govern with reason and justice, for long experience has demonstrated this to be the sole virtue without which no city can in any way endure. And certainly, if there is some good law or institution in our city, this ceremony holds first place, since it repeats and frequently calls to mind all that which constitutes the secure foundation of any public and private good.

Acciaiuoli continues in terms that are drawn strictly from the fifth book of the *Nicomachea*, which had inspired the speeches of *his* Giannozzo Manetti and which later was to be used as a model of its kind. Justice appeared to Donato nearly to represent the meeting point of philosophy, law, and theology.

> I do not doubt that, if this divine virtue which God has sent to earth and placed into our hands and those of others who rule and govern could be seen with our eyes, its splendor would appear so great that it would entirely overcome our senses, and would set our minds afire with an ardent love and desire to achieve its beauty and dignity, for it is said to be the star Hesperus, it is called Lucifer, it is known as the queen of all the moral virtues. . . . It is the rule and measure of every action. It is what makes us happy and blessed.

Justice, which represents a calm inner measure and a composed public equilibrium, is truly the meeting point of the righteous man and the well-governed city: "If our happiness is nothing else, as Democritus understood it . . . , than the peace of mind, the calm that forever guides the spirit of the just man. In line with this is what Xantippe used to say of her husband, Socrates, that she saw him come to and leave the house always with the same countenance, which showed that he had a very serene spirit free from any troublesome care."

Justice is the highest norm of public life, as it is the foundation of human life and the rule in the family:

> Just as the physician considers the health of his patient to be his aim, the general, victory, the captain of a ship, a fair voyage, so the good ruler in normal government always has as his evident purpose the observance and administration of justice. This is the judgment of the supreme and divine Plato, who in his works on the republic praises this excellent virtue so highly that he does not hestitate to say that just as the soul is in our body, so justice is the soul of the city. The body lives through the soul, the republic lives through justice. O, noble clear judgment of the philosopher! But still not content to place so much dignity in the republic . . . , he also gives it the great honor of raising it to the heavens, affirming that if there were any virtue which might be properly attributed to God, then it is none other than justice.[63]

This was, it is well to repeat, the custom in oratory. These were rhetorical themes that should rightly not be overestimated. But it was still a custom whose prevalance is significant, whose decline was clearly to indicate a crisis. In the ideal of serenity and of measure—the "serenity" of Socrates on departing from and returning to his house—lies the tone of a society which had found its equilibrium and had established its way of life. There is a special grandness about this fidelity to an order which at base had already been outlived, consumed by a mortal disease.

These men did not stint in their duties as public citizens; in the magistratures and in business, in the politics of their city and of Italy their object was to maintain a rational balance that could adapt to various exigencies without suffocating them. They were men who believed in "justice" or, rather, in the possibility of a wise and careful calculation in order to harmonize "liberty" and "peace," and yet they upheld a nobility worthy of respect. Because they had a singular faith in man's reason and believed in wisdom, the subtle expedient and, I would almost say, honest business, they were in the end able to order the lives of men and states and to bring prosperity to all without harm to things or persons. The "men of antiquity" were for them this paradigm of the supremacy of wisdom, the triumph of "form," that is, of measure; they were a well-ordered political cosmos. In their school order and perfect equilibrium had to be "reborn."

> You have kept safe and integrate not only the freedom of a great state, but that of all Italy, which would have been subjected to the power of one man alone. The rashness of some having been brought under control, all the discords composed, all the wars pacified, this state has finally reached the goal that the sages advised to the best rulers. As the physician's goal is health, the general victory, the navigator, a safe voyage, so the ruler of states desires happiness, economic security, renown, and an honest and virtuous life for the citizens.[64]

Thus Acciaiuoli, in the dedication to Piero di Cosimo of his version of the life of Demetrius, translated into Latin the ideal he extolled in the vernacular in 1469. He remained faithful to this ideal in the most trying moments of his life, as well as throughout his magistracy, "aiming to follow reason rather than sentiment in accordance with the practice of prudent men." When he was a magistrate at Poppi in 1462, he was obliged to prosecute friends of his friend, Piero de' Pazzi, and he wrote to Piero explaining that justice must rule over friendship: "*in hac re, que magni ponderis est, me non solum bonum virum sed etiam bonum civem esse, equo animo patiaris.*"* Two factions had broken sworn agreements in a bloody clash. "To violate the peace is the same as to break faith; when this happens, society, friendship, and the community of men are destroyed. If the mutual faith among people is broken, no one may longer maintain his way of life. Even pirates and savages are in the habit of respecting a truce, of keeping the faith and honoring an oath. These traitors, who preferred to obey their angry passions rather than to follow reason, have forgotten the rights of nations and of common humanity."[65]

* "In this matter, which is of considerable consequence, you should be well content that I am not only a good man but also a good citizen."

This was not rhetoric; though interests, friends, relatives were at stake, since the rule had been established he remained loyal to it: "and the city depended on his fidelity, and found it was inviolably served by him." What is important is not so much the honesty of a life, but how it was conceived and identified with the ideal of a society and of a period. With a "well-ordered community" the Florentines aimed to rival the wise and prudent people of antiquity, who conducted themselves according to the law of reason.

In this spirit Acciaiuoli collected and summarized Argyropulos's lessons on the *Nicomachea* and published the commentary together with the new translation by the learned Byzantine, thus joining the company of men whom he venerated most, from Palla di Nofri Strozzi to Leonardo Bruni to Giannozzo Manetti. Addressing himself to Cosimo de' Medici, who was an assiduous reader of Aristotle's works (*cum vidissem hos libros a te libentessime legi*), he wrote an eloquent eulogy to the ancient treatise (*habent libri ii summam dignitatem admirabilemque doctrinam ordinem vero prope singularem*). He presents both the translation and the commentary as the mature fruits of a society, expressions of a way of thinking and of an order of life. Acciaiuoli, who was celebrated by his contemporaries as the perfect example of the citizen philosopher ("governing the Republic, he applied himself to philosophy, and philosophizing, he governed the Republic") and whose constant aim was to unite in himself moral rectitude, practical activity, political wisdom, and speculative insight, saw in the *Nicomachea* the solemn expression of a type of complete man.[66]

When Louis XI ascended the throne of France in 1461, Florence sent an extraordinary diplomatic mission to pay him respect. It included Filippo de' Medici, the Archbishop of Pisa, Piero de' Pazzi, and Bonaccorso Pitti. Donato Acciaiuoli took advantage of this occasion to dedicate to the new sovereign a copy of his life of Charlemagne, "a worthy homage from a Florentine to the King of France." The choice of Charlemagne was not accidental; "we have read," Filippo de' Medici declared in his solemn speech to the king, "that Charlemagne, your predecessor in this kingdom, who was called to Italy on the appeal of Pope Adrian, restored our cities, which had been ruined by Totila, king of the Goths, and for two centuries turned into a desert." Acciaiuoli's dedication of the book is in several respects noteworthy. He was grateful to the king of France not only for the former benevolence to the Florentines, but also for the kindness shown the Acciaiuoli family:

In thinking of what you might appreciate . . . , Charlemagne came to my mind, who in his time was not only the crowned ruler of the French, but the light and glory of the whole world. I see it as a duty to write about his life, customs, and noble deeds, and to place before all men the image of a prince, who was not fictitious, as Xenophon's Cyrus, but truly by nature endowed with many extraordinary gifts, and who appeared by divine will, so that he might serve as an example and a mirror of virtue for all the princes of the world to follow in their private and public rule.

Greater than Marcellus, Fabius, or Scipio, he strived tirelessly "not for one state alone, nor for the glory of the Roman people, but for the common freedom of all Christians."[67]

It was Charlemagne, we read in the *Vita*, who made Florence and Italy rise again, liberating them from the barbarians who had held them in subjugation for three hundred and thirty years (*tot enim ab Augustolo ad Carolum Magnum fuere*). Passing through Etruria after his coronation, "he restored the city to its ancient grandeur, induced the nobility, who had been dispersed in their surrounding castles, to return to it, encircled it with new walls, and adorned it with churches." But, above all, Charlemagne gave new life to letters and culture:

His teacher had been Albinus, who later took the name Alcuin, a very learned man and a well-known philosopher, from whom he acquired not only wisdom but also the precepts of oratory and the art of speaking. It was due to the work of Alcuin that, it is said, Charlemagne founded the school of Paris, which was later preserved and expanded under his successors, and achieved such prestige and fame that it is now known throughout the world as the seat of cultured men.

Acciaiuoli's conception of the Carolingian renaissance and his predilection for a legendary tradition dear to the Florentines are not so important as the picture he gives of this ideal figure of the learned and wise prince, who seeks in culture, and classical culture, the necessary doctrines to rule the state ("liberally educated, not only in Latin but also in Greek letters, he entrusted the education of his own sons as well to learned men, so that from the time of their birth they were schooled in the noble arts").[68]

Acciaiuoli not only derived pleasure from history (*ex clarorum hominum memoria non mediocrem voluptatem*), but everywhere he sought to establish the ideal ruler of the state, a prince who would correspond in reality to that image that the philosophers he revered defined in their treatises on morals and politics. For him this ideal was embodied in Charlemagne in the Middle Ages and Scipio in antiquity—Scipio and not Caesar (*quantum enim Scipio Romane libertati consuluerit* . . .). This explains why he continued to stress the thesis that there is no duty that is higher, holier, or nobler than to work to assure that justice may reign in the state (*nihil . . . in hac vita preclarius, nihil excellentius, nihil sanctius quam in administranda republica patrie sue pietatem officiumque prestare*). This duty seemed to him to be an inherent part of his own inner formation, his own culture: "What can be more worthy to be desired than that culture be joined with good habits and with a model life?"[69]

These words appear in a letter written in June 1461 to Filelfo, a letter that revealed the writer's deep affection for Argyropulos, whom he loved "not only as a teacher, but also as a father." Beside learned letters, in this same period, we find business letters and letters preoccupied with the Italian situation, with the affairs of Genoa, Naples, and Milan, and with the French menace. "I am very much afraid," he wrote on 29 June 1461 to Lorenzo Acciaiuoli, "that if God does not intervene, there will be great dissension in Italy. The transalpine nations have never invaded this side of Gaul without the gravest consequences. The Gallic people are very ferocious, as others are aware, and as Italy herself has often experienced. . . . *Quid si sapientes viri non sapiunt?*"[70] Nor, on the other hand, did the danger of the Turkish advance escape him. "If ever there was a time," he wrote to the Pope in 1463,[71]

in which the savage attacks of the barbarians had to be combatted, this is the moment. With Byzantium taken, and Sinop and Trebizond defeated, all of Greece annexed, all of Christendom is threatened by war, massacres and slavery. Once the Goths, Vandals, Herulians and other barbarian peoples overran Italy with equal violence, and held her slave more than was fitting for a country that had been the master of all people. Hence if we want to prepare wisely for the future, we should consider the events of the past.

After 1462, following his magistracy at Poppi, his official posts multiplied: he became prior in 1463, gonfalonier in 1474; he was sent as ambassador several times to the Italian states, to Rome for the election of Sixtus IV (1471), to Milan (1475), and to France (1473). He was governor of Volterra (1470–77), podestà of Montepulciano (1472), podestà of Pisa (1476), and an official of the Florence Studio (March 1473–October 1474). His speeches enjoyed great success. The dual motif of his activity is constantly reflected in his private correspondence: his preferred studies and an attentive and active interest in Florentine and Italian problems.

With Ammannati he discoursed about books, and he accepted the latter's advice and criticism. The old master apologized—*si imperiose loquor, ex veteri magisterio hoc imperium est*—while continuing to discuss with him frankly, giving his honest opinions. Ammannati wanted a Latin Plutarch. He had found one, but an expensive one (*pretium minus LXXX aureis esse non potest*), in three volumes, which the owner did not intend to sell separately. The cardinal was ready to pay; what made him hesitate was not the price, but the mistakes of the translators (*precium non terret, terrent . . . traduciones*). He had consulted several of them: "Antonio Tudertino, whom you knew well, has translated them very badly; I liked the translations of Leonardo Aretino, as well as those of Francesco Barbaro. You have translated only two lives, both of which I fully approve." But Ammannati did not approve otherwise of the style of Acciaiuoli's letters. It would be well, he reprimanded him, if he wrote with more care; if he did not know how to write, or if he were careless, he was wasting his time, and his teacher really had no cause to rejoice.[72]

Donato answered ironically: "I have learned from your letters that you are now entirely dedicated to the Holy Scriptures, and that you are immersed in the comments of Saint Thomas. This has convinced me that, elegance and richness of expression aside, you consider only the content; and concentrating entirely on broad questions, you neglect the small ones." At any rate he thanked him for the reproof:

For a long time your admonitions have convinced me that in this our mortal life nothing is so beautiful as culture united with an honest life. Perhaps I have lacked the talent and zeal to achieve this; but the will never, nor will I ever lose sight of the fact that it is more often your teaching, when I was very young, that continues to guide me. How much I would like to see you, speak to you, and listen with pleasure to your beautiful conversation. This is the greatest desire of my life. But since this is denied me, write to me at least, kind as you are, a little more often. The longer and more frequent your letters are, the more they will be appreciated and fill me constantly with new joy.

This was in mid-1465. The interchange of affectionate advice, reproaches, and apologies, the lesson in style, was to continue at a distance. In 1467 Ammannati was overjoyed that Donato had finished the lives of Scipio and Hannibal—"But for pity's sake, do not be in a hurry; correct and revise everything with care. Remember that in Florence I hardly glanced through half a page and I found several things that would not do." But then, from Siena, he wrote that he and Campano had read Acciaiuoli's copies of the translation of the life of Demetrius and the biography of Charlemagne *tua opera ex diversi collecta.* Campano, a man of fine taste, praised the style (*ornatum laudat, et genus dicendi illustre et purum*). And he, Ammannati, the old teacher, had taken delight in recognizing traces of his former teaching (*antique institutionis nostre sum contemplatus vestigia*). The dialogue continued; Campano praised Demetrius and Charlemagne "brought from obscurity to the light, one from the heart of Greece, the other from the depths of barbarity."[73]

This exchange was uninterrupted despite the fact that Ammannati had written an indignant letter, already mentioned, from Rome in November 1478, a letter that should be read in its entirety—proud in its reproof, human in its request for money, which the elderly teacher, who had known poverty, asked of the excellent scholar for his children, in the name of their old affection (*mitto tibi ex reliquiis praeteriti naufragii mei aureos viginti et quinque papales, qui en calceandis filiolis te adiuvent*). Finally, the teacher was again placated and praised his pupil's work: *Scipione e Annibale.* Continue the work, he said: the times and the vigor of the mind, the lucid style, and the esteem of all, demand it.[74]

When Acciaiuoli was far from Florence on official duties, the scholarly conversation was kept up in letters. From Poppi, on 20 November 1462, he discoursed amiably with Landino on this need to keep the dialogue alive. From Volterra, on 5 November 1469, he joked with Melior Cresci and Lilio Tifernate on the same question. Friends had written him about the peace of solitude and the wisdom it would instill. But friends are more stimulating, Donato answered, "than the hills, the mountains and the broad horizons of this country.

Socrates, the greatest of all philosophers . . . , said that it was not the mountains and not the trees that taught him wisdom. . . . Study and an upright life, rather than mountains, are beneficial to man." Acciaiuoli did not complain:

The people here are meek; the city is strong, built on a steep rock with a wide view that spreads out on all sides; the country is rich in saffron, wine, oil, wheat, and every other victual. There are bathing places here, veins of sulphur and salt, mines of copper. . . . And I am attending to the duties of my position. I study and take walks in the fashion of the peripatetics, and plan to go hunting game, the time and opportunity permitting. You . . . write to me often, and do not be deterred by my possible disagreement. Differences sharpen the wit and provide material for the exchange of letters."[75]

The ambiguous Antonio Ivani and prominent men from Volterra entered the dialogue; so did Federigo, Duke of Urbino, who asked him for his comment on the *Politics;* and later Oliviero Arduini, Lorenzo da Colle, Fonzio, Cantalicio, Ficino, Platina, in addition to his old friends.[76] Donato's grief over the loss of his son—*caro mea et filius meus erat!*—and of his brother Pietro, and his humility in the face of the "Lord of Death," reverberate in his letters. In the dispatches to the Studio we encounter the usual academic disputes, the divergences and conflicts among scholars; in the official dispatches to the Medici is shrewd, precise diplomatic information. These latter also contain news of what had by then become public functions. A good example is a letter of recommendation, sent to the Magnificent from Milan on 23 March 1475, by the "orator" Acciaiuoli on behalf of Bernardo di Vieri del Bene whom he advises he made a prior.[77]

Acciaiuoli's last literary works were the commentary on the *Politics* and the Italian translation of the *Storie* by Leonardo Bruni. It appears almost as though he was the vertex around whom had gathered all the old Florentines, bent on exploring the histories of the "free peoples" and penetrating the significance of their systems of government. The dates follow close together: on 3 August 1472, he dedicated the *Politics* to Federigo da Montefeltro; on 27 August 1473, he finished the translation of Bruni. The famous oration to Sixtus IV was delivered in 1471.[78] On 17 August 1471, he wrote the last letter—at any rate the last of which we know—to Argyropulos, who had left Florence. From 1473 on, his ambassadorial missions followed one another without a break: twice to France, then to Milan, twice to Rome, and to Volterra and Pisa. His public life had gained the upper hand.

The letters that Donato wrote himself stop in October 1474, and in the last one, to the physician Matteo Moreto, he speaks specifically of Argyropulos's translations, "*vir excellentissimus.*" In the next to last, also written in October and addressed to Giovanni Nesi, he discourses on hunting partridge and mentions a lunch that Griso had attended. This letter, dated 5 October, is playful: "*ut recreatione aliqua sublevati melius deinde gravioribus rebus vacare possimus.*"* Faced with these *studia delectationis*, we are reminded of Platina, the great master of *honesta voluptas* (as he called the culinary arts), in which he was so well versed that he wrote a treatise on the subject. A letter was addressed to Platina on 5 May 1474; there is no reference in it to *de honesta disciplina*, but to *de optimo cive*, which had pleased the Magnificent. Shortly before this, in April, Ficino had recommended to him the son of Marsuppini, the same Marsuppini whom Donato had admired so much as a young man: *non decet Musam fieri mendicam.* The names are the same, but the new world had superseded the old. That partridge dinner described to Nesi sets one thinking. Griselli, Giannozzo Manetti's secretary, was present, and with him the memory of a time when Cosimo the Elder was in the ascendant. Nesi, first a Ficinian, then a Pichian, and finally a Savonarolian, was the future author of *Oraculum de novo saeculo*, in which he sang the praises of the Ferrarese Socrates for restoring Florence to its ancient measure. Standing apart, but not detached, was Rinuccini, who then was against the Medici as in the future he would be against Savonarola, as opposed to the Medicean "tyranny" as he was to the popular advance.

In his human and cultural attachments Acciaiuolo remained true to his noble position. He worked as a good citizen for the citizens of his Florence in his own time, even though he did so with aristocratic detachment. Just as he had accepted the most profound tenets of Argyropulos, whom he had wanted in the city, without following the Platonic fashion which the Byzantine had helped to promote and which fascinated Lorenzo so much, so in the new period, with its new

* "Refreshed by a little diversion, we are the better able to deal with graver issues."

politics, he served loyally the "*res publica*" while following the old golden mean.

When the Pazzi, with whom he was tied by many bonds, made their ill-fated attempt against the Medici, he was in Rome on an official mission; and it appeared that even he and his family would be overthrown by the harsh reaction against the unsuccessful conspiracy. But faith in his loyalty prevailed: "He was the cousin of Agnolo; nevertheless the city trusted him, and it was served by him inviolably." In this tragic moment, he hurried back from Rome to Florence and was dispatched immediately as ambassador to France on a mission which the circumstances rendered most delicate. Lorenzo kept posted on his trip. He was to stop in Milan, and on 29 July the Magnificent wrote anxiously to Girolamo Morelli: "Donato should have arrived." Donato had arrived, but he had fallen ill. On 20 August, Lorenzo wrote: "We are waiting to hear . . . whether Donato will recover."[79]

Acciaiuoli died in Milan on 28 August 1478, before his fiftieth year. His funeral tribute was written by Cristoforo Landino, whom he had once called a student *etiam pratensi oppido indignum.**[80] His death, which ended a still promising career precisely in the year of the Pazzi conspiracy, might be taken as a tangible sign of the passing of a type of culture and learning that by then was on the wane in Florence. Ficino and the Ficinians, Pico and his friends, and Savonarola and the scholars who gathered around him were to represent something entirely different, even though some of the personages remained the same. Acciaiuoli was of the same caliber as the humanist chancellors of the early Quattrocento, of Bruni, and of Manetti. And if one could converse as a friend or opponent with Piero and Lorenzo "*frater meus,*" one would find himself on another level if contronted with a Landino or a Ficino.

When Cristoforo Landino, a good and honest schoolmaster, delivered the customary funeral eulogy to Donato Acciaiuoli, he no doubt meant to praise the prominent personality, descendant of a great family, who had been for a number of years an "official at the Studio," who had influenced the nomination of professors and had been a force in Florentine academic life. With him certainly disappeared a man of great culture, but, above all, a figure who was

* "unworthy even of the city of Prato."

distinguished for his noble birth, his adherents, and his rare integrity. Yet, at the moment in which many of his best friends, even his relatives, had fallen into disgrace, been killed, or been banished, it is probable that not a few followed the example of the "divine" Marsilio, who, after the Pazzi conspiracy, refused to recognize those who had been compromised, even though previously he had fawned over them with all his obsequious flattery.

For the rest, Donato Acciaiuoli did not leave a heritage of remarkable works. His letters, though significant, were not circulated; his writings were almost all of little importance. His major works were the commentary on the *Nicomachea*—which in substance everyone knew to be that of Argyropulos, and his translation of Bruni's *Storie*. The interest of the world of Florentine culture was now directed elsewhere. Acciaiuoli's reputation was linked to the ideals of an earlier time; his name could serve at best for dialogues or treatises whose purpose was to describe the old Florence.[81]

It would be a serious error to believe that his writings, which in large part were unpublished and not worthy of publication, should reveal to us a thinker of rare depth or a writer of singular stature. He was neither, even though he was well informed on philosophical questions, especially well acquainted with Aristotle and Plato, and not without knowledge of medieval and contemporary thinkers. He wrote a polished Latin; he was a careful student of the classics, interested in rhetorical devices, and a not negligible writer of Tuscan prose. Besides the translation of Bruni, which is a pleasure to read, his original drafts in the vernacular of many of his Latin writings, some of his dispatches, and his lively and well-expressed official letters testify to this.

If one discards an old prejudice and begins to read the works in the vernacular of the Latin writers of the Quattrocento (which were often first drafts later turned into Latin), one will certainly find no rare undiscovered gems but will find some beautiful passages. One would then be able to discuss on a more solid basis the literary production of the century and also the unique character of its learned language—that is, of that "Latin" which, with its artifices, at times achieved rare effects and a certain very refined and profound reasoning, an exceptional index to a whole world of understanding and way of life that is not easy to gather from a conventional formula.

These considerations apply to such a writer of modest scope as

Acciaiuoli, in whose notebooks one may find a scholarly construction—labored, studied, and step-by-step—of the Latin of the period. For example, a text by Cicero or Quintilian is broken down into its component parts and its construction punctiliously analyzed and scrutinized. We get the impression that it was exactly the same procedure an artist would follow in studying a Roman building, a temple, or a cupola, the way it had been put together, its "quality" and secret "reason." These are certainly well-known matters, but perhaps the echo of certain terms, too often interpreted in the light of later discussions, has obscured the original sense of some attitudes and hence their meaning.

At that time, by "imitating" one sought in reality the key to a certain rhythm, the law of a harmony. And one asked of the ancients —that is, of certain perfect achievements—the profound reason for that perfection, with the aim of discovering that quality or, as Patrizi said, those *logoi* that had governed the works of antiquity. In certain human expressions, considered to be models, one hoped to discover the processes by which humanity achieved outstanding results. The heroes of Plutarch do not constitute "ideas," but celebrate a humanity from which it is possible to learn a way of life. The old "histories," political events of the past in this sense, were more than models; they were "experiences" to be treasured.

Thus Acciaiuoli, the reader of Plutarch but also of the medieval biographers of Charlemagne, the translator of Bruni, hoped to integrate modern experience with the lesson of antiquity and formally to perfect and extend his style to encompass an elegant classical Latin and the good Florentine of the *Storie* by Messer Leonardo of Arezzo. Despite the teaching of Argyropulos, as a man of politics and history Donato always put greatest stress on Aristotle's ethics, economics, politics, history, and moral life. He was interested neither in Aristotelian metaphysics nor in the rising Platonic "theology."

A good Christian, he saw in religion a worldly tie among men, an everlasting hope, but he had no predilection for "very subtle theologians." "We will ignore the many ingenious researches conducted by holy doctors . . . and many other speculations which the most clever theologians are seeking." In the presence of Christ the incarnate the only human possibility is a quiet faith: "If all my limbs . . . were converted into tongues, and all the parts of my body could speak with human voices, I would have faith in my power to explain or to relate an infinitesimal part of the most sacred mystery," in whose presence "there is no mind that is not wanting, no sense that does not remain confused, and no tongue that does not become mute."[82]

These words, taken from the "oration of corpus Christi" given by Donato Acciaiuoli on 13 April 1468 "*nella compagnia de' Magi*"* contain the usual rhetoric, somewhat overblown and "baroque" as was often the case with religious oratory if it was not impassioned by the chaste sincerity of a San Bernardino of Siena or the civic vigor and apocalyptic force of a Savonarola. It was of no use to force the limits, but useful to confine them within the milieu representing a way of life in which it was a "civic" duty to participate even in lay societies and to celebrate in them the absolute "sacred" value of the "wise and discrete life." According to what one reads in the oration on justice, the principle of justice was also an aspect of religion; for if there is a virtue under heaven, it must be that of justice.

Donato once made a friendly reference to Luigi Pulci in a letter to Lorenzo.[83] It was indeed Pulci who expressed better than any other, in these years, this way of conceiving religion as an essential force of human society, independent of any sectarian religious cult:

Mentre lor cerimonie e divozioni
Con timore osservarono i Romani,
Piaceva al ciel questa religione
Che discerne le bestie dagli umani.†

And one believed that absolute justice was at the heart of religion:

e la giustizia, sai, così concede
al buon remunerazio, al tristo pene;
si che non debbe disperar mercede
Chi rettamente la sua fede tiene.‡

At one time, despairing in the face of war and the Turkish advance, Acciaiuoli wrote: "How unhappy I am! What is there to hope

* "before the Society of the Magi."
† "While the Romans observed their ceremonies
And devotions in dread, this religion
That distinguished humans from beasts
Pleased the heavens."
‡ "and justice, you know, so dispenses
recompense to the good, pain to the bad
that one need not despair of reward
Who honestly upholds his faith."

for? It seems that there is no greater pleasure now than bloodshed, carnage and massacre" (*"miserum me! Quid . . . sperare nos oportet? . . . nullus ludus videtur esse iocundior quam cruor, quam cedes, quam trucidatio hominum"*). Savonarola was to translate this sense of tragedy into apocalyptic visions; in Acciaiuoli it was to nourish a precise sense of the citizen's duties.

It may be understood in this perspective how Argyropulos's teaching became reduced to limits that in part distorted the original intention of the learned Byzantine. He had succeeded in giving an impetus to the movement Platonizing "idealism," which until the middle of the Quattrocento had been substantially ignored in Florence. Later Ficino, who aimed to be recognized as the true initiator of the Platonic cult, took pleasure in misrepresenting history: he said that it was Cosimo who made the authentic Plato of Marsilio correspond to Argyropulos's authentic Aristotle, of whom he himself approved. The Ficinian profile later crystallized into a false image of Florentine Aristotelian culture, in which Ficino's Platonism *ex novo* was inserted. Ficino always had a taste for classifying and establishing hierarchies, which induced him to make another subdivision—as imprecise as it was fortunate—of his period into Alexandrists and Averroists. This had been to some extent a commonplace in polemical use that little corresponded to the situation of Italian culture in the late Quattrocento. And yet this too was emphasized by Ficino and presented with new force to those who were attempting to evaluate the philosophical positions of the period.

In reality, if we approach the important work of Argyropulos, the translator and commentator—and there is no better access to him than through Acciaiuoli—we perceive the weight the latter carried in cultivated Florentine circles among philosophers, philologists, and men of science. If we want to illuminate the work of the Byzantine master, we must necessarily alter the picture that Ficino hoped to impress upon us of the speculations of this period and of the origins of his interests.

On the other hand, if Acciaiuoli was a friend and faithful disciple of Argyropulos, it is no less important to point out the way in which he himself narrowed the scope of the Byzantine's teaching in continuing the line that started with Salutati and led through Bruni to Manetti. Acciaiuoli confined himself to the three subjects of morals, politics, and history; even his "dialectical" studies were undertaken for their practical function, with a strong leaning toward "rhetoric." In sum, what was important to him was the study of the process of argumentation, the articulation of speech, and the invention of dialectics—not a vision of the structures of being. As Politian was to say in one of his opening lectures, it was not the sublime, divine, and serene dialectics of Plotinus, the queen of metaphysical knowledge, that interested Acciaiuoli, but dialectics as the art of speaking, as discussion that is in turn applied to concrete research.

With all this, when Acciaiuoli died in 1478, not yet an old man, he was already out of fashion. There could have been no exchange between him and the Ficinians; and he would not have been either politically or culturally at home later among the Savonarolians. Even in politics, having detached himself from the many who openly or not so openly agreed with the most active opposition to the Medici, he had collaborated too much with the "tyrant" to be approved without reserve by men like Rinuccini, and he remained too much tied to certain positions of the *Florentina libertas* to be accepted without reserve by the Mediceans.

It was precisely his position that in the end limited his activity and effectiveness, even though traces of his presence were to be felt for a long time. Nevetheless this man, who was certainly in no sense of first rank; who was tied to a world which, although it had been outlived a few decades earlier, did not for this reason appear any less distant; this good Donato who died just at the ascent of the Magnificent helps us to understand the foundation of a culture and civilization, its habits of life. The glimpses he gives are in part different from the customary picture given of Medicean Florence under Lorenzo. It was a serious, almost severe way of interpreting life, knowledge, and the arts; if at times the mode of expression had a certain rhetorical bombast, it was always the tone of a moral seriousness not yet degenerated into moralistic preaching. Ethical-political reflections and historical narrations were nourished by broad experience. The "ancients" were listened to for their solemn "lessons" in order to achieve a better understanding and to live in their own time with clearer reason. One gained a more solid awareness of the contemporary period by comparing it with the past. In antiquity one could not be misled; confronting the present with the past, one could usefully discover what traits had changed in man and what had persisted, as one turned from ancient Latin to the Florentine vernacular "in order to bestow greater benefit on the city."

If we pass at once from here to the Ficinian prose that flourished in these same years; if we consider all the baroque splendor of his images and his enthusiasm for the magnificent world of eternal ideas, for the raptures in celestial deeps of in those mysterious and evocative depths of inner man, we are reminded of Dante's description of old people clad in leather and bone. Nevertheless, if we allow ourselves to be seduced by that remarkable Ficinian grandeur and neglect any other voice, we rob that period of not only valid but profoundly effective themes. If indeed we were to judge the thinkers and problems of the entire Quattrocento as motivated by the "Platonism" of the Magnificent's court, we would distort the truth.

Notes*

1. *Vita di Donato Acciaiuoli descritta da Angiolo Segni, e per la prima volta data in luce dal cav. avv. Tommaso Tonelli* (Florence, 1841), p. 35. The handwritten manuscript is conserved in ms. Naz. 2, II, 325, cc. 91r III v of the National Library of Florence (and also in Palatino 493).

2. Alamanni Rinuccini, "Oratio in funere Mattaei Palmerii," in F. Fossi, *Monumenta ad Alamanni Rinuccini vitam contexendam* (Florence, 1953), p. 81.

3. C. Landini, *Eulogium in funere Donati Acciaiuoli.* In 1455, when the question arose of filling the chair that had been Marsuppini's, one of the candidates (along with A. Rossi) was Cristoforo Landino, who was supported by many ("a great many felt that [he] should be elected in preference to all others, and they affirmed that his teaching was not in the least abstruse . . ."). His supporters included A. Acciaiuoli (". . . my cousin Angelo worked hard for Landino; he supported him publicly and helped him generally . . .") and hence by the Medicean party (". . . the supporters of Landino . . . are considerable, but none of them are among the leaders of the republic"). Donato Acciaiuoli opposed Landino's nomination and deplored the "singular impudence" of those who "had the gall to go up to that assembly hall where only lately we heard the voice of Carolus Arentinus [Marsuppini] and, before then, the voices of so many other profoundly learned men." It was a thing unworthy even of Prato (*hoc . . . etiam pratensi oppido indignum!*). The very forceful letter to Andrea Alamanni, dated 15 April 1455, is contained in Magliab. 8: 1390, in various drafts (cc. 16r–17v and cc. 96v–97r, with the many deletions). Correcting it later on, perhaps in view of possible publication, Acciaiuoli systematically deleted Landino's name, substituting for it the expression "*familiaris vir.*" A friendly letter to Landino, sent from the Casentino on 20 November 1462, is printed in part by della Torre, *Storia,* p. 411. However, the entire letter, as it appears in Magliab. (8: 1390, 46v), indicates that Landino had turned to Acciaiuoli to raise again a question that interested him deeply: "As for that matter . . . on behalf of which you pleaded with me so

* In this introductory study to an edition of Acciaiuoli's collected letters, my purpose has been in part to fulfill the need, already pointed out by Tiraboschi and in our time by Marchesi, to better illuminate the work of Acciaiuoli, which I believe to be singularly representative of that type of Florentine civic humanism which Baron (among others) has described so well. At the outset I would like to call attention to two works to which I am especially indebted and which every student will appreciate for their integrity: A. della Torre, *Storia dell' Accademia Platonica di Firenze* (Florence, 1902) and G. Cammelli, *G. Argirupolo* (Florence, 1941).

persuasively, although it had seemed simple enough at first, the stupidity or, rather, the stubbornness of those who were debating the issue among themselves exaggerated the matter to such a point—much against my wishes—that it became difficult thereafter to find a way out. Be that as it may, in writing to you about it I don't have to go into every detail, for you know how important your letters are for me and how much I can learn from your suggestions and those of your wise and noble father, as well as from the development of the issue itself." For Acciaiuoli's activity at the time in the Casentino, see State Archives of Florence in Med. av. il Princip., 10: 401, 414.

4. Ms. Riccardiano 1166, c. 56 v. (Niccolò della Luna and Leonardo Dati): "I am lingering a while at the Dominican cloisters, not unlike Tytius in the underworld, since my circumstances here are in no way better." Another letter of special note from della Luna to Palmieri clearly illustrates the contemporary state of mind: "Niccolò della Luna sends greetings to Matteo Palmieri. The other day I learned from your so kind and welcome letter with how much forethought the senate had decreed that every single citizen be subject in the future to the public census. It seems that this is little better, if at all, than the usual frenzy, especially so since we are now witnessing how our citizenry is bent on rushing headlong into a precipice. If we have no choice and do not know how to defend our freedom with our own power, then we should do it with the aid of foreigners. If it would further the common welfare of the republic, it might indeed be better if we were to deliver ourselves to a superior foreign power. . . ." It is difficult not to be reminded of Rinuccini's *De Libertate.* When Acciaiuoli became closer to the Medici later on, he upheld his ideal and exalted Scipio, the guardian of liberty (ms. Magliab. 20: 154, c. 76r), but at that time he considered Cosimo the man who had saved "not only the freedom of this illustrious republic, but also that of all Italy, which might have been suppressed by a certain power well intent upon just that" (*Proemium in vitam Demetrii,* ms. Magliab. 23: 95, written in his own hand). And it was Acciaiuoli who was to draft, on 20 March 1464, the public decree which established Cosimo as the father of his country ("There is nothing . . . more glorious in this life, nor more excellent, nor more sacred, than, in administering the common weal, to discharge one's filial duties to one's country and to render it service"). This is written in his own hand in the cod. Naz. 2, II, 10, cc. 23r–24r, and in the copy of Jacobus Nicolai Cochi Donati ("the scribe . . . of said council") in Magliab. 8: 1439, cc. 57v–59v.

5. In his life of Pandolfo Pandolfini, Vespasiano says that "Pandolfo and younger people made much of messer Carlo d'Arezzo, who read Aristotle's *Politics* to them. . . . He first heard Aristotle's *Ethics* from maestro Battista de Fabriano, and in part from messer Giovanni Argirolupos." We would assume that he read them with Argyropulos's and Donato's commentaries. The son of Manetti, Angelo, speaks at length of the translations and readings of his father in the dedication to Montefeltro (Magliab. 8: 1439, cc. 17r sqq.; Vat. Urb. lat. 223, f. I sqq.).

6. Politian, *Epist. X,* 4 (Angelus Politianus Marquardo Breisacio). See also F. Buonamici, *Il Poliziano giureconsulto* (Pisa, 1863), pp. 94 sqq.

7. Acciaiuoli speaks of the loss of his father in a letter of condolence to Pandolfo Pandolfini, which is quite moving (it is contained in the cod. Magliab. 32: 39, cc. XXXI–XXXIV): "See how different your fate is from mine. I was barely born when I lost my father; I never once set eyes on him, nor did I ever know him. I could not draw on the experience of his life, cut short as it was by premature death, nor did I know any happiness thanks to him, nor did I receive any aid in my career, nor inspiration to lead a virtuous life." His recollection of his mother is also present in his letters. To Griselli he wrote, on 8 July 1448, "Remember me also to our mother, Lena. Although I do not write to her, neither she nor her concerns are ever forgotten" (Magliab. 8: 1439, c. 98v). In a touching letter to Angelo Barga (Magliab. 8: 1439, c. 25r), written in September 1449, he expressed his warm gratitude for the help Barga gave his dying mother. He wrote another affectionate letter to Palla Strozzi in August 1449 (Magliab. 8: 1439, c. 23r-v and della Torre, *Storia*, pp. 325–26). He wrote to Ammannati in October 1454 of his great affection for Michele Brancacci (Magliab. 8: 1439, c. 90r) and to Niccolò da Cortona: "Exiled from home and country, without parents, without friends, destitute of all worldly goods, he led a life of misery ever after. At one time, however, his ancestors lived in this very city as highly honored citizens, and his father was one of the most famous leaders of our republic."

8. J. Picolomini Cardinalis Papiensis, *Epistolae et Commentarii* (Mediolani, 1506), c. 168v. The letter, dated Rome, 5 November 1468, also alludes to the difficulties of the Acciaiuoli family: "Act in such a way as not to neglect the property of your friend, who, God willing, is going to live with you for many years to come and who in the future may be useful to you. Whatever eventuality you and your brother may encounter, remember the refuge which is nowhere safer nor more readily available to you both than it is with me. . . . I am sending you twenty-five papal gold pieces, which I managed to salvage from my past shipwreck and which may help to keep your children in shoes. If I succeed in improving my own fortunes, an annuity larger than this . . . may some day be forthcoming . . . as a token of my esteem. . . ."

9. Magliab. 8: 1439, c. 98r. The letter, which was reprinted in part by della Torre (*Storia*, pp. 335–37), was used by Gutkind in his very valuable work *Cosimo dei Medici il Vecchio* (Florence, 1949, pp. 178), to document the discontent of the Florentines. Erroneously, he dated the letter 1458; it should be 6 July 1448. In it he describes very well the situation during that tragic summer, with the attack of the Arragonese, the fall of Piombino, the burdens imposed by the support of the Sforza against Venice, the plague. There are many letters to Baldesi, all with a political tenor, which in part escaped the notice of della Torre. A Baldesi di Mateo Baldesi completed the transcription (at eight o'clock on 10 December 1467) of the *Vita di Carlo Magno* by Donato, which is conserved in the cod. Naz. 2, I, 62 (formerly Magliab. 6: 95; Gaddi no. 24, a.c. 36r–43r).

10. Many letters testify to his friendship with Griso. But see also, in Med. av. Princ., 12, c. 304, Lorenzo's letter to Piero: ". . . Donato Acciaiuoli of your party recommends ser Griso, who desires this time to be notary of the signori.

. . . I will for this reason recommend him to Luigi Ridolfi and I beg you to notify me of similar matters and do me this honor, because this charge has been given me by the entire Academy. . . ." See Magliab. 8: 1439, v. 98v. 100r (to Griselli); 99r, 101r (to Manetti). The report of the Venetian embassy is contained in Laur. plut. 90 sup. 89, c. 32r–70r (della Torre, *Storia*, pp. 279 sqq.).

11. The origins of the *Dialogus in quorundam amicorum symposio Venetiis habitus dum ibi Florentini populi nomine legatione fungeretur* come from Venice and this mission. The work is dedicated by Giannozzo *ad Donatum Acciaiolum.* The dialogue, to which della Torre refers, is not very significant—except, perhaps, for some allusions. Here is the beginning of the justification for the existence of all animals: ". . . since neither God nor Nature ever act without purpose, according to that famous saying of the philosopher, approved by sacred and divine writers alike, and, moreover, if we agree—in accord with the views of the heathen Stoics, later taken up by Catholic writers—that everything was created for the benefit of man, then, indeed, it follows that all animals are useful and wholesome for man. . . ."

12. The rough draft (Magliab. 8: 1439, c. 100v) is deleted.

13. Here is information on the codices which might be of interest, all the more in that Sabbadini did not use the correspondence between Acciaiuoli and Vespasiano da Bisticci. In the name of Vespasiano, Acciaiuoli wrote (1448) to Filippo Podocataro of Cyprus (on whom see Sabbadini, *Epistolario di Guarino Veronese*, [Venice, 1919], 3: 508–10): "I would like to let you know that I have been able to obtain Lactantius's [book] on Statius only with immense difficulties, but in a passably good and corrected condition." (On Lactantius Placidus and his commentary on Statius, see Sabbadini, *Le scoperte dei codici*, 1: 28–29, 33; 2: 186, 231.) Shortly afterward he asked him for *Lycurgi et Nume vitas eleganter conversas* (Magliab. 8 1439, 102r and v). To a certain Guglielmo, Acciaiuoli wrote (30 December 1448): "The works of Tertullian, Athanasius, and Gregory of Nazianzus, written on papyrus . . . I have sent. . . . As to the *Lives* by Plutarch and other works, I am waiting to know your offer. For the moment there is nothing else left . . . save some fragments of Diogenes Laertius . . . " (Magliab. 8: 1439, c. 103v). To Ammannati (1449): "As for the little work of Plutarch about which you wrote, if you transcribe it, you will be doing something that will also reflect renown as well on you. . . . As for the lives of Nicias and Crassus, I am doing my best to have them transcribed. . . . The other day, searching in the library of San Marco, I came upon a certain volume written in Greek letters, which contained these and many *Lives* of Plutarch . . . " (c. 104). To Manetti (1449): "I hear that you possess Cicero's work entitled *The Orator*, well corrected and in a good condition . . . " (c. 27v). In 1451 Filelfo wrote to him (*Epistulae*, ed. 1502, f. 65v): "I am informed that you have certain old books on the art of grammar. . . ." To Ammannati (1451) Acciaiuoli wrote: "The commentary on Donatus begun . . . to be drawn up by you. . . . The book *De Oratore*, which I have here. . . . Your *Tusculanae* I gave to him (to Marsuppini). . . . I see that George of Trebizond has retranslated Demosthenes's speech [in defense of]

Ctesiphon [*On the Crown*] . . . " (c. 35r). To Filippo Ugolino (1453): "I gave your book *De Oratore* to Giorgio Antonio Vespucci . . . " (c. 84v). In 1454 he asked Filelfo for "that certain commentary on *I Trionfi* by Petrarch, once written by you . . . " (c. 86r). He asked (87v) for the *de officiis;* in 1461 Filelfo wrote to him (*Epistulae,* c. 116v [126v]), sharply criticizing Traversari's translation of Diogenes Laertius; in 1462 (c. 41v) he received from Vespasiano the *Filippiche* of Cicero and other codices ("on the First Punic War, the history by Leonardo, the life of Charlemagne, and Aemilius Probus, and other works"). In 1465 Ammannati (*Epistulae,* c. 52r) asked him for the *Summa* by Saint Thomas, *omnia opera Senece, omnes vitas Plutarci in latinum traductas et insuper de viris illustribus.* Concerning all of Seneca Donato answered that it was "Nowhere in Florence . . . , except at the library of the Abbey at Fiesole" (cod. cit. c. 49r). Ammannati (*Epistulae,* c. 65r) answered that concerning the Plutarch "the cost does not deter, the translations, however, do. . . . Antonius Tudertinus, so ineptly. . . . [Those by] Leonardo Aretino [Bruni] are acceptable, by Francesco Barbaro . . . acceptable; "*De remediis utriusque fortunae* by Francesco Petrarch, not his *De viris illustribus.* . . ." In regard to this Donato wrote to him (c. 50v): "The book *De remediis utriusque fortunae* was nowhere to be found in Florence; the sons of Giannotto Manetti had it. . . ." Among the letters to Acciaiuoli from Antonio Ivani, conserved in the cod. Magliab. (8: 10, c. 8r), we read: "The letters of Cicero *Ad Atticum,* which you had sent over to me. . . ." On the subject of Vespasiano's codices in the Naz. 2, IV, 192, c. 211 of the National Library of Florence, the following note may be found: "Hermas, whom the Apostle Paul mentions while writing to the Romans, wrote a book entitled *The Shepherd,* which Vespasiano arranged to have sent to him from England to Florence, and which he is now keeping in his villa in Antella."

14. Ms. Magliab. 8: 1390, cc. 109r–110r: "Much forbearance should be shown to the young men of these times; the genius of those who dedicate themselves to the study of fine arts should not only be tolerated but admired. . . ." The two teachers indicated here are mentioned in a file of the Studio of 1451, published by A. Gherardi, *Statuti della Università e Studio fiorentino* (Florence, 1881), pp. 461–62.

15. Magliab. 8: 1390, cc. 94r–94v. A letter to Ammannati of 10 October 1451, alludes to the interruption of his studies in philosophy (see della Torre, *Storia,* pp. 342, n. 351–52; C. Marchesi, *Carlo Marsuppini d'Arezzo e Donato Acciaiuoli. Uno scandalo nello Studio Fiorentino* (Catania, 1899), pp. 5–6. For the Chiarenza-Fazio wedding, loc. cit. c. 34v: "To be truthful, I don't care too much for the handbook on dialectics . . . , for our study of dialectics and philosophy has had to be put aside and postponed for a while if—as we hope it may work out—we may hear Carolus Aretinus this year."

16. The Magliab. codex cited, 8: 1390, a.c. 22r, under the date of 6 July 1449, begins with "*exercitationes pro exiguitate ingenii.*" All the notes are in Magliab. 21: 150. The notes contained in Magliab. 6: 162, are posterior (here a date is given, 25 November 1456).

17. Magliab. 8: 1390, c. 103v.

18. Magliab. 8: 1390, cc. 29r–30v (see della Torre, *Storia*, pp. 339–41).

19. On this discussion, see Vespasiano da Bisticci, *Vite*, ed. Frati, 3: 336–39; della Torre, *Storia*, pp. 346–47. Donato's letter, Magliab. 8: 1390, c. 33v–34v (*ex Chufonensi, XII kal. Octobris 1450*), which also expresses his thanks for the *Dialogo*, cited above. "That dialogue you recommended to me a long time ago was of inestimable benefit to me, not only because I could read your authors, but also because, thanks to it, I have come to realize that I should have become such a man as I saw myself judged to be by one of the most learned men of our time.") The original letter in Manetti's hand, "*Generosissimo atque eruditissimo Adolescenti Donato Acciarolo tamquam fratri honorando*," is in Naz. 2, IV, 109 (formerly Magliab. 39: 72; Strozz. in fol. 538).

20. On this discussion, see Segni, *Vita*, pp. 47–48; della Torre, *Storia*, pp. 412–13; and, mainly, n. I, p. 413. But both sources are inexact, and della Torre is the more surprising inasmuch as he had the originals of the drafts, as he says, in front of him. This has come down to us in three editions. Magliab. codex 6: 162, contains, in the hand of Acciaiuoli, the Italian text (cc. 87r–94v), and the Latin text (c. 95r). These are the rough notes, as is clearly evident from the constant corrections throughout. The Italian text indicates the genesis of the written document, relating it to the conversations that took place when he was a prior with Rucellai; the Latin text begins: "When the question was recently raised as to whether it is easier to perform a good deed or a bad one, a certain friend of ours expressed the opinion that to perform a good deed was easier; he put it down in writing, substantiating his view with a good many arguments and citing various authorities. . . ." In reality, Acciaiuoli elaborated the Latin text at a later time. Following the first discussion, Fra' Giovanni da Viterbo sent his opinion, in writing, in Italian, to Rucellai. The text of the letter in his neat handwriting is contained in the miscellaneous codices Naz. 2, IV, 192 (formerly Magliab. 8: 1400, c. 195r). This is followed by Acciaiuoli's handwritten text "in our vulgar tongue," which is dated 20 August 1464 (*Vale Florentie xx augusti 1464*), in the same "notebook" sent to Giovanni Rucellai, whose name it bears. Rucellai evidently showed Acciaiuoli's answer to Fra' Giovanni; the friar added to it, hastily ("please excuse my writing thus . . . "), on a blank sheet a not very conclusive postscript, ending with his greetings to Acciaiuoli: "My salutations to my adversary, whom I love the more, having seen him defend himself so piously, and I offer him each of my works in all that pleases him, because he is virtuous and also because he is your relative and well disposed to the order, according to your letters and his notebook, declared to be of the Acciaiuoli family, who had been friendly to the order. And finally out of love of his forebears and your and his human excellence, I am always at your service to the best of my humble abilities. I recommend myself to you" (c. 209r).

21. Ms. Naz. (Florence) 2, IV, 192, c. 202r. Acciaiuoli cites Hesiod, the tale of the prodigious Hercules at the crossroads, St. Basil, St. Augustine, the *Nichomachea* ("to better confirm the aforementioned, one may refer further to the highest philosopher, Aristotle"), and the Thomistic commentary.

22. Magliab. 8: 1390, c. 83r–84r.

23. Magliab. 8: 1390, c. 82r (-106r); Marchesi (*Uno Scandalo*, pp. 7–9; della Torre, *Storia*, p. 353. "If it were proper for immortals to shed tears for mortals, the divine Camenae would weep," Matteo Palmieri wrote (Magliab. 8: 1437, c. 16r).

24. Magliab. 8: 1437, c. 82v.

25. Magliab. 8: 1437, c. 91r.

26. Magliab. 8: 1437, c. 94v (cp. II r-v), 95r (13r), 95v (13v).

27. On Lianoro, see Sabbadini, *Epistol. di Guarino*, 3: 534–35 (Muellner, *Reden und Briefe Ital. Humanisten*, p. 97). In 1454 he was in Florence, as may be gathered from a letter of Donato, c. 90v (Florence, 4 November 1454): "Your gentleness, your learning, your conduct, and all the virtues with which you are so prodigiously endowed and which are so much in evidence, inspire me to think of you very often indeed. Hence I am already writing this letter to you, although you have barely left; but I am writing it to assure you beyond any doubt that my promises are ever present on my mind, no less than your kindness toward me. . . ."

28. A. Rossi, *Oratio* . . . ; Magliab. 6: 183 (formerly Strozz. in quarto, n. 175). See especially c. 9, the praise of poetry: "This [poetry] encompasses all of the liberal arts and the harmony of its rhythmns penetrate the human spirit so profoundly that one is easily moved to wherever it may lead. . . ." Acciaiuoli's letters to Rossi are dated from the end of 1454 to 1455.

29. Magliab. 8: 1390, c. 18r. It is interesting to follow in their various minute stages of elaboration the most lively of Donato's letters to Rossi.

30. Magliab. 8: 1390, c. 95r.

31. Magliab. 8: 1390, c. 85v, 87v.

32. A. Rinuccini, *Lettere ed orazioni* (Florence, 1953), p. 18. On the subject of the children of Argyropulos as well as this information, see Perosa's observations in "Leonardo," 15(1948): 261–66.

33. Ms. Magliab. 8: 1439, cc. 47v–48v. See Fossi, *Monumenta*, pp. 60–63; and Marchesi, *Bartolomeo della Fonte* (Catania, 1900), pp. 13–14: "If there ever was a time when this our republic truly delighted you or anyone else, then, indeed, this is that time. . . . The study of letters has never been so flourishing in this city. We find adolescent and youthful scholars in Greek and Latin letters and the majority are so learned in Platonic and Aristotelian disciplines that they appear to have been educated at the Academy [of Athens]. Immediately following the death of Pope Nicholas, Argyropulos of Byzantium, a man of outstanding genius and learning worthy of ancient Greece, arrived in our city. Here he taught the Florentine youth not only Greek letters, but also Greek arts, which contribute so manifestly to a wholesome and happy life. Moreover, he has taught here—and still does—the philosophy of life and of morals, as well as the philosophy of nature, displaying an exquisitely refined taste, worthy of the ancients. He is supposed to have translated into Latin various works of Aristotle, and to have explained with brilliant scholarly insight the opinions,

the famous mysteries and profound doctrine of Plato, to the great admiration of his listeners. His teaching has thus enabled a number of young scholars, who were already thoroughly trained in Latin letters, to master in addition Greek letters and philosophy so well that they could write the language and eventually publish eminently praiseworthy works of scholarship. Our city, with all its new buildings, becomes more beautiful every day. It is remarkable with how much enthusiasm the Florentines apply themselves to the construction of superb homes and public buildings. Cosimo himself, this extraordinary man, is building private homes, churches or monasteries, within the city limits and beyond, and all this at such a fabulous cost that he may very well be put on par with the ancient emperors or kings. In addition to all these, he is building a magnificent library and to this end he is collecting books wherever he can get them. I have myself employed a large number of copyists who, at his expense, are now copying sacred as well as secular works. Greek books are also sought after wherever they may be, and he, this magnificent man, purchases them with rare discrimination, not so much for his own glory or as an ornament for the city, as for their being put to use in scholarly research. Thus Florence is flourishing more than ever before, and this not only with regard to the study of letters and the fine arts, but also of painting, sculpture, and numerous other pursuits, which I need not enumerate, lest it be said that, in judging ourselves, we are displaying too much conceit." The letter also contains the interesting information that Vespasiano had commissioned a translation into the vernacular of the *Saturnali* of Macrobius ("Although that book by Macrobius on the *Saturnalia* will be most difficult to translate into Tuscan [Italian] because of its subject matter, I shall try to do so, nevertheless").

34. Giovanni Cavalcanti, *Istorie Fiorentine* (Florence, 1839), 2:210. Cavalcanti, referring to the gossip that was circulating in the city, said, "His hypocrisy, which is full of ecclesiastical arrogance, is paid for by emptying our pocketbooks. . . . He has filled the private coffers of the friars of his order; and now that he can no longer build as a friar, he has started to build a palace, one side of which is reported to be the unused Colosseum of Rome." As is known, it was Donato who drafted the public decree proclaiming Cosimo as father of his country; it appears in his minute handwriting in Ms. Naz. 2, II, 10, c. 23–24. A copy of the official draft is contained in Magliab. 8: 1439, cc. 57v–59v ("Donato Acciaiuoli, a gentleman and man of letters, has promulgated the above decree, which on this day, Monday, the 18th of March, 1464, was approved in a final vote by the assembly, which is known as the most honorable Council of the Hundred. I, the scribe Jacobus Nicolai, was present as the seal-bearer of Donato, having arrived at this very time from that council session").

35. See Rinuccini's letter to Argyropulos (Florence, 4 August 1455), Giustiniani, p. 14: "You are coming to a city that for its beauty and amenities may be favorably compared with any other in Italy. The wages you will be receiving, although hardly commensurate with your unrivaled scholarship and erudition, are not to be despised, especially in our day. And, I should say, it will not be beneath your dignity, nor damaging to your reputation—which you so justly earned by your efforts—to teach the humanities in our city. Since this

city has no peers in all Italy—and I say this by the others' leave—even in other fields of endeavor worthy of commendation, I might say that in this particular branch of learning it has long since surpassed all the rest by a wide margin."

36. Argyropulos's opening lectures, contained in Ms. Riccardiano 120, cc. 1–36, were published by Muellner, *op. cit.* His entire course on the *Soul* may be found, in Acciaiuoli's handwriting, in Mss. Magliab. 5: 41 (trans.), V, 42 (commentary). Argyropulos wrote: "There were three men of outstanding genius. I do not count Zoroaster and many others before Anaxagoras, who were teaching philosophy in a rather vague way and in verse. Thus, then, there were really three; that is, Socrates, Plato, and Aristotle. Socrates, who taught moral philosophy and how to reason, was mistakenly called a moral philosopher, although in reality he was preeminently a speculative philosopher. He realized that the men of his time dedicated themselves to forensic oratory; he attempted to discourage them from its practice and sought to induce them instead to take up the study of philosophy and to strive for self-perfection. Man is born imperfect, but, potentially, he is capable of perfecting himself, so that he may then perfect others. After Socrates came the divine Plato, who reached a peak of perfection in every one of his faculties. He was supreme in poetry, unexcelled in rhetoric, and, as we may gather from his writings, a moral philosopher and a philosopher of nature, a mathematician, and, above all else, a speculative philosopher who was not so much concerned with teaching a system of philosophy as with the practical application of the Socratic method. Plato was followed by Aristotle who had studied under Plato for twenty-one years, and who then bequeathed to us a matchless system of philosophy and the sciences."

37. *Petrus Philippus Pandulphinus Donato Acciaiolo* (Ms. Magliab. 6: 166): "I will show you the prudence and wisdom of Plato. . . . I will expound to you the dialogue entitled *Meno* . . . " (cc. 108–9). The letter to Santo Vireto is in Magliab. 6: 166, c. 112r. I included Pandolfini's letter, which is a very vivid and telling portrayal of Argyropulos and his teaching, in the collection of the "Archivio di Filosofia" of 1951, devoted to texts on the *Soul*, pp. 28–29. On Santo Viriati, a poet of the house of Ordelaffi and a teacher at Forli (for some of his writings, see Ms. Class. 201), see especially G. Raimondi, *Codro e l'umanesimo a Bologna* (Bologna, 1950), pp. 32–33.

38. Ms. 2, I, 104, of the National Library of Florence, c. 15r, *de ideis:* "On this point the philosopher meant to challenge the view of Plato, who proposed that the highest being is the Idea. Argyropulos argued his point at great length in the following manner. He stated that Plato assumed there is a supreme being beyond all heavens, the ruler of all there is, in whose mind are subsumed all archetypes of subordinated things [and beings], but only causatively, not in essence. Aware of himself, he creates eternally, out of himself, another, second god, who encompasses in his mind all there is, that is, the causes for the forms of all archetypes of beings that are within him in their essence and that are of his own substance; thus, he has within himself, first of all, the archetype of the universe, and, thereafter, the archetypes of all other

things. Contemplating them, that is, understanding himself, he creates all other archetypes of all subordinated things and beings; he creates thus third and fourth gods, and, thereafter, not only male but also female ones. This fact should be understood to mean that nothing at all can be created without the concurrence of two agents—matter, of course, and form—and that, for each of the two there exists a corresponding idea, the one appertaining to the form likely to be given a masculine designation, and the other, pertaining to matter, a feminine one. . . ." (*Marginal note in Acciaiuoli's hand:* "In the first instance, they are called *rationes* [causes], in the second, *exemplaria* [models, archetypes]. They are called causes in that, in the philosopher's mind, they are causative, just as it is said of the sun that it creates causatively the frog, the horse, and other animals.") With regard to Argyropulos's study and knowledge of Plotinus, see P. Henry, *Les manuscrits des Ennéades* (Brussels, 1948), pp. 91–96, on Par. gr. 1970, which is in the handwriting of Acciaiuoli. (See also how eloquently Cilento speaks in the note to his translation: Plotinus, *Enneadi* [Bari, 1948], 1: 257–58.) But the chronological conjectures tending to establish connections with Laur. 87, 3, annotated by Ficino, are not acceptable. In fact, Henry affirms that Argyropulos had made use of the Laur. after Ficino had annotated it—that is, after 1454. Now we know that again, in 1456, Ficino outlined the lost *Institutiones* only on the basis of Latin sources, and that Landino urged him to wait "*quoad Graecis litteris erudirer*" ("until such time as I receive instruction in Greek letters"), as he himself admitted. And his thorough knowledge of Plotinus appears later, in 1460. Hence the chronological connection established between the two codices—or, rather, between Ficino's conjectures and Argyropulos's transcription—are not convincing.

39. The position of Niccolò Tignosi da Foligno (on whom see Lynn Thorndike, *Science and Thought in the Fifteenth Century* [New York, 1929], pp. 161–79, 308–31) would also be worthy of more careful consideration with regard to Ficino's education. The *opusculum de ideis*, dedicated to the Magnificent, in Ms. Laur. 82, 22, and in a different version in the Vat. lat. 3897 (ex Tuderto die Xa Jan. 1470), was published by Thorndike (but see also Ms. 606 of the Oliv. of Pesaro). The commentary on the *De anima* (Florence, 1531) is also dedicated to Lorenzo. Important for our purpose are the accounts of the method according to which Aristotle was read and commented upon (Naz. Florence, Conv. C, 8, 1800), dedicated to Cosimo the Elder: "In commenting upon and expounding various authors, great care should be taken that an interpretation of the true meaning, reflecting the author's intent, be given, and that there never be a false ring to it. Nothing should be left dangling or ambiguous in the construction, so that anyone reading the text can readily understand it and see what the author intends. The subject matter itself should therefore not be merely read and understood, but mastered to such an extent that it may be taught to others." And here is his condemnation of the "conservatives": "Nor do they allow Cicero, a man almost divine, to be counted among the sages. . . . They also hold in contempt that outstanding man, Giannoffo Manetti, who in his time was counted among the most erudite rhetoricians, and they slander Matteo Palmieri. They abuse Donato Acciaiuoli and

Alamanno Rinuccino in secret, because, as philosophers immune to offense, the latter openly and eloquently discourse on and expound their views. . . ."

40. See G. Breen, "Giovanni Pico della M., on the Conflict of Philosophy and Rhetoric," *Journal of the History of Ideas* 13(1952); Breen, however, admits that there is a change in Pico's ideas after 1485, on the basis of an unfounded assertion by Ferriguto (*Almorò Barbaro* [Venice, 1922], p. 321). In a letter of 30 September 1489, Pico countered that what was important was to open the door to the truth, nor was the golden key of more avail than the wooden one ("*praestat omnino aperire lignea, quam occludere aurea*"). See the letter in *Giornale critico della filosofia italiana*, 31(1952): 523–24, from Ms. Conv. D, 2, 502 of the National Library of Florence. The question of the *genus dicendi philosophorum* had, moreover, become common; one of the more precise syntheses is in the dialogues on love, by Lorenzo, a Pisan priest (Ms. Magliab. 21: 115): "There are two principal ways of approaching an issue . . . ; one is open-minded and to the point, worthy of a learned gentleman—which I for my part heartily approve and which I hope will prevail, but which has fallen into disuse and which the philosophers of our time reject. To my way of thinking, Plato is the foremost exponent of this approach, and here in Italy our Cicero far surpassed anyone else in it. The other approach is the one our native philosophers claim to be using, wherein they say they are emulating Aristotle; it is shallow, dry, sly, and thorny, as well as dubious, and not only does it preclude all subtlety in reasoning but it takes recourse to soothsayers and oracles. . . ."

41. Politian, *Praelectio de dialectica*, in *Opera* (Lugduni, 1528), 2: 460.

42. R. Curtius, *European Literature and the Latin Middle Ages* (New York, 1953).

43. See letter of dedication to Piero de' Medici in a small treatise on dialectics, G. Cammelli, *G. Argirupolo*, pp. 222–23 ("Cicero, prince of orators, whom we emulate"). In the first chapter of his *Miscellanea*, Politian included a glowing eulogy to Argyropulos ("Argyropulos of Byzantium, our former teacher in philosophy, who is as thoroughly versed in Latin letters as he is in all those disciplines of learning encompassed by the *Decreta* that go by the name of "the goat's hair shirt of Martianus' [play upon words: *capella* means goat; actual title of the work is *Disciplinae* by Martianus Capella]"). Nonetheless, he added, Argyropulos could not forget that he was a Greek and, hence, did not tolerate Ciceronian eloquence, which for him was contrary to Hellenic culture: "Annoyed by the verbose style of Latin letters as exemplified by their founder and foremost author [Cicero], the Greek master dared to charge—again and again—(and we hardly dared believe our ears) that Cicero was ignorant not only of philosophy, but (may it please the gods) of Greek letters as well!"

44. On the subject of the Platonic tradition and its continuity, see the account given by Klibansky of Ficino's celebrated letter to Martino Uranio (R. Klibansky, *The Continuity of Platonic Tradition in the Middle Ages* [London, 1939], pp. 45–47); see also the academic discourse of J. Koch, *Platonismus im Mittelalter* (Scherpe-Verlag, Krefeld).

45. For Salutati's reading of Plato, see *Epistolario*, Novati, 3: 144, 515. For his knowledge of the *Timaeus*, see also ms. Magliab. 29: 199, which belonged to him and in which (cc. 117v–123r) there is a fragment of the Ciceronian version. For his research on the *Phaedo*, see *Epistolario*, 3: 444, 449. On his first reading of the *Republic* and of Vergerio, see *Epistolario*, 4: 366; on his knowledge of Vergerio and his reading of the *Gorgias*, see *Epistolario* (ed. L. Smith), pp. 241–42. The copy of the *Philosophia* of William of Conches, which had belonged to Giovanni da Ravenna, may be found in the Laur. Ashb. 173. The codices of the *Timaeus*, now at the National Library of Florence (Convent of San Marco), were in the possession of Niccoli. With regard to Ficino, Caponsacchi wrote in the *Vita* (conserved in ms. Palatino 488 of the National Library of Florence): "having copied in his own hand Calcidius above the *Timaeus* . . ." (The codex is now at the Ambrosiana). The extract of the *Timaeus*, an autograph by Vergerio, is contained in the Marciano lat. 14, 54 (*Allegabilia dicta collecta ex Thymeo Platonis*).

46. Chalcidii, *Comm.*, ed. Wrobel (Leipzig, 1876). The comments of William of Conches are contained in Ms. Marciano Lat. 10, 4 (which had been in the possession of Bessarion: "Plato, in dealing with natural justice, included everything Socrates had said about positive justice, thus establishing one single and cohesive treatise on justice, natural as well as positive" (c. 9r).

47. Uberto Decembrio wrote these lines in the preface of his translation of the *Republic:* "Not being permitted to take any liberties,/we accept the political works of Cicero as though they were law [play on words: Cicero's books entitled *De legibus* (*On Laws*) and several *De Lege* . . . (On the Law of . . .)]; the work of Plato, however, the fount from which Tullius [Cicero] is said to have drunk,/we might as well put to the test . . ." (Laur. 89 sup. 50 = Ambros. B 123 sup.). In his prologue Decembrio refers to the judgment of Macrobius, which was destined to become widely used: "According to Macrobius, the books of Plato and Cicero, both writing on the republic, differ fundamentally from each other . . . , in that Plato ordered his republic in a manner he himself thought fit, whereas Cicero had the order imposed on the republic by its foremost citizens. . . . " It is a theme that was put into verse by Palmieri (*Città di Vita*, 3: 22): "But the combination that Plato had envisaged/which would be present in a just, wise and learned people,/cannot be found in a corrupt people. For this reason Tullius chose this city/since it could be governed and ruled with sense./And he did not give it laws that were theoretically perfect,/but only the best humanly possible. Thus one imagines it, while the other describes it as it is,/one dreams and the other demonstrates. . . . "

48. *Leon. Ar. ad Cosmam Medicum* (Laur. 76, 57; Magliab. 8: 1424): "The translation of these letters gave me so much pleasure that I imagined Plato himself was present and that I could look into his very heart. . . . In his letters, I see Plato not so much teaching others as taking action himself. . . . Thus, I urge you, please, to read these letters often, and to commit their individual passages to memory, especially dealing with the republic." The begin-

ning of the letter is quite beautiful: "Between noisy and turbulent public gatherings which flow in and out of the assembly halls of Florence at all times like the tide at Euripus, [my work] constantly interrupted, not only by various errands but also by idle talk, I have translated Plato's letters into Latin as best I could." It would be useful to keep in mind that the translation of the *Republic* was attributed to Bruni by Giovanni Dominici (*Lucula noctis,* ed. Coulon, p. 408: "In that book, *De Republica,* . . . by that proficient disciple of yours, the man from Arezzo, worthy of every respect, who rendered it from the Greek tongue into ours." And on p. 165: "That man from Arezzo, who translated the above named booklet by Plato from the Greek into Latin in so graceful a style . . . "). That Dominici alluded to the *Republic* there can be no doubt (he speaks of the condemnation of Homer), as there is no doubt that the work is not a *libellus,* and that the Aretine, for all that we know of him, did not translate it. Did he mean perhaps to allude to a single book of the work?

49. Ms. 199 of the Archiginnasio of Bologna (*In libros Platonis de legibus ex greca lingua in latinam versos ac illustri Venete reipublice senatori Francisco Barbaro Sancti Marci Procuratori, et per eum ipsi reipublice dedicatos, Georgii Trapensutii prefatio*): " . . . Anyone who inquires, thoroughly and objectively, into those laws which Plato declared inviolably sacred if his republic were to endure in freedom must agree with me that it was Plato who inspired the founding fathers of Venetian freedom to form the republic, and subsequently gave them the courage to carry on. . . . And I am not at all surprised that they read Plato and appreciated him, for in those times almost all of Italy was conversant with the Greek language. The Italian noblemen—thanks to whose concurrence the city of Venice was founded, in the face of all the adversity of the time—were in no way less proficient in Greek letters than in Latin letters. It also seems quite remarkable to me that everything that 'bears out this origin and is thus more persuasive than any testimony of Plato himself corresponds perfectly! . . .' " (And in Barbaro's letters, Brixiae, 1743, see p. 297.)

50. *Cest Liure est a moy Homfrey de Gloucestre du Don P. Candidus Secretaire du Duc de Mylan* (Ms. Harl. 1705; see also Cat. 2: 177–78). The Duke of London wrote to Decembrio in April 1439: "We read and reread it [*The Republic*], for indeed so impressive are its discerning and profound thoughts, and so pleasing is the dignity of your commentary and its elegant style. We propose that we will never be without it, at home or on a campaign . . . that we will always have it handy to offer delight and give us respite in hours of leisure; and, moreover, that it may be our constant companion as well as counsellor in the conduct of life . . . " (Ricc. 827, 63r; M. Borsa, "Correspondence of Humphrey Duke of Gloucester and P. C. Decembrio (1439–1444)," *English Historical Review* 19(1904): 515–16).

51. On Vergerio's knowledge of the *Gorgias,* of which he made a thorough study, see, besides the correspondence (ed. L. Smith, [Rome, 1934], p. 241: "I read Gorgias twice, from beginning to end"), the *De ingenuis moribus.*

C. Bischoff stresses this in *Studien zu P. P. Vergerio dem Alteren* (Berlin-Leipzig, 1909) ["Abhandlungen zur mittleren und neueren Geschichte," Fasc. 15], pp. 31, 82, 83. F. P. Luiso denies that there is a translation of *Gorgias* by Vergerio ("Commento a una lettera di L. Bruni e cronologia di alcune sue opere," in *Raccolta di studi critici, dedicata ad Alessandro d'Ancona* [Florence, 1901], p. 93).

52. The dedication to the Cusan of the translation of *Parmenides* by Trapezunzio was published by Volter. 6201, 61r sqq., by Klibansky, "Plato's Parmenides in the Middle Ages," *Mediaeval and Renaissance Studies* I, 2 (1943): 291 sqq. In the prefatory letter addressed by Bruni to Loschi on the subject of the partial translation of the *Phaedrus,* he says that he had finished it "above all because the power and essence of poetry is described in it." The translation of the *Convito* (Alcibiades's eulogy to Socrates) is among the letters of Bruni (ed. Mehus. Flor. 1741, 2: 70–76); on the *Cratylus,* see Mehus. Flor. 1791, 1: 53. Ficino, as is known, in the preface to the translation of Plotinus (Flor. 1492), attributed Cosimo's decision to restore the Academy of Florence to the influence of Pletho, "*quasi Platonem alterum, de mysteriis Platonicis disputantem*" ("as though he were another Plato, discoursing on the Platonic mysteries"). But his presentation of the facts leaves one perplexed. Pletho made an impression primarily because of his religious position and because of his announcement of the imminent end of Christianity (as well as of Islam) and the restoration of the true Hellenic religion. ("[He foretold] that, a few years after his death, Mohamedanism as well as Christianity would lapse into decay and that pure truth would then shine forth from one end of the world to the other," George of Trebizond wrote.) Pico referred to his interpretation of classical myths, and the Sienese Dati mentions him with regard to the same subject.

54. A. Rinuccini, *Lettere ed orazioni,* pp. 187–90.

55. Ms. of the National Library of Florence, 2, III, 373, c. 2r (autograph).

56. Ms. of the National Library of Florence, 2, III, 54 (formerly Magliab. 25: 277, from the Bibl. Gaddi, no. 13).

57. Today it is ms. 2, III, 55 (formerly Magliab. 25: 41) of the National Library of Florence. See ms. 2, III, 53 (formerly Magliab. 25: 506 Strozz. in vol. 278).

58. On the subject of Argyropulos's son, I refer to what is said above. And on the subject of his stipend, see Rinuccini, *Lettere,* p. 14.

59. For the discussion on entelechy, see what I have written on "Atene e Roma," Series 3, anno 5, fasc. 3, 1937 (*Endelécheia e entelécheia nelle discussioni umanistiche*), in which the texts are also indicated.

60. A precise classification of the sciences may be found at the beginning of the lessons on physics (ms. of the National Library of Florence, 2, I, 103, formerly Magliab. 12: 5 Strozz. fol. 589) begun on 3 November 1458: "It seems obvious that philosophy should first of all be defined before being subdivided. Only then can one comprehend what it is all about, can one grasp

the subject matter to be dealt with, understand the objective toward which one is to proceed, and see the ultimate goal of one's endeavors, the name by which it is known, and its import or significance. . . ." For the dichotomic divisions, see the same ms., c. 2r sqq. (the date of the end is given at c. 252r: 2 August 1860). The *Panepistemon* of Politian is also an introductory lecture, and the author refers to the usage, to which he himself conformed, of preceding the commentary on Aristotle by a classification of the sciences: "Those engaged in the interpretation of Aristotle's works were accustomed to start out by breaking down the body of philosophy into its component parts." In the same way as Argyropulos, Politian chose medicine as a model, and declared that he proceeded through division: *divisionem istiusmodi aggredi* (Politian, *Opera* [Lugduni, 1528], 2: 306 sqq.). Also within the sphere of Argyropulos's influence, Fonzio's classification in the *Oratio in bonas artes* of 8 November 1484 (Frankfurt, 1621, pp. 329–42) should be consulted.

61. See Garin, "La fortuna dell' etica aristotelica nel' 400," *Rinascimento* 2(1951): 321–34. On Argyropulos, see in Vat. lat. 5811, ff. 1–31, the treatise *de institutione eorum qui in dignitate constituti sunt* (mentioned by A. Perosa in *Leonardo,* [1946], pp. 265–66).

62. *Protesto fatto da Donato di Neri di Messer Donato Acciaiuoli oratore di compagnia a dì 15 maggio 1469.* I use the text contained in Magliab. 6: 162 (formerly Strozz. 1093): *Orazioni e dicerie di Donato Acciaiuoli scritte di propria sua mano e fragmenti di altre sue opere pure di sua propria mano* (but I have compared the text with Ricc. 2204, cc. 9r–14v, with Naz. 2, II, 50, c. 180r, and with Magliab. 8: 1389 and 8: 1433).

63. The platonist referred to by Acciaiuoli was—according to Platina (*De optimo cive,* 2 [Parisiis, 1530], f. 90v)—often mentioned by Argyropulos ("Precious, indeed . . . is the saying of your doctor Argyropulos that justice is as much a part of human society as the soul is a part of a living being").

64. Ms. Magliab. 23: 95 (autograph). The same subject is treated, practically in the same words, in the dedication of the *Politics.* On the subject of the single "tyrant," see Platina's *De Optimo cive,* 1: f. 75r: "He is putting to death the scholars, he has prohibited banquets and fraternal reunions, he is abolishing schools and any public gatherings where citizens could exchange news or find mutual support; he believes it is in his interest to divide the citizens as much as possible."

65. Ms. Magliab. 8: 1390, c. 43 r–44v.

66. The definitive form of Acciaiuoli's commentary, as it later appeared in print, is given in the ms. of the National Library of Florence, 2, I, 80 (formerly Magliab. 21: 8), which had belonged to one of the Acciaiuoli family (*Alexandri Acciaioli et amicorum*): "Commentary by Donato Acciaiuoli on Aristotle's work on ethics as translated by J. Argyropulos of Byzantium, with a dedication to Cosimo Medici." The ms. of the Naz. 2, I, 104 (formerly Magliab. 12: 52 Strozz., in fol. 602), an autograph contains the original draft of Argyropulos's course. Notes and rough drafts are conserved in ms. 6: 102. If one compares carefully the editing of the commentary by Acciaiuoli with Argyropulos's

course, one is forced to recognize that the Florentine writer merely ordered and retouched the work of the Byzantine professor. What is original, if anything, is entirely in what he accentuates.

67. On the diplomatic mission, see G. Canestrini and A. Desjardins, *Négociations* (Paris, 1859), 1: 118. For the life of Charlemagne, I use the signed draft (ms. National Library of Florence, 2, II, 325, formerly Magliab. 8: 1401) and the Latin text (ms. Naz. 2, II, 10). But see also ms. 2, I, 62 (formerly 6: 95), the copying of which was completed "the day of the 10th of December 1467 at eight o'clock" by Baldeso de Matteo Baldesi.

68. We find the identical theme, with very similar expressions, in the preface to the *Politics* (ms. 2, III, 373 of the National Library of Florence): "Formerly, it was considered the greatest distinction of famous men, above all others, to have pursued the study of letters and to enjoy the friendship of scholars . . ."

69. Ms. Magliab. 8: 1390, c. 37r.

70. Ms. Magliab. 8: 1390, c. 37v.

71. Ms. Magliab. 8: 1390 47.

72. Ms. Magliab. 8: 1390, c. 49r (and in the collected correspondence of Ammannati the letters on pages 52r, 53v, 65r, 65v). On Antonio da Todi and his translations, see A. Zeno, *Dissertazioni vossiane* (Venice, 1752), 1: 358–60.

73. See J. Antoni Campani, *Epistole et poemata* (Leipzig, 1707), pp. 182–86, 300.

74. J. Picolomini Cardinalis Papiensis, *Epistolae et commentarii* (Rome, 1584), c. 168v.

75. Ms. Magliab. 8: 1390, c. 51r. (See della Torre, *Storia*, p. 545).

76. A large selection of letters from Ivani to Acciaiuoli is contained in ms. Magliab. 8: 10; a letter from Fonzio is in Magliab. 6: 166, c. 115v and in Palat. Capp. 77, c. 4r (published by Juhasz, 1931).

77. Among the letters written when he was an official of the Studio (Archives of the State of Florence, Uff. Studio, 9–11), are some supporting Lorenzo da Colle (9: 163): "In the time I have been here I have had the opportunity to know Messer Lorenzo da Colle, who lectures on poetry and the art of oratory, and I have found him so well versed in the Latin language as well as in Greek that I have devoloped a great respect for his talent. . . ." (Pisa, 22 March 1475); (2: 105): "I believe the ability and competence of Messer Lorenzo da Colle, who lectures on poetry and the skills of oratory here, is known to you. I did not know about him at first, but later when I became acquainted with him, I found him so competent in Greek and Latin that I felt his salary was insufficient. . . ."; (9: 166): "It seems to me that I do not praise too highly Messer Holiviere Arduini, who . . . deserves to be favored for the experience he has demonstrated in this university, because he understands so well every subject and dedicates himself to his student listeners and to me during discussions that have taken place here in my room, and I can testify in the best of faith that he has proved a great honor to himself and to the city . . . " (Pisa, 3 April 1476). And here is the recommendation for

Del Bene (State Archives of Florence, Med. av. il Princ., 48,9): "I did not have time when I left you to recommend an intimate friend of mine who has great faith in me and who desires, one time, if possible, through my intercession and your grace, to be made prior. He is Bernardo di Vieri del Bene, who is fifty years old, and who has had a successful career as a merchant. Not long ago he returned from Constantinople, and aware that he is growing older, he expressed a great desire for this honor. For this reason I ask if you would please arrange it in such a way that he may receive this recognition and I this pleasure, for which I would be most grateful considering the affection I have held for him since our boyhood. The charge will be well placed in him, for he is a person of means and from a good family. In sum, I recommend him to you and ask you please to grant him your favor when you have received my letter. . . ."

78. For the commentary on the *Politics*, see also F. Da Montefeltro, *Lettere di stato e d'arte (1470–1480)*, ed. P. Alatri (Rome, 1949), p. 106 sqq. The oration to Sixtus IV is conserved in a great number of manuscripts (Magliab. 32: 39; Naz. 2, VI, 17; Magliab. 8: 1437, etc.).

79. State Archives of Florence, M.a.P., 96, 83; 96, 238.

80. The *Eulogium in funere Donati Acciaioli* is contained in mss. Ricc. 671, 914, 1199 (and translated among the *Diverse orationi . . .* collected by Francesco Sansovino [Venice, 1561], 1: 2). Politian wrote these dystichs:

> Donato by name,
> from Azarola's stock,
> I was known for my gift of speech
> at home in my native Florence.
> Despatched as my country's spokesman
> to the king of France,
> I yielded my last breath
> in the walled town
> of the duke of the serpent.
> Thus I gave my life for my fatherland. . . .

81. See Fonzio's *Donatus, de poenitentia*, pp. 264–87. And, pp. 390–92, the elegy "In obitu Donati Acciaioli."

82. *Oratione del Corpo di Christo*, ms. Ricc. 2204, c. 180r.

83. State Archives of Florence, M.a.P., 21, 79 (2 August 1468).

IV
Paolo Toscanelli

Paolo dal Pozzo Toscanelli was born in 1397 and died in 1482. His long lifetime spanned one of the most impressive periods in the history of Florence, primarily in the history of Florentine culture.[1] When he was born into the home of the Toscanelli on the other side of the Arno, the Chancellor of Florence was Salutati, who up until a few years before had been in the habit of crossing the river nearly every day on his way to the nearby church of Santo Spirito to study, meditate, and converse with Luigi Marsili, the Augustinian friar whose severe conduct and sharp criticism of the church precluded him forever from being raised to the dignity of bishop, much to the disappointment of the Florentines. The convent had become revered as a seat of learning for the great men of the Trecento. It was here that their republican pride, their rigorous studies and their ardent faith had been nourished.

Marsili died in August 1394. In 1397, just at the time of Toscanelli's birth, the Visconti were launching their aggressive campaign against Florence with the inflammatory invective of Loschi, and Coluccio was drafting his letters in defense of the *florentina libertas* —letters that Gian Galleazzo feared more than mounted horsemen. It was a mortal duel, in which the civic culture of the Florentine humanists took the field with unwavering determination. Uberto Decembrio, a distinguished writer and Lombard statesman who entered the lists in the service of the Visconti, confessed that he had visited Florence only once in order to make the acquaintance of the chancellor who fought with so much courage for the freedom of his fatherland: "The walls, the towers, the palaces of your Florence will fall in ruin, Coluccio; the day will come when the old peasant will point out to new colonists the land on which your town once stood. But the glory of your name will live eternally, because you have fought for your country like Camillo and Curio, Horatius Cocles and the Scipios, the Catos and the Fabi."

The prophecy of Uberto Decembrio did not come true; Florence and republican liberties did not fall. A few decades later, as though consecrating the city's greatness, Brunelleschi's cupola rose, "ascending above the skies, large enough to embrace in its shadow all the people of Tuscany"—as Leon Battista Alberti, a great friend of Toscanelli, wrote feelingly. The mathematical calculations that Pippo, the architect, had learned from the physicist Paolo—who had become a scientist of such repute that he earned the respect of such men as Johannes Müller and Nicholas of Cusa—also contributed to building it "without the aid of a girder or a wooden model."

Born at a decisive moment in the history of the Italian states, Toscanelli in the prime of his life saw the reunion in his city, amid all the splendor of the East, of the delegates to the Council for the unity of the Church. He listened with great curiosity to the descriptions of distant lands, and he offered in exchange to the most revered of the Greeks, Georgius Gemistus, his detailed knowledge of mathematics and physics. The contemplative and withdrawn years of his old age paralleled those of the somewhat corrupt but vital and vigorous pomp of Lorenzo the Magnificent. He died after the tragedy of the Pazzi conspiracy, when Ficinian Platonism, abounding in beautiful imagery and turgid with fantasies part Oriental, part baroque, had become the fashion among the refined artists and decadent intellectuals who flirted with Hellenic mysteries and magic rites.

Florence was a great capital; it was perhaps, at that moment in history, the world's most important cultural center. Parisian scholars —even professors at the Sorbonne—awaited with impatience and greeted with enthusiasm the latest word from Florence. But all this was foreign to the aged recluse Toscanelli, who had been a schoolmate and lifelong friend of the Platonist and mystic Cusan but who had the mind of a spice merchant. Paolo was enamored with measures and numbers—not in order to contemplate them in the heavenly spheres of divine mathematics but in order to use them in his accounts, to determine the ways of the stars that guide navigators, to forecast births and harvests, and to calculate the equilibrium of the great structures in which the rich Florentine burghers liked to unite luxury with good taste within the framework of a strange devotion that ranged between Venus rising from the sea and Virgins adored in ascetic meditations.

"They measure the forms of things with their genius alone, apart from any matter, while we who want to build things to be seen will use the most crass Minerva." Thus Alberti spoke of the mathematics of the painter and other similar devices of the craftsman, contrasting them with pure mathematics, which was considered beyond material application. But it would be a fitting epigraph to indicate the distance between the most recherché culture of the Ficinians, who regarded with the superior disdain of a highly aristocratic academy even the technical nature of university science, and this knowledge, born in a different world. The new knowledge had different aims, hard-working and modest, almost self-effacing, mundane and hence disillusioned, frequently bitter, and far from pleasant diversions and easy optimism. In substance, the comparison would be akin to comparing a sublime philosophy, proud of its absolute perfection, with the honest, very approximative artisan who discovered America "by mistake," who constructed "by coincidence" the cupola of Santa Maria del Fiore, or who calculated the trajectories of the comets solely to improve harvests and vintage times with a good horoscope.

Leon Battista Alberti was a great friend of Paolo Toscanelli. He dedicated to Toscanelli his *Intercenali,* one of the most astounding documents of the century, a book that is still entirely contemporary, whose pages traversed Europe anonymously and were mingled and confused with those of Lucian and Erasmus but which at times were more beautiful, more serious and profound. Although characterized by the commonplace of a parallel between the medicine of the body and the medicine of the soul, this dedication is not extraneous. The same comparison appears again in Ficino's more celebrated dedication to Cosimo. "As other physicians, my dear Paolo, you offer sick bodies bitter and nauseating medicines; I, on the contrary, in my writings seek to cure the sicknesses of the spirit with a cheerful smile." It was not a cheerful smile, however, but a cruel irony, a bitterness at times morose and almost desperate, a profound dejection that permeated much of Alberti's writings.

Alberti's dedication of another work to Toscanelli must also have been affectionately ironical. The work has not come down to us, nor do we know whether it was indeed written; it was to be an imaginative and prophetic series of letters in which he predicted the future fortunes of the world and of Florence, events to befall princes and popes.[2] They may have been "fables" or "visions" of the kind that pleased Alberti so much, and in which he mockingly parodied the astrologers and their prognostications. They were sent purposely this time to a friend, a famous astrologer as well as physician who was engaged in studying the infallible forecasts of the comets about future grave events.

Paolo could not have taken his art completely seriously, even though it is difficult for these men who were always teetering between a crisis in faith and an uncertain science to determine to what point they would go in ridiculing even their own certitudes.[3] It is probable that, all things considered, Toscanelli preferred the doctrines of Albumazar on the great conjunctions or cycles of history to the learned dissertations of Ficino about the soul of the stars. It was not a coincidence that in the same years in which the great Marsilio wrote the *Theologia platonica* and was taking delight in mystical wanderings among idyllic worlds, Christopher Columbus was transcribing for the king of Portugal a letter sent by Paolo Toscanelli in 1474 to Canon Martins.

Certain chronological references speak at times a strangely persuasive language and give an almost corporeal sense to this mobile fabric of human life that characterized the period. In 1474 Ficino wrote from Florence to Francesco Bandini that he had finished the draft of his great book destined to appear in 1482—the year of Toscanelli's death. On 25 June 1474, Paolo "the physicist" sent to the king of Portugal his nautical map and the no less famous letter about a shorter way by sea to the "spices"—the letter that Columbus transcribed in his own hand on the front page of his copy of the *Historia* by Pius II.[4] If we look at the end of that century (which for Florence was already a period of decline, perhaps the most beautiful that a civilization could hope for), it is difficult not to give an almost paradigmatic meaning on the one hand to the grandiloquent poetic theology of the Hellenized Platonists who adorned the court of the Magnificent with oriental embellishments and, on the other, to the calculations that emerged from Toscanelli's house. The latter, if they were not to guide, were at least to comfort and inspire the future admiral of the ocean fleet.

On the one hand was the flowery rhetoric of the literati, court philosophers, theoreticians, and propagandists of the new princely regime; on the other were the figures of a son of rich merchants: Domenico, Paolo's father, registered at the Catasto in 1429 eleven families in his service, one footman, two bailifs, a horse and a mule.

Paolo himself, anything but poor, at the time of the death of his brother Pietro in 1469, was occupied with managing an important commercial house that Pietro apparently owned in Pisa and was studying navigation, transport, and ship routes, not out of erudite curiosity but for specific material interests.

The culture of Toscanelli and that of Ficino and Landino seem to belong to two different, far-removed worlds. One was peopled by artisans, politicians, and merchants, for whom knowledge, art, and faith formed one whole in a soiety for which the city was its living, vital synthesis. In contrast was the detached culture of intellectuals in the service of a lord, who at times engaged in embellishing his court, at other times served as his shrewd advisers in the techniques of government. Yet if we study the situation more closely, we see a specification of tasks, a more articulate organization, a more developed rationalization in the process of substituting professionals for dilettantes, specialists for the universal man. The ideal of the complete man of action and thought, engaged in an active productive life as well as in politics, was being replaced by the rigorously trained technician: here the soldier and there the ruler; here the merchant, there the artist; here the man of action, there the intellectual. At times the man of letters, who was removed from laborious duties, tended to become confounded with the courtier and the clown.

In Florence of the Quattrocento, if there was a distinction between the types of culture, there was no declared antagonism. Those historians who exaggerate the conflicts and give rise to grossly distorted misconceptions have been and continue to be very much mistaken. Alberti and Toscanelli, Ficino and Landino were certainly profoundly different, and yet they moved about on the same cultural horizon; they maintained constant relations among themselves and were not always cognizant of their profound divergences. The fecundity of these years cannot be understood if this wealth of contrasting motifs, manifest in different temperaments, is not understood. Thus Paolo the physicist appears bathed in glory in Ficino's writings, as suited a man who, beside being learned, was also rich and influential. Landino, who wrote a very touching eulogy to Toscanelli—*veneranda immagine d'antichuita* (venerable image of antiquity)—linked him to the memory of that Alberti to whose "architecture" Angelo Politian was to write the preface.[5]

The differences—and they were great differences—were inherent in the tension which stirred an epoch and in a society which animated and formed them, whose political struggles and prophetic visions, heroic evocations, evasions, and compromises were united at times in the same persons, just as astrological superstitions, the voices of God, magical beliefs, and brilliant scientific intuition were linked in the minds of these men. Everywhere there were conflicts and contrasts, heroism and weakness, the most astute concepts and the most crass illusions. It should be emphasized that the same phrases struck different and far removed people in their readings—people who were drawn together by a spiritual life marked by the same anxieties, disturbed by the same doubts and the same passions.

Around 1481 Christopher Columbus transcribed on the margin of his copy of the treatises of Cardinal Pierre d'Ailly the verses of the Psalm: *caeli enarrant gloriam Dei, et opera manuum eius annunciat firmamentum. . . .** He regarded nature with awestruck admiration; at the same time he felt the sense of destiny willed by the stars and by God. A few years later, in Florence, under the influence of the inspired prophet Savonarola, Giovanni Pico was to write, on the same subject (*caeli enarrant gloriam Dei*), pages worthy of the scientific rigor of his friend Toscanelli in order to debunk the sibylline astrology which was Toscanelli's official profession.[6] At the same time the Lord of Mirandola was indignant to see the Virgin Mary disguised as an astral image, Columbus was coyping in his own hand the famous text of Albumazar: "at first glance the constellation of the Virgin emerges as a girl full of grace, honesty and purity, with long hair and a beautiful face; in her hand she holds two ears of wheat, and she is seated, . . . and nurses a baby."

Ut Albumasar testatur
Inter stellas declaratur
Virgo lactans puerum. . . .

The mystical song of the Stella Maris by Giovanni di Garlandia sanctifies an *astrologia spiritualis* capable of attributing to the Virgin in precise correspondences the properties of the stars.[7] Among Toscanelli's papers we may read a letter by a famous professor at the university of Ferrara, Pietro Bono Avogaro, who, with regard to the

* "The heavens tell of the glory of God, and the firmament attests to the work of His hands."

comet of 1456, promotes Albumazar's doctrines in order to predict dreadful catastrophes in store primarily for Italy.[8] Paolo followed the course of the comet and established its movements with unusual precision to determine exactly the fatal influences which rain from it onto the earth.

Concepts of ingenious originality were joined inextricably with old and time-worn exigencies. Among the books annotated by Columbus, besides the theological-astrological fantasies of Cardinal d'Ailly, we find the Italian translation of Pliny by Landino, the work that fascinated Leonardo da Vinci so much. Toscanelli, Landino, Columbus, Alberti, and Leonardo were closely tied to those themes that animated Florentine culture and Florentine life; the city was kept in a state of ferment between sidereal prophecies and the voices of the Lord, between subtle calculations and the residues of ancient superstitions, between flights of sublime metaphysics and corporeal earthly interests. Indeed something great was stirring in the world: a momentous change was taking place in the relations between man and reality. Among the men who were contributing to it there was a vague awareness of a radical upheaval in process. Leonardo was drawing and observing appalling cataclysms; Savonarola was predicting in terrible words the advent of the Apocalypse; Toscanelli was reading in the comets the dire forebodings of changes in laws and empires; Columbus was seeking in Joachim of Fiore and Albumazar the proof of a new epoch of the world, which he felt the call to discover.

This age, which is so easy to imagine as full of harmony, joy, reasoned measure, ancient and modern wisdom, was shaken by a dark sense of tragedy. It was not many years later that Philip Melanchthon of Nürnberg was to address with quiet eloquence a solemn thanks to Florence in the name of all of learned Europe. If the new century was a century of light, for this men gave thanks to Florence and to the work of its scholars. But there was no peace in the Florence of the second half of the Quattrocento, and the new century was to be ushered in by the followers of Savanarola beyond the flames of the stake. Its inception was not untroubled: the new equilibrium was not to be achieved without a struggle. It was not by chance that the measure of such men as Leonardo, Machiavelli, and Michelangelo seemed to conceal something ambiguous beneath an almost tragic greatness.

All this must be emphasized in order to understand Toscanelli's activity in his time—as well as the activity of his friends—beyond those curious hagiographic and conventional fashions to which a historiography of positivistic flavor was no less inclined than the subsequent idealistic historiography.

In fact, Toscanelli would be discussed a great deal at the time of the celebrations of Columbus's discovery of America at the end of the nineteenth century. Having been neglected for four hundred years, he was officially declared in solemn learned assemblies to be the "forerunner" of the discovery of America: the mind that had conceived the great voyage, the author of an ingenious and fruitful misunderstanding, the thought preceding the action. Cesare de Lollis, the deserving editor of the writings of Columbus, fell so in love with this image that at the end of 1923 he again repeated: "The thought of one, a man of study, became the action of the other, a man of the sea and of adventure, . . . the intuition of one . . . came to obsess the mind of the man of action." And this, to some extent, at least symbolically, may even be true.

What is less true is the image of Columbus as an ignorant and credulous sailor by comparison with Toscanelli, the flawless scientist, immune to "medieval" superstitions, the accomplished man, integral and free from human foibles. Nevertheless this was the figure sanctified by the epigraphic publications of the *fin de siècle,* imposing in their bulk and scientific or pseudoscientific display, which laid the Quattrocento doctor, apothecary, and astrologer to rest in a fine mausoleum of ministerial and umbertine taste, destined to fascinate all of subsequent historiography up to our time. Since astrology was in the eyes of these worthy men a medieval superstition, they covered his shameful parts with a modest veil, and everything was done to demonstrate that Toscanelli was in reality not an astrologer, that he calculated the course of the comets for purely speculative purposes. The folios containing his calculations have been separated from the context in which for centuries they had been handed down.[9] The venerable Strozzi codices have been dismembered, so that prescriptions against baldness should not contaminate the sublime mathematical truths. The clearly astrological aspects of the few surviving texts have been left in the dark. In the lists of towns and climates the latter-day scholars looked for extraordinary sources, and it did not occur to anyone that similar notions abounded in the common astrological manuals. Finally, not content with having constructed the purest of scientists, a prophet more than a "precursor," a seer, they tried to attribute to him moral virtues, impeccable habits, and heroic qualities. First it was discovered that Toscanelli was pious and a vegetarian; then it was found that, after eighty-five years of earthly exile and almost a decade of student life in Padua, he died a virgin.

In reality Paolo Toscanelli started studying medicine in Padua; how could a good physician at that time, as he was, not be interested in herbs and imported medicaments and not be concerned with astrology? Or how could he not consider Don Ferrante, whose theory of crises and of the critical days of diseases was a topic of fundamental importance in medical discussions? On three points astrological theories appeared easily to have the upper hand over some opposing theories; the lunar phases exercized influence on the life of plants, on certain human functions, and on the tides. The critical days for pruning, grafting, harvests, women's periods, together with the tides, were the warhorses of the promoters of astrology. When Galileo, on the fourth day of his dialogues, wrongly scoffed at De Dominis and gave an erroneous interpretation of the tides, it was his aversion to astrological doctrines on astral influences that led him to make the mistake.

The battle over astrology, between 1400 and 1500, is one of the most important chapters in the history of scientific knowledge, as well as an extremely delicate one. The case of Galileo and his evaluation of Kepler, who defended astrology against Pico's attack against it, shows how dangerous an indiscriminate condemnation of the "astrologers" can be, whether it is on the level of astronomy or on that of geography, medicine, or even history. Galileo summed up very well astrology's defects in principle: the insertion of fantastic causes and of mythologizing processes into scientific investigation was at one time, as Pico had already pointed out, a process in which people took recourse to the most generalized and far removed causes without considering the nearest and intermediate processes.

In reality, astrology had a double aspect: on the one hand, it was a survival of astral cults; on the other, a complex of research, observations, and scientific theories which were frequently inexact and more frequently vitiated by erroneous procedures. To attribute to a constellation or a planet, or to their reciprocal encounters, a disgrace, a fortune, or a character trait was to assume that Mars or Gemini were in reality not physical bodies but the ancient pagan divinities whose names they bore and who were identified with the stars. But to connect certain earthly phenomena (such as the tides) to celestial movements, or to assume in general that, considering the tie that links physical phenomena, the heavens too influence the earth, was not in itself a fallacious hypothesis, even though it was wrong to relate the mortal and final crisis of a disease, which tends to recur within a certain period of days, simply to the stars.

Recourse to a remote and very general cause, common to disparate phenomena, merely signifies ignorance of the true "causes" and their relationships. And yet, if we isolate the religious component—even though it too is important, the scientific or pseudoscientific aspect of astrology appears both complex and worthy of consideration. If we set aside the generic reference to celestial causes, there remain to astrology the observations, descriptions, calculations, and hypotheses about the stars and their behavior—that is, an astronomy that is anything but contemptible. What remains is the attentive and accurate study of the "climates"; the description of the earth, of towns and peoples; the exact location of places, undertaken in order to specify as precisely as possible the knowledge of the relationships between the heavens and the earth. Given the regularity and the periodic nature of celestial phenomena, it becomes a study of all periodical phenomena, of the problem of the periodicity of world history and of the life of man: the search for constant and variable aspects and the problematics of their relationships. Whoever believes that the books of Albumazar or Guido Bonatti, of Ibn Ezra or Pietro d'Abano, of Al-Kabisi or Cecco d'Ascoli contain only the relics of ancient superstitions or the phantasmagoria of sick minds, will be very much surprised to find there, besides important documentation on distant religions and echoes of primitive creeds, remarkable pieces of profound psychological analysis, important chapters on geography, astronomical observations, theories on historical cycles and on the characteristics of nations and men, and so on. Nor would it be a mere pleasantry to affirm that in a good book on astrology by some Ali or Omar there is still more to be learned than in many books by so-called philosophers.

At any rate, Paolo Toscanelli, who studied medicine in Padua between 1417 and 1424 and who was a man of serious bent, integrated astrological research into his preparatory studies, and in order to probe them more deeply he rounded his education out with a thorough study of mathematics. All the information we have on his activity and culture, rather than giving us a picture of the abstract universal man so dear to a certain common rhetorical conception of the Renaissance, confine us within the framework of a scholar concerned with mastering a chosen discipline. His study of agriculture and of perspective—that is, optics—did not place him outside a well-defined area of research, while his knowledge of Greek was, in itself, indispensable for access to the most important scientific works which were reappearing at that time in the original. We should remember that this was the period in which Ptolemy, Strabo, Galen, and Archimedes (to mention only some of the authors known to Toscanelli) were being read again.

The fact that Toscanelli studied in Padua should also not be overlooked. Padua was significant for its lively interest in scientific knowledge, in medicine and physics; the ancients were neither scorned nor ignored, although their scientific writings were read more than were their works on history, morals, politics, or poetry. Studying medicine in Padua between the second and third decade of the Quattrocento meant reaping the benefits of a specific cultural patrimony, reading certain books, listening to certain teachers, and learning certain methods.

It was not that Florence ignored science; there were noted physicians and scientists among the Florentines or among those who lived and taught in Florence. Among the physicists and logicians it is enough to mention Pelacani, one of Buridan's outstanding pupils; and among the astronomers, Dagomari, who was celebrated by Boccaccio and Villani and mourned by Salutati, and whose writings were probably well known to Toscanelli. Among the physicians was the great Ugo da Siena, and so on. But the climate of Florence, which was artisanal and, at the same time, inclined to the political-moral disciplines, never encouraged the flowering of an equivalent unprejudiced science, which (even though in the end it became enclosed and conservative) aristocratic Padua fostered.

The "freedom" of Padua was basically that of scholastic boldness bordering on heresy. This was specifically the spirit in all the high-level intellectual circles and mainly in the university—a spirit that was erosive and often sterile, refined and played out, basically not dangerous, and extremely conservative. The humanistic Renaissance culture of Florence was not universitarian, and it was antischolastic. On the one hand, it touched the world of the men of letters and men of action; on the other, it touched that of the artists, artisans, and technicians. It was no coincidence that Florence was a city which, all things considered, had no university tradition, even though it was the seat of a Studio that was the most important center of the new culture, as much in the field of science as in that of the arts; and that out of its climate emerged Leonardo, Machiavelli, Michelangelo, and Galileo. However, Toscanelli's Paduan preparation is important if only because it was translated into fruitful action and concrete projects, hence into new thought. His subtle academic knowledge contributed not little to the material needs of Tuscan merchants and to the requests of such friends as Filippo Brunelleschi and Leon Battista Alberti.

But Toscanelli's student sojourn in Padua was most noteworthy for one primary reason: at Padua he met and befriended a fellow student, Nicholas of Cusa, and this friendship lasted throughout his life. Paolo was among those present at the bedside of the dying cardinal in the palace of the archbishop of Todi, in August 1464; he placed his signature at the bottom of Nicholas's testament beside that of Canon Fernam Martins, the canon of Lisbon, to whom he later sent the letter and map that were to have so much significance for history.

The Cusan, in complete agreement with certain fanciful historians, did not have much to do with Italian or with Florentine philosophy of the Quattrocento. His most important philosophical works had no reverberation in Florence in the fifteenth century. Ficino appears to have ignored him. But the contacts that the philosopher did not have with philosophers, the mathematician had with his friend Toscanelli, whose doctrines he valued highly. From 1450 on Nicholas continued to send Toscanelli his works on the problem of squaring the circle. In a letter to Toscanelli written from Rieti on 12 July 1450, and in his dedication to him of *de geometricis transmutationibus,* Nicholas recalled the emotion of their first youthful encounter and the ties that had never been broken. In the name of their long friendship he asked Toscanelli "to correct his work." That these were not rhetorical exchanges, but a genuine dialogue between scientists, can perhaps be inferred from the fact that in the *de quadratura circuli,* completed in

Bressanone in 1457, Nicholas introduces Paolo as his interlocutor, placing into his mouth a frank criticism of *de arithmeticis complementis*—"an obscure book, of dubious interpretation."

In 1464 the dialogue was enlarged to include Johannes Müller, the famous Regiomontanus, who on 5 July 1464, about a month prior to the Cusan's death, attacked Nicholas's writings on the squaring of the circle. He addressed himself specifically to Toscanelli, stressing the latter's great competence in mathematics and philosophy and opposing it in a way to that of the Cusan, on whom he was to pronounce, in 1471, a very harsh judgment ("a ridiculous geometer, whose vanity has led him to fill the world with humbug"). Toscanelli he praised highly:

> You have the fullest knowledge of geometry; you are the most expert and rapid at numerical calculus. . . . In you I recognized the gentle, sweet spirit. . . . If there were someone whom the study of philosophy should celebrate and the glory of mathematics sanctify forever, you before anyone else in our time, Paolo the Florentine, are the only one among the Italians worthy of so much honor, since you possess all the disciplines in such perfection that if you wanted to measure yourself with Archimedes, you might win the palm. Philosophy has made you, a docile pupil, into a most learned teacher; nor have you ever been satisfied, best among men, for, after gaining a thorough knowledge of medicine, you have learned Greek.

Regiomontanus wrote two letters to Toscanelli. Their pretentious style and rheorical manner must be discounted, in the same way we diverge from the old historians in attributing unqualifiedly to Paolo the theses that the Cusan put into his mouth.[10] But there can be no doubt that Toscanelli was considered an outstanding scientist and that, in 1464, when he was nearly seventy, he had attained the reputation of an oracle. Regiomontanus continued to refer to his astronomical observations as well as to those of Alberti, and his comparison with Archimedes was intentional. The study of Archimedes was in this period a very important part of the progress of scientific knowledge, and it is almost symbolic of the reciprocal influence of technique and science.[11] Moreover, the very learned Toscanelli remained a man of precise investigations rather than of words: observations, calculations, possibly advice and suggestions.

In 1450 the Cusan had asked him for a revision; the same was demanded of him by Müller in 1464: "*in manus tuas depono gratissimas limandum*" ("I entrust my work to you, so that you may correct it"). His personality may be gathered by the impact he had on others, according to witnesses. A man of unusual reserve and great humility, he only entered into conversation with others to give them the results of his own research. This was true in his relations with Nicholas of Cusa, with Müller, later with Columbus, and earlier with Brunelleschi.

If the writings of the Cusan and of Regiomontanus give us a picture of Toscanelli as a great mathematician and a student of Archimedes, the relationship with Brunelleschi reveals the fruitful collaboration among scientists and artists that was a unique feature of the Florentine cultural environment. Vasari relates that "on returning from his studies one evening maestro Paolo dal Pozzo Toscanelli was at dinner in a garden with some of his friends, who to honor him had invited Filippo: the latter, after hearing him discuss the art of mathematics, became so friendly with him that he learned geometry from him. And although Filippo was not a man of letters, he reasoned things out so well from his practice and experience that he astounded him [Paolo] many times."[12]

Filippo, like Leonardo later, was an "*omo sanza lettere,*" that is, a man without great culture, mainly in Greek and Latin. But his discussions with the Paduan doctor were nonetheless fruitful. Experience and reason met and collaborated. Pippo, Alberti, and Paolo are three names linked by reliable sources and precise documents; they seem to epitomize the interchange of ideas and the collaboration between science, the mechanical arts, and technique; between ancient wisdom and modern constructions: Toscanelli, the new Archimedes; Alberti, the student of mathematics and artist; and Brunelleschi, the remarkable engineer. It is interesting to reread the malicious Giovanni Cavalcanti's report of a very Leonardian plan of Brunelleschi's and other "geometers' "—and Toscanelli comes to mind—with which they aimed to submerge Lucca in the waters of the Serchio in 1430. "Some of our fantasts," Cavalcanti wrote, "among them Filippo di Ser Brunellesco, . . . advised, and with their false and lying geometry . . . demonstrated that the city of Lucca could be flooded; and they presented the plan with their ill understood arts in such a way that the stupid masses cried . . . : 'We touch with our hands what you the speculators design; but you want the war to last so that you will keep your positions forever.' "[13]

The picture is lively: the people of Florence allied with the scholars against the magistrates, who were accused of wanting to prolong the war. But more interesting is the convergence of art (and what art!) and science, of theories and techniques, in the setting of a return to the ancients—the reading of venerable works and the lessons of things; experiences and discussions, as Machiavelli was to say in his incomparable way. The divorce claimed between letters, sciences, and arts is pure fantasy on the part of careless and prejudiced contemporary historians.

Cristoforo Landino places Paolo Toscanelli in perspective as the venerated figure of the sage of antiquity, in the background of Calmaldoli's philosophical conversations dominated by Alberti, living in the midst of a dialogue with scientists and technicians, with men of letters and artisans. With Alberti he studied the movements of the stars; with an instrument constructed in the Duomo he studied the movements of the sun;[14] he made solar clocks; he gathered information from travelers about distant countries; he discussed with Georgius Gemistus the text of Strabo, which in these years found an unexcelled student in Guarino Veronese.

He observed and studied the comets of 1433, 1449–50, 1456, 1457, and 1472. *Immensi labores et graves vigiliae Pauli de Puteo Toscanello super mensura comete** may be read on page 244 of the Magliabechian Codex XI, 121, which at the end of the last century was imprudently torn out through a pious wish to isolate the little group of writings presumed to be in the hand of Toscanelli. The sum total of his observations in the barren language of ciphers, some lists of cities indicating latitude and longitude, some astrological notations, and a brief note to the Cusan are all that remain of the work of the scientist. Eminent astronomers have discussed the precision and value of the observations on the comets, pointing out the surprising exactitude of his calculations, but without taking into account the cultural context in which the investigations took place. Numerous observations and writings on the comets existed prior to Toscanelli. In fact, the attention of astrologers had been focused in particular on the *stelle cum caudis,* which are described and listed in the *Centiloquio,* the famous text attributed to Ptolemy which notes their

* "The indefatigable work and sleepless nights of Paolo dal Pozzo Toscanelli in the measurement of the comet."

influences on the death of kings, of rich gentlemen and noblemen, and similar misfortunes (*inducit mortem regum et guerras et mortem multam et decollationem et mortalitatem et mortem naturalem et mortem per gladium*).

Toscanelli's calculations, in the Magliabechian Codex, are preceded by the transcript of a letter written on 17 June 1456 by Pietro Bono Avogaro, the well-known professor at the Studio in Ferrara, in which the properties of the comet of 1456 are recalled. This is followed by a short astrological treatise on the same star, whose attribution to Toscanelli, though at times accepted without discussion, is far from tenable. But it is important to stress the aim and character of this research: the determination of relationships between celestial phenomena and earthly events. This is stressed not so much in order to support or minimize Toscanelli's astrological beliefs as to insert his observations in their place in a rich and noteworthy literature composed not only of superstitious conclusions but also of very important investigations and calculations. In other words, Toscanelli's work on the comets is not some kind of miracle isolated in a desert, but a happily accurate result which stands out from a very large production. In the same manuscript that had originally contained Toscanelli's papers are other treatises on the comets, conjunctions, and eclipses, which are probably directly linked with Toscanelli's activity.

If people had been agitated for centuries by prophecies and portents, in the second half of the Quattrocento in particular they lived in an incubator of great events. Just as the plague of 1348 had been tied to the contiguities of the stars, so the comets and their conjunctions seemed to mark the Turkish advance and the great crisis of Christianity. The anguish of the new century permeated the commentaries on the Apocalypse and the preaching of inspired prophets. The ancient astrological theory of the great conjunctions—that is, of the periods of world history, included in the widely disseminated works of Albumazar, penetrated and disturbed fifteenth-century minds. The myth of rebirth—that is, of the new cycle about to begin, with that whole complex of practical consequences which accompany a forecast that is believed and that tends to become realized to the extent that it is believed—and the idea of a radical change which must come about in the fifteenth century—that is, the idea of the Renaissance itself, which has given rise to so much frenzy on the part of historians—may have a not inconsiderable astrological component.

This astrology (to return to Toscanelli) was not limited to research on the comets, but was extended to include that famous list of cities, with its measures of latitude and longitude, which has exercized the minds of so many historians and geographers. In reality, they are not very original lists; they are transcribed (the sources of some were even indicated in the same Toscanelli codex) from medieval astrological treatises, among which was the famous *Speculum astronomiae.*[15] The source of one list—the most important for the number of European, African, and Asian localities—was until recently sought in vain, and it nurtured all sorts of speculation. It has been located in a Trecento vernacular text, probably the work of Paolo dell' Abbaco, which includes along with many others this famous list of towns, almost identical, together with quite remarkable observations on an essential subject: the relationship between dry land and the sea on the earth's surface. The text contains an uninterrupted discussion of the Alphonsine Tables which is along the same lines, according to Villani, as Dagomari; at one point it attacks Ptolemy's theses and those of his commentators: "With all due regard for Tolomeo, he does not distinguish well the quarters of the habitable earth. . . . Neither does Ali. . . ." And the author continues to discourse on calculations of distances made "in the *mappamondo*" and on the "infallibility" of the "geometrical demonstrations."[16]

Instead of separating Toscanelli's notes from the context of astrological research and from their rather complex history, we will have to return them to Florence with the aim of specifying at least in part the same themes of his geographical research. If it was absurd to separate medicine from astrology in the Quattrocento, it was even more absurd to separate geography and astronomy from astrology. Ptolemy, who was the highest authority, was at the same time a geographer, an astronomer, and an astrologer, and his works cannot be separated from one another. The interweaving, in Columbus's notes, of Pliny and Albumazar, of Pierre d'Ailly and Pius II, is not a sign of a strange ignorance, but an index of participation in the current fashion in culture.

Original geographical investigations were attributed to Toscanelli on the basis of Landino's testimony, who describes him as questioning travelers from distant countries. But such "scientific" curiosity about remote lands, combined with specific commercial interests, was everywhere present in the Quattrocento. If we stop to consider the men who lived in Toscanelli's milieu and who were linked to his circle, why not cite, among the records of voyages and the letters and notes of merchants and missionaries, the unforgettable passages of Cyriacus of Ancona, with their taste for distant countries and stormy seas, the cities and peoples of the East? And what about Poggio? What of the official letters of Bruni on foreign and business relations with the countries of Africa and Asia?

The Portuguese were not the only ones looking for new maritime routes; nor, in Italy, were Venice and Genoa the only such seekers. Florence too, with its access to the sea through Pisa, was increasingly interested in problems of communications with eastern ports. Toscanelli, who was not only a scientist but also a businessman, made practical use of the results of his studies and of his thoughts on the evidence of travelers. In July 1459 he met the ambassadors of the king of Portugal in Florence; on 25 June 1474 he sent Fernam Martins, the canon of Lisbon and "an intimate friend" of the king of Portugal, his famous letter:

> I am transmitting . . . to His Majesty a map made with my own hands, which indicates the contours of your shores and the islands from which the voyage should be begun, always westward, and the areas which should be reached, and how much of an angle should be deflected from the pole and from the equatorial line, and how much distance, that is, how many miles would need to be covered in order to reach the places that are richest in every kind of aromatic spices and gems. And you should not be amazed that I call the harbors where the spaces are, *western,* while normally they are called *eastern,* because those who sail steadily west, by navigating toward the antipodes, will reach these regions.

His reflections on the map of the world, borrowed from Francesco Castellani, bore their fruit. Paolo the teacher paused to dream of new countries and great royal edifices, of rivers marvelous for their width and length, of two hundred cities along the banks of one river alone, of huge marble bridges lined on each side with columns, of temples and palaces covered with solid gold, jewels, and pearls, and of learned men, "philosophers and astrologers whose arts and inventions" have made these wide lands flourish. Whoever reads this letter forgets the scientist and dreams of cities and ideal worlds, like the drawings of Filarete on the pages of Thomas More.

The rest is known. Whether the correspondence between Columbus and Toscanelli is authentic or not, it is certain that Columbus was acquainted with Toscanelli's idea, that he copied in his own hand the letter to Canon Martins, and that he carried out the dream that had been dreamt in the shade of Brunelleschi's cupola. On the frontispiece of the first edition of the *Novum Organum* by Francis Bacon is a famous engraving symbolizing the new science and the new civilization: ships that face the open sea, beyond the column of Hercules. Science, with experience and reason, formulated an hypothesis and drew a navigational map; the navigator verified it; or, rather, he made it come true, to the extent to which he integrated it, corrected it, and realized it with great risk and effort. Thus Columbus turned the mistaken measures of the geographers into the true reality through a fruitful joining of knowledge and action.

Thus the greatest event of the fifteenth century appears to have been the ideal result of Toscanelli's activity, of the work of a man whose influence we see in so many and such great works of others, but strangely enough of whom we are unable to grasp a single feature. He is present in the measurements of Brunelleschi's cupola, in the bitter prose of Alberti, in the mathematical reflections of the Cusan, in the astronomical discussions of Müller, in the astrological polemics of Pico, in the philosophical conversations of Landino and Ficino. He accompanied the ships of Columbus. And yet his figure is truly more tenuous than a shadow: a few numbers that express his long sleepless nights and his dreams of fabulous lands. Perhaps he was the ideal sage of this new era, inclined not to thrust his own personality to the fore, but rather to make the world a better place to live in and life more humane. Intent on his work, and therefore alive in the works on which he collaborated, he was not apart from the others but together with them in a common task.

Notes

1. On Toscanelli, his activity, and the episodes in his life, the massive work by G. Uzielli, *La vita e i tempi di Paolo dal Pozzo Toscanelli, Ricerche e Studi* (Rome: Ministry of Public Instruction, 1894), remains essential despite its unnecessary length and many inexactitudes. Uzielli discourses for nearly 800 folio-size pages *de omnibus rebus et de quibusdam aliis,* but he managed nonetheless (although with a singularly distorted perspective), to gather together all the scanty information we have on Toscanelli. The most important part of the work is without doubt Chapter Six, by Giovanni Celoria, the successor to Schiaparelli at the Specola di Brera, where Toscanelli's findings on the comets were demonstrated. The essay by Celoria was later reprinted separately (*Sulle osservazioni di comete fatte da Paolo dal Pozzo Toscanelli e sui lavori astronomici suoi in genere* [Milan, 1921]) with a photographic reproduction of Toscanelli's tables, which appeared in Uzielli's work without the astrological charts of the constellations, evidently in a frank attempt to "modernize" the author. Thorndike (*A History of Magic and Experimental Science* [New York, 1934], 4:432 sqq.), referring back to Celoria, warns us against the attraction of the Toscanellian "myth," even though he remains conditioned by Celoria's research, which has also been reproduced with some attenuation of the less acceptable parts, by Abetti, *Storia dell' Astronomia* (Florence, 1949), p. 56 sqq. But much more will be said on the subject of Toscanelli the astrologer. With regard to the thorny question of Toscanelli as the "forerunner" of Columbus, see, among others, H. Vignaud, *La lettre et la carte de Toscanelli sur la route des Indes par l'ouest. Étude critique sur l'authenticité et la valeur de ces documents et sur les sources des idées cosmographiques de Colomb* (Paris, 1901); G. Uzielli, "Toscanelli, Colombo e Vespucci," taken from *Atti del IV Congresso Geografico Italiano* (1902); G. Uzielli, "Antonio di Tuccio Manetti, Paolo Toscanelli, e la lunghezza delle miglia nel secolo delle scoperte," *Rivista Geografica Italiana* 9(1902) (very important for the marginal notes of Antonio Manetti to ms. Conv. Soppr. G. 2.1501, of the National Library of Florence, in which Toscanelli is mentioned); C. De Lollis, *Cristoforo Colombo nella Leggenda e nella Storia,* 3rd ed. (Rome, 1923); and N. Sumien, *La correspondence du savant Florentin Paolo dal Pozzo Toscanelli avec Christophe Colomb* (Paris, 1927).

2. "Leonis Baptistae de Albertis Vita," in *Opere Volgari,* ed. Bonucci, (Florence, 1849), 1:102: "There remain of his works the *Epistolae ad Paulum Physicum,* in which he predicted, years in advance, future events in his country. . . ." The dedication of the *Intercoenales* is contained in *Opera inedita pauca separatim impressa,* ed. G. Mancini (Florence, 1890), p. 122 sqq.

3. Much has been said (frequently erroneously) about Toscanelli's astrological beliefs. Pico wrote, as quoted in Garin, ed., *Disp. adv. astrol. div.* (Florence, 1946), 1:5–12, 60: "Paulo the Florentine was thoroughly at home in medicine, but even more so in mathematics, Greek, and Latin. As often as he was questioned about these [astrological] pursuits of his, he would pointedly reply that the results were quite unreliable and even fallacious; he referred among others to himself as a case in point. Having completed by then his eighty-fifth year of life, he said he could not find in his nativity, which he had minutely examined, the least trace of a stellar configuration presaging a more than ordinary life expectancy." Similarly, Ficino, in his commentary on Plotinus (*Opera* [Basle, 1576], 2:1626) wrote: "Paulo the Florentine, an outstanding authority on astronomy, used to make fun of it, for he had studied his nativity with utmost care and yet could not discover in it anything that would augur longevity, although he had lived five years beyond eighty." In the *disputatio contra indicium astrologorum* (Kristeller, *Suppl. ficin.* [Florence, 1937], 2: 66–7), in a text not used by Uzielli, one reads: "Paulo of the City of Florence, a scholarly astronomer and physician, told me that the reason why he preferred not to draw any conclusions was that judgment in forecasting events was most difficult to reach since antecedents are of no help at all. There are so many different factors to be considered that only a sage or one specially gifted by nature could foretell some specific event by following the rules of this science. Then, he said, an event need not occur in the expected manner if the one whom the event concerns knows of it beforehand. A man of moderation, informed ahead of time, may quite often be immune to the influence of the stars. For instance, he said, he had treated Nicola Populesci, a man forty-five years old who was suffering from pleurisy, which had been correctly foreseen by an astrologer. The astrologer had also foretold that the patient would die of this pleurisy; but, thanks to his [Toscanelli's] treatment, the patient did not die. He affirmed, moreover, that it was possible to avert many deaths that were prognosticated for a certain day simply through persistence, and that, on the contrary, it was the incontinent and the fearful who usually fulfilled the prognostications of the astrologists. As to some definite ruling on life expectancy, the astronomers have hardly anything to go by; on this issue, each proceeds in his own fashion. He said, besides, that, having studied his own horoscope with extreme care, he had never come upon anything indicative of life expectancy, nor any factor adding to one's life span, nor even any aspects that could be said augur continued life. Yet, he said, he had outlived all his kin. He had completed his eighty-fifth year, glowing sound in body and mind. From his horoscope he had foreseen that at certain times certain illnesses were to befall him; being a physician, he could prevent them, paying special attention to his food and drink and taking plenty of exercise."

Lucio Bellanti, on the contrary, in his answer to Pico (*De astrologica veritate. Responsiones in disputationes Johannis Pici adversus astrologicam veritatem* [Florence, 1498]), declared: "As for Paulo the Florentine, who I am told was a distinguished mathematician, I never spoke with him myself, nor did I ever see him. From several of his friends, however, I have heard that there was nothing he put greater faith in than astrology. But as a man of profound wisdom he did not go about preaching it from the housetops, although he did reveal the mysteries of the spirit to his close friends; and whatever he came to know of future events, he told them. . . . [Leon] Baptista Alberti, a Florentine and very close friend of Paolo, as well as one of the foremost writers of our time, confirms this in his work *De Architectura*. . . ." Pico himself supplies very interesting information elsewhere (and generally overlooked) in the *Disputationes*, 2:19–24, 310: "In epistographic notations [written on the back of Mss.] by Paulo the Florentine, physician and mathematician, I found two different dates given for the reconstruction of the city of Florence; the first, the year (A.D.) 801, and the other, the year 802, whence we have a totally different position of stars for each date."

4. *Scritti di Cristoforo Colombo pubblicati e illustrati da Cesare de Lollis* (Rome, 1894), pp. 186, 364–5. It should be kept in mind that Martins is the Aristotelian interlocutor of the *de non aliud* of the Cusan.

5. For this and other evidence, see Uzielli, who collected them with a certain diligence.

6. Columbus, *Scritti*, p. 409 sqq.; De Lollis, *Colombo*, pp. 25 sqq. The "astrological" commentary of Pico on Psalm XVIII is conserved in a manuscript in the city library of Ferrara (in which see Garin essay in *Riv. critica di Storia della Filosofia* 12(1957): 5 sqq.).

7. Columbus, *Scritti*, p. 437. See also Albumasar, *Introductorium in astrologiam* (Venice, 1506), 6:2, c. 4v; E. F. Wilson, ed., *The "Stella Maris" of John of Garland* (Cambridge, Mass., 1946), p. 146 (and pp. 99 sqq. for the *astrologia spiritualis que proprietates signorum Virgini tribuit*).

8. Ms. Magliab. 11:121, c. 237*r* sqq. (now Banco Rari, 30). Avogaro's text figures now with Toscanelli's calculations, even though written in a different hand; it bears the date of 16 June 1456, and is a brief astrological note on the comet. There follows, in the same hand, the beginning of a small treatise of a rather unoriginal nature on the comet. This incomplete treatise has been attributed to Toscanelli (Uzielli-Celoria, *La vita*, p. 327), but without serious grounds. Moreover, in concept it resembles an analogous writing on the comet of 1472 contained in the same codex (Magliab. 11:121, c. 235*r*), and it is no coincidence that it should initially have been combined with Avogaro's writings. The name of the author is not easy to read; Thorndike believed it to be Laurentius Viterbiensis, but, if "Viterbiensis" is certain, "Laurentius" is not (which would read rather something like Annius; and the dates and inspiration would not be in contradiction). So far as the comet of 1456 and the impression it made in Florence are concerned, see a note written by Guglielmo Becchi to Pietro de' Medici, dated 15 June 1456 (Magliab. 11:40: Ghuglielmi Becchi, *de cometa ad Petrum Cosmi de medicis civem clarissimum*), written in the course of the great debate that was current in the city ("On my way to the San Marco Library I met a friend of yours who was about to return to you; it was a pleasure to me rather than a mere courtesy to inquire after you and your health. When I took leave of him, I begged him to remember me to Your

Highness, unworthy of you though I am. Meanwhile, here, the entire population has been inordinately perturbed by the threatening portents in the skies, and various rumors as to the meaning of these phenomena have been circulating among the simple people as well as among the educated classes . . . ").

9. Precisely in this way ms. Magliab. 11:121 (formerly Strozzi 1127) was unfortunately split up and placed together with related and possibly connected texts, not without reason. It is no coincidence that we find here codices of the *Speculum* to which Toscanelli refers.

10. G. Uzielli, *La vita*, pp. 268 sqq.; "Joannes Germanus Paulo Florentino," in *De triangulis omnimodis libri V: accedunt Nicolai Cusae quaedam de quadratura circuli ecc.* (Nürnberg, 1533), pp. 29, 56, etc. For the relations between the Cusan and Toscanelli and for a short letter from Paolo to the Cusan, see *Die mathematischen Schriften* of the Cusan (Hamburg, 1952), pp. 128–31.

11. See A. Rey, *L'Apogée de la science technique grecque. L'essor de la mathématique* (Paris, 1948), pp. 306–09. With regard to his interest in Archimedes, see among others the manuscript of Conv. 1, V, 30 (San Marco). This manuscript originally belonged to Filippo de' Ser Ugolino Pieruzzi, whose library, rich in scientific texts, should be more thoroughly studied. Incorrectly described by Heiberg (Archimedis, *Opera* [Leipzig, 1881], pp. 86–88), it contains passages from *de sphera et cylindro* in the Latin (see also L. Thorndike and P. Kibre, *A Catalogue of Incipits of Medieval Scientific Writings in Latin* [Cambridge, Mass., 1937], p. 126); the *de isoperimetris propositiones septem* of Jordanus; *Milleus romanus de figuris sphericis*—that is, the three books of Menelaus of Alexandria (see also M. Cantor, *Vorlesungen über Geschichte der Mathematik* [Leipzig, 1880], 1:349–604); the globe of Theodosius of Tripoli (Cantor, *Vorlesungen*, 1:346–47); the *Epistola Abuyafar Ameti filii Josephi de arcubus similibus;* and so on.

12. Vasari, *Le vite* (Florence, 1878), 1:333 (in 1550 edition [ed. Florence], 1:296).

13. G. Cavalcanti, *Istorie fiorentine* (Florence, 1838), 1:328.

14. L. Ximenes, *Delvecchio e nuovo gnomone fiorentino e delle osservazioni astronomiche fisiche et architettoniche fatte nel verificare la costruzione libri IV* . . . (Florence, 1797).

15. The four lists were formerly contained in Magliab. 11:121, c. 254, and are now among the isolated sheets among the rare books; Uzielli (*La vita*, pp. 463 sqq.) invented all sorts of fantasies about them. In the same work (p. 464), Wagner showed how one was derived from the *Speculum astronomiae*, which appeared, not by chance, precisely in the same codex from which (due most likely to the initiative of Uzielli), Toscanelli's texts were torn out. That the term *decani*, which appears in the other list, was related to the decani, and hence referred back to an astrological text, is likely, and it is difficult to understand why Uzielli should have resolutely excluded it, and why he should, of all things, have gone so far as to believe that the book had belonged to a Giovanni de' Cani da Montecatini. The curious thing is that the most important list of the cities, on which Uzielli dwelled, may also be found in a lengthy astro-

nomical work in Italian, which appears before Toscanelli's texts in the Magliab. ms. 11:121; and it is unusual that so many worthy gentlemen, among so many elucubrations, should never have taken the trouble to study carefully that huge collection, which in fact does not appear to have been brought together by coincidence.

16. Magliab. 11:121, c. 74r sqq. They are observations on the eclipses dating from 1300, mixed in with other writings. The author, while he also refers to observations made by a master Lando in Siena (c. 79r: "maestro Lando writes that he considered in Siena . . . "), states that he undertook careful observations in Florence in precisely the period in which we know that Dagomari worked in the city ("it was assiduously observed by me in Florence . . . "). The author, who was a scholar, vigorously attacks the Alfonsine Tables and boasts several times of his "new and true correction" (c. 84r). Today this affirmation is confirmed by as much as we know of Paolo from Boccaccio (V. Romano, ed., *Genealogie*, 15, 6 [Bari, 1951], 2:762–63, in which Paolo is mentioned by Filippo Villani as still living; G. Boffito, *Paolo dell'Abbaco e Fabricio Mordente* [Florence, 1931]; and Giovanni Villani, *Cronache*, 12:41), and from Salutati (Novati, ed. *Epistolarae* [Rome, 1891], p. 15, in which the date of his death, assumed by Novati, does not seem tenable). Nor does the fact that, at a certain point, references to celestial phenomena after Paolo's death are included in the context constitute a serious challenge to the attribution. It occurs in other writings that are certainly his—in Ashburn. 1308 and in the ms. Plimpton (formerly Buoncompagni) studied by Thorndike (*History of Magic*, 3:207 sqq.). On the other hand, there is another work (again in ms. Magliab. 11:121, cc. 115r–165r), clearly astrological and also quite remarkable, by Paolo Dell'Abbaco. The fact is that this Paolo was an author of considerable importance, whose works deserve to be seriously investigated for their own merits, as well as for the purpose of "situating" Toscanelli historically.

V
Images and Symbols in Marsilio Ficino

Hear, Florence, what I say to thee; hear what God has imparted to me: from thee shall spring the reformation of all Italy.

The promise of renewal and peace ("a token of Paradise/this city seemed/with all united/great peace was seen") had been extinguished on the stake in front of the Palazzo Vecchio. Savonarola had perished, and the street urchins of Florence roamed along the dry riverbed of the Arno, gathering the relics of the friar for the pious veneration of not a few remaining superstitious Piagnoni.

Canon Ficino was writing his *Apologia* against the poor dead monk, maintaining that not just one devil but a whole host of demons had been incarnated in him. It was rare in this period, (though quarrelsome invective was quite common) for so much abuse to be directed in so little space against the memory of a dead man. The authenticity of his scandalous "*Apologia* against the Ferrarese anti-Christ," has often been denied, and attempts have been made to prove in many ways that Ficino could not have sullied his reputation with such an ungenerous act. In reality, however, the style, the quotations, a certain treatment of the argument, lead us to consider these pages as the work of the great Platonist.

But we are inclined even more to believe that the tract was his when we know more of his character. At the time of the Pazzi conspiracy he had been a friend of many of those involved in the plot. But when it failed, when the Salviati had died tragically and the rest had been torn to pieces in the streets of Florence by the fury of the mob, the devout Marsilio was quick to forget and to have others forget his compromising relations.[1]

He was ready to flatter his powerful protectors in any way. He said in the preface to the *Libro della Vita* that his body had been born at Figline on 19 October 1433, sired by the physician, Diotifeci Ficino, in order to direct him toward the curing of bodies. But he called

Cosimo de' Medici, the father of his country, the father of his soul, the true physician who had regenerated his spirit, turning him away from Galenus and directing him through Plato to the healing of souls.[2]

Thus in Ficino we are confronted with the first great Quattrocento Florentine prototype of the court philosopher in all its luxuriant and recherché style. This was something novel. The first Florentine humanism had been sober, almost severe; its florescence had been characterized by the great culture of the chancellors of the republic, the men of the government, the members of the great families, monks known for their piety, prominent prelates, and even celebrated university teachers. High culture, especially in the field of the moral and political sciences, was truly natural to those who constituted the ruling class of the commune, which was being transformed into a signoria. Yet among Ficino's friends we find the eminent figure of Giovanni Pico, one of the most aristocratic and richest men in Italy, a friend of lords and sovereigns as before him the wealthy Giannozzo Manetti or the powerful Donato Acciaiuoli had been the worthy heirs of the tradition of Coluccio Salutati and Leonardo Bruni.

With Ficino appears the learned man of the court who was not a university professor but in the service of a lord who used him, not only to add luster to his own house, but also undoubtedly for the subtle purpose of political propaganda. It is therefore interesting to note that while leading Florentines for more than a half-century had sought standards of life and of government in the *Ethics*, the *Nicomachea*, and the *Politics* of Aristotle, when Cosimo came to power he suddenly discovered his enthusiasm for Plato. His adversaries, defeated and retired to their conventual or country retreats, took comfort in a severe and ascetic stoic wisdom. To the Florentine youth, who had been habituated to being exhorted from university chairs and in official speeches to pursue the dignity of worldly action and civic life, the Ficinians now preached the raptures of contemplative mystical practices.[3]

On the other hand, that special objectivity in religious matters which accompanied the spread of the Platonic fashion under the protection and with the approval of the Medici, cannot be dissociated from the political conflicts between Florence and Rome that exploded after the Pazzi conspiracy. And it was very often much more the cultivated criticism of exclusive aristocratic, intellectual circles than a strict moral commitment. When Florence was divided, the true rebels were to be found in the ranks of the Piagononi of Savonarola.[4]

In this environment, alongside the noble intransigence of Girolamo Savonarola or the exuberant sincerity of the Savonarolian Pico della Mirandola, the obsequious and rather unctuous Canon Marsilio Ficino cannot but be considered of inferior rank. Even in his style—at times almost baroque—we feel the great distance between him and the great men of the Quattrocento.

Yet when we consider the enormous range of his work, the repercussions it caused for more than two centuries in all of Europe, and the profundity of some of his principles, we can understand the enthusiasm of his contemporaries and of posterity. And we understand why that noble and unhappy figure of a man, Pandolfo Colenuccio, in praising the glory of Florence, chose Marsilio above all as the personification of its thought. The sincerity of his spiritual torment truly redeemed the undeniable failings of an unheroic disposition.

His biographers tell us that he was educated according to the customs of the time by the Aristotelian texts and in the school of an Aristotelian, a physician and philosopher, Niccolò Tignosi da Foligno. A clear record of these youthful experiences is contained in his first writings. Yet it is probable that the Florentine Aristotelianism that followed the teaching of Argyropulos (whom Tignosi himself esteemed highly) was already something very different from scholastic Aristotelianism. How can we forget the portrait of the Byzantine scholar given us by Pier Filippo Pandolfini, describing Argyropulos completely absorbed in reading *Meno* and full of enthusiasm for Plato? And how can we forget that one of the most authoritative Quattrocento codices of Plotinus, the *Parigino greco 1970,* was transcribed by John Argyropulos himself?[5]

Ficino's initial love for Lucretius is, on the other hand, more subtly significant. Later, in his mature years, he was to burn what he had written about the grandiose and tragic Epicurean concept.[6] And yet, even in certain pages of the *Theologia platonica*—which plays upon the horror of a world without hope, a world in which it would be impossible to conceive of a physical existence without purpose and significance—we can conjecture the process of development that led Ficino from Lucretian desperation through Platonic hope to Christian certainty. It was a certainty, however, that never completely obliterated the difficulties he had overcome, the remembrance of which he always carried with him; a note of lingering doubt runs through the loftiest passages of the philosopher, giving them uncommon force.

If Plato was for Marsilio Ficino more than the master incarnate of divine wisdom, a decisive influence in his formation had been the reading of hermetic *opuscula,* which he translated into Latin and which constituted one of the major literary successes at the end of the Quattrocento. The wisdom of the "thrice greatest," mysterious and allusive, presented in an admirable form, uniting poetry and prophecy, conquered all the minds that yearned for a religion liberated from the rigidity of formulas and from the narrowness of the traditional authorities. The idea of a perpetual revelation, as old as humanity, spread by way of hermeticism, made slow but sure progress. Hermeticism taught that the most obscure mysteries of being, unrevealed to man since his origin, accompany him as a treasure given without distinction to all; whoever is able to find it must habitually question himself and things in all sincerity and modesty. Man is presented as an exceptional being, the living image of God in the world; due to this very close tie with the Creator, he is himself a creator and capable of bringing together in himself and making use of all the forces of the universe.

At one time hermeticism satisfied the most subtle religious needs as well as that thirst for the magic dominion over things which had permeated the entire subsoil of medieval culture: the divine man of the *Pimandro,* the "hermetic" man, the magic man, capable of mastering the whole world of the elements, the forces of the heavens and the demoniacal powers themselves. It would suffice to read the *Libro della vita,* which is perhaps the most strange and complex of Ficino's works, in order to understand the fascination which hermeticism exercized over him, a hermeticism understood more as a theology than as a key to every mystery.

To philosophize for Ficino did not mean in fact to understand rationally certain aspects of experience, or to devise perfected tools of logic, or to rediscover the value and the sense of human behavior. True philosophy is something quite different: it is to surprise the mysterious nature of being, to uncover its secret, and, through a kind of perception that is beyond scientific knowledge, to arrive at an understanding of the ultimate meaning of life, liberating man from the dread of his mortal condition.

According to Ficino's philosophical masterpiece, the *Theologia platonica,* man would be the most unfortunate of all the animals that live on earth if he could not gain the certainty of his salvation. For only man has had the fortune along with the misery of his finiteness, the anguishing awareness of his immutable limits. To the *imbecillitas corporis,* which he has in common with all living beings, he alone joins a spasmodic *inquietudo animi,* an *anxietas,* a thirst that cannot be quenched at earthly founts because—and Ficino returns to this theme constantly—death and pain impend over him; more subtle still, he has a sense of the extreme insubstantiality of things, a sense that we live in an inconsistent world, a world of shadows and illusions, that we move on the surface of a reality whose secret escapes us. There are two ways out of this painful awareness of something wanting in our own nature, this need for what we do not know, this sense of bitter desperation which is always with the serious philosopher: either the conscious acceptance and recognition of a closed situation; or the hope that everything here on earth is only a bad dream, that this insignificance of things is the sign that beyond these senseless things exists a level of meaning, a light that is never extinguished and that reveals everything, a fount that truly quenches all thirst.

At the time of his initiation into Aristotelian and Lucretian thought, Ficino considered the possibilities implicit in taking the first course—that is, accepting the ineluctability of an exclusively earthly fate. Beings for a day, transitory individuations of a species that is the only one of its kind: nothing remains for us but to live out our day and to ensure the survival of the species. We may take delight in the divine *voluptas* that is honored and spent in the act of generation; we may rejoice at the sight of this beautiful family of plants and animals; within allowed limits we will achieve our own modest joy. And through our domination over self, supported by a clear conscience and resignation, we will be content to conclude a life which will have the meaning that we give it.

For Ficino the perspectives of Aristotle and of Epicurus correspond: both are basically physicists and do not go beyond nature, but their faithfulness to these limits condemns man to a situation without meaning. Aristotle—be he that of Alexander of Aphrodisias or of

Averroes—debases man as an individual person. It is of little importance whether I commit myself to the bosom of universal matter, or resign myself to the unity of an intelligence which is the form of the human species. In either case, I lose myself—that is, my personal individuality.

If we read the *Libro del piacere*, Ficino's first complete work after his Aristotelian notes, which is entirely interwoven with Lucretian references, we find it permeated with the need to find a solution that would transcend nature and give a positive meaning to man's doubt. We suffer because we are in exile. What we seek is not the *voluptas* that Venus finds in the embrace of Mars, but the *gaudium* of the soul which comes home, finally liberated from its earthly prison. Our endless search does not point to an incentive to worldly tasks, but is the unknown call of the infinite: advance notice that beyond all finite things lie truth and life.[7]

Ficino's constant thesis is that Aristotle's philosophy was valid only with respect to physical matters, while that which counts is beyond the physical, beyond the world, beyond the signs, in another world; this thesis had its roots in his attempt to radically resolve human uncertainty—that is, to give an absolutely positive value to our desperate appeal, interpreting it as an absolute need that has issued from an absolute real good and is turned again toward an absolute real good. Any one of us, precisely because he is the bearer of this call, is therefore revealed as an undeniable syllable of God. The ancient myth of ambiguous man, the child of wealth and poverty, outstretched, prone, forever reaching out beyond the little he owns toward the most beautiful distant land, is reiterated. But the true wealth consists precisely in that lack and in the present nostalgia for the lost infinite good—as Plotinus said, in the memory of our father's house.

The beginning of Ficino's interest in Hermes, Plato, Plotinus, Proclus, and the pseudo-Dionysius proceeded from his rejection of the physical Aristotle and the mundane Epicurus and his desire to pass from nature to something else, to abandon earthly lust—exiled and tragic, as Seneca had found it, forever inadequate to man's needs—in order to gain the bliss that surpasses desires. In this regard the invocation, painful to the point of physical anguish, which we find at the heart of the *Theologia platonica*, is characteristic: "Make it so, O my God, that all be but a dream; that tomorrow awaking to life, we may know that up to now we have been lost in an abyss, where all was dreadfully distorted; that, as the fish in the sea, we were creatures inclosed in a liquid prison which oppressed us with horrible nightmares!"

At this time Ficino was preoccupied with reading Hermes, and this passage should be understood precisely in this light. Hemeticism, in fact, was not then being introduced for the first time into the culture of the Latin West. It had always been present in the *Asclepius*, attributed to Apuleius, and in Lactantius so full of references and quotations from the *Logos Teleios*. The humanists had been deeply moved reading the famous praise of human power in the *Asclepius*, and they adopted the concept as their own: "*magnum miraculum est homo, animal adorandum atque honorandum.*"* Giannozzo Manetti had included in his *De dignitate et excellentia hominis* whole pages of Lactantius, brimming with hermeticizing aspects. Ficino's use of these terms later, however, was to be entirely different, in the same way that his understanding of man's worth was basically entirely different.[8]

In the main, for early humanism the sign of human greatness was the activity that man carried out in this world. Human power was solemnized in man's work on earth, engaged in building his city. The general line of Manetti's thought is permeated with Aristotelianism. His preferred texts were the *Nicomachea* and the *Politics;* his ideal was the dignity of an active life. One of Manetti's most beautiful passages is the one in which he extols the splendor of Florence as a monument to man's nobility: the statues, Brunelleschi's constructions, the paintings, poems, the sumptuous palaces; the commercial activity, the great wealth—these are our works. And he continues, with emphasis: "Ours, that is, human because they are made by men, and all are things that may be seen, all the houses, the villages, the cities, and all the buildings of the earth. . . . Ours are the paintings, the sculptures, the arts, the sciences; ours is the wisdom . . . ; ours are the infinite inventions, our work is in all the languages and letters." But this real *miraculum magnum* is understood and spent in an earthly horizon. Even when an allusion is made to a higher and secret power—that is, a mysterious dominion magically exercized over natural forces—even then it is physical work, in which the sage who

* "It is marvellous to be a man worthy of reverence and honor, who takes on the character of a god, as though he himself were a god."

had penetrated to the core of the *Logos Teleios* understands its hidden cipher and dominates its forces in order to direct them toward his own ends.

However, in translating the *Pimandro* and the other theological works, Ficino restores the whole tone of their religious message of salvation. The greatness of man lies in his divine essence, in his being intimately, substantially, a god; he may perhaps be a fallen god, and forever an exile on earth, mindful of his remote home, to which he must but cannot return.[9] The indelible sign of the dignity that sets him apart from the fatal necessities of the natural world, from the terrible inevitability of death, is to be sought in his ontological structure. But his nobility is basically a nobility of birth and not his achievements in works nor an award for virtue.

On the other hand, the hermetic *opuscula* taught Ficino to look beyond this world, to rise above the dominion of nature, to understand the secret language of God. They spoke to him of a redeeming *gnosis* which may be attainable by breaking through the bonds of the perceptible world, by looking beyond the deceptive surface of false appearances. They spoke to him of a liberating knowledge, conceded by God to wise and pure men but withheld by Him from ordinary minds, a knowledge symbolized by allusive images, in signs that the sage must interpret. They spoke to him of the perfect awareness that grasps the profound value of every book, its mystical sense: to understand it means to be united with God. And it *may* be understood, on condition that we do not limit ourselves to the flesh, the body, the earth; on condition that we heed the call of all our being, inviting us to penetrate the veils that hide the divine face, so that the tormenting anguish that consumes us be dissipated in that other world, our true world wherein resides the only good that can console us, where there is no flight of time and no decline to death.

Hermeticism taught—and this explains its enormous success—that God had revealed himself to man since the most ancient times; it taught the existence of a perpetual revelation, of which every religion is merely an expression and partial translation; it offered religious peace in a cult in which Moses, Plato, and Christ would be in accord. This harmony on the one hand makes us certain of the one and only truth which is sufficient unto itself and eternal; on the other hand, it divests religion of all its impediments, of all the obstacles that the mortifying letter or the crystallization of rites seem to raise for the critical philosopher as well as for the devoutly faithful. It teaches us to go beyond the exterior trappings to attain the soul of truth which pulsates within us, which lives in things, which is everywhere present, and which is realized in an almost exemplary fashion in a Christianity interpreted in the light of that Platonic tradition that constitutes the key to all mysteries.

The teaching that Ficino believed to come from ancient Egypt, that he found in agreement with the Pythagorean, Platonic, Stoic, and Neoplatonic traditions, together with the books of the pseudo-Dionysius, gave him the comforting sense of a profound communion with all men, of a communion of all faiths, of a harmony of all revelations, a sure sign of the solid foundation of a doctrine. And he drew from it an inspiration and a basis for his apologetics, the highest expression of which was his book on the *Religione Cristiana*. In this work, Christianism is presented as the synthesis and the culminating point of this continuous revelation of God: a perpetual religion and philosophy united by a secure faith in the supernatural destiny of man, in the respect for the indestructible values which are the proofs of this divine vocation. In his apologetics Ficino found his happiest expression; he invites all peoples to religious peace in the cult of the good, "since" (as he says) "God does not wholly reject any cult so long as it is human and is directed in some way to Him. . . . God is the highest good and truth, the light of the intellect, and the ardor of the will. Those therefore . . . who sincerely honor God revere Him constantly through their good works, the truth they speak, the clarity of the intelligence that they possess, and as much charitable will as they should have."

Hence, beyond the literal sense lies the one and only truth, which, however, in order to manifest itself, must be perceived, must be clad in flesh, must become substance. The Platonic tradition, which offered Ficino an answer to his most urgent demand, invited him to go beyond the appearances of things, taught him to see in the reality that surrounds us symbols that allude to and refer back to another reality. The physicist Aristotle, as does every scientist, stopped at the body of the data; Plato, the theologist, discovered everywhere, in clear relief, an ideal direction, a hidden sense. For science, which is worldly, things remain corporeal in their weight; for philosophy, which is divine, they become transfigured, established in a superior harmony. Philosophy is therefore this subtle vision that captures the rhythm of being and surprises its secret, that with its knowledge liberates hidden powers and gains freedom for whoever follows it.

The fascination of Ficino's work lies precisely here: in the invitation to look beyond the opaque surfaces of reality in order to understand everywhere the sign of a hidden harmony which animates and unifies all—in seeing not the body but the soul of the universe. As true man is not his mortal raiment, but his immortal soul, and as only the one who sees this soul sees man, so all things have their truth and this is their soul, whether they be plants or stones or stars in heaven. This soul, then, is their secret life, or rhythm, a form, a light of beauty, because truth is not a logical term, a conceptual abstraction, but a soul—that is, a principle of living life, of order, and of grace. Just as the Being is He who above all is life and goodness—that is, God the Father, the fount of light and love.

All of Ficino's philosophy—if indeed one should continue to call it a philosophy—is in this percepton of reality as life, as order, as beauty. Hence it is expressed in and proceeds from symbols, images, and forms. When our mind becomes conscious of the fact that the perceived object is but a sign and goes beyond it, we do not thereby attain truth through logical deduction; this would, on the contrary, be a regression and hence an extreme estrangement. The truth is understood by grasping the number and rhythm with a mental vision—that is the soul of beings which the artist achieves in his creations where he does no more than translate the act itself by which the divine artist creates all. To know is to see directly the constitutive act of every real being, that life in the process of being born which is the source from which each thing springs; in each thing there is life and a soul—that is, the furthest prolongation of a divine ray.

In the book *Dell' Amore*, in which he teaches us explicitly that "universal beauty is the splendor of the face of God," Ficino shows the various levels of reality, and he scans the rhythm of the universe in its evolution from the divine source (the rest being no more than a reverberation and refraction of the light of the Lord).

The divine power, supreme over the universe, mercifully infuses with his ray, as though they were his sons, the angels and spirits created by Him. This divine ray, in which there is the fecund energy of creation, depicts the order of the entire world, in the Angels as more akin to God, much more clearly than in worldly matter. Hence this picture of the world which we see in its entirety is better expressed in the Angels and in men than what appears to our eyes. In the latter is found the shape of all the Spheres, the Sun, the Stars, the Elements, rocks, trees, and animals. In the Angels these images are called ideas and prototypes; in the spirits, reasons and knowledge; and in worldly matter, appearances and forms. These images are clear in the world, more clear in the spirit, and clearest in the Angel. Hence one and the same face of God is reflected in three mirrors in order: in the Angel, in the spirit, and in the human body. . . . The splendor and grace of this visage, as it is reflected either in the Angel, in the spirit, or in worldly matter, whichever it might be, must be called universal beauty, and the desire that is attracted to it, universal Love.

In this translation of all of reality into rhythms of light and love, in this poetic vision of the world—a poetry in the fullest, richest sense of the term—lies Ficino's originality. Whoever attempts to understand his thought by placing it in a certain conceptual framework handed down to him by tradition, and which offers nothing new in itself, loses in a tenuous logical web the force of this singular writer. Ficino loved to express himself in figurative terms, through images and myths, precisely because his philosophy is not abstract reasoning or physical science but rather this profound vision of the face of a most beautiful God, imprinted in the innermost core of things, this rediscovery in everything of that God who lives in us, completing with our knowledge the circle that constitutes us. As Tommaso Campanella was to write:

I fill the universe
contemplating the God within all things.

To philosophize is to love God and to return to God: it is religion; it is that moment of spiritual life in which we achieve a communion with God in supreme contemplation.

Only when we grasp all this firmly can we understand the method of Ficino's teaching. For him to teach philosophy meant to love in order to awaken love. "There is one way only," he wrote, "for the salvation of youth: and this is Socrates's conversation with himself"; that Socrates who "makes of himself an old child so that through a domestic and playful familiarity he may sometimes make old people of children."

A strictly rational statement is of use to science. To "see" God it is necessary to mount the stairs in an ascent that is a reconquest and an inner regeneration, a "rebirth." Ficinian philosophizing is in essence only an invitation *to see*, with the eyes of the soul, the soul of things: an exhortation to love through the telling of a personal experience to be imitated; an incentive to plumb the depths of one's own soul so that the whole world may become clearer in the inner light. From this derives the process through forms, refining the corporeality of the empiric data to a beautiful image, but always transforming the abstract into the concrete, the static and dead into the live and personal. True to the Platonic thesis that the root of every reality is a form, Ficinian thought says the movement of knowledge is the process directed from the perceptible impression to the idea that approximates it, not in a verbal-conceptual term, but in the rich fluidity of an image that guides the mind to the perception of the supreme light:

> When man sees man with his eyes, he creates in his imagination the image of man and proceeds to judge that image. For this exercise the soul uses the mind's eye to see the reason or the idea of man, which is in essence itself the divine light. Whence a certain spark immediately alights in the mind, and the nature of man is truly revealed; this occurs in other things in the same way.

Only by passing Ficino's images in review can we faithfully follow the trend of his thought, even if the purpose of it escapes us, placed as it is in this union of love which is the death of the sage—who, as the philosopher says, "grows through this death to a more sublime life."[10]

The central figure is without doubt man, his inner life, his soul as master of his body and free from the body (which it contains in itself, as Plotinus averred, rather than being contained within the body). Here suddenly the discourse slips into Avicenna's image of the flying man, suspended in space and devoid of resistance, without stimuli or sensorial requirements, where the body seems almost to have fainted and to be dissolved in a total separation from all things while the soul succeeds in asserting itself as pure and autonomous activity.

Here then is the reason for man, the eye of the world, the mirror of the universe, who understands and brings to consciousness the image of God everywhere diffused: "He raises himself up to regard the face of God, which shines within the soul." And all this is configured as reflected light that is received and mirrored by seeing eyes, themselves alive with a secret light of their own: "So one ray of the sun is painted with the colors and forms of all the bodies that it strikes . . . ; the eyes with the help of a certain natural ray catch the light of the sun, painted in this fashion, and since they possess it, they see the light itself and all the paintings that are in it. The reason for all this order of the world is thus received by the eyes." All is an irradiation of the light of the Father; it is as a smile that animates it, and sparks are born of it, and they are the souls. The entire world is like a discourse pronounced with looks and glances, "whence it follows," Ficino concludes, "that all the ornament of this world, which is the third face of God, offers itself incorporeal to the eyes through the light of the incorporeal sun."

And this is the theme of man, the link or marriage tie of the world, in which all the orders of reality and all the levels of being are wed, and the inferior world is united with the superior. Man, gathering all within himself in his conscious vision, is extended into the cosmos and leads back to the one and only source—the dispersed streams, in a continuous circuit, into which the pulse of being, arising from the center of its own unity and renewing itself, is translated.

Here the themes of light and love are joined together; the light indicates the ontological basis and the descending moment in the act of divine emanation, while love is the ascending conversion, which in the desired and achieved recurrence celebrates the value of the harmony of things. In this fashion the *Theologia platonica* presents as fused together and renewed the most cherished assumptions of Hellenistic thought: the world is the lyre played by God, and all is musical and animated, "because the work of the living maker must be alive and one" (*unius viventis opificis unum debet esse opus vivens*). The soul of the earth is one and makes plants and rocks grow, which when uprooted are reduced and dissolved. And over all the souls one supreme soul governs, and that is all one with the total unity, with the light which, transforming itself into heat, is lovingly converted into God.

From God to God, Ficino attempted to penetrate the ultimate mystery, to thrust his eyes into that dazzling light which shades itself from whoever attempts to probe its splendor:

Do you want to gain the reason of light more easily? . . . Seek it in the light of every reason. . . . What is the light of God? It is the immensity of his goodness and of his truth. What is in the angels? It is a certainty of intelligence that comes from God, and an abundant fulfillment of will. What is in celestial things? It is a copy of the life that comes from the angels and a declaration and manifestation of human excellence which proceeds from the heavens, a smile of the heavens. What is in fire? A certain vigor of celestial things that is infused in it, and an active propagation. And in those things that are devoid of feeling is infused a heavenly grace. In the things that have feeling is a joyfulness of spirit and a strength of mind. And finally, in all things is an effusion of an intimate fecundity, and in every place is an image of divine truth and goodness. . . . But this God is an immense light which consists of itself and for itself, in all things and most intensely outside of all things. He is that source of life, from whose light, as David says, we see the light: it is an eye which regards all things in each thing, and truly sees all things in Himself, while He sees Himself to be all things.

Born as light, the universe is converted into love: "The mind is moved and charmed by the search for its own light to recover the divine light: and this attraction is true love. . . . When God infused his light into the spirit, he ordered it above all so that men be guided by it to beatitude, which consists in the possession of God."

Among the most beautiful passages of Ficino are the many pages on the light, including a commentary on an oration by the Emperor Julian which pictures humanity plunged into a night without stars, in total darkness. Here suddenly the splendor of the sun is hailed in chorus as the true image of God.

These are texts which later became models and commonly known through the natural hymns of the Greek Marullo, or the "*lalda del Sole*" of Leonardo da Vinci, ending with the powerful elegy of Campanella. But in Ficino all the celestial themes attained a rare loftiness; whoever has become accustomed to him will never forget his heaven, at one time mysterious and remote, full of fearful menaces and dreadful monsters, at another all harmony and promises and beautiful faces, overflowing—as he once wrote to Bernardo Bembo—"with the fertility of life and the abundance of grace."

If at this point someone were to ask what theoretical value this construction really has, the argument would be lengthy and varied. The great merit of Ficino is that he was the translator and interpreter of all of Plato, all of Plotinus, all the major texts on Platonism up to

Psellus. To have bequeathed this philosophy—or rather this *forma mentis,* this speculative horizon to all of Europe, with reverberations that were still felt at the height of romantic idealism—was a remarkable feat. After Ficino there is no writing, no thought, in which a direct or indirect trace of his activity may not be found. Without Ficino that renewed sense of inner life and those new tones which moral and religious life acquired in the European culture of the sixteenth and seventeenth centuries would be incomprehensible. In all this the heir of the most scholarly humanistic philology was one of the masters of the modern conscience; it would be time well spent to retrace all of his arcane and remote contributions.

So far as his original writings are concerned, then, it is necessary to distinguish the practical religious, moral, and political importance as reflected in the ideals of religious tolerance, peace among the peoples of different faiths, and a loving human coexistence. Without taking into account the diffusion of an apologetics, founded on new bases, which after having wrought changes in the Catholic Church through Egidius of Viterbo and Seripando, converged through the most varied channels of the Protestant world to become the most vital positions of modern religious thought.

Of Ficino's metaphysical concepts, finally, it behooves us to speak as of a beautiful consoling fable, of a poetic transfiguration of things, in which the needs of the heart are answered by the heart's reasons. Fear, pain and death are not syllogistic conclusions: they are the experiences of all men, which pose grave questions to all men. Scientific reason—and Ficino the physician and scientist knew this very well—operates within its limits but does not go beyond the limits of the human condition. There remains then no other remedy than the one to which Socrates had recourse nearly at the end of his life: fables. *Forsitan in praesentia somniamus, forsitan non sunt vera quae nunc nobis apparent.**

Thus Ficino always maintained the attitude of a theologian on the border of a poetic transfiguration. In the face of the Averroists who deny the immortality of the soul, Marsilio exclaims: it is not possible, it would be too sad! He too knew perfectly well that his was no answer but only a protest. But if the answer is perhaps impossible,

* "Maybe we are only dreaming of the present, maybe all that appears to us now is not true."

why not comfort with hope the brief hours of these condemned that are men?

Boetius once quoted a text of Aristotle, which became famous throughout the Middle Ages: "How ugly it would be, if among the beautiful forms of Alcibiades, we also saw his entrails!" And then, why not cover the horror of disintegration with the veil of a poetic fantasy? Why not admit that the heart goes beyond the mind? Why not accept the promises of metaphysics beyond the brief certitudes of science? "Knowledge," Ficino said and the Magnificent repeated, "aims to enclose the infinite into our thought; love extends the mind to receive the vastness of divine mercy."

This does not change (we should take care to note) the fact that Ficino the philosopher had as an implacable heritage the melancholy of one who feels the flight of time and who knows the risk of transforming a need into a hope, a hope into a certainty. But, like his artist friends, he too wanted to change his own sadness into song. This, I would say, is the real value of his "theology": a few poetically effective passages. And it was perhaps in this that he was a true disciple of Plato, who wrote that "philosophy is the highest music," and that the philosopher has no more to do than to compose music.

Notes

1. With regard to the relics of Savonarola, see J. F. Pici, *Vita R. P. Fr. Hier. Savonarolae* (Paris, 1674), p. 95 (" . . . a bone, which fell into the Arno from the boat on which it was being ferried, and which a certain boy brought to his mother . . . "), and L. Landucci, *Diario fiorentino del 1450 al 1516* (Florence, 1883), pp. 178–79 (" . . . the one who picked up those bones that were floating"). The *Apologia pro multis Florentinis ab Antichristo Hieronymo Ferrariensi hypocritarum summo deceptis ad Collegium Cardinalium* is conserved in the single codex Magliab. 8: 1443 from the sixteenth century, from which Passerini took it (*Giornale storico degli Archivi Toscani* 3[1859]: 115), and Kristeller included it in *Supplementum Ficinianum* (Florence, 1937), 2: 76–79. Ficino had praised Savonarola's "holiness and wisdom" in 1494, and had called him *divinitus electum* ("elected by God"). E. Sanesi, in *Vicari e canonici Florentini e il "caso Savonarola"* (Florence, 1932), p. 15 sqq., denies the authenticity of the writing, but it was recognized by Kristeller, *Supplementum,* 1: 141. It is curious that Ficino's friend, the Calmaldolese Paolo Orlandini, in a short poem written not long after the philosopher's death, unites in one perspective the blessed spirits "Messer Marsilio di Ficino and Savonarola" (ms. of the National Library of Florence, Conventi, G. 4. 826). But on this question, see the study by A. Chastel, "L'Apocalypse en 1500. Le fresque de l'Antéchrist à la Chapelle Saint-Brice d'Orvieto," *Bibliothèque d'Humanisme et Renaissance* 14(1952): 124–40 (*Mélanges A. Renaudet*).

2. "I, the least of priests, had two fathers: Ficino, the medic, and Cosimo Medici. To the first I owe my birth, to the second my rebirth. The first dedicated me to Galenus, a physician and Platonist; the second, however, consecrated me to the divine Plato [himself]. . . . Galenus healed bodies; Plato, however, healed men's souls. . . . "

3. Vespasiano da Bisticci said of Giannozzo Manetti that he had the *Nichomachea* in mind, "out of long habit." His orations in praise of "justice" may be found, among others, in Palat. 51 and 598. But it would be worthwhile to consult the collection Ricc. 2204, taking the "protest" of Pier Filippo Pandolfini of 13 July 1475, which was already entirely platonizing, as a point of departure. And among the autographs of the same Pandolfini we read (ms. Naz. 2, IV, 192, c. 241): "non contenti adunque de la civile, non de la purgatoria virtù, conseguite la purgata iustitia. . . ." At one extreme is the stoic reserve of a Rinuccini; on the other, platonic flight. So far as Cosimo's infatuation with Plato is concerned, at the time of the Council of Florence and under the influence of Pletho, see Ficino's introductory comments to Plotinus's translation.

4. For the attitude of Florence, one should read again, for example in the *Synodus Florentina,* the violent invective against Sixtus IV, written probably by

Gentile Bechi (" . . . the guardian of the heavens has opened the doors to all of hell. . . . He calls peace war, this our vicar of truth . . ."). Lorenzo's protection of Pico after his condemnation should be placed in this context, as well as his complete sympathy for a certain anti-Roman intellectual rebellion. With regard to the tenor of the relationships betwen the Medici and Ficino, see the rough draft of a letter to Ficino (in Med. av. il Principato, 88, 202) containing references such as the following: "Your letters have in fact no less an effect and authority in soothing the ferment of our soul than the behest of Neptune in allaying a storm at sea. . . . Much as Alexander would suffer Lysippus only to sculpt him or Apelles to paint, thus would I like to be praised by you alone—provided, that is, that the virtues of my spirit are at all comparable to the features of Alexander. . . . "

5. Ficino's first philosophical essays, still Aristotelian, were published by Kristeller in *traditio* 2(1944): 274–316 (cod. Palagi 190 of the Moreniana) and in "Rinascimento," 1950. However, the whole general conception of his relationships with various Florentine cultural positions and currents (which according to Della Torre was canonical) will probably be modified. At the same time the position of Tignosi, who argues strongly against the scholastics in the *Opusculum in illos qui mea Aristotelis commentaria criminantur* (Laur. plut. 48, 37 and Naz. Conv. C. *8.* 1800), should be altered. Pandolfini's letter is contained in Magliab. 6:166, cc. 198r–109v. On Paris. greacus 1970, see Henry, *Etudes plotiniennes,* Vol. 2, *Les manuscripts des Ennéades* (Paris-Brussels, 1948), pp. 91–96.

6. On the *commentariola in Lucretium, quae puer adhuc nescio quomodo commentabar* ("small commentaries on Lucretius, which I was still too young to know how to develop"), see Kristeller, *Supplementum,* 2: 163 (and *Opera* [Basle, 1576], 1: 933). But a letter to Politian is also important—a letter in which he defends himself and which certainly does not contain the entire truth, although it is entitled *laus veritatis:* "It is reported, as you say, that certain letters over my signature are written in the style of Aristippus and somewhat in that of Lucretius rather than of Plato. But, Angelo, if these letters are indeed mine, they can't be written in this manner; if, however, they are written in this manner, then, indeed, they are not mine but were fabricated by my detractors. As everyone is aware, I have been following the divine Plato from my earliest youth. . . . "

7. In the *Theologia platonica,* 14: 7, Ficino wrote: "Sensual gratification will be sought so long as there is need and desire." But it is important that the *Liber de voluptate* ends with a text by Epicurus, who, in physical agony and at the point of death, declared himself to be blessed by an inner serenity ("He says he spends a happy day, and yet he is tormented by excruciating pain . . . "). The *de voluptate* bears the date 1457, *anno aetatis suae XXIV.*

8. Of great value for an understanding of the hermetic tradition is Vol. 4 of the *Hermetica* by Scott (completed by Ferguson and published in 1936). Knock's statements (*Corpus Hermeticum* [Paris, 1945], pp. 264 sqq.) are entirely insufficient for the medieval tradition of the *Asclepius.* It is enough to consider that he ignores the important citations of Vincent de Beauvais in the

Speculum naturale, which are singularly important considering the wide circulation of the work. I have been waiting for some time for the appearance of a study of the humanistic tradition.

9. *Theologia platonica,* 14: 7: "In the midst of our pursuit of pleasure we are sometimes despondent, and when the curtain falls we leave sadder still than before. . . . Whenever there is nothing to keep us busy, we feel out of place and overcome with sadness, although we can not tell why. . . . "

10. See E. Gombrich, "Icones Symbolicae: The Visual Images in Neo-Platonic Thought," *Journal of the Warburg and Courtauld Institutes* 11(1948).

VI
The Cultural Background of Politian

Politian departs from his usual mild tone once, in his *Miscellanea,*[1] to caution us that in order to understand and truly "read" a poet we should know many things: philosophy, medicine and law, all the "arts," and philology. Nor is it enough to remain on the threshold of these subjects; we must plumb their innermost recesses, study them thoroughly, acquire a daily familiarity with them, absorb them into our blood.[2] But, above all, he says, we must keep awake to the light of Cleanthe's lantern, because the doctrines of the philosophers are full of the works of the poets.[3] The passage ends with a reference to Pico as *noster amor*. It is intended as a relevant allusion but can be taken as a cryptic reminder of the way in which, according to Politian, the connection between poetry and philosophy must be understood.

The friendship between Pico and Politian is well known. It was sincere and profound and lasted throughout their lives. The philosopher (Pico) had so much influence over the poet that the latter, who as a young man had drunk but a small draught from the fount of wisdom and had then fled from it as the dogs from the Nile, returned to it later at a mature age with his friend and drew on it to such an extent that he ended his days teaching ethics and logic on the basis of the Greek originals at the Studio of Florence. What Pico thought of "poetic theology" is known, though not even fragments of a book by him that bears this title are extant. However, his commentaries on the *Genesis* and the *Psalms,* and his writings on the love songs of Benivieni, largely bridge the gap and show us in a brilliant form that anguished search for an elusive wisdom.

As the Egyptians placed the sphinxes to guard the sacred mysteries, so the prophets and saints enveloped the revelation of God in images. This was not a new way of interpreting poetry, but the young philosopher gave it a new accent. Giovanni Pico was a sincerely religious man. He believed in the Word, and he believed that the

Word was living and that it spoke to all men. He fought for the unity of men under the banner of harmony. He wrote one of his hymns to peace because he wanted philosophy to be more than a hymn to peace. He was persuaded that Moses, like Christ, Zoroaster and Mohammed, Plato and Aristotle, Avicenna and Averroes, Saint Thomas and Duns Scotus, said only one thing: that the world is for man, that man is working freedom—the builder of himself and of his worldly dwelling. Pico had studied languages and was interested in the most remote ones; he had spent a fortune on books, but not in order to adorn a library; he sought knowledge because knowledge unites, because knowledge will show men that divisions and wars arise out of error, deceit, and superstition.

It is not easy to understand Pico and to distinguish in him ancient principles and new quests; but then it is not easy to understand any of the complex spirits of this complicated period. He wanted to assemble in Rome scholars from all over and draw up the bases for a universal peace and the reign of man; it is difficult to say whether this could be called the last council of church fathers or the first international congress of scientists. He certainly believed, with the most steadfast faith, in the liberation of humanity through science, which, discovering the roots of truth as well as of error, would conquer fanaticism and restore the brotherhood of men.

He continued to fight throughout his life, with a cavalier sense of his mission, on the border between illusion and truth, perhaps because man himself lives on this border. He was always as one who fights on a frontier: the frontiers of magic and not magic, astrology and not astrology, cabala and not cabala, superstition and not superstition. He was condemned by the Church of Rome, which sought to brand him a heretic. Savonarola hoped to make him a pillar of his order, but when Pico died still young, Savonarola announced from the pulpit to his followers that the count was thereafter consumed by the flames of divine castigation, his own anguish. Yet, at San Marco, at the side of the Ferrarese prophet who was not always able to dispel these ironical spirits, Pico appeared instead as the true prophet when, in order to achieve "harmony," he dreamed of wandering through the land preaching. Pico was a cross between the utmost critical potential of the Quattrocento and an ancient missionary spirit; one never really knew whether he spoke the religion of the fathers or the faith of the new times, the poetry of the ancients or the science of the moderns; whether he was an unusual poet, an inspired prophet, or a clear-sighted scientist.

One cannot speak about Politian without mentioning Pico, united as they were beyond death in their love of knowledge and in the habitual daily customs of life, in the collations of codices as well as in family preoccupations and walks in the hills of Fiesole. "*Is igitur,*" wrote the poet, "*continuo me, cum quo partiri curas dulcissimas et nugari suaviter interdum solet, et quem sibi studiorum prope assiduum comitem. . . . adlegit; is me instituit ad philosophiam, not ut antea somniculosis, sed vegetis vigilantibusque oculis explorandam quasi quodam suae vocis animare classico.*"*[4]

They were both followers of the new faith in man, but in a different fashion. Pico gathered around him Greeks, Jews, and even Indians in order to discover in all one sole aspect, to draw from this the basis on which to preach mutual understanding and peace. Politian, with the curiosity of the man of science, looked for the differences in order to understand their origins and history. Pico had the soul of a missionary and a reformer; Politian, that of a critic and historian. Pico was always preoccupied with transforming a discovery into a program of action; Politian's activity took the form of an essay, a lesson, or a poem. They lived at the wane of the century, on a chronological border when grave events were pending: "and in the meantime the cold, bare facts made the wheel of fortune turn mercilessly," Politian wrote. The Turks were advancing from the south, "so that it always seems to me as though the funeral cross is borne in front of me, . . . while these barbarians are in Italy."[5] They both died at the time Charles VIII was entering a divided Florence. And beyond Florence and Italy, the face of Europe and of the world was changing.

At the opening of the century, a great cultural movement was being realized in a program of civic renovation. Guarino was teaching: "Raised and educated from childhood under the aegis of the Muses, you have learned to administrate, reinforce, and maintain yourself

* "Thus, he is still with me, with whom he used to share his intimate personal thoughts and occasionally engage in merry banter. He chose me for his constant companion in his studies. He introduced me to philosophy, so that I began to take an interest in it, but not in the half awake state of mind I was in before, but with my eyes wide open and my mind watchfully alert, almost as though it had come to life at the call of his voice."

and the city that is yours. And thus it behooves you to ensure that the Muses are not only the masters of sweet harmony, but also the arbiters of states" (*musas ipsas non modo chordarum et citharae, sed rerum etiam publicarum moderatrices*).[6]

Henceforth only two possibilities were left for humanism: to exhaust itself in an ever more empty and evasive rhetoric, which later was explicitly to become the humanism of the Jesuits; or to nourish with its strong cultural heritage the new science of nature and of man. At the time Politian was reducing to a strictly critical level the active and effective impetus of the *studia humanitatis* and transferring all its pedagogical and political functions to the foundation of the moral sciences. Pico, who was to prepare the ground for the elaboration of concepts essential to the new natural research, was at the same time to reaffirm the validity of this knowledge as an instrument of struggle—as later Bruno was to invalidate the secrets of magic as a means of persuading and fascinating men. Politian understood human freedom in the field of criticism and poetry; for Pico, poetry and philosophy, science and religion must serve a liberating purpose.

The heritage of Pico was later to be found among the scientists on the one hand and the reformers and heretics on the other; that of Politian, in the new schools of philologists and historians, but also among the statesmen and jurists and the new logicians of the Cinquecento, up to and including the works of Ramo. They were different and complementary expressions of the possibilities of a new fruitful culture, but both were still quite divergent. Pico and Politian were very far apart in their individual understanding of the tie between philosophy and poetry. For Pico, poetry was philosophy veiled in images; for Politian it was the moment in which humanity molded itself, the painful birth—and hence, according to etymology, *poetic*—of man, the builder of himself:

> *Sic species terris, vitae sua forma, suusque*
> *Dis honor, ipsa sibi tandem sic reddita mens est.**[7]

* What earth brought forth,
the flower of its life,
the noblest that its gods have wrought,
the mind [of man]
now, at long last,
pays homage to itself.

For Pico poetry was a revelation and a vision of the truth; for Politian it was the builder and molder of the world of men, the creative synthesis that also governed the sacred celestial dwelling. What he said of poetry reflects faithfully what Pico had already said in his *Oratio* about free man, the creator of himself. This image of man is incarnated in his *poeta*. Pico's Adam corresponds exactly with Politian's Orpheus:

An vero ille ferox, ille implacatus et audax
Viribus, ille gravi prosternens cuncta lacerto,
Trux vitae, praeceps animae, submitteret aequo
Colla iugo aut duris pareret sponte lupatis,
Ni prius indocilem sensum facundia victrix
Vimque relectantem irarum flatusque rebelles
Carmine mollisset blando, pronisque sequentem
Auribus ad pulchri speciem duxisset honesti?
Quippe etiam stantes dulci leo carmine captus
Submittit cervice iubas, roseamque dracones
Erecti tendunt cristam et sua sibila ponunt;
Ille quoque umbrarum custos, ille horror Averni,
Cerberus, audita getici testudine vatis,
Latratum posuit triplicem, tria sustulit hiscens
Ora, novo stupidus cantu qui flexerat atram
Tisiphonem, saevo lachrymas conciverat Orco.
Ipsum fama Iovem, cum iam cyclopea magna
Tela manu quatit insurgens tonitruque coruscat
Horrisono et caecis miscet cava nubila flammis,
Ut tamen increpuit nervis et pectine pulcher
Delius alternumque piae cecinere sorores,
Placari totumque sua diffundere mundum
*Leticia et subito coelum instaurare sereno.**[8]

* What if that rough, that intemperate man—so ready
to use his force, and to rudely thrust aside all in his path,
of so savage a mood, so reckless a mind—should meekly bow
his neck to the yoke or willingly submit to rough harness?
What if the never-tamed mind should yield to persuasion,
restraining fury, and should lead, won over by winsome words,
the angry rabble—listening intently with both ears—
to things of beauty and gentleness?
[Wild beasts] may even halt in their tracks;
the lion, charmed by a beguiling air,
may be led captive by his mane; and the dragons,
ruffling their ruby-red crests, will cease hissing.

Such diverse perspectives necessarily imply diverse means of approaching poetry. The "Lord of harmony" sought through allegory a convergence of concepts; Agnolo almost had a feeling of the sanctity of the Word. If man is, according to Ficino's formula, the *copula* of the world, the Word is the *copula* of men. To approach it and to understand it for what it really is takes on the seriousness of a rite, but it also requires long and rigorous study of an entire science. Every element has value up to the last orthographic detail; it must be resought and reconstructed in all its phases and developments. The literary monuments consolidate this human tie: to restore and understand them is truly to integrate the whole science of man.

On the other hand, to thus consider "poetry" and "philology" also involved, for Politian, a genuine separation from the entire Platonic climate out of which the reconstructions of "poetic theologies" emerged and with which the famous commentaries of his teacher and later colleague, Cristoforo Landino, were interwoven:

*Landinus, homo et eloquens et eruditus, et Florentiae iam diu doctor bonarum litterarum celebratissimus, cui se praeceptori adulescentiae meae rudimenta magnopere debent, et qui nunc in professione quasi dixerim collega, locata iam in tuto sua sibi fama, nobis adhuc in stadio laboriosissime decertantibus ita favet, ut quicquid ipsi laudis acquirimus, quasi suum sibi amplecti atque agnoscere videatur.**[9]

Even that guardian of the shades below, that terror of Hades,
Cerberus, on hearing the bard's sweet lyre, roared thrice,
opening wide three of his cavernous mouths,
the heavenly melody striking him senseless,
making the gloomy Tisiphone veer around,
and bringing tears to the eyes of Orcus.
It is even told of Zeus that, when he rose to wield
the giant bolts of panic-striking thunder,
convulsing the vault of heaven with blinding flashes of fire,
he heard afar the fair Apollo plucking the chords of his lyre,
and gracious Muses joining him in response;
his anger died forthwith, and he spread gladness upon the earth
and let serenity rule again the cerulean skies.

* "Landino, a man of eloquence and learning and of now undisputed fame, a renowned scholar of belles-lettres in Florence, to whom as the teacher of my youth I am profoundly indebted for implanting in me the first rudiments of knowledge, and whom at this time I might almost call a colleague in my profession, has been helping us, while we are engaged in this most trying contest, so that whatever glory might be awarded to us should rightfully reflect upon him."

The simplification of Landino, of Ficino, and to some extent also of Pico, in dissolving the poetic image into the philosophical concept and understanding the latter as the word of God, eventually led poetry back to theology; thus it burned, in the flame of divine love, all of human creation and with it all earthly events, all of history and philology. The diversity of languages, the distinction between periods, the particularized concreteness of the terms were losing their sense. Politian's adherence to the text, on the contrary, signified in the end the most rigorous faithfulness to the humanity of language and to its history and loyalty to the critical application advanced by the *studia humanitatis*—in contrast to the evasive culture of the more orthodox Florentine Platonists, to whose circle, under the auspices of Lorenzo, Politian belonged but from which he must be clearly distinguished.

It was not a coincidence that Lucio Fosforo, in a letter written in 1485 to Alessandro Cortesi, observed that, in his view, three figures stood apart from the culture of the time: Lorenzo Valla, Domizio Calderini, and Angelo Politian ("*Laurentio Vallae, Domitio Calderino Angelum Politianum adiicio, et quasi triumviratum creo*").*[10]

Much could be said of Calderini, a man of subtle genius, and of Politian's attitude toward him—from that rather "impious" epigram in which the poet compares Ficino attending mass with Calderini's reluctance to turn *ad popularem errorem* (to the common error),[11] to the harshest judgment of the *Miscellanea,* in which, although he recognizes Calderini's acumen and doctrine, Politian also emphasizes the vanity of the man who had gained the Roman chair too soon, who was contemptuous of everything, obstinate in his errors, deluded, *praestigiosus.* It had been more than ten years since Calderini had died, while still young, *ille, ille doctus, ille quem probe nosti . . . mira eruentem sensa de penu vatum*† (to use the words of the epigraph attributed to Politian himself for the tombstone which Baccio Ugolino and Angelo Mafferi had built for him on the shore of the Garda Lake).

Iacopo Antiquario, on receiving the *Miscellanea,* took objection to it. "You should not have been so pitiless toward a dead man," he

* "By joining Angelo Politian to Lorenzo Valla and Domizio Calderini, I would create a kind of triumvirate."

† "He, the learned man I used to know so well . . . behold the wealth of wisdom he found in the shrines of the masters."

wrote to Politian in November 1489. "His untimely death," he added, "prevented him from correcting. . . ." *Fuit inter nos Domitius, et monimenta reliquit famae non poenitendae.** And Politian replied: "You say that to fight with the dead is not nice, and is as useless as a war against ghosts. And yet all the major thinkers have done it, and the dead were their masters. Only criticism of the dead, by then free of animosities and personal interests, serves the truth": *Ego vero sic Domitium studiosis quasi foveam viatoribus ostendo, nec autem oblivisci videor humanitis, quin potius . . . melius aliquanto de vita merebor censura ista mea, quam forsan alius indulgentia.*† The entire letter, which would merit the subtitle "On the Duty of Not Respecting the Dead," and which is a fine example of Politian's quite objective argument, indicated his low regard for Calderini.[12]

Lucio Fosforo's judgment of Valla was most pertinent.[13] As important a thinker as Politian was a poet, Valla was close to Politian in the clear critical awareness that he applied to cultivating the *studia humanitatis* and in the need to understand philology as a rigorous historical science rather than as the attraction of rhetorical simplification. The distance between the two men was related to the diversity of the periods in which they lived.

Politian was by then situated in an age in which the new culture was no longer an active force in the city; Florence was no longer the city of the humanist chancellors and merchants but, from that time forward, of the courtiers and professors, who were more often professors of the court. Lorenzo and Giovanni Pico, both of whom ideally belonged to the period of the "literate" rulers of states, also contributed to building the *respublica litterarum.* At the moment when the Platonists were asserting themselves, the Platonic dream that rulers should be wise men had ended. The Platonic city was no more than an academy. This was the moment in which Politian was at the height of his career, "without any other republic than that of philology."[14] Yet that antiquity which had been the school of free men was not transformed with him into rhetoric, but became a science of antiquity and criticism of poetry. It was not the criticism of Valla, in which a historical essay had been converted by the force

* "Domizio left us, but what he left behind is to his fame, not to his shame."
† "Hence, I am pointing out Domizio to the students as I would a pitfall to travelers; nor would it seem to me that I lack charity, for . . . I would rather deserve myself this my censure than perchance another's indulgence."

of the argument into an unexcelled instrument of political and religious reform; it was a no less important critical science, unaccompanied by an equal "civic" passion but leading to no less valid works of poetry and history. And it is precisely this that distinguishes Politian from his teachers and Florentine colleagues and that reunites him ideally, as Lucio Fosforo claimed, with the great Valla.[15]

Politian and His Teachers

Politian frequently mentioned a few of the men who had been his teachers in Florence or who had contributed to his education. His relationship with Bandino has been noted. He was to write warmly of Andronico Callisto in a letter to Lorenzo (*"O quantus ab illo Spiritus in nostri pectoris ima venit!"*) *[16] In the *Miscellanea* he singled out for special praise his teachers Ficino and Argyropulos, referring to the latter as the prince of the Aristotelians and to the former as the restorer of ancient Platonic wisdom and "much more fortunate than the Thracian Orpheus in having succeeded in restoring to life the faithful Euridice with the sound of his lyre." Later Politian declared that their teaching had induced him to abandon philosophy in order to let himself be seduced by the poetry of Homer, which he began to translate into Latin *miro ardore, miro studio*† when he was still a youth. He returned to the study of philosophy—in reality another philosophy, no longer *"ut antea somniculosis, sed vegetis vigilantibusque oculis,"*‡—under the influence of Pico.[17] The *Miscellanea* and the *Epistole* are full of Pico.

Ficino is not so much in evidence. Politian's epigram on hearing the mass is perhaps somewhat ironical. Certainly irony is intended when he thanks Ficino for comparing him in his *de vita libro tres* to Hercules: "My weak shoulders cannot support so much honor, and hence clearly I am not Hercules, who bore the heavens on his." There is perhaps something more than irony in his letter on astrology, in answer to Ficino's denial that he had formerly had a weakness for magic and astrology:

* "How deeply our hearts were stirred by this sublime mind!"
† "with admirable zeal, admirable scholarship."
‡ ". . . in the half awake state of mind I was in before, but with my eyes wide open and my mind watchfully alert."

I am happy to hear you say so; at any rate today you no longer believe in them. If in the past you have made some concession to the vulgar tongue, Aristotle also wrote popularizing books. If then you changed your opinion, many respectable philosophers have preceded you, since through investigation they discovered new things (*nec mutare sententiam turpe philosopho, qui cottidie plus vide*).*[18]

Nor is there much trace of Ficinian Platonism in Politian's work, even though Plato is often in evidence; it is Plato and not "Platonic theology," Plato rather than that aspect of Socratic morality which could have converged with the teaching of Epictetus. Thus Agnolo preferred such dialogues as the *Charmides* or the *Lysis*, and he lovingly translated the *Enchiridion*. He did not love or desire that lantern which cost three thousand drachmae because it had belonged to the philosopher, "*sed eius imaginem animi, quae multo plus lucis habeat.*"†[19] One should reread the entire *Defensio Epicteti*, which was addressed to Scala following tragic events "between death and wars, the pain of the past and the fear of the future" and, as he wrote to Madonna Lucrezia, mortal "tedium." (This stoic reading of Politian should be tied to other returns to stoicism during these grave years of political crisis. Perhaps then some conventional judgments on the cultural attitudes of this society might have to be discarded.)[20]

The wisdom of the *Enchiridion* was invoked against the turbulent times—the medicine of the soul corresponding to that of the body. Here the intentional reference to medicine has a perfectly stoic quality, but it is also characteristic of the man who had translated Alexander of Aphrodisias, who had translated and commented on Hippocrates and Galenus, who had among his "authors" Dioscorides and Pliny, and who had read Pliny studiously.[21]

A great deal more should be said about Pliny in order to illuminate the reasons why the humanists were so taken with him, from Landino who translated him (and not well) to Barbaro who gave loving attention to the text, to the elder Beroaldo who made him the object of daily meditations. Politian's interest in Alexander of Aphrodisias, Pliny, Dioscorides, Hippocrates, and Galenus (all physicians), and later in Aristotle, reveals his considerable curiosity about "science"

* "Nor should a philosopher ever be ashamed to change his mind, for he learns more with each passing day."

† ". . . but rather a likeness of his mind, which shed so much more light."

and "physics." This curiosity could also explain his scarce sympathy and his youthful annoyance with the "great" Ficino. If, beyond the knowledge of nature, man is left only dreams and illusions and the beautiful mythical adventures that they express, these are to be found in poetry and not disguised in complex "theological" constructions!

Politian's relation with Argyropulos, who instructed the Florentines in more than peripatetics, presents an entirely different problem. If in public Argyropulos read and commented on the original works of Aristotle, interpreting them in the light of the entire history of Greek thought, encompassing in his lectures the pre-Socratics to Proclus, in private he commented on Plato, edited the writings of Simplicius, and transcribed the whole of Plotinus, revising the text. He commented on the tragedians, and he always integrated his courses on Greek philosophy with a total vision of the Hellenic world. At the same time he did not neglect a discussion of the positions of Western thought as well as of the Arab commentaries which he as a student of Padua knew very well. Politian spoke of Argyropulos always with great respect, at times even affectionately, but he loved to polemize with him. The *Miscellanea* opens with a famous discussion of the learned Byzantine, and it ends with his name. Thus the beginning and the end of Politian's philological masterpiece, the *summa* of his teachings, is united with the name of the great Argyropulos and is ideally contraposed to the work of Pico.

In appearance, the argument of the day turned about a question of the spelling of the world "entelechy" (*entelechia* or *endelechia*), but in reality it involved a radical difference between two concepts of the soul: was it a perfect action or perpetual motion, a part of the body or a separate motor? Platonism or Aristotelianism?[22] Again, since it was Cicero who spoke of the *endelechia,* the argument pitted the Greeks against the Latins and encouraged the arrogance of the Byzantine refugees toward the Italians who were their hosts. Argyropulos took advantage of the occasion to criticize the Latins, who had produced few philosophers since the time of Cicero.

Politian, in his turn, exaggerated Argyropulos's attitude in order to write a clever literary piece. That the Byzantine did not press his criticism of Cicero we can infer from the "lecture notes" on his course which are extant, transcribed in the hand of his pupil, friend, and protector, Donato Acciaiuoli. But Politian did not like the Byzantines much and he never missed an occasion to speak ill of them. He found them spiteful and quarrelsome among themselves ("*acerbissimae inter hos Graecos inimicitiae*"),* and petulant and presumptuous toward the Latins: "*vix enim dici potest quam nos aliquando, idest Latinos homines, in participatu suae linguae doctrinaeque nos libenter admittat ista natio. Nos enim quis quilias tenere litterarum, se frugem; nos praesegmina, se corpus; nos putamina, se nucleum credit.*"† He did not even spare Gaza, who it was commonly agreed was a man of superior stature and whom he himself had celebrated in elegant Greek dystichs, and he showed indulgence toward the sarcastic and acrimonious Trapezuntios. (In the end he devalued the work of both, to whom he opposed his Venetian friends Ermolao Barbaro and Girolamo Donato: "*nunc in isto quidem genere, vel nitore vel copia, vivimus ex pari cum Graecis.*")‡[23]

With all this, the opening chapter of the *Miscellanea*, measured against the solemn figure of his teacher Argyropulos, is a very fine essay, practically a model for a reconstruction of Politian's method of investigation. The question arises over a term, even a letter: should *endelechia* be corrected to *entelechia*? Its solution forms a chapter of cultural history, which broadens into a discussion of high metaphysics, immanence, and transcendence. Politian passes from the Greek to the Latin commentators in a lordly fashion. Here we find Plato's *Phaedrus* and the relationships between Plato and Aristotle, the questions of the Platonism of the early Aristotle and of the constitution of the Aristotelian *corpus*. He then turns to the nature of the soul—that is, immanent, and to the soul as a self-propelled motor—that is, "separate." This was the great question of the synthesis, for the entire world of antiquity as well as for the early Christian and the medieval world. The argument involved two consonants which appeared to have been an error in transcription and easy to correct. But behind the argument lay hidden a secular struggle of ideas and unending historical problems. Politian concludes the work by thanking

* "the feuds among those Greeks are bitter indeed."

† "No one can tell for sure how willingly that [Greek] nation will allow us—Latins that we are—to share in its language and its learning. They think our literature so much rubbish, whereas theirs is beyond compare, that ours is but the parings, theirs the fruit, ours the empty husks, theirs the kernels."

‡ "Now, at any rate, in this respect we are no worse off then the Greeks, be it with regard to gracious living or to affluence."

Pico, who led him to rediscover philosophy in history and in philology.

What is important to us is Politian's method, his scholarship, his ability to see the problem always as a historical problem: that is, his constant, systematic, conscious application of a logical criterion. It was a question of a diphthong, and he presented the considered arguments of his contemporaries, selecting examples not at random but according to a rational order, to well-documented contemporary epigraphs, and to coinages of the period. But, truly, he asks ironically, can the imperial mint always have made the same mistake? For us it does not matter if his conjectures do not stand up, and that a more accurate exploration of the codices should have disproved him. What is valuable is his historicizing of an entire history in which, in order to clarify a term, orators, historians, legal documents, epigraphic testimony, and the human life of a period are called forth as witnesses. There are times when the rules of the founders of a new logic come to mind! And his history does not stop at the classics; it pursues a cultural tradition of the Christian world. He checked so far as possible the hands through which a codex had passed. In the *Miscellanea* and in his letters (the necessary integration of the *Miscellanea*), he explicates, for whoever is able to see, the first great strictly "scientific" investigation in the field of literature, of law, and of history in general.

The exchange of letters with Leoniceno, on medical-pharmaceutical questions connected with Dioscorides, Pliny, and Avicenna, confronts us with a conscious criticism that is truly the dawn of a new scientific attitude. If we attempt to locate the great moments in the progress of western knowledge, we see them tied to two attempts to recuperate the knowledge of antiquity: one medieval, in which the Arabs played the preponderant role; the other humanistic and renaissance. The first, with its religious veneration of the text as the authority and the truth, gave way to commentary and even to commentary on commentary. Recourse to experience, which was not lacking and which led some historians to err, was one more *case* within a formulation already considered definitive and hence irreversible. The humanistic revival was historical and critical and tended to place a text within a period, within a well-defined situation out of which the inducement to new research necessarily springs. At the moment when Aristotle or Ptolemy are seen tied to a particular period, at that precise moment their absolute, timeless authority ends. This is the point of departure for the bases of a logical, scientific revolution. For this reason Politian the philologist is a great name in the history of the progress of human knowledge.

Thus we can return to Argyropulos, who, despite his Greek character, was in reality neither contemptuous of the Italian world which played host to him nor linked with the quarrels of his compatriots. Politian was indebted to him more than he admitted, specifically for his fruitful way of approaching the ancients, and in part for his feeling of national continuity with the Romans, corresponding exactly to that which the learned Byzantine manifested with regard to ancient Greece, his homeland. Argyropulos already sensed the solidarity of the various aspects of the culture, and was preoccupied with resolving the problems of the texts and the difficulties of interpreting them as historical problems.

But the influences of the learned Byzantine are better attested to where Politian, in his teaching at the Studio, again goes through, in dissenting agreement, the same stages as his master. Still, to discover agreements beside original views, as Politian did in his famous opening addresses on the *Nicomachea* and the *Organon*, is also of use in making a concrete evaluation of the contribution of the Greeks to Italian humanism, which is frequently presented in an erroneous perspective. An initial position, in which the entire new culture was seen to derive from the contribution of the Greeks between the Council of Florence and the fall of Constantinople, was later reversed to its extreme opposite, a complete negation, only to be reactivated in the stress on the determining function of the knowledge of the Greek language. Sufficient thought has never been given to the fact that the process was really of a dialogue, not altogether new, at times greatly animated, profitable to both sides—a dialogue in which the Greeks drew from the Latins and vice versa. This was not only a question of a linguistic phenomenon, nor of a quantitative contribution of texts.

A prominent victim of a web of errors in perspective was Argyropulos himself, who carried no less weight than Bessarion and certainly more than Pletho. He introduced the Florentines to a new work of Aristotle, but he also introduced Neoplatonic theology, ending with his commentary on the *Ethics* in 1456. At the same time, having lived in the environment of the exiled Palla di Nofri Strozzi and later among the anti-Medicean Florentine groups, he did not remain alien to the ethical and political concepts of these groups. These he voiced in a small treatise on the duties of the magistrate, which contains passages on tyranny not unworthy of the most important antityrannical literature of the Florentine Quattrocento. They include a definition of the corrupt magistrate who lays the foundation for tyranny at the precise point when he dissociates his own interest from the common good. They further include a very effective portrait of the courtiers who surround a man of wealth and power. Finally they include a hymn to justice, the soul of the republic which more than echoes—even imitates—the customary orations pronounced by Florentine magistrates from the ringhiera.[24] Certain of his minor writings also give us a picture of Argyropulos as a master of rhetoric. The *compendium de regulis et formis ratiocinandi,* dedicated to Filippo Valori, contains an interesting glimpse of his inductive processes.[25]

The New Philosopher

The most famous opening lectures of Politian are in the center of this fertile exchange between Greek and Latin culture: the lecture on the *Nicomachea,* with its well-known classification of the sciences, and those on logic with the *Strega* and the *Dialectics.* In the opening lectures on Aristotelian ethics (on which he gave a course in 1490–91), the famous *Panepistemon,* he recapitulates analogous lectures —those of Argyropulos could have provided him with an exact model, but he also integrates them with unusual effectiveness, including along with the *artes liberales* not only the *machinales* (technicians) but also the *sordidae ac selullariae, quibus tamen vita indiget.** [26] The extension of classification is original in these lectures, and they reveal an almost sensuous pleasure in terminology, a rare taste for words along with an interest in reality. At times the lectures digress, like letters, to give a detailed description of an instrument or of a machine.[27]

This very cultivated humanist continually breaks into conventional images with his penchant for "physical" problems, with his interest in "factories," and with his curiosity about natural phenomena. The

* "servants and artisans, of whom life nonetheless has need.

violets of his exquisite Latin dystichs and the roses of his Italian verses flower (if the image may be allowed) in a minute observation coupled with a keen study of scientific descriptions. The melancholy of his poem on the setting stars remind us of his astronomical observations or of his careful analysis of the Greek treatise writers whose codices still reveal traces of his hand.

This solid foundation, this grasp of reality, this recherché taste for the concrete are at the center of Politian's considerations of history, his fine passages on rhetoric, his reflections on dialectics. They should serve to caution all those who seek his doctrinal premises within the framework of Ficino's "theology," to which he did not burn the necessary grain of incense at the court of Lorenzo. *Platonica ista remota nimis,** he once exclaimed, addressing his listeners: let us abandon the too pure divine contemplation, *materiae sordes reformidans,*† and cultivate a logic that does not fear contact with things, *volutare in eis logicam sinit.*‡ Descendants as we are of poor men, *de fastigio in planum,*♯ let us be satisfied with the arts of speech, with the tools of research, with the means to convince, in place of the rhythms of the eternal.[28]

From this we see once more that Politian's return to philosophy after his initial contempt for it signified, not a palinode, but the discovery of *another* philosophy, united with "letters" and with the *studia humanitatis* and in fact crowning them: *ad usque lares philosophiae semita patebat.*△ We should reflect on the whole of his sparkling irony in the most beautiful of his Latin lectures in prose, the *Lamia,* with which he introduced his course on the *Analytics* and which is an answer to his critics: *inter se detortis nutibus consussurarunt: Politianus est; ipsissimus est; nugator ille scilicet, qui sic repente philosophus prodiit.*φ

It is not very difficult to imagine who those witches could have been who not only lingered around the Fonte Lucente in the hills of

* That Platonic world is too remote
† which shuns sordid matter
‡ but that brings some thought to bear on them
♯ having come down from the heights into the plains
△ The road to the shrine of philosophy stood open.
φ who, without knowing gestures and nods, whisper to one another, "There goes Politian! That's he! That's the imposter who turned philosopher overnight!"

Fiesole, but who also promenaded in disguise in the city: *homines credas, Lamiae sunt.** They were witches who repeated to him: How could you, a grammarian who has never even listened to the masters of philosophy, have become a philosopher? It is curious that the same sentences recur in the opening lecture on the *Dialectics*—not unintentionally, but obviously as a quotation. It is a meaningful quotation, because here Politian says clearly who his schoolmasters had been and how he left them for the true teachers who later made a philosopher of him. The old teachers had been both the scholastics who sometimes amused him and sometimes nauseated him, and the commentators and repeaters of the ancients. Via "letters" he discovered Aristotle by himself—*Aristotelis puritatem*—and the convergence of linguistics and dialectics; he emerged a philosopher. The witches derided him, but he knew well that there are many ways of being a philosopher. His philosophy was critical, logical, a moral liberation.

In his emphasis on Aristotle and on the logic which the well-known philosophers neglected, not because it was of little importance but because it was too difficult; in his stress of ethics; in his defense of the *grammaticus* as a *litteratus* and as a *criticus* ("It is we who have relegated it to the little schools of the trivium, as though in punishment"); in the polemic against the malicious Florentine "witches" who denied him the title of philosopher, there is an intent that cannot be disregarded: "There were wise owls at the time of the ancients; today there are many owls, with feathers and eyes and an owl's beak, but wisdom, that they do not have." Did this final remark of the *Strega* allude only to the "scholastics"? Did the many owls refer only to some lean friar still lost behind the terminist logic? Can we ignore the fact that at that time Pico too discussed the excesses of the theologizing interpretations of Ficino in a small work dedicated to Politian? And didn't Ficino, in the commentary on *Parmenides,* deplore the impudence with which the youthful scholar allowed himself to criticize him?

The pattern of Politian's critical thought and the direction in which its problems were oriented are apparent in a particularly happy way in his collected letters, which he compiled in the year of his death.[29] In these the interlocutors of his dialogue—his true

* "One takes them for human beings; yet they are witches."

teachers and colleagues—are introduced in the most important passages. The letters give an unusual panorama of the literary culture of the second half of the Quattrocento, whose focal center was Florence.

An important chapter of literary history could be written on the composition of this work, which differs so much in style from the correspondence of the fifteenth century—on its inspiration, its aims, its vicissitudes, and the alterations made in it after the death of the author. Without any doubt the zeal with which Politian labored to determine the significance of the anti-Barbaro argument and the return to and imitation of the ancients would become clear in such research. It is not a coincidence that the discussion between Barbaro and Pico on the relationship between linguistic expression and conception, between logic and language, is included in this correspondence; it also contains the polemic on imitation between Politian himself and Paolo Cortesi, which is no less essential and in some ways complementary. Cortesi stressed the thesis that art is imitation—an imitation of nature in its highest expression; hence the Ciceronian style was to be taken as the model of a perfect individualization, almost an incarnation itself of human nature in one of the activities that are natural to it. Cortesi was proceeding (much more than it would seem) with a scholasticizing simplification of humanist imitation, applying on the rhetorical level to Cicero the same process that tradition had applied on the speculative level to Aristotle. The example won support inasmuch as its absolute perfection posed it as a metahistorical objectivation beyond which no progress was possible.[30]

Politian's argument was articulated in two stages: to imitate the style of another, he said, meant to sacrifice one's own individuality, to lose oneself in a lifeless uniformity. The imitators "*carent viribus et vita, carent actu, carent affectu, carent indole, iacent, dormiunt, stertunt. Nihil verum, nihil solidum, nihil efficax. Non exprimis—inquit aliquis—Ciceronem. Quid tum? Non enim sum Cicero.*"* Here also is an indication of Cortesi's tendency toward an objectivity which negated individuality—exactly where, for Politian, the *studia*

* "lack creative force and life, they lack originality, they miss the mood, they are out of style, they take things as they come, they snooze, they snore. There is nothing genuine in whatever they are doing, nothing substantial, nothing that in any way would impress one's mind. 'You are not expressing Cicero,' someone remarked. 'So what? I am not Cicero.'"

humanitatis (far from being directed toward nullifying the individual purity of each man by changing it into a group mask or, as he said, into the monkeys of the ancients) tended to bring forth in all its entire originality the personality of each individual.

The individual matures specifically in his constant contact and confrontation with the most precise and hence the most noble personality of others. In this way the entire past (in the matter of style Politian extended his attention to Christian writers) serves to make the present emerge as newer and more original. The recuperation of the entire Latin world—and, beyond Latinity, of that Greek world on which the Latins were nourished—was no more than a reconquest of one's own history (which for the Italians was a national history interrupted by the barbarians) in order to achieve the purest production of the present from the study of ancient events. To use Politian's metaphor, it was the flintstone, which when struck showered the sparks by itself. It is not by chance that we find included in the *Nutricia,* in classical poetic tradition, Cavalcanti and Dante, Petrarch and Boccaccio. It was not a coincidence that Landino, in his opening lectures on Petrarch, saw the study of classical Latin as an introduction to a broader and better articulated vernacular language. It was not by chance that Politian passed from Greek to Latin to the vernacular in refining his style. His most cultivated vernacular later became, through popularization, Florentine Italian. *"Cum Ciceronem, cum bonos alios multum diuque legeris, contriveris, edidiceris, concoxeris et rerum multarum pectus impleveris,"** then, and only then, in such abundance will you find that supreme purity, simplicity and nakedness which appears to be little but is everything. All of reality descends into the description of a rose, and hence its totality is accessible to all, the most artistocratic and the most plebeian, supremely ideal and entirely real: *umanissima.*[31]

Something like a modest but singular proof of this process of reconquest of self through a laborious mastering of a very elaborate style exists in those "Latins" that Politian, in accordance with practice, prepared with the vernacular in front of him for the elementary exercises of Piero de' Medici. The popular vocabulary corresponded

* "After you have read Cicero and other classical authors, thoroughly and often enough, after you have compared them with each other, absorbed them, and in this way filled your mind with a great many thoughts."

to the most solemn work; *auriga* finds its counterpart in *mannerino*. A Latin prose passage on the transiency of life, which reflects the rhetorical gravity of the word in common usage, is as though transfigured in this vernacular text:

> This life of ours flows like the water of a river; and human things waver and are finally destroyed. . . . If we had as much treasure as the wealth of Croesus, we could not prevent our banishment from this country; and we would go to a country not knowing whether it is west or east, nor would we know whether horses are sold there, nor whether one could say that some lovely garment is being sold on auction, nor whether the inhabitants of that country marry their daughters to foreigners, nor how much they appreciate our people. I have such great fear when I see the earth opened to swallow our bodies that I do not even dare open my mouth.[32]

Confronted with this scholastic exercise, the mind begins to think curious thoughts. That "fatherland" of ours, from which we will be "banished" by death, is the earth; Ficino at the same time wrote heartfelt words on the heavenly "fatherland" and on this worldly "exile." Apart from the irony of that doubt about whether in this other world there are markets and auction sales, the passage clearly alludes to those Florentine merchants of whom Politian had stated on another occasion: "They have a soul like merchandise, which though not yet on sale, is well placed to be sold"—an original way of teaching the small Piero the difference between *vendibilis* and *venalis*.

Even more than the attack against the monkish hypocrisy of the prologue to the Plautine *Menechmi*,[33] which was the fashion, the passage recalls to mind the epigram on hearing the mass, which in truth had the flavor of impiety. But (in order not to deviate to the question of humanistic "piety," which cannot be resolved with one more text, against which many others could immediately be opposed, and which, moreover, is entirely the result of an attitude) it is more useful on the stylistic level to quote the letter to Lucrezia de' Medici of 18 December 1478:

> I stay at home by the fire in wooden sandals and I would seem melancholic to you if you saw me, but perhaps I seem so in any case; and I do nothing, nor I see anything nor feel anything that pleases me. . . . I remain alone with myself, and when I have enough of studying, I ruminate about death and wars, and the pain of the past and the

fear of the future; nor do I have anyone with whom to sift these fantasies of mine . . . and I am dying of boredom.

Politian's Modern Thought

Language, style, problems of human communication in the city and throughout time: this in the end is the core of Politian's thought, always tied to a moment; an almost punctilious analysis of the texts, in order to understand the variation in style from author to author, from period to period, and in order to explain the change in taste and judgment: Demosthenes, who some consider dry; Cicero, whom they sometimes call "bloodless and boring," and again "insipid and weak," and "flat," but also "turgid and rambling." This "philological" research constantly tended toward an integrated history, although it would be wrong to isolate on a formal level Politian's investigations on the text of the *Pandette* and those on the history of Roman law, which are important not only as a free and objective return to the sources and to critical discussion, but especially as an indication of the need to relate every aspect of human history.[34]

On the lesson of the ancients a modern "conclusion" flowers in the vernacular: "New arguments make new cases, and new cases require new methods." And so the great wisdom is born: "An old man told me recently that these injustices cannot endure; and that justice is like water: that when its course is impeded it breaks over the dam, or it swells so much that it overflows its banks." Here is a Politian recalled in Guicciardini's *ricordi* and of whom it was said, correctly, that "a modern feeling and reasoning has found here a full and victorious formal expression." A poet "without any other republic but that of philology" rediscovers in his critical activity "a serene civic meditation."[35] This was no longer the magnanimous "rhetoric" of the republican ideal of "civic life"; it was perhaps the birth, in the disappointment of failure, of Machiavelli's political science.

Whoever has a penchant for harmonious processes would find it difficult to resist the temptation to place the ideal line of Politian's development under the sign of Orpheus, uniting the theme of the popular drama with the *Nutricia, de poetica et poetis* and the *Sylva.* Together they would form a kind of profession of faith in the formative virtue of poetry. The myth of Orpheus was dear to the humanists; it was something of a commonplace in their rhetoric. From Fonzio to Landino, the song of the poet who tames beasts and lifts rocks is elevated to a symbol of the word which educates, which constitutes man cementing society to himself, and which then makes him master over material things. Ficino had projected the savor of the fable into the infinite and had dissolved the human into the divine. Politian remained faithful to that limit which wraps in melancholy every one of his poems. The divinity of man is limited by the world and closed by death: "When I see the earth opened to swallow our bodies . . . I do not even dare open my mouth."

The song of Orpheus can conquer many earthly things:

Svolger l'orfica lira addietro i fiumi
Trar con le cupe lor tane le belve,
E co' faggi le rupi, e a mezzo il volo
*Arrestar suso in aere gli augelli.**

And it could tame what was beneath the earth ("I see the wheel of Ission made fast . . ."). It may invoke, not redemption from the inexorable law of death ("All things in the end return to you/each mortal life passes back to you"), but Euridice's right to fulfill her earthly course. "But the tender life and the bitter grape/you have cut with the hard scythe/Who is he who harvests seeds of grass/and does not wait till they mature?"

The elegant hexameters of the *selva,* published in 1491 after having waited in vain for several years (since 1486) for those commentaries which were to integrate it, compose the "orphic" themes into an ideal story of human education under the banner of the poets:

Intulerat terris nuper mundoque recenti
Cura dei sanctum hoc animal, quod in aethera ferret
Sublimes oculos; quod mentis acumine totum
Naturae lustraret opus, causasque latenteis
Eliceret rerum . . .

* "The song of the orphic lyre behind the rivers
lures beasts from their dark caves,
from cliffs and beech-woods,
and arrests the birds in mid-flight."

Quod fretum ratione animi substerneret uni
Cuncta sibi . . .[*36]

But these were not acquired gifts; they were only latent possibilities. Humanity was savage; and only the word and the song gave men marriage, laws, religions, and civilization. The history of man is scanned in a history of poetry, and poetry is the entire laborious history of man, which in the end seems to approach the great Tuscan poetry:

Nec tamen Aligerum fraudarim hoc munere Dantem,
Per styga per stellas mediique per ardua montis,
Pulchra Beatricis sub virginis ora volantem;
Quique cupidineum repetit Petrarcha triumphum;
Et qui bisquinis centum argumenta diebus
Pingit; et obscuri qui semina monstrat amoris:
Unde tibi immensae veniunt praeconia laudis,
Ingeniis opibusque potens, Florentia mater.[†37]

Poetry: For Politian the life of man oscillates between a painful preparation which pours out in song and poetic liberation; between the most rigorous reason of the most studied culture and that point of absolute freedom in which in the end man creates. Works of art and of poetry are born of this process—a most lucid process in which all is dissolved and reawakened to new life, in which study is as though transfigured and is no more. All becomes the spontaneous voice of

* "Of late, there stepped onto the earth and into
modern times—by the design of God—
that blessed being who can raise to heaven
his searching gaze; whose questing mind may scan
all nature's works, who seeks the hidden
causes of things and . . .
who, basing himself on reason,
submits all to himself . . ."

† "Nor would I desist from paying tribute to Dante,
who with fair Beatrice to guide him
sped through the nether and upper realms
to the loftiest peaks of the mountains;
and Petrarch who renews the triumph of love;
those who in ten days create a hundred tales
and those who reveal the origins of an obscure love.
Hence, eternal glory reflects forever upon you,
inexhaustible in genius, unsurpassed in art,
Mother Florence!"

feeling; every word and every rhythm conclude an age-old labor, like those in Politian's love poetry, which is perhaps the most graceful of his Latin verse:

Puella delicatior
*Lepusculo et cuniculo . . .**

Along with his friends, the theoreticians of humanism, Politian sang the praises of man the creator. But since he did not limit himself, as the professional philosophers did, to rhetorical statements about creation, but actually created something—even if it was only cantos—and spent his time in philological and historical research in order to understand the poets, his poetry of man perhaps goes further and captures that rhythm of toil and triumph. As he said in the epigraph for Giotto: first the toil, then the tower ringing high in the sky (*turrem egregiam sacro aere sonantem*).†

Poetic creation, laborious research: in the rhythm of philology-poetry he essayed, Agnolo concluded his own work. He did not have Pico's faith in a renewal or the prophetic fervor of Savonarola. He had something of the courtier, of the court professor who feels burdened by his work and would like to free himself from it to lead a more satisfying life. He had every kind of human weakness. But he never had that of Ficino: he did not confuse beautiful dreams and myths with the reasoned truth of thought. A classical scholar, he drew from the classics a sense of man's limits and observed the distinction between the risk of the poet and the analysis of the philosopher. And he asked comfort and salvation from verse, since only poetry and the arts "liberate men from death and make them eternal." The poets will live "until the stars shine on a world made silent."[38]

* "A maiden more graceful
than a small hare or a tiny rabbit . . ."

† "the tall tower resounding to the peal of sacred bells."

Notes

1. Reference is made, for convenience, to Politian's works in Latin in the edition of Lyons, Apud Seb. Gryphium, 1(1539) (*Epistolarum libri XII ac Miscell. Cent. I*) and 2(1528) (which contains other writings, including the translations and the Latin and Greek poems); but the text is given according to the Aldina of 1498. For the Italian prose and the unedited writings, see I. Del Lungo, ed., *Prose volgari inedite e poesie latine e greche edite e inedite* (Florence, 1867) and L. D'Amore, *Lettere inedite di A. Poliziano* (Naples, 1903). For a history of the criticism and bibliographical references included, see the chapter by B. Maier in W. Binni, ed., *I classici italiani nella storia della critica* (Florence, 1954), pp. 231–56. For certain of his Latin prose writings, see Politian, *I prosatori latini del Quattrocento* (Naples-Milan, 1952); for the Greek epigrams, see the Ardizzoni edition of the same work (Florence, 1951). On the correspondence, see the excellent article by A. Campana in *La Rinascita* 6(1943): 437–72. And see the now rare edition of [author unknown], *Sylva in scabiem,* brilliantly edited by A. Perosa (Rome, 1954), which among other things rightly stresses Politian's "taste for certain harsh aspects of reality"; see also J. Cotton Hill, "Death and Politian," *The Durham University Journal* 46(1954): 96–105.

2. Politian, *Opera,* 1: 517 sqq. (*Miscell.* ch. 4: "*quam multa poetarum interpretibus legenda . . .*"): "Whoever wants to understand the poets should burn the midnight oil, as we say, going back not only to Aristophanes but even to Cleanthes. And he should study not only the writings of the philosophers, but also those of the lawyers and even the physicians and logicians, and of anyone else who has contributed to the body of learning known as the 'encyclia,' but mainly the writings of all men of letters. And he should not only research but meditate upon all this and not be content with a mere nodding acquaintance; he should fathom the innermost depths and make himself thoroughly at home there."

Politian, *Opera,* 1: 517 sqq.: "In any event, you will find that a great deal, primarily from the writings of the philosophers, has been incorporated into the works of our poets; for example, we pointed out a few years ago when lecturing publicly on the poet Persius [A. Persius Flaccus] that his fifth satire appears to be modelled on Plato's dialogue entitled *Alcibiades I.* . . . " For the course on Persius, see I. Del Lungo, *Florentia. Uomini e cose del Quattrocento* (Florence, 1897), pp. 178–79. The *Praelectio in Persium,* in *Opera,* 2: 462–71, which Del Lungo dated 1484, is entirely taken up with the problem of the relationship of poetry with philosophy: "Especially, however, we should look—as attentively as though into a mirror—into those authors who point as with a finger to a rule of life for good or ill. . . . The ancients were right in saying that philosophy was, first of all, a kind of poetry; hence they believed it was especially suited to inspire the very first beginnings of wisdom. . . . That most profoundly learned man (Persius) . . . added a great deal to philosophy from his uniquely personal experience of life, and quite often he expressed himself in a dialectical manner." For a more common position, see the *praefatio* to the *Miscellanea, Opera* 1: 490: "Just as in dying wool it should first be steeped in certain solutions, in order to prepare it to absorb the purple die, thus it would seem to me that the human mind should be conditioned likewise by exposing it to suitable literature and teachings, to prepare it fully (as Cicero said in his *Hortensius*) so that it may absorb wisdom."

4. Politian, *Opera,* 1: 697 (*Miscell. Coronis*). The *Miscellanea* ends with praise of Pico and is full of references to him, many of them explicit recollections; even when Pico's name is not mentioned, his influence may be felt: "This truly noble prince, Giovanni Pico della Mirandola, a man so outstanding that he may be properly called a hero, so richly is he possessed with all the gifts of fortune in body and mind; a young man with nearly divine features, bearing his stately body with the dignity of a king, with a keenly discerning mind, an exceptional memory, tireless in his studies, and endowed with a rich and clear eloquence, which one cannot say whether more extraordinary for his voice or his manners; learned in all philosophy but also a most erudite and profound scholar of literature in the [Greek and Latin] languages, and of all the noble arts."

5. Del Lungo, ed., *Prose volgari,* pp. 32, 36.

6. This is a letter written in 1519 to G. N. Salerno (ed. Sabbadini, [Venice, 1915], 1: 261).

7. Politian, *Nutricia,* 114–15 (in Del Lungo, ed., *Prose volgari,* p. 375).

8. Politian, *Nutricia,* 116–38 (in Del Lungo, ed., *Prose volgari,* pp. 375–6). For a relationship between *Orfeo* and *Nutricia,* see Del Lungo, *Florentia,* p. 331.

9. Politian, *Miscellanea,* ch. 77, *Opera,* 1: 647. See also *Epist. Barpt. Scalae* (*Opera,* 1: 139): "Landino . . . once my teacher, now, however, . . . a colleague of mine, a man of undisputed authority and renown in the field of letters. . . . "

10. *Epistolarum, Opera,* 1:75 sqq.

11. Del Lungo, ed., *De Domitio et Marsilio,* p. 119: "Marsilio attended mass, it's true, but that mass was said/by you, Domizio; seeing that, which of the two of you is therefore more devout?/Who can doubt? You are more devout than he/as it is better still to do a good deed than to hear about it."

12. See Miscell., 9(*Opera,* 1, 524 sqq.), and *ibid.* the epigram cited; see also among the epigrams, ed. Del Lungo, pp. 151 and 153. The letter exchanged with the antiquario is in *Opera,* 1, 86–92.

13. See in Fosforo's letter to Cortesi (Del Lungo, ed., *De Domitio,* p. 74), the quotation of Valla's famous preface to the *Elegantiae:* "For who does not know that, after Rome was sacked and the Empire lost, Italy was taken over by barbarians, and that all Roman learning, indeed, all knowledge of letters

and arts then fell into disuse? This then was the will of your Emperor, that all this should be laid in ashes and be lost forever. But, at length, there arose once again a man of genius, as though new flames had burst forth from ashes. . . . " For the resemblance to Valla, see the explicit comments of M. Santoro, *Poliziano e la sua fede nella retorica,* "Stoa," 1948 (p. 10 sqq. of the extract); and for certain characteristics of Politian's philology, see the valuable study on "La polemica Poliziano-Merula," *Giornale Italiano di Filologia* 5(1952): 212–33.

14. See the beautiful passages by G. Folena, "Umori del Poliziano nei Detti piacevoli," *L'Approdo* 3(1954): 24–30, from which the quotations from the *Detti piacevoli* are also taken (see *Angelo Poliziano Tagebuch* [*1477–79*], first published in Jena, 1929).

15. For the unconventional view, one should proceed very cautiously in situating Politian within the ambiance of Florentine "Platonism" (see A. B. Ferruolo, "A Trend in Renaissance Thought and Art: Poliziano's Stanze per la Giostra," *The Romanic Review* XLIV, 44(1953): 246–56). See also Ida Maier, "Une page inédite de Politien: la note du Vat. lat. 3617 sur Démétrius Triclinius commentateur d'Homère," *Bibliothèque d'Humanisme et Renaissance* 16(1954): 7–17, and my "note" on the subject in issue of the *Giornale Critico della Filos. It.* 3(1954): 439–42. Russo, in L'Orfeo del Poliziano, *Belfagor* 8(1953): 269–81, rightly takes issue with the tendency of Momigliano, "Ritratto di Poliziano," *Belfagor* 5(1950): 281–87, to "disengage" Politian too much.

16. See the elegy *ad Laurentium Medicem* (Del Lungo, ed., *De Domitio,* pp. 227–28). So far as Fonzio is concerned, in addition to the famous epigram ("Study once delighted me;/but insidious poverty, with its tattered garments, frightened me./Now, however, that the bards are again acclaimed by the people,/I might as well suit the times"), the elegy includes among the works of Pannonio, *Poemata* (Utrecht, 1784), 1: 674–87 (Folena, *Umori,* p. 24).

17. *Miscellanea,* Coronis, *Opera,* 1: 696–99: "In fact, under the guidance of two outstanding men, Marsilio Ficino of Florence (whose lyre was more fortunate than that of Orpheus, the Thracian, in recalling to life from Hades the true—if I am not mistaken—Eurydice, that is, the profound wisdom of Plato), and Argyropulos, the Byzantine (without doubt the most famous peripatetic of his time), I dedicated myself from my earliest youth to the philosophies of both, but not too assiduously, being by nature and age more receptive to the blandishments of Homer. . . . Thereafter, however, since various other matters and endeavors became more pressing, I imbibed philosophy only occasionally and left it—much as the dogs drink in the Nile and then run away—until Giovanni Pico returned to this city. . . . " This testimony should be combined with the other, fundamental one of the *praelectio de dialectica* (*Opera,* 2: 459–61), parallel to the *Lamia.* Here Politian indicates his *true* masters: "Theophrastus, Alexandros [Alexander of Aphrodisias], Themistius, Hammonius, Simplicius, [John] Philoponus, and all the others of the Aristotelian school . . . whose place (as it pleases the Gods) is now taken by Burleus [Walter Burley, 1275–1345], Erveus [Hervaeus Natalis, d. 1318], [William] Occam [d. 1349],

Entisberus [William Heytesbury, Chancellor of Oxford, fl. 1340–71], and Strodus [Ralph Strode, 1350–1400]. At all events, as a youth I labored over certain doctors of philosophy and rhetoric—and not obscure ones, either, some of whom proved to be so ignorant of Greek and Latin letters that they sullied the pristine purity of Aristotelian writings with a flood of fearful nonsense emanating from their own benighted minds. They sometimes made me laugh, but more often they even turned my stomach. On the other hand, those few who had mastered Greek appeared to be dealing with some unheard-of and sensationally novel matters; there was nothing at all, however, in what they had to impart that I had not met with before in those very books with which I was even then so amply supplied . . . thanks to Lorenzo de Medici. . . . " Del Lungo (*Florentia,* p. 129), for those who teach *ex commentariis,* mentions the names of Andronicus Callistus (who commented on Aristotle) and of Calcondila, a colleague of Politian. With regard to Argyropulos, besides the Greek epigrams, see the spirited letter of Michelozzi (*Florentia,* p. 220): "Messer Giovanni Argiropilo arrived yesterday. . . . He is younger than ever and gayer. . . . He came without a beard, which I know will not please Agnolo, and does not look at all Greek; and he has not forgotten the *or bene,* but inserts it on every occasion. Tell this to Agnolo. . . ."

18. *Epistolarae,* pp. 298–302.

19. *In Epicteti Stoici enchiridion e graeco interpretatum, ad Laurentium Medicem epistola* (*Opera,* 1: 182). Do these words display a certain irony toward some Platonic infatuations? For the *defensio Epicteti,* see the same work, pp. 205–13.

20. Del Lungo, ed., *Prose volgari,* pp. 67–68. How can we not be reminded that Giuseppe Rensi, in a bitter period and with a clear purpose, republished with the translation of the Epictet the collection of Politian's writings?

21. On the translation of Hippocrates and Galenus, see the letter in Italian of 5 June 1490 to Lorenzo (Del Lungo, ed., *Prose volgari,* p. 77), in which he requests him to ask Pier Leone, the famous physician, to look it over again: "If master Pier Lione would like to take the time to correct this translation of mine of Hippocrates and Galenus, which is almost finished, as well as the commentary above, in which I explain all the medical terms that derive from the Greek. . . . I think it would be a fine and useful work, if devotion does not deceive me in it. Messer Ermolao and the count [Pico] show their good opinion of it." But he speaks of it also in the *Lamia,* in which there is a hint of those many "waking hours," of which Crinito also was to speak ("a great deal of work went into it and many sleepless nights . . .") in his letter to Gian Francesco Pico (*Opera,* 1: 272).

22. *Miscellanea,* 1 (*Opera,* 1: 505–14). On this question and its lengthy history, see the article concerning who spells the word one way or the other, "Ἐντελέχεια and ενδελεχέια nelle discussioni humanistiche," *Atene e Roma,* series 3, 5 (1937).

23. *Miscellanea,* 90 (*Opera,* 1: 675 sqq.). Here Politian mentions Pietro d'Abano with much respect (p. 679), although he takes cognizance of his faulty

knowledge of classical languages. He criticizes the praise of Trapezuntios, who had written vicious things about Gaza: "Anyone carefully examining these books [the *Problemi,* attributed to Aristotle, translated by Trapezuntios and later by Gaza] would scarcely put great faith in Gaza, stepping as he does, quite literally, into the other's footprints; if that man were outspoken, he would rather take Theodoro to task, I am sure, for plagiarizing. . . . "

24. *De institutione eorum qui in dignitate constituti sunt* (Vat. lat. 5811): "If someone holding public office seeks his own advantage rather than tends to the welfare of those for whose benefit the office was entrusted to him, then, surely, a tyrant is bound to take power. It follows automatically that anything done to favor such a tyrant is to the detriment and ruin of the commonwealth. If there is one thing certain, it is that flatterers and sycophants will always adore a man of means or someone in public office or other position of prominence, for they are totally lacking in self respect and independence of spirit. Obsequious and servile, they feign goodwill and friendship, and they unhestitatingly put themselves at such a man's service. Whatever he says or does, however contemptible, or exceeding all bounds of propriety, they praise to the skies, as a matter of course. Whatever he finds pleasing is proper and human. . . . Whatever he says, they nod assent to; whatever he frowns upon, they deprecate; and, if he laughs, they simply burst into fits of laughter. . . ."

25. Argyropulos's writings on logic are contained in ms. 2, II, 52 of the National Library of Florence, which is one of the most noteworthy and complete sources.

26. *Opera,* 2:306–31. See I. Maier, "un inédit de Politien: la classification des arts," *Bibl. Hum. et Ren.* 22(1960): 338–55.

27. *Opera,* 1: 121–24.

28. *Opera,* 2: 458–61.

29. Del Lungo, ed., *Prose volgari,* p. 85.

30. *Opera,* 1: 250 sqq.

31. See Pernicone's "Sul testo delle Stanze del Poliziano, *Giornale Storico della Letteratura Italiana* 129(1952): 1–25; and with regard to Pernicone's edition, the notes of G. De Robertis, "l'Edizione delle Stanze," *Il Nuovo Corriere* of Florence, 5 August 1954.

32. Del Lungo, ed., *Prose volgari,* pp. 38–40.

33. *Epistolarae* (*Opera,* 1: 213); *Epigr.* (2: 611); Del Lungo, ed., *Prose volgari,* p. 283.

34. A. M. Bandini, *Ragionamento storico sopra le collazioni delle fiorentine Pandette fatte da A.P.* (Livorno, 1762); F. Buonamici, *Il P. giuresconsulto o della letteratura nel diritto* (Pisa, 1863) (which also contains related texts and translations).

35. G. F. Folena, *Umori,* p. 30.

36. *Nutricia,* pp. 34 sqq. (Del Lungo, ed., *Prose volgari,* pp. 372–73).

37. *Nutricia,* pp. 720 sqq. (Del Lungo, ed., *Prose volgari,* pp. 422–23). It is hardly necessary to point out the reference to Cavalcanti's song.

38. *Manto,* 339 (Del Lungo, ed., *Prose volgari,* p. 303).

VII

Giovanni Pico della Mirandola

To speak of Giovanni Pico della Mirandola without descending to the level of rhetoric and without understating his importance is not a simple matter. Nor is it easy to account for his fame and for the extraordinary impression he made on his contemporaries. Still, we cannot ignore the words of Erasmus, written on 29 September 1516, from Antwerp to a famous friend: How can you dare speak of unhappiness, you who have had the good fortune to visit Italy in those wonderful years when Angelo Politian, Ermolao Barbaro, and Pico della Mirandola flourished?[1] Erasmus was not a lenient judge. At the time he wrote these words, the men he spoke of had been dead for some time—descended to the grave too soon, as he observed on another occasion, as though consumed by their own restless spirits. Yet in his eyes they were men of such magnitude that an encounter with them seemed sufficient to give meaning to life.

Erasmus's observation reflects faithfully an idea then widespread in Europe: that the Italian cities were crowded with uncommon geniuses who were difficult to classify, somewhat enigmatic, endowed with exceptional capacities and a strange fascination, reaching out toward elusive goals. They were men about whom it would have been easier to spin a legend than write a history. The most unusual of all was probably Giovanni Pico. In his time he was very nearly the symbol of an entire epoch; with time his real consistency was effaced. A Faustian image, with romantic and decadent overtones, has consigned the solid figure of a very human thinker to oblivion. In the minds of most he has remained a phantom with prodigious gifts, shrouded in mystery, on the border between magic and occultism, heretical temptations and mystical aberrations. Today, even after so much research the work of restoration is sometimes difficult; it is not easy to restitute the complex perspective in which he lived—a northern nobleman who ended his days in Florence, the city of proud popular traditions.

Among the papers of the Benivieni house is an account of the first meeting in Florence between the gentle Girolamo, who later became Pico's dear friend, and the sensitive poet from a family of learned theologians and scientists who was destined to join the ranks of Savonarola.

From the start the traits of the knights of the North contrasted with the ways of the Florentine merchants in the young count.[2] The lords of Mirandola and Concordia, rich and quarrelsome, predisposed to war and family strife, were well representative of that northern nobility with its lordly pretensions and feudal nostalgia to which Giovanni's brothers remained faithful. For Giovanni, who was born in the ancestral castle on 24 February 1463, another destiny was intended. His father, Gian Francesco I, died shortly after his birth, and he was reared by his mother, Giulia Boiardo, the aunt of the poet by the same name. Apparently, Pico was very close to his mother.[3]

He was oriented very early toward study in a society permeated with culture. At the turn of the century the Italian cities, although shaken by a historical process that was undermining their power, were expressing in art and science the perfection of a civilization that had matured with so much effort. It was an age of economic and political crises of every kind. Europe was in the throes of transformation; the Turkish menace was emerging in the East; the discoveries of new lands were to revolutionize commerce; religious unrest, ever more widespread, was pointing to a profound upheaval. The Italian Renaissance was a splendid era of world history, but it was not a happy season. Savonarola, Machiavelli, Leonardo, and Michelangelo have a tragic, not a joyful, aspect. Their greatness was awe-inspiring; their serenity was beyond pain, beyond any illusion. The enchanting impressions of the Florence of the Magnificent, the images of Botticelli and Politian, certain embellishments of oriental or baroque taste dear to the prose of Ficino and the Ficinians, all constituted a sort of charm that dispelled the wounds of reality (although Lorenzo, who was at base a rude commoner, remained profoundly tied to this reality, to material things, as opposed to the "ideas" of the Ficinians).[4]

The young Lord of Mirandola's upbringing was not Tuscan. It took place in a different climate in the great centers of the North where the humanistic revival had been introduced and was united in various ways with the tradition of the oldest universities of

Europe. When we consider Giovanni's youthful voyages in search of the fine golden thread of a model history of knowledge, we encounter the great crossroads of fifteenth-century culture. In the Mantua of Vittorino da Feltre (and later of Isabella and Mantegna), Pico could for the first time meet Politian. He would study in Bologna and Padua and sojourn in Pavia. The heritage of the juridical schools of Bologna had for some time been linked to the *studia humanitatis*. Filippo Beroaldo the Elder, a philologist worthy of the esteem of Erasmus and Politian, was to be Pico's companion at play and table. Ferrara, which had witnessed the greatness of Guarino, was to give Pico a guide and friend in Battista Guarino, the son of one of the most important teachers of Europe. In Padua the ancient tradition of Aristotle was losing its austerity in the humanistic elegance of the refined and pious Venetian patricians like Ermolao Barbaro, the friend of Pico's mature years. Pavia, where the echo of the lessons and polemics of Lorenzo Valla had persisted for a long time, remained a prominent center for studies in logic and science.[5]

In this experimental environment Pico began his studies, following the classical *iter* of a university student. His considerable wealth and multiple friendships facilitated not only his moving about but also the ease of his sojourns and provided interesting contacts as well as a limitless opportunity to read. He thus acquired one of the most important libraries of a century that witnessed many splendid collections,[6] while his facility with languages was soon complemented by the work of paid translators of remarkable erudition. Pico was able to read Greek, Hebrew, and Arabic, and he was later to attempt translations of the Old Testament. But when he was interested in reading texts that were inaccessible to everyone, he commissioned their translation, and sometimes even explanations and summaries, from leading orientalists who were themselves celebrated: Elia del Medigo, a Jew from Candia and a teacher in Padua;[7] Guglielmo Raimondo di Moncada (Flavio Mitridate), a converted Sicilian Jew who worked for the Pope and for Federigo da Montefeltro and whose fame as an expert in languages was known throughout Europe from Louvain to Heidelberg;[8] Jochanan Alemanno, whose important writings remain extant.[9] If it was to Pico's credit that he demonstrated the necessity of broadening to the languages of the Orient that curiosity which had focused on Greek and the classics of Hellas since the time of Petrarch, his collaborators should not be ignored. His activity was frequently that of an organizer whose conspicuous wealth helped defray the extensive costs involved in the research and acquisition of codices and the remuneration of scholars.[10]

He was also a pioneer, comparable to the greatest, in doing for oriental culture what Petrarch, Boccaccio, Bruni, Aurispa, and Traversari had done for the Greco-Roman world. If others like Giannozzo Manetti, preceded him, he was still to accentuate and invigorate a renewed taste for all the knowledge that could be gathered from the East, giving an impetus that was to have incalculable consequences for biblical studies on the one hand, and for the return to basic sources for philosophical and scientific knowledge on the other. It is not an exaggeration to say that for centuries, in connection with important research in these fields, Pico was nearly always referred to as to the common founder of a family. Nor can it be denied that his curiosity about the East as the cradle of truth led him to nourish an ever broader view of history and an ever richer understanding of humanity, beyond the narrow limits of any one tradition. Truth can and must be served by every contribution, from whatever side it may come.

The restless wandering of the young count among the university centers of the North should not be misconstrued. It was more akin to the custom of medieval *clerics* than to the mania for travel that was so characteristic of the humanistic age. Pico did not travel as did Poggio, Ciriacus, or even Aeneas Sylvius, with a taste, beyond learned discovery, for landscape, nature, and peoples. He was to go from school to school following a precise itinerary whose stops were as serious as they were compulsory: Bologna, Padua, and Paris.[11] Gradually he harvested personalities, in addition to books.

It was precisely his insatiable curiosity and his humanity that led him to discover, through his contacts with eminent men, the world of the new culture that was about to affirm itself more often outside than within the universities—at times even in opposition to the universities. In the courts, in the liberal circles of scholars, in schools renewed by the humanists like that at Ferrara, the myth of the old university tradition—serious but often expended, without resilience, wasted on formal questions, and too easily satisfied with empty formulas—was breaking down. Pico cannot be understood without taking into account his particular position in this conflict. He belonged in truth to two worlds. Though formed in the most illustrious citadels of ancient knowledge, he was open to new tendencies and new methods. He came to argue in favor of tradition against renewal, but he did so in order to conclude with an attempt at conciliation that would salvage the conquests of the past—not what was commonplace but what could be taken up again in a more vital orientation of study.

His own youthful education was probably instrumental in forming Pico's role as a mediator. In Bologna, where his mother had joined him, he studied canonic law.[12] When he lost his mother in 1478, he went on, in 1479, to Ferrara, with a short stay in Florence.[13] We could call it a kind of rapid passage from the old university world to the most famous centers of humanism. Again, if we attempt to reconstruct from among the records and conjectures the human contacts of young Pico, we are struck by his function as a focal point of encounter between conflicting tendencies.[14] His friends and companions in Bologna, to whom he remained loyal, conserved their taste for student life; they were lighthearted, although they were famous scholars, and more inclined to discuss women and feasting than the problems of existence. The Florentines, even the most innocent like Girolamo Benivieni, caught up as they were in the great world of art, never lost sight of their city's heritage of civic values, political involvement, and religious seriousness.

The beginning of Pico's brotherly affection for Girolamo Savonarola (with whom he became acquainted early and whom he always loved) probably dates from these years. It was a decisive tie for both, and it may have marked the destinies of both. It was Pico, in fact, who induced Lorenzo de' Medici in 1489 to summon the great Dominican to Florence. It was also his adherence to Savonarola, perhaps, that induced his enemies, in the autumn of 1494, to have Savonarola poisoned by his secretary Cristoforo di Casalmaggiore. The two were men of very different temperaments, the learned philosopher and the friar, but they were united by an equal passion—by a kindred sense of the seriousness of life and the sacred value of the truth. They did not always travel the same road, but they were together in the fight against hypocrisy and lies, corruption and conscious error, and in the defense of the dignity of every man.[15]

Pico remained two years, from 1480 to 1482, in Padua, where he studied the bases of Aristotle's philosophy and his medieval, Greek, Arab, and Latin commentators. These were the years he was to remember always, years of long sleepless nights spent on the scholastic doctors. The eccentric Nicoletto Vernia taught at the university. He was a good Aristotelian but not very original, noted more for his odd ways and for a certain penchant for Averroism than for his soundness of thought. He passed into history with a reputation superior to his merit because of his entirely unorthodox theses on the soul and the subsequent sensational recantation he made rather readily to the bishop. Vernia, like other contemporary Aristotelian scholars, was essentially representative of the sterile decadence of a school whose technical refinements were not accompanied by any speculative vigor nor a passion for research.

Nor did Pico draw any major contributions from his acquaintance with Agostino Nifo, whom he entertained as a guest on his estate at Corbula; Nifo was a vain though celebrated professor. He was the author of innumerable works in which infinite erudition was joined with supreme speculative incompetence. A shadow of the fame that had surrounded him during his life remained after his death, due mainly to the great men whom he had flattered, slandered, and fought in vain.[16]

Elia del Medigo was a man of quite different substance: a Jewish scholar of profoundly religious bent, who translated philosophical texts for Pico from the Hebrew or summarized and discussed them. He furnished Pico with explicit information on cabalistic currents for which he personally had little sympathy, being a lover of clear thought and rational discourse. It is certain that Pico received from Elia his penchant, never abandoned, for Averroistic mysticism—for the idea of a conjunction of the human intellect with the absolute, achieved through knowledge.

Ermolao Barbaro was not in Padua at the time Pico was there. Later the two were to keep up close relations marked by harmonious disagreement. Barbaro was a Venetian patrician from a great family, at home with humanistic culture. Could one forget Francesco, the friend of the Florentine groups which had gathered around Salutati, or the solemn dignity and cultivation of the bishop of Verona? These were men who had been present at the baptism of the new Plato, clothed in the garments of an ancient prophet and surrounded by the austere grandeur of the aristocracy of the Venetian republic. In humanism they had recognized an ideal of life capable of transforming the sobriety of a profound wisdom into superbly elegant forms.

Pico asked something more of culture. He was more naive, if you like, but he was certainly more sound. He sought the truth, the secret of matter, the revelation of the mystery of life. Ermolao Barbaro was interested in Christ and classical literature; Giovanni Pico sought Christ and the truth—the meaning of the evangelical word according to which Christ is reason become man. Hence their first meeting was rather a shock. In the course of time their relationship was to become a fraternal dialogue, but it was never without some conflict. Pico never achieved Ermolao's lofty detachment, and Ermolao was never to feel the dramatic passion of Pico.

In a way the years at Padua concluded a painstaking formation. Not yet twenty, Pico possessed an unusually mature culture. At the same time he did not spurn love affairs, poetry, and student life. The testimony of friends, and even macaronic verse, depict him in the streets of the old university city as a rather formal but polite figure, with a certain solemnity even in youthful pranks, full of grace and dignity.[17]

If Elia del Medigo had introduced him to the more subtle seductions of the mysticism of Averroes, giving him a clearer idea of the complexity and wealth of Arab and Hebrew thought, the Greek Manuel Adramittenos taught him to seek the Greek Hellenic tradition in the authenticity of the originals. In 1482 Pico studied Ficino's Platonic theology. In 1484 he decided in favor of a sojourn in Florence. To cross the Appenines, to insert himself into the cultural climate of Florence in the last quarter of the century, was a major and difficult matter. It should be recalled that, at exactly the time Pico was discovering a homeland by choice on the banks of the Arno, Leonardo was going North. The artist was seeking between Milan and Pavia a more solid reality with more material substance, away from the Florentine delights—delights which, on the contrary, were to seduce Pico more and more.

Pico recalled this later in Bologna when he was making observations on the stars and celestial movements with his friend Beroaldo. In Florence he was fascinated by the Platonic and hermetic mysteries of Marsilio Ficino more than by the rigorous knowledge of Paolo Toscanelli. The conviction matured in him that the truth lay hidden beyond the secret of numbers: enigmatic languages were the heavens in which the glory of God was written—nature with its phenomena, and living beings; enigmas were the books in their variety of signs and tongues—the more obscure they were, the richer in promise. The mystery of reality, Pico wrote a little later, is guarded by the Sphinxes; it is hidden in the penetralia of a tomb whose entrance is sealed and barred to the unworthy. He was obsessed with the idea of finding the key capable of opening the door to the one and only truth, which in its infinite expressions is sometimes unveiled and sometimes hidden.

As a pupil of the great universities of the North—of Bologna, Padua, Pavia—he regarded Florence as a promised land. The philosophy and science of the northern schools were refined but sterile; they taught one how to discuss, but they were losing the sense problems in dialectical devices. In Florence there was no university; Lorenzo's cautious policy had relegated it to Pisa. In Florence were the Platonic circles in which philosophy was translated into images capable of rivaling those that were set on canvas and that issued without pause from the shops of the artisans. It is difficult to find anything in history that could come close to that remarkable alloy of image and concept, of reason and incarnation, of number and body, which the Florentines had by then achieved. It may sound rhetorical, but it is certain that Brunelleschi's cupola, like certain of Ficino's passages, succeed in rendering perfectly the sense, now of a huge corporeal mass which sufflates itself in its own reasons, now of a most subtle reason which translates everything into forms.

Ficino brought to full fruition the process that had been maturing from the time of Cosimo the Elder and the Council: the rebirth of a Christian Plato. He began with the allusive passages of the hermetic books that suddenly bloomed everywhere like a kind of miraculous revelation. He went on to integrate and comment on the texts of Plato, Plotinus, Porfirius, and the later writers down to Psellus, including the Emperor Julian.

The wave of the new philosophy spilled over from Florence into all Italy, and from Italy to Europe. It was limited frequently to beautiful passages, composed of ardent discussions on problems capable of stirring everyone: death and immortality, good and evil, love, the just state, the destiny of man, the secrets of nature. All this was set down, not in weighty tomes to be read only by experts, but in simple and human essays, in the dialogue initiated by Socrates with the artisans of the town squares and streets of Athens. Together with these essays, other works were circulated, composed of symbols, allusions, and metaphors. These were filled with the occult fascination of magical ceremonies and theurgic practices, rich in mysterious and subtle promises, and enveloped in the mystical halo of widespread religiosity. Under this halo, it seemed as though conflicts and differences could be resolved in a universal peace, while the idea of a world made up of numbers and secret harmonies deluded those who studied nature with the hope that they could conquer extraordinary powers.

The poetic philosophy of the courts, of groups and circles of learned nonprofessionals and of noble ladies, of academies that arose to compete with the universities thus came to oppose the difficult philosophy of the schools, insipid in its jargon and arid in its highly virtuoso logic—the philosophy of the professors who had nothing more to say, either to men who longed for spiritual comfort or to those who were seeking the truth of the real world. Looking at certain paintings or reading certain lyric poets of the Quattrocento and Cinquecento, one often recognizes clearly the passages of the Platonists; one never thinks of the quarrelsome disputes of the Aristotelian masters.

Between 1484 and 1485 Pico lived in this Florence, among poet-philosophers and philosopher-poets. He too discussed philosophy and poetry. He also wrote, as was the custom, and continued to write (at least until 1486) Latin poems and Italian verse. It appears that he burned part of them, despite the benevolently critical judgment of Politian. Whatever remains does not place him in the ranks of the great poets, on the subject either of love or of religion. Many of the sonnets are no more than exercises; not a few of the Latin verses frankly reveal the model imitated. However, at little more than twenty years of age Pico succeeded at times in evoking the halo of melancholy that envelops first loves and a somewhat bitter sense of the incomprehensibility of life. At times he almost seemed to have a presentiment of his destiny; happy is he who dies young, he wrote; happy is he who dies in the morning: "to complete our day then is better than to await the evening."[18]

Later, after the dramatic years, a great scholar who came to visit him from France recalled that once Pico had been suddenly overcome with emotion and had wept after listening to music. A dark sense of the end and of naught already permeated his youthful existence. With all this, Pico was no poet, at least not in verse; if at all, then in some great page of prose whose high rhetoric appears to attain the summit of formal art.

On the subject of Pico's his first long stay in Florence, two famous letters, writen in 1484 and 1485, are worthy of note. The first was to Lorenzo on the subject of poetry. It is slightly adulatory and is important for its opinions on Dante and Petrarch. The second, to Ermolao Barbaro on the relationship between philosophy and beautiful style, is an epoch-making document, which in a certain sense constitutes an unforgettable reaction against the grammatical preoccupations of literary humanism and its rhetorical degeneration. Ermolao Barbaro sought beautiful passages even in the books of thinkers. Pico looked only for civic, moral, intellectual, and religious values. The words of the Bible, he wrote, are simple, at times crude but alive, animated, flaming, incisive, and capable of transforming men. Socrates's speeches were bereft of adornment, he said, but Alcibiades preferred them, and rightly so, to the great orations of Pericles. The philosopher does not desire the gardens of the Muses; he seeks the famous cave in which the truth lies hidden. These were very same words used by Leonardo da Vinci.[19]

Here was a rebellion against humanistic refinement, a movement of scornful impatience. Pico went from Florence to Paris in the summer of 1485—to the Sorbonne, the citadel of theology and of the "Parisian style," sharp and spiny, but still solid. He soon returned, in March of 1486; too much dialectical jousting and linguistic severity prevailed at the Sorbonne. The men who were his friends, like Robert Gaguin, were turning toward humanism.

Back again in Florence, he defined the goal of his research and applied himself feverishly to tumultuous projects. He was twenty-three. He had discovered the cabalistic books, bought them, and had them translated by that extraordinary figure Flavio Mitridate, who was as temperamental as he was learned and who lived a disorderly, complicated life. Pico really believed that the texts of the cabala contained the *other* revelation—the mysterious and secret one through which, for the initiates, it was possible not only to secure the key to reality, but also to find the method for reducing all faiths, all doctrines, all languages of the Lord to one unity. The cabalistic method, according to him, would have resolved every problem and have brought all research to an end. If all is the Word of God; if the stars in heaven and the elements, the phenomena of life and the voices of nature, the senses of men and their concepts are letters of the Lord; if the various religions are the way in which different peoples have translated the one divine summons; whoever then learns the alphabet of God, in the correlation of letters and numbers, will find not only the common root of things and hence of universal science, but also the foundation of the harmony between religions and philosophies. The eye of the sage will eventually discover the hidden harmonies between the different levels of being, between the heavens and the earth, between man and the world, and he will be able to make himself understood by all peoples and all material things by coordinating the natural forces and drawing the living closer together. Situated from that time on at the magic meeting point of the infinite lines that converge toward the infinite, he will truly be at the center of the cosmos.

It is easy to guess how much soothsaying and magic operated in Pico's mind: turbid dreams of the most impenetrable past and happy intuitions of the future were strangely combined in him. But at the same time, fruitful aspirations animated him. What had been the great dream of the Cardinal of Cusa glowed in Pico's heart: peace among men, religious harmony. A vision of philosophical research that would placate divergencies, that would be capable of integrating the various conceptions then contested, was taking shape before his eyes: Plato and Aristotle, Averroes and Avicenna, Saint Thomas and Duns Scotus. He was discovering the sense of man and his central position in the universe, as well as a knowledge that could become operative and dynamic. Over all was the sense of unity, of love as a force uniting matter and men.

These were months of impassioned, almost inspired, work: the philosophy of love, poetic theology, the harmony of doctrines, a universal synthesis of knowledge, the dignity of man. A bold project was maturing by which he hoped to render his own meditation effective. He planned to propose a meeting of scholars who would convene at his expense from all over Italy in Rome to discuss publicly a number of propositions or theses, arguments and theories, in order to verify his ideas and put them into practice. He would then have his theses printed and disseminated in all the schools. The convention was scheduled to take place after Epiphany in the year 1487.

Pico, despite his untiring research, was no savage recluse. He did not forego friends and festivities, women and feasts. The most sensational episode of his life occurred just at the time when he was preparing the great Roman meeting. While he was visiting relatives near Arezzo, in May 1486, he attempted to abduct the beautiful Margherita, wife of Giuliano di Mariotto de' Medici, of a far-removed and penniless branch of the Medici family. The affair was much discussed for a long time, and its reverberations are conserved in solemn texts. In one of the manuscripts of Cardinal Egidius of Viterbo, now at the Biblioteca Angelica, the gossip in connection with this scandal is dwelt on with such malevolence that it almost appears as though the Cardinal intended to discredit even Pico's doctrines.[20]

It is worthwhile to follow the affair in the official dispatches and diplomatic correspondence. From the notes of one of the Este orators, Aldovrandino Guidoni, we know that Margherita was widowed in 1486 and that her husband had been a certain Costante Speciale, a fairly wealthy man who bred racehorses. Soon after his death she had remarried Giuliano di Mariotto, an exciseman of no means in Arezzo. She was, it seems, already "enamored" with Pico. What is certain is that on 16 May, when the count was on his way to Rome, the lady, who had attended mass accompanied by a footman and a child, was lifted to a horse and carried away, by Pico and his brigade of twenty, in the direction of the Sienese border. It is diverting to reread the various versions given in the dispatches; for some it was abduction, for others an escape. Guidoni was not the only one to write to Ercole d'Este that Margherita "was inflamed with love for the count" and mounted the horse on her own initiative. Luigi della Stuffa also explained to the Magnificent that the lady, "enamored and blinded by such a fine figure of a man, voluntarily" followed him. It is certain that they were seen. The tocsin was rung. The captain of Arezzo assembled more than two hundred armed men. Eighteen of Pico's relatives were apparently either wounded or killed, the lady was recaptured, and Pico and his secretary, Cristoforo di Casalmaggiore, were saved only "due to the sturdy legs of the horses" but were overtaken in Marciano.

The magistrates of Arezzo immediately declared to Lorenzo that they considered the event an offense against the entire people. Giuliano was mainly distraught at the loss of eighty-four florins, and he immediately took back his beautiful, rich wife, who, in his words, had been badly deceived. According to Costanza Bentivoglio, Pico's sister-in-law, it was Giovanni who had been seduced; the "woman followed him willingly," she said. Francesco Baroni was of the opinion that Pico had lost his reputation; Guidoni concluded that "although similar mistakes had been committed by many who were inflamed by Venus," the count, previously regarded as a saint, in the eyes of many had become a Lucifer.[21]

When the incident had died down, due to the Magnificent's intervention, Pico retired to Umbria. Later, in October, he wrote of his repentance in veiled terms to a friend; he compared his temptations with those of the Anchorites and proposed to lead a life that would erase the memory of his guilt.[22] During stops at Perugia and Fratta he wrote a commentary on a song by Benivieni, competing with Ficino's Italian treatise on the philosophy of love of no little importance. He established the theses to be discussed in Rome, whose number grew from seven hundred to nine hundred. He drafted a major commentary on Plato's *Symposium*. He wrote the opening address to the Roman convention, the famous "oration on the dignity of man," one of the noblest works of Quattrocento thought, which was never published or disseminated during his lifetime.

The theses appeared on 7 December in Silber print, and immediately provoked a scandal. Many of Pico's affirmations sounded dubious to Roman circles, and the count's entire project must have appeared suspect.[23] It was indeed easy to accuse this young man of little over twenty of vanity and frivolity—even Pico's friends did so. His aim was to announce publicly in Rome, before a large assemblage of scholars, the harmony of the philosophies and of all doctrines; he planned to speak with enthusiasm of the cabala and magic, quoting authorities that were (to say the least) doubtful as well as many pagan thinkers, both ancient and modern.

Stirrings of religious unrest were frequent during these years, and extraordinary events had been attributed to those same mysterious writers to whom Pico appealed. A strange hermetic rite celebrated by Giovanni da Correggio on Palm Sunday, 1484, had astonished the Romans. On 4 July 1486, the same Este orator who a short while before had described Pico's adventures in Arezzo communicated to the Duke Ercole that "Giovanni da Correggio, known as Mercurio and the latest prophet," had already been investigated as a heretic by the inquisition in Bologna; that, dear to the king of France, he had come to Florence for Easter and had remained there with letters from the king and under the protection of Lorenzo de' Medici, notwithstanding the fact that he had been arrested in July as a heretic, exposed to the public in chains by the Inquisitor of Florence, threatened with death on the stake, and as a consequence had attempted to commit suicide.[24]

The hermetic ideas of Giovanni da Correggio, though crudely expressed, were circulating in the environment of Ficino and Pico and in the same circles, linked as they were with the curiosity for fascinating and prolix subjects. Even more suspicious was the talk of the cabala, the Platonism, and those oriental mysteries. The discussion in Rome was suspended on 20 February 1487, and a breve of Innocent VIII deferred the "conclusions" to the examination of a commission of theologists and jurists. The panel emphasized their captious obscurity, the novelty of the terms which had never been heard, and their equivocal character. Pico's explanations were judged insufficient; seven of his propositions were condemned on 5 March, and six of the rest were declared of doubtful orthodoxy.

Then came the drama. In a breve dated 6 June the philosopher was accused of not having awaited the pontifical decision, of having written new texts, and of having sought the support of imprudent theologians. The Pope initiated a process against Pico for heresy. The condemnation was pronounced on 5 August: the conclusions "are in part heretical, in part they savor of heresy; some are scandalous and offensive to pious ears; the majority repeat the errors of pagan philosophers. . . ; others are intended to encourage the obstinacy of the Jews; lastly, many disguised as natural philosophy aim to favor arts that are inimical to the Catholic faith and to the human race."

Despite the fact that the records of the trial have been rediscovered, it is difficult to establish from them the basis of certain accusations against Pico. The accusations are also hard to ascertain from the gossip gathered on the spot by Florentine ambassador Giovanni Lanfredini; the ambassador kept Lorenzo, who was anxious about the fate of his friend, informed. The *Apologia*, written effortlessly in twenty nights, in which the philosopher forcefully defended himself, often accusing his judges of ignorance, is dated the end of May. Was it printed at the end of May, or was it instead printed "in a grotto at Naples" and back-dated, as the Pope accused (according to Lanfredi's report)? Was the condemnation itself published immediately or was it made known only on 15 December, as Pico claimed? What was the true sequence of events? On 31 July Pico had submitted under oath to the decisions of the commission. Two of the commissioners who had upheld him, Jean Cordier and Jean de Myrle, later did the same. How did his subsequent rebellion, which aroused the Pope's indignation, manifest itself?[25]

In January Pico left Rome for France, perhaps in order to seek the support of his friends at the Sorbonne. Jean de Myrle publicly pointed out that among the theses that had been condemned were some upheld at the Sorbonne. It was then that Innocent VIII made public the condemnation of Pico, of the *Tesi,* and of the *Apologia,* and proclaimed the order for his immediate arrest. On 16 December the injunction was transmitted to the Grand Inquisitor Torquemada in Spain, on the assumption that Pico would look for refuge there. On 19 January Lorenzo de' Medici sent a dispatch to Innocent showing great concern: "I am advised that there are papal bulls and all sorts of persecutions [in preparation] for the Lord Count Giovanni della Mirandola." He admonished the Pope not to cede to his passions and not to make "some great scandal in the church of God." "Learned and religious persons" in Florence had read the *Apologia,* he wrote, and had found nothing reprehensible in it.[26]

Events were developing precipitously. Having escaped capture in Lucca, Pico was arrested near Lyons by Philip of Savoy, the Lord of Bresse. The order for arrest, which was also valid for lay authorities since it concerned a recidivous heretic, had been transmitted by the pontifical nuncios in France—Lionello Chierigato, Bishop of Traù, and Antonio Fleres—who then continued on their way to Paris. Pico was to be transported later to the fortress of Vincennes and held there. Just before his arrest he had burned his books and papers.

The affair had repercussions all over Europe: at the Sorbonne, at the court, in the parliament of Paris. The ambassador of Milan requested Pico's immediate release; when this was refused, since it was a question of heresy, he threatened to have it appealed to the court of parliament. The king and his royal council, as well as some members of parliament and not a few at the Sorbonne, sided with the philosopher. After delicate temporizing with the papal nuncios, who wanted to have the prisoner transferred to Rome; after the Bishop of Paris had solemnly published the breve of condemnation; after the *Apologia* was banned in France; after subtle negotiations by Lorenzo, until now overlooked by historians; after all this, Pico was liberated (his imprisonment at Vincennes had lasted about a month) and expelled. But he was provided with a safe conduct by the "most Christian king," and was the object of universal sympathy. Eventually even the nuncios sympathized; they recommended Pico's good faith to the Pope and pointed out the advisability of avoiding a scandal. In Turin, on 30 May 1488, while he was considering a trip to Germany to see the Cusan's library, Pico received a letter from Ficino, who invited him in the name of Lorenzo to come to Florence. In Florence he was to spend the last years of his short life.[27]

"Two days ago, while I was riding horseback outside Florence, I met by chance the Count of Mirandola, who has been living befittingly in the surrounding country, and who applies himself diligently to study," Lorenzo the Magnificent wrote, on 11 August 1488, to the orator in Rome. He wrote in order that the orator might intervene with the Pope, who, Lorenzo advised, should stop listening to the slander of others.[28] Pico lived as a good Christian and studied; and his works were not those of a heretic.

This was the beginning of an extensive correspondence from Lorenzo to Lanfredini; it continued for about a year and a half, defending Lorenzo's friend Pico against intrigues and attempting to obtain an honorable pardon for him and the peace of meditation. It is an important historical episode, which as yet has not been completely written—at times punctuated by expressions of warm friendship and at times by the echo of a deep conflict of ideas. There were matters on which Pico would not compromise. However strong his faith and sincere his sense of obedience, his adherence to certain principles was equally firm. When he learned that someone in Rome was preparing a book against him, he rebelled and announced that he would answer. The Magnificent wrote with fraternal affection; he added postscripts of unusual warmth in his own hand to the letters to Giovanni Lanfredini: "Giovanni, I beg you, as much as possible . . . these things with the Count I do not consider less than if they concerned my own person." When the ambassador insisted that this was a case of heresy, the Medici exploded indignantly, observing that Innocent was no Sixtus and that famous theologians had not discovered errors in Pico.

Despite all this, the Pope remained adamant and transmitted a sarcastic reply to the Lord of Florence. It is one thing, he said, to make one's own son a cardinal, but it is something quite different to absolve a heretic: "Lorenzo writes so much about the religion and the exemplary conduct of the Count, I doubt that Lorenzo is not deceiving himself. But anyone who wishes to deceive himself may do so. I intend not to deceive myself, and Lorenzo should take care not to let himself be swayed by these heresies."[29]

The absolution did not come from Innocent VIII. It was conceded by Alexander VI on 18 June 1493,[30] after Lorenzo, whose affection for Pico had never been shaken, had died. Lorenzo had ordered books from the Vatican library for Pico, claiming he wanted them for himself. He helped him obtain a permit to reside in the city. In order to please Pico, he welcomed Savanarola to Florence. As he was dying, he asked to have Pico one more time at his side.

The last years of Giovanni Pico's life, from the summer of 1488 to his death, were marked by a new austerity, a more solemn overtone. He continued his studies, and he in no way altered the substance of his concepts. But he was more self-contained, more cautious. His religious conversion, which was profound, brought him ever closer to Savonarola, although he never identified his work, which was that of an intellectual, with that of the Dominican, which was first and foremost moral and political.

Pico did not feel close to the fullness of the time. For him the new century, that of spiritual peace and of the reunification of peoples, must come through the enlightenment of minds paralleled with a reform of customs and the scientific refutation of errors. The first mistakes to be overcome were for him errors of the intellect: false sciences and erroneous interpretations of the books of the Lord—that is, the wrong reading of the book of revelation and the book of nature. Savonarola proceeded with ever greater force to announce the imminent new century and worked simultaneously for a reform of the religious customs and structures of Florence, the new Jerusalem; Pico fought for the destruction of spurious sciences and for a correct interpretation of the Scriptures and of nature. His activity was that of a commentator on the one hand and of a polemist on the other, even though in his battle he felt himself entirely on the side of Savonarola and increasingly detached from the Medicean and Ficinian circle.

He continued his study of Hebrew with the noted scholar Jochanan Alemanno. He commented on the *Psalms*[31] and at the same time on the beginning of the *Genesis*, the verses on the creation. From this work issued the *Heptaplus* dedicated in 1489 to Lorenzo. This work best expresses Pico's cabalistic tendency; in it his vision of reality is most organically composed, in its order, in the correspondences of its levels, in its view of man the nexus and the ideal center of creation.

Pico had tempered the vehemence of his *Apologia;* the acceptance of natural magic, the idea of man as understanding nature and active in nature, are quietly inserted in a context that harks back to patristic and scholastic literature on the divine work of the six days—conserving its noble language, full of biblical intonations, but also containing a thread of rigorous logic. The commentary on the *Psalms,* however, remained uncompleted. It was in part dispersed, and the material gathered was possibly used by others who had access to his books and papers.

Of his major work on the harmony of the philosophies, nothing remains but an essay, *sull' Essere e sull' Uno,* which appeared in 1491. Pico's most speculatively subtle work, it was dedicated to Politian and was later interpreted in a broad discussion by a famous Aristotelian, Antonio Cittadini of Faenza, a professor at the most celebrated Italian universities. Here Pico was engaged in his most important metaphysical effort, a conceptual analysis tied with the new reading of Plato, Plotinus, Proclus, and Avicenna. Unfortunately, the great discussion on the significance of the various philosophical traditions is missing.

This work constituted the ultimate point in the erosion of the idea of a sole authority in philosophy and of the privileged position of Aristotle. Pico saw clearly the conclusive importance of the new historical awareness, which became predominant in the fifteenth century. His premature death cut short his attempt at a critical systematization. Fortunately, it did not prevent the near completion of his work attacking sibylline astrology, which was to become the first part of an extensive investigation with the aim of distinguishing between rigorous scientific research and pseudoscience. Not enough can be said of the methodological value and the basic repercussions of the book. If it is true that Pico also gathered results already understood by scholastic masters, it is also true that he broadened these and coordinated them into a new awareness of problems and research. Many passages of this last work stand not only at the threshold of new science, new logic, and new methods of research, but also, as Savonarola believed, on the threshold of a more serious and more felt religious experience.[32]

In the last years of his life Pico's moral and religious quests appear more thoughtful; they have the old passion, but with a new depth.[33] The most elevated and sincere, the most vital and liberal figures of the sixteenth century, from Erasmus to Thomas More, found in Pico's last writings a kindred soul. The great letters to his nephew Gian Francesco, whom he loved as a son and whom he wanted to be his heir, were circulated in Europe and translated into the national languages by some of the most important men of the time: Thomas More in England, Robert Gaguin in France, Jacob Wimpheling in the German-speaking countries.[34]

Thomas More declared that the life of the young count was a model to be followed. "A great philosopher and a good theologian," Gaguin said, whose edifying pages should be read and reread as a vital nourishment. First-rate scholars could not elude his influence. Serious thinkers like Lefèvre d'Etaples turned to him as to an oracle. Pico had seen the men closest to him die: Lorenzo de' Medici, Ermolao Barbaro, and Angelo Politian. The storm predicted by Savonarola was then gathering over Florence. As Leonardo Salviati wrote, destiny intended that Pico die on the day when foreign troops were entering the city which had become his fatherland. His last will is laden with significance. He left his money to the hospital Santa Maria Nuova and his body (clad in a Dominican habit, just like his Savonarola) to San Marco.

His works were in large part collected and published through the devotion of his nephew. The future historian, however, must still investigate (in addition to the details of his life) the exact fate of the notes and drafts: how many of these went to lend vigor to the works of Gian Francesco; how many of Pico's plans were put into practice; how many others were served by his work? The extent of Pico's presence in the consciousness of learned Europe from 1500 on remains to be ascertained. It was very broad and frequently unsuspecting among scientists, philosophers, men of action; in great religious consciences; in diverse times, from the Cinquecento to the Ottocento; in the most diverse and opposite forms, but always as a vital ferment.

At least one of his writings is among the great works of all time: the oration on human dignity. It was written to be presented formally at the Roman convention. It was printed after his death, at the end of the century. It did not circulate while he was still living, and only one manuscript copy of the draft is extant. It contains few pages, but these stamp an epoch which, though past, is forever present. It appeals for peace among doctrines, harmony among beliefs. It speaks of the continuity and the convergence of human efforts toward the light; it takes note of man's importance in the world and of his singular and troubling vocation.

The pronouncement of the Lord to Adam has not been dimmed by time, Pico wrote. Man's value resides in his responsibility, in his freedom. Man is the only being of the reality who chooses his own destiny; he alone carries out history and frees himself from the conditions of nature; he dominates nature. He alone is the son of his own works. The conscious image of man, which is characteristic of the modern world, was born here: man exists in the act that constitutes him, he exists in the possibility of liberating himself. In this concept is an implicit condemnation of every oppression, of every slavery, of every conditioning. Here, along with the evangelism of peace, is expressed the evangelism of the radical freedom of man.[35]

It is not coincidental that, as a Dutch scholar observed not so long ago, Pico's writings reemerged from the past as most current, after the 1930s, in all of Europe. They were reedited, translated, and commented on as a new barbarity threatened to submerge the world.[36]

Historians and philosophers can continue to discuss medieval and modern Pico, his science and his faith. In times of tragedy men have sought in him the profound theoretician and the eloquent defender of a just peace among men and of freedom as the constitutive structure of man.

Notes

1. Des. Erasmi Roterodami, P. S. Allen, ed., *Opus Epistolarum* (Oxford, 1910), 2: 350 (letter no. 471 to John Reuchlin). See also (same work) 5: 237 (letter 1347, to Jodocus Gaverius): "Pico della Mirandola and Angelo Politian (the glory of their age) died when they were still young."

2. State Archives of Florence, Arch. Leonetti-Mannucci-Gianni, ms. 43, c. 35 (from the life of Girolamo Benivieni, written by Antonio Benivieni, the younger): " . . . on the occasion of his first discussion, which, as Girolamo related it, was on the subject of types of weapons, for whose use, it seemed to the count, still imbued with those gentlemanly concepts of lords, Piacentini, and other Lombards, Florence, an industrious and mercantile country, had no regard; but Girolamo, who could not tolerate this city being outclassed in any honorable profession, discoursed even more about Florence in these first talks with the count. . . . "

3. For the dates of birth and death, see also the horoscope in ms. 46 of Arch. Leonetti-Mannucci-Gianni (State Archives of Florence). On his life, the most remarkable source is the biography of his grandson Gian Francesco, which predates the editions of the works (which are quoted here in sequence), according to the Basle printing of 1572. (Other sources are quoted in Garin, *Giovanni Pico Della Mirandola* [Florence, 1937], p. 3, nos. 1 and 2).

4. André Chastel has written very competently about the different "tones" of the Florentine cultural world in *Art et humanisme à Florence au temps de Laurent le Magnifique* (Paris, 1959). Specifically on Pico, see pp. 51 sqq., 85 sqq., 104 sqq., 191 sqq., and 198 sqq.

5. On Pico's primary education and on his first work ("an oration of thanks"), see *Elogio al Principe Giovanni Pico . . del Padre Lettore Riccardo Bartoli* (Guastalla, 1791), pp. 57–65. A description of Pico just after he was born may be found in a letter written to him by Giorgio Merula (published by the well-known Vat. Capp. 235, f. 43, in L. Dorez, "Lettres inédites de Jean Pic de la Mirandole, 1482–1492," *Giornale Storico della Letteratura Italiana* (GSLI) 25(1895): 356–57): "It was about twenty years ago when, on my way to Bologna, I made a detour to Mirandola, to pay my respects to Peter of Calabria, who was then teaching there and who later became a judge. Your mother, Giulia, welcomed me with exceeding kindness; your father was then off to the wars in Calabria and Apulia, serving in the pay of Piccinino [Niccolò, 1375–1444, a condottiere], and your brothers were absent. While we sat at the dinner table, your nurse brought you over in your swaddling clothes and, between the kisses and caresses of your mother, when your sisters quoted I don't remember which of the epigrams of Martial, the nurse jokingly asked,

'What if this child should fancy letters more than arms?' How right she was, that nurse of yours!"

On Pico's first trip to Ferrara, see the detailed description of Raffaele da Volterra, *Commentariorum Urbanorum octo et triginta libri* (Basle, 1544), p. 246*v*: "On a trip to Ferrara in the company of the Cardinal of Aragon, the papal legate, I saw there this youth, who, although yet a novice, was clad in the robes of a protonotary and, to the profound admiration of the audience, was engaged in a debate with Leonardo Nugarolo." The less quoted reminiscence of Rome is no less interesting (p. 247*r*): "A few years later, I saw him again in Rome. He had given up the priesthood, and he was attired then in a nobleman's silk clothes, wearing a neckchain. There, his teaching, including some of his propositions judged not quite acceptable by the school of Paris and rejected at the behest of Pope Innocent, was vindicated." A record of his stay in the cities indicated above is contained in the correspondence and memoirs of contemporaries.

6. Two copies remain extant of the inventory of Pico's famous library, which was left to San Marco in Florence, then inherited by his brother Anton Maria, bought by Domenico Grimani, passed on to the Convent of San Antonio in Castello in Venice, and finally dispersed. One copy, dated 1498, which lists 1,190 volumes, is contained in the archives of Modena, and a later one is contained in a Cinquecento ms. of the Vatican (Vat. 3436). The inventory of 1498 was drawn up by Antonio Pizamano, a Dominican, a friend of Pico and Politian, and a representative of Grimani. It was published by F. Calori Cesis in an appendix to his *Giovanni Pico della Mirandola*, entitled "Memorie storiche della città e dell' Antico Ducato della Mirandola" (Mirandola, 1897), 6: 32–76 (on which see the review by R. Renier, *GSLI* 31(1898): 127–31). An excellent illustrated copy of the Vatican inventory was published by Pearl Kibre in the work *The Library of Pico della Mirandola* (New York, 1936), pp. 119–297. Useful references may be found in the essay by Th. Freudenberger, "Die Bibliothek des Kardinal Domenico Grimani," *Historisches Jahrbuch* 1936, pp. 15–45. The volume of Giovanni Mercati, *Codici Latini Pio Grimani Pico* (Vatican City, 1938), is especially valuable; it retraces Pico's codices which finally ended up in the Vatican.

7. On Elia del Medigo and his importance, see U. Cassuto, *Gli Ebrei a Firenze nell'età del Rinascimento* (Florence, 1918), pp. 284 sqq., and J. Dukas, *Recherches sur l'histoire littéraire du Xème siècle,* (Paris, 1876). Elia translated for Pico the *Summa Averrois in libro metheororum* (the ms. is in the Vatican 4550, with the dedication and footnotes in Pico's handwriting, on which see G. Mercati, *Codici,* pp. 34–35), published in 1488 by Andrea Torresano in Venice, and dedicated to Grimani (*IGI,* 1108); he also translated the *Quaestio Averrois in librum primum* (15 July 1485, Florence), conserved in Vat. lat. 4552, with copious notes by Pico (and printed by Aldo Manuzio in 1497). He compiled an *Expositio Averrois de substantia orbis,* contained in the autograph sent to Pico (Vat. lat. 4553) and written in 1486 ("I completed the exposition in Bassano, on the fifth day of October, 1486, according to the Roman calendar, having begun it after taking leave of aforesaid noble lord [Pico], who was then

residing in the resplendent city of Florence, on the fourth day of September of the same year, after promising him that I would get it done"). Elia's *Liber de proprietatibus elementorum,* a *Tractatus de intellectu speculativo,* and a treatise *de partibus animalium,* again with notes by Pico, are contained in Vat. lat. 4559 (interrupted at tr. 14). Elia also composed for Pico "in the year 1485, according to the Roman calendar, at the end of July, in Florence," in the *Annotationes in dictis Averois super libros physicorum* ("The Most Illustrious Lord, Count Giovanni della Mirandola, having expressed the desire to possess some . . . , I could not possibly refuse him. He is, indeed, a man of profound wisdom, with a natural bent for true philosophy or, rather, I might say, that in him we have a most noteworthy philosopher . . . "). In the same period he wrote a *Quaestio de esse et essentia et uno* ("When I was in Perugia in the company of the learned count, the gracious Lord Giovanni della Mirandola, the renowned philosopher, we spoke much about Being, about Essence, and about Oneness . . . to all of which I could contribute but little myself . . ."). These last two works were frequently republished in the Cinquecento as an appendix to the commentary on the *Fisica* by Giovanni di Jandun, together with a *Quaestio de primo motore* compiled by Girolamo Donato ("who once, during his student years in Padua, had convincingly argued this issue in public"), in which the discussions on the argument with Pizzamano and Grimani are included ("as we discussed it in those days with the most distinguished doctors, the gracious Lord Antonio Pizzamano and Lord Domenico Grimani"); it follows a *Quaestio de mundi efficientia,* which is dated 1480, Venice. An important letter from Elia to Pico (at the time of the Roman disputation), including references to cabalistic texts, is conserved in the Latin ms. of the Bibl. Nat. of Paris 6508 (folio 75 is reproduced in the edition of writings edited by Garin [Florence, 1942]; the text is on pp. 67–72).

8. On the complex and somewhat enigmatic figure of Flavio Mitridate, who is to be identified with the converted Jew Guglielmo Raimondo da Moncada, see R. Starrabba, *Ricerche storiche su Guglielmo Raimondo Moncada, ebreo convertito siciliano del secolo XV*, taken from the "Archivio Storico Siciliano," N.S. 3(1878): 15–91 (which does not identify Moncada with Mitridate and follows him only until 1483); U. Cassuto, *Gli ebrei* etc., pp. 299 sqq.; and U. Cassuto, "Wer war der Orientalist Mithridates?" *Zeitschrift für die Geschichte der Juden in Deutschland* 5(1934): 230–36. Very important for the chronology of the relationship between Mitridate and Pico is the letter from Rodolfo Agricola to Adolf Rusch of Heidelberg, 13 April, 1485 (K. Hartfelder, *Unedierte Briefe von Rudolf Agricola. Ein Beitrag zur Geschichte des Humanismus,* "Festschrift der Badischen Gymnasien gewidmet der Universität Heidelberg zur Feier ihres 500 jährigen Jubiläums," [Karlsruhe, 1886], p. 32): "It is the eminent Guglielmo Raimondo who returned to you those writings of mine; if my memory serves me right, it was he about whom I spoke to you at Worms and of whom I then said I had heard that he had been teaching in Louvain and that thereafter he had gone on to teach in Cologne, but that he had left there to go to Italy. . . . Apart from being an accomplished linguist in Latin, Greek, Hebrew, Chaldean, Arabic and I do not know

how many other languages, he is, moreover, a scholarly theologian, philosopher, and poet, and, in sum, he is one in all and all in one. . . ." His works and translations for Montefeltro (translations of astrological texts and of the *Koran*) are in Vat. Urb. lat. 1384. For the translations of Hebraic texts for Pico (the commentary on the Psalms of Gerson and the *de resurrectione mortuorum* of Maimonides), contained in Vat. lat. 4273 with some unusual statements by Mitridate, see Mercati, *Codici*, pp. 22–23. The translation of the cabalistic book *Bahir*, completed in 1486 for Pico, is contained in Vat. ebr. 191 (on which, besides Mercati, see G. Scholem, *Ursprung und Anfänge der Kabbala* [Berlin, 1962], p. 42). On the complex question of the three cabalistic codices translated by Mitridate for Pico and described by J. Gaffarel, see *Codicum Cabalistorum Manuscriptorum, quibus est usus Joannes Picus . . . Index* (Paris, 1651). On whether they correspond or not to the three Vat. ebr. 189–91, see M. Steinschneider, "Jochanan Alemanno, Flavius Mithridates und Pico della Mirandola," *Hebr. Bibl.* 21(1881): 109–115, 130–32; Th. Freudenberger, "Die Bibliothek," pp. 35 sqq.; and G. Mercati, *Codici*, pp. 22–23.

After the break the name of Mitridate comes up again in relationship to Pico in a letter written by the secretary of the count to the chancellor of Lorenzo, after his return from France, with regard to "various books" which "a Guilelmo Mitridate" had in Viterbo (D. Berti, "Intorno a Giovanni Pico della Mirandola. Cenni e documenti inediti," from *Rivista Contemporanea* 16(1859): 32). In addition to the document published by Berti, there is a letter of request from Lorenzo to Lanfredini dated 28 March 1489 (State Archives of Florence, MAP, file 51, no. 445) in which he asks for "the books of Mitridates." Finally, in the *Carteggio umanistico di Alessandro Farnese*, published by A. Frugoni (Florence, 1940), pp. 39–41, we find a second letter, from which we learn that in 1489 Moncada was a public professor at Viterbo, that he was a friend of Gregorio da Spoleto, and that he requested the Florentine edition of his *de Machabeis*.

9. On Jochanan Alemanno, his stay in Florence, and his works, see J. Perles, "Les Savants Juifs à Florence à l'époque de Laurent de Médicis," *Revue des études Juives* 12(1886): 245–48, and primarily U. Cassuto, *Gli Ebrei*, pp. 301 sqq.

10. For his expenses for cabalistic books, see *Opera*, p. 178 ("books I acquired at tremendous cost").

11. "Visiting not only the schools of letters in Italy but also those of France," according to his grandson. In Italy he frequented Bologna (1477–78), Ferrara (1479), Padua (1480–82). In France he stopped only in Paris, although Alessandro Cortesi, writing to him in 1487, says that while travelling through the Provence, along roads already taken by Pico, he heard talk of the count everywhere (the letter is published by Vat. Capp. 235, f. 35, in L. Dorez and L. Thuasne, *Pic de la Mirandole en France (1484–1488)* [Paris, 1897], pp. 106–08).

12. Gian Francesco records that "when he [Pico] was in his fourteenth year he did in fact go up to Bologna to study law, in deference to his mother,

who so ardently wished him to take the sacred vows; but having applied himself to it for two full years . . . he turned to another subject." And yet he had already compiled " . . . from the papal epistles, called Decretals, a compendium or breviary, . . . no mean accomplishment."

13. Pico asked of the Marquis of Mantua on 14 April 1479 that he be permitted to travel freely across his territory in order to go to Ferrara to the Studio where he would like to remain "four or five years." At the end of May, he was in Ferrara (F. Ceretti, *Giulia Boiardo*, "Atti e memorie delle RR. Depp. di Storia Patria per le prov. dell' Emilia," N.S., 6, 1(1881): 225). A sojourn in Florence in 1479 is confirmed by the correspondence with Politian and by the poetic testimony of Benivieni (see Garin, *G. Pico*, pp. 5–6). Pleona, Misona, Delia, and Floria, who meet during the seventh eclogue of Benivieni are, in the author's commentary, "various figments of his imagination" (abominations, superabundance, moral virtues, justice), even though there probably is an echo here of less abstract loves.

14. In an attempt to reconstruct Pico's relations with various groups and circles, I have sought to order his correspondence, taking into account not only what has been published by him and to him, but also the not inconsiderable unpublished material, a part of which I uncovered in the expectation of being able to complete the publication of his entire correspondence (see *La cultura filosofica del Rinascimento Italiano* [Florence, 1961], pp. 254–76). I will publish another "contribution" shortly.

15. For some aspects of the relations between Savonarola and Pico, see Crinito's texts (*De honesta disciplina*, 3: 2, 5: 1, 8: 3, referred to in the edition cited of Pico's writings, pp. 79–84). For reverberations of the meetings of San Marco, see Leonardo Salviati, *De' dialoghi d'amicizia* (Florence, 1564).

16. For this part, so far as Vernia is concerned, see also P. Ragnisco, "Documenti inediti e rari intorno alla vita ed agli scritti di Nicoletto Vernia e di Elia del Medigo," taken from *Atti e Memorie della R. Accademia . . . di Padova* 6(1891). Nifo's references to Pico are collected in the volume of Pico's writings edited by Garin (Florence, 1942), pp. 84–86. So far as Corbula is concerned, in which the conversation with Pico mentioned by Nifo took place (Garin, *G. Pico*, p. 84), this concerned the land and the Ferrarese residence, of which the grandson speaks in the biography ("purchasing land in order to draw sustenance for himself and his family, he bought himself property in Corbula, in the countryside of Ferrara, paying several thousand gold pieces for it"), and of which there is already a mention in a letter of 1483 from Ferrara to the Duke Ercole, published by Calori Cesis ("they gave me one of their properties in Corbola, which bordered on mine, and without which it would be impossible for me to raise cattle"). On Pico's thought concerning Averroism, and on Pico and Nifo, the passages of Bruno Nardi are essential (*Sigieri di Brabante nel pensiero del Rinascimento Italiano* [Rome, 1945], pp. 159–70); see also "La mistica averroistica e Pico della Mirandola" in the volume *Saggi sull' aristotelismo padovano dal secolo XIV al XVI* (Florence, 1958), pp. 127–46.

17. The macaronic references are in the *Nobile Vigonce opus,* published in Venice in 1502 ("and the *primicerius* came with Count Mirandola"); of interest is the dispatch to Pico of the *Fabella epirota* of Medio and the exchange of letters that followed (see Garin, *La cultura filos. del Rinascimento italiano,* pp. 257–58, 266–68).

18. The Italian poems were published in part by the very deserving Felice Ceretti (*Sonetti inediti del conte Giovanni Pico* [Mirandola, 1894]), who took them from the Magliabechian and Este codices; in part, integrating Ceretti, from L. Dorez ("I sonetti di Giov. Pico della Mirandola per Leon Dorez," *Nuova Rassegna* 2, no. 25 [1 August 1894]); and from a Parisian manuscript. Dorez discourses on various subjects, although the question about the text and authenticity of some sonnets published by Ceretti remains open (but see G. Renier in *GSLI,* 1898, pp. 127–31; and N. V. Testa, "Sull' autenticità delle Rime di P.d.M.," *Rivista Abruzzese* 20(1905): 12–23). On the Latin rhymes, see G. Bottiglioni, *La lirica latina in Firenze nella 2 metà del secolo XV,* taken from *Annali della R. Scuola Normale Sup. di Pisa* (Pisa, 1913), 25: 182 sqq., 228 sqq.

19. The two letters of Pico are in *Opera,* pp. 348 sqq., 351 sqq. The answers of Barbaro are in V. Branca, ed., *Epistolae, Orationes et Carmina* (Florence, 1943), 1: 100–09.

20. Ms. Angel. 1253 (*Tractatus de anima*), f. 18*r*–19*r* (" . . . a man should not attach himself to the wife of another, lest he commit fornication, as Pico with Margherita . . ."; "Admit it, Pico, neither you nor I have ever been perfect . . ."; "Who, indeed, can be free of jealousy? Even Mithridates could not"). It was wrongly said of Margherita that she was "the wife of Lorenzo."

21. We have various documents on the incident, some published and some as yet unpublished. The "Lettera a fra' Ieronimo da Piacenza" of Costanza Bentivoglio (16 May 1486) was published in *Memorie Storiche Mirandolesi* 2(1874): 167–68. The dispatch of Aldovrandino Guidoni to Ercole d'Este of 12 May 1486 was published by Antonio Cappelli in his *Lettere di Lorenzo de' Medici detto il Magnifico conservate nell' Arch. Palatino di Modena con notizie tratte dai carteggi diplomatici degli oratori estensi a Firenze* (Modena, 1863) (taken from vol. I of *Atti e Mem. delle Depp. di Storia patria per le provincie Modenesi e Parmensi*), p. 54 (not the other documents that are mentioned in the note). Thus D. Berti in an appendix to his *Cenni e documenti,* pp. 45–48, published only one part of the dispatches of the Florentine archives—not, for example, the protest of the Aretine magistrates. The Florentine documents which I refer to here (and which, together with the others concerning both this incident and the serious question of the condemnation from 1487 on, I will publish elsewhere) are: State Archives of Florence, MAP, 39, 487; 39, 490; 39, 492. It is interesting to note how in these documents Pico's secretary already appears in a rather dubious light.

22. *Opera,* pp. 376–78. It is the most important letter to Andrea Corneo da Urbino. On this, and on what follows, as well as on the composition of the speech, Benivieni's commentary, and some other projected works and works

already begun, I refer to what I have written previously and which I summarize briefly here, with a few corrections and inclusions relating to the passages on Pico in *La cultura filosofica del Rinascimento italiano* (pp. 231–89).

23. On the first editions of Pico's theses, see E. Valenziani, *Les incunables de Pic de la Mirandole. Contribution à une bibliographie*, in *Pensée humaniste et tradition chrétienne au XV et XVIe siècles* (Paris, 1950), pp. 333–38, which also contains information on prior research.

24. The document, which does not seem to me to have been used by earlier scholars, is worthy of note (see P. O. Kristeller, *Studies in Renaissance Thought and Letters* (Rome, 1956), pp. 221–47, but already published in 1938 and included here; L. Lazzarelli, *Testi scelti*, ed. M. Brini (Rome, 1955), taken from "Archivio di Filosofia"; P. O. Kristeller, *Lodovico Lazzarelli e Giovanni da Correggio*, taken from the work *Bibl. degli Ardenti della Città di Viterbo. Studi e ricerche nel 150 della fondazione*, Viterbo, s.d.); see also A. Cappelli, *Lettere di Lorenzo*, p. 55: "Messer Giovanni da Correggio, known as Mercurio and the newest prophet, the son of the late Mess. Antonio da Correggio, came to this city this Easter to approach his Majesty the King, whose counselor he was, and he possessed letters written by his Majesty and his Majesty's secretary who were very anxious to see him. And this last orator of his Majesty, whose name was Mess. Bernardino Marchese, had explicit instructions to bring about a meeting between the former, [Mess. Giovanni] and his Majesty; but being uncertain of the road, he could not leave. It appears that Messer Giovanni had been investigated earlier by the inquisition in Bologna as a heretic, and then freed. Again, on this day, he was arrested at two o'clock at night in his house, and two of his servants were taken and roped together. The said Mess. Giovanni was conducted to the Bargello at the request of the Signori X, in spite of the fact that the whole affair had originated with Lorenzo the Magnificent, and he was then turned over to the Inquisitor of San Francesco. The latter seems to have taken very harsh measures against Mess. Giovanni, ordering all the people to come and see him in chains and to treat him like an animal, threatening to see him burn. So that the aforesaid Mess. Giovanni, in desperation, struck his head against the block, and tore all the flesh from his head with his hands, and for this reason it is doubtful that he will be condemned to die. And since he will not die, it is believed that he will not come to a bad end; not so much perhaps because of his error as from the wish of others who had him arrested." It might be interesting to note that in the spring of 1486 Pico, Flavio Mitridate, and Giovanni Mercurio da Correggio arrived in Florence together with the French envoys.

25. In addition to citing Berti's study which is dated but should not be overlooked, the work of Dorez and Thuasne is still basic; the acts of the trial and the various documents referred to are published in it. It appears that Lorenzo received the *Apologia* in February 1488, since a letter of thanks was registered at that time in the protocols (12 February) (*Protocolli del Carteggio di*

Lorenzo il Magnifico per gli anni 1473–4, 1477–92, ed. Marcello del Piazzo [Florence, 1956], p. 370).

26. State Archives of Florence, MAP, 57–15, 19 January 1488: "I have been informed that they are preparing edicts and all forms of persecution against the count Jo. Mirandula. It appears to me that you should remind Our Lord to beware of arousing passions . . . not to make a big scandal in the Church of God; that the Lord of Mirandula is in fact most learned in the opinion of men, and I do not think it would be wise to drive him in desperation to take some wrong road. And I believe he would be more amenable to gentleness than. . . . Look at this apologia of his, which is in part a justification of conclusions . . . of religious and learned people, and I understand that these are not against the faith, for which he could reasonably be reproved . . ." (*the ellipses indicate missing passages in a very damaged text*).

For the reactions of various Florentine religious circles, and for the relations they were later to have with Pico, see the works of the Dominican Giovanni Caroli of Santa Maria Novella, *Super quibusdam conclusionibus Johannis Pici Mirandulae principis* of 1498 (in ms. Conv. C. 8.277 of the National Library of Florence, from Santa Maria Novella); the many works of Orlandini of the Camaldolese, who speaks of Pico constantly in verse and prose (the manuscripts of his works have been transferred from the Florence National Library to the Laurentian Library); the works of Giorgio Benigno (primarily the two small works which contain evidence of a theological discussion which took place at the Magnificent's home on 31 June 1489, at which Pico, Politian, Ficino, Bianchelli, Niccolò dei Mirabili, and others were present: *Disputatio nuper facta in domo Magnifici Laurentii Medices,* of Mirabili, Flor. 1489; and *Septem et septuaginta mirabilia reperta in opusculo Magistri Nicolai de Mirabilibus,* of Benigno, printed in Florence without other indications).

27. Lorenzo followed the affair anxiously and attempted to persuade Roman circles, also through the intervention of Pico's brother, Antonio della Mirandola. He wrote on 3 February 1488 to Lanfredini (MAP, 57, 22): "You know how warmly I have written to you recently on the subject of Count Giovanni della Mirandola. Count Antonio, his brother, who is there, should have had news of him, and it comforts me to persevere in writing to you to intervene with N.S. [Nostra Signoria] in order that the aforesaid count may leave. His departure would please me, if S.S. [Sua Sanctità] agrees that it would perhaps absolve him from the calumny, and I would appreciate it if N.S. would reinstate him in its grace. In agreement with Count Antonio in this matter, help him as much as possible and give him the letter enclosed." On 22 March (MAP, 57, 36), the agreement with Rome is imminent: "I have heard with great pleasure and satisfaction of the decision you have come to with N.S. with regard to Count Giovanni della Mirandola, and on the basis on which you write to me, I will make the aforementioned count understand that he is to leave. I am certain of my opinion that S.S. will decide in such a way that N.S. will be satisfied, and to this effect I will direct my careful effort. In order that you understand everything, I am sending you a letter from his chancellor, who writes my Ser Piero. . . . Advise me again of the judgment of N.S. . . . "

Neither Berti, who does not always situate the interventions of Lorenzo exactly, nor Dorez has correctly evaluated the specific role played by the Magnificent in the resolution of the crisis.

28. State Archives of Florence, MAP, 59, 203. The letter was published in the *Adnotationes et monumenta ad Laurentii Magnifici Vitam pertinentia* (Pisa: Fabroni, 1784), pp. 293–94, but with a curious mistake in the date, which becomes 1492. Many mistakes have also arisen in similar fashion in the dates of Pico's activities.

29. As I have indicated, I will publish elsewhere the complete set of documents which have only been published in part and used by Berti. On 13 September 1488, Lorenzo asked for permission for Pico to live in the city (MAP, 59, 224): "I am anxiously awaiting some positive answer as to the affairs of Count Giovanni della Mirandula, whom, as you know, I could not have closer to my heart, for the reasons I have stated. I recommend him to you as highly as I can and I beg of you that you at least obtain this grace from N.S., in order that he might be able to remain this winter in the city. He is outside and would not move one step without the order of S.S. . . . " On 16 October, he insists (MAP, 59, 29): "I remind you again and I recommend the Count of Mirandula. I beg you to attend to those actions that I have written you about at other times, because I could not wish them more and the winter is coming." On 15 February 1489, Lorenzo asked in haste for "a Chaldean psalmist, whom I would greatly need for a few days" (MAP, 59, 120). Pico was then commenting on the Psalms. On 13 March (MAP, 59, 134) he passed on a note expressing the desires of the count ("please do something about it, and so that it be done, you need not mention the count's name"). On 28 March (MAP, 51, 445), he asked for the books of Mitridate. On 19 June 1489 (MAP, 51, 515), Lorenzo made a new attempt to obtain an absolution for Pico. The letters of the Magnificent, of Lanfredini, of Pico himself (MAP, 88, 77; 51, 534; 51, 535; 51, 536; 51, 538; 58, 88; 58, 89; 58, 98), between July and October, are very important and, at times, highly dramatic; they show the warm affection of Lorenzo (the words in his own handwriting were added to the letter of 21 August, MAP, 51, 535. Pico's letter reached Rome on 27 August; MAP, 51, 534).

Mention of the writings against Pico and of the trial initiated by the Master of the Sacred Palace is made in MAP, 51, 535 (21 August 1489) and in Lanfredini's answers.

Pico was referring most likely to a volume by Pietro Garsia, Episcopus Ussellensis, who on the order of the Pope examined the *Apologia* ("the *Apology* by Giovanni Pico . . . has been given to me, to be read and examined at your request, since the falsehoods and the superstitions of the Magi and the Cabalists are resuscitated in it . . ."). The work, entitled *Determinationes magistrales*, was printed in Silber type in Rome and dated 15 October 1489 (IGI, 4177). The conclusion is important: "Written in the city of Rome [in 1488], in the residence of my Most Reverend Lord Rodrigo Borgia. . . . Concerning the aforesaid inquiry, however, it had been my intent throughout to judge not so much the person of Giovanni Pico as his reasoning. I am well aware and have taken cognizance of several debates that took place in the presence of the Most Reverend Father Johannes, the Bishop of Tournay, the Majordomo of Your Holiness, an inquisitor singularly qualified to deal with issues of this nature, who maintained that the man in question [Pico] was endowed with prodigious genius matched only by his learning."

30. For Pico's letters concerned with obtaining the pardon after the death of Innocent VIII, see L. Dorez, *Lettres inédites*, pp. 358–61. Another recapitulation of the question of the condemnation with an analysis of theses, is contained in Domenico Bernino, *Historia di tutte l'heresie* (Venice, 1711), 4: 222–27.

31. As is known, the commentary on the Psalms was not finished. Parts were dispersed. I have attempted to indicate elsewhere what remains of them (Garin, *La cultura filosofica*, pp. 241–53). It may be that others used other passages.

32. At the end of 1497 Savonarola wrote a compendium of the *Disputationes* of Pico, the *Trattata contro l'astrologia* (Florence), which appeared after 1497. Ms. Conv. Sopp. D. 8.985 of the National Library of Florence also contains a compilation by Savonarola of the notes of Pico (*Ex libro Concordia Jo. d. Mirand.*).

Bellanti maintains that Pico wrote the book against astrology on the advice of Savonarola. L. Bellantius, in *De astrologica veritate; responsiones in disputationes Johannis Pici adversus astrologicam veritatem* (Florence, 9 V 1498, cp. IGI, 1443), wrote, although imprecisely: "It seems remarkable that in so short a time he should have come to realize that that fallacious astrology should be repudiated. Perhaps the friar Girolamo Savonarola, with whom he often took counsel, may have induced him to see the light, and that he then embraced the unadulterated and indivisible truth; and it may have been at the friar's urging that he then wrote this work."

33. The commentaries on the *Pater* and the other short works, which were to have so much success in the following centuries, are from this period. On his death, see L. Dorez, *La mort de Pic de la Mirandole et l'édition Aldine des oeuvres d'Ange Politien (1494–1498)*, *GSLI*, 32(1898): 360 sqq. The text by his grandson testifies to his state of mind: "While taking a walk through those long parallel rows in the orchards of Ferrara and discoursing on the love of Christ, he stopped abruptly and said: 'I am telling this to you, but it should remain a secret. Whatever is left of my fortune, now that my quest has come to an end and been consummated, I shall give away to the poor and, taking only my crucifix, I shall go forth into the world, traversing the country on my two bare and unshod feet, from castle to castle, from city to city, preaching Christ.' I learned subsequently that he had changed his mind and had decided to take the vows in the Dominican order."

34. The first edition of the French translation of Gaguin (*Counseil prouffitable contre les ennuys et tribulations du monde*) is from 1498 (19 April). That of Wimpheling was published in Strasbourg in 1509. The English text of Moore appeared in London in about 1510 with the life of Pico. (Pico's bi-

ography is contained in the third volume of the complete edition of the works of S. Thomas Moore, published by Yale University Press).

35. A serious study of Pico's vicissitudes and an evaluation of his thought has yet to be made. Interpretations have been quite varied, and in this century have been subjected at times to overly "modernizing" influnces, and at times overly "conservative" reactions. A brief mention of the most important and characteristic works (not previously cited): Ch. Sigwart, *Ulrich Zwingli, Der Charakter seiner Theologie mit besonderer Rücksicht auf P.v.M.* (Stuttgart-Hamburg, 1855); G. Dreydorff, *Das System des Johannes Pico, Grafen von Mirandola und Concordia. Eine philosophisch-historische Untersuchung* (Marburg, 1858); G. Massetani, *La filosofia cabalistica di G. Pico della Mirandola* (Empoli, 1897); A. Levy [Liebert], *Die Philosophie des G. Pico della Mirandola. Ein Beitrag zur Philosophie der Frührenaissance* (Berlin 1908); I. Pusino, *Ficinos und Picos religiös-philosophische Anschauungen*, ZKG, 44 (Gotha. 1925), pp. 504–43; H. Baron, *Willensfreiheit und Astrologie bei M. Ficino und Pico d. Mirandola*, "Kultur-und Universalgeschichte. Walter Goetz Festschrift" (Leipzig-Berlin, 1927), pp. 145–70; Pusino, *Der Einfluss Picos auf Erasmus*, ZKG, 46(1928), pp. 75–96; E. Cassirer, *Individuum und Kosmos in der Philosophie der Renaissance* ("Studien der Bibliothek Warburg," 10), (Leipzig-Berlin, 1927); A. J. Festugière, "Studia Mirandulana," *Archives d'histoire doctrinale et littéraire du Moyen Age* 7(1932); G. Semprini, *La filosofia di Pico della Mirandola* (Milan, 1936); E. Anagnine, *Giovanni Pico della Mirandola. Sincretismo religioso-filosofico* (Bari, 1937); B. Kieszkowski, *Studi sul platonismo del Rinascimento* (Florence, 1936); A. Dulles, *Princeps Concordiae. Pico della Mirandola and the Scholastic Tradition* (Cambridge, Mass., 1941); E. Cassirer, "Giovanni Pico della Mirandola," *Journal of the History of Ideas* 3(1942): 123–44, 319–54; G. Barone, *L'umanesimo filosofico di G. Pico della Mirandola* (Milan, 1949); G. Di Napoli, *L'essere e l'Uno in Pico della Mirandola*, "Rivista Italiana di filosofia neoscolastica" (Milan, 1954), pp. 356–89; J. Slok, *Tradition og nybrud. Pico della Mirandola* (Copenhagen, 1957); F. Secret, "Pico della Mirandola e gli inizi della cabala cristiana," *Convivium* N.S. (1957): 31–47; E. Monnerjahn, *Giovanni Pico della Mirandola. Ein Beitrag zur philosophischen Theologie des italienischen Humanismus* (Wiesbaden, 1960). The most general works on the subject are not cited here, such as those of Della Torre, De Ruggiero, Carbonara, Saitta, or also, for another reason, those of Dilthey, Renaudet, Chastel, Thorndike, even though they contain basic contributions.

36. See J. Kamerbeek Jr., "La dignité humaine. Esquisse d'une terminographie," *Neophilologus* 41(1957): 247–51. With regard to what is said of the editions and translations of *de hominis dignitate*, published and translated in English: by E. L. Forbes in *Journal of the History of Ideas* (translation) 3 (1942): 347–54 and in *The Renaissance Philosophy of Man* (Chicago, 1948); by C. G. Wallis in "View," 1944 (and, earlier, Annapolis, 1940); again by E. L. Forbes, (Lexington, 1953) (text edition of E. Garin, edited by P. O. Kristeller). In German: edited by H. W. Rüssel, 1940 (and 1949); and in the work "Studia Humanitatis, Beitrag und Texte zum italienischen Human-

ismus der Renaissance," *Agora* 5, 12(1959): 121–4. In French: P. M. Cordier, *Jean Pic de la Mirandole* (Paris, 1957), pp. 121–91 (text and trans.). In Italian: G. Semprini, *La filos. di P.d.M.* (Milan, 1936), pp. 211–57 (translation); G. Pico D.M., *De hominis dignitate* etc., ed. *E. Garin* (Florence, 1942) (text and trans.); and in the work *Filosofi italiani del Quattrocento* (Florence, 1942), (text and trans.); B. Cicognani, ed., (Florence, 1942) (text and trans.); F. Battaglia, *Il pensiero pedagogico del Rinascimento* (Florence, 1960) (extracts and text by Cicognani and trans. by G. Barone).

VIII

Girolamo Savonarola

The greater part of the literature concerning Savonarola—if we refer not so much to scholarly research, which has made very important progress, but to works that are properly speaking historical—is located, and not just chronologically, among those critical perspectives of the last century which do not derive directly from preoccupations or arguments wholly extraneous to our more current interests.[1] Apart from the value of the documents which they have brought to light, scholars have too often remained tied to apologetic demands of various kinds, whether their eyes have been turned nostalgically toward the past or whether they have looked boldly to the future.

Representations of Savonarola as the "precursor" as opposed to the "vestige"; descriptions of the medieval man who survives and who like the knight of Berni's burlesque poem does not notice that he is dead and still combats modern man; and portrayals of a modern man who, on the contrary, because he is too alive ends up not acting either in his own time; this whole manner of transfiguring memories of the past into a hypostasis of one's own ideals and passions, although not devoid of effective rhetoric, is nonetheless very far from being history. Nor did Francesco de Sanctis write history, in 1896, when he made the felicitous analogy that became compulsory reading on the subject: "Savonarola was the last ray of a past that was setting on the horizon; Machiavelli was the dawn, the forerunner of modern times. One was the last of his kind of medieval man; the other, the first representative of modern man." This explicit and simple image was bound to become established, and de Sanctis pressed it home, reiterating, "Savonarola was an evocation of the Middle Ages, a prophet and apostle of Dantesque style," whereas "Machiavelli, in his Roman robes, was a true modern *bourgeois.*"

Carducci enjoyed accentuating once again the contrast on purpose in his eloquent lectures at the University of Bologna "on the evolution of national literature," in which he emphasized Savonarola's medievalism: "and he did not feel that the reform of Italy was the pagan renaissance, that the purely religious reform was reserved for other peoples who were more sincerely Christian; and he did not see, poor friar, amid the tumult of his piagnoni the piteous smile on the pallid face of Niccolò Machiavelli in some corner of the Piazza."[2]

Perhaps no less significant among all these documents are the opening pages of the appendix to the twenty-third "Archivio Storico Italiano," in which, in 1849, padre Vicenzo Marchese, a Dominican of San Marco, presents a noteworthy collection of material on Savonarola:

Three great Italians, who emerged at different times from the same monastery, led a tragic life, had their fame put in doubt and challenged, and two among them suffered the cruelest death. Giordano Bruno, Tommaso Campanella, and Girolamo Savonarola have left the question unanswered as to which was the greater or the more unfortunate. All three were builders or cultivators of a new philosophy in Italy; all three were enemies of every kind of tyranny. . . . All three in their genius and misfortune had to suffer the wrath of powerful enemies, who after disturbing the serenity of their lives aimed to revile their memory after death, charging the first two with atheism and the third with having profaned religion. But if history has been unable to clear Bruno's name of all fault, it has quite revindicated that of Campanella, and the name of Fra Girolamo Savonarola, unstained by the gallows, will shine forever in the writings of Nardi, Segni, Machiavelli, and Guicciardini, and will be remembered by Italians with reverence and affection as long as they hold religion and freedom dear.[3]

If the historical comparisons of padre Marchese appear strange and the trinity Savonarola, Bruno, Campanella seems rather unusual, his eloquent writing expresses very well the same attitude that led Tommaseo, in 1853, to have published, under the title *Opuscoli inediti di Fra Girolamo Savonarola,* his own works, *Dell' Italia.* He chose the name intentionally, thinking specifically of the ideal of the friar: *unus ex potissimis vitae christianae effectibus est animi libertas.** Tommaseo liked to make the friar appear almost as the saint of the Italian risorgimento:

* "One of the most significant consequences of the Christian way of life is the freedom of the soul."

Rare is the man to whom is given the power to unite teaching and example, contemplation and action, the life of religion and that of civic society, science and love, the authority of an orator and that of a writer, not in order to turn the ringhiera into a pulpit but the pulpit into a ringhiera. . . . A theologian and artist, and a poet even in argument; haughty and humble, serene in his gentleness, gentle in his vehemence, precisely because he was strong, worthy to be venerated by that affectionate ardent soul, Filippo Neri, who kept in his room his image crowned with the halo of the saints. . . .[4]

Heretic or saint, forerunner or survivor, but always detached from his time, Savonarola always seemed destined to remain irreconcilable with a culture which yet felt his fascination and with a world which he bitterly fought, but only after having devoutly listened to it as to a sincere expression of its own profound quests. The conventional idea of the renaissance in general and of the Florentine Renaissance in particular—pagan and lighthearted, carefree and merry, completely captivated by classical myths as well as the most worldly festivities—has erased the memory of that Marcian Academy which gathered "pagan" poets and philosophers around the Dominican of San Marco, who seemed to convey a new religious inspiration to the artists, while Verino sang:

Non haec finxerunt veteres mendacia vates,
Nullaque tartareos commenta est fabula manes.
Veridico at nobis Deus haec praenuntiat ore,
Dum veniae est tempus, dum libera nostra voluntas,
Dum coelum virtus, dum pariunt crimina mortem,
Quaeramus summi vestigia tuta magistri.
Quicquid mortale est Christi spernamus amore.
Blanda serenati fugiamus murmura ponti.
*Religio est tranquilla quies portusque salutis.**[5]

* The ancient bards did not invent myths,
Nor is chastisement in hell a fairy tale;
The Lord let us know the truth:
While this is the time of grace, while our will is free,
While virtue still leads to heaven and sin to death,
Let us follow the stern admonition of the Master;
For the love of Christ, let us spurn whatever is mortal,
Let us flee the insidious lure of the deep.
Faith leads to the peace of the blessed, to our heaven of salvation.

The thoughtful judgment of Guicciardini has not been sufficiently noted: "And thus, having done so much of benefit with regard to spiritual matters, his works with regard to the wellbeing of the city and the public good were no less important." It seemed to Guicciardini that Savonarola was endowed "with a very sound judgment, not only in his writings, but also in practical, worldly matters, in the universals which he understood very well." Universals he certainly understood, though not particulars and not historically well-defined situations; that is, moral questions and good habits rather than genuine political problems: "his works on the observance of good habits were most saintly and admirable, nor had there ever been so much goodness and religion in Florence as in his time." Guicciardini could also feel the precise limits of the Dominican's preaching, but he did not, because of this, underestimate their sense; in fact, he was to study his sermons carefully and to express "the apocalyptic themes in the angry polemics of the *Ricordi*."[6] "Such a man," Machiavelli was to say, "must be spoken of with reverence."[7]

One thing above all should be stressed: Florence of the late Quattrocento, even in the most cultivated circles, did not feel that insurmountable abyss between the city and the friar which historians of the nineteenth century later assumed. Guicciardini's judgment could well be placed beside the modest testimony of Luca Landucci: "And he preached always on matters of state, that one should love and fear God, and cherish the good of the commune; and that no one should longer want to lift his head and to become powerful. He was always for the people."[8]

Confronted with the "evil" tyranny of the Medici, Fra Girolamo, the restorer of "liberty," felt himself tied (more than it would appear) to the tradition of "civic life" in which "good habits" and "religion" were joined, in accordance with the ideal cherished by "Aristotelians" like Bruni, Manetti, Acciaiuoli, and Rinuccini as well as by such "Platonists" as Palmieri. It was the old "republican" tradition of the chancellors and magistrates, who, though defenders of the new culture, had strict customs, and who, at the side of their priests, had upheld Florentine policies when necessary even against the popes. Such had been the case at the time of Marsili or of the great Coluccio who crossed the Arno in the afternoon to seek advice on every serious matter with the friar of Santo Spirito. These "ancients"—to use a word dear to Vespasiano da Bisticci, convinced as they were that God does not pardon those who go beyond the "measure" in affairs of the world and who become tyrants, would probably have placed Savonarola's Thomism in the same line as that of Dominici or Saint Antonio. His predictions might well have been linked with the prophecies of many other Dominicans and become accentuated as a result of the perils that seemed to impend over Italy at the end of the century and that harassed Florence.

It was not by chance that in the same period in Genoa another Dominican, Fra Giovanni da Viterbo, the famous Annio da Viterbo, a strange type of humanist-parodist, preaching on the Apocalypse in March 1480, tied the advent of the Antichrist to astrological predictions and the Turkish advance.[9] He also announced the downfall of the church (*flagellanda Ecclesia*) and, after this test, a universal union under one Shepherd (*totius Ecclesiae ad universalem unionem sub uno pastore Christo . . . et victoriam contra bestiam et pseudoprophetam . . .*).*

The augury of great events, of the mutation of the world, was spreading increasingly at the end of the century. Astrologers studied the heavens for the conjunctions of major stars, which foretold changes in reigns, empires, and religions. Leonardo da Vinci imagined immense cataclysms, floods, and the "razing of cities." For Marsilio Ficino the stars denoted the rule of Saturn and the golden age; his discipline, Egidius da Viterbo, was to see their sign also in the discovery of America. For Savonarola men must first suffer the trial of fire and water; only after expiation would they attain the "new century." The Ficinian and *piagnone* Verino sang:

Quicquid agam, pavidis semper tonat auris horror
Temporis extremi, crebrisque tremoribus imo
Depressa aequabunt umbrosas culmina valles,
Astrorum lunaeque nitor tunc fiet opacus.
Pallescent solis radii lucemque negabunt.
Bella fameques prement miserandis caedibus urbis,
Cum pecus atque homines consumet tabida pestis.
Bellua nascetur pejor serpentibus afris;
Antichristus erit, vas perditionis iniquum . . .

* "the universal union of the entire Church under one shepherd, Christ . . . , and victory over the beast and the false prophet. . . ."

Omnia mox diris ardebunt oppida flammis,
*Quae nunc tam vano surgunt constructa labore. . . .**[10]

In the subsequent period Fonzio was to discuss the signs of the Antichrist. Leonardo was to draw his prophecies: "Darkness, wind, high seas, floods, burning forests, rain, lightning, earthquakes, avalanches, the leveling of cities." Visions of imminent earthly paradise and visions of appalling cataclysms converged at times in the same writings, were current in the same cultural circles, were sometimes uttered by the same writers. They represented two poles of one tension that passes through a moment of crisis; in the expectation of future events, decisive for all of humanity, prophets emerge with ever greater frequency and become more agitating; in the universal fervor their sayings more often appear as though they are proving true. Hence, Savonarola was not outside of his time but entirely within it.[11]

Non so se sai che 'n Fiorenza è venuto
Un gran servo di Dio predicatore
Vero profeta, e dotto e ben saputo . . .
"Fiorenza, io son venuto a predicare
Dentro da te, come da Dio inspirato.
Di qui mio dir per tutto ha resonare.
Sarà tuo popol manco flagellato

* Wherever I turn, there resounds forever in my ears
the unspeakable horror of the Last Days of Judgment,
when amid tremors and quakes the mountain heights
shall be leveled and the green valley laid bare,
when the glittering stars and the shining moon will turn dark,
when the rays of the sun itself will pale and refuse their light.
Wars and famines will then oppress the cities, causing pitiful carnage,
and cattle as well as men shall be carried off by pestilence.
The beast shall then arise, far worse than the African dragon,
and Antichrist shall come, the vector of iniquitous perdition,
all the towns shall quickly be reduced in fearful flames,
those very towns that even now are being built in vain by arduous labor. . . .

Di tutti gli altri, perché se' eletta.
Così son dal Signore illuminato.
Con fede questo don divino accetta,
Ringrazia Dio, e fa grande orazione,
Di poi con penitenzia alquanto aspetta.
O quanta fia la tua consolazione!
Più ricca e più potente che mai fussi
Sarai di regno e di persone buone. . . ."*[12]

If it is true, as Savonarola's last biographer wrote, that the land of martyrdom is the fatherland of martyrs, it is also true that the Ferrarese had become a Florentine long before that tragic day in May 1498. He held a passionate love for the people of this contradictory and remarkable city, sinful and inclined to every mystical practice, cruel and yet most generous. He had come as a barbarian to a flourishing Athens, and he soon conquered it—all its scholars and all its strange and capricious populace:

Florence, I believe that thou remember when I began to preach to thee several years ago. I started out simply without philosophy, and thou wert complaining that I preached simply. Yet these sermons bore fruit among simple people, whom it was necessary to tend to first. But the learned then began to object, and I was contradicted by poets, astrologers, philosophers and the worldly wise, who were contesting and tormenting me, giving the impression that our simple preaching was ignorance. I do not say this to praise myself, but because they believed this. Then I started preaching on the basis of reason, to explain both the natural and scriptural reasons for what I was saying, and I began to

* I do not know whether you know that
A great servant of God has come to Florence,
A preacher, a true prophet, learned and knowing . . .
"Florence, I have come to preach
Within thy walls, as inspired by God
From whom my word for all resounds.
Thy people will suffer the scourge less
Than all the others, for thou art chosen.
Thus have I been enlightened by the Lord.
Accept this divine gift with faith,
Thank God, and raise a great prayer,
Then with penitence await whatever comes.
Oh how great will be thy consolation!
More wealthy and powerful than ever,
Thine will be the kingdom of the good . . . ."

preach to thee of faith, and to demonstrate it in many ways, and then thou touched the sores, as Saint Thomas.

These words are from a 1496 Lenten sermon on Amos and Zacharias, which Girolamo pronounced at a decisive moment of his life, purposely choosing the text of Amos, the prophet who was killed. "This is the aim of the prophets," he said to his listeners, "this is our goal and our gain in this world."[13]

He resumed his preaching, which had been interrupted by a pontifical interdict, on Ash Wednesday. The signoria of Florence had decided that the voice of the prophet should be heard again in Santa Maria del Fiore, and Alexander had given his ambivalent permission. It was a day of great festivities in Florence. During the carnival young boys had abstained from the barbaric custom of cracking each other's skulls in a game of throwing stones. "It appeared indeed extraordinary," Iacopo Nardi was to write later, "that at that time this stupid and bestial custom was voluntarily abandoned."[14] Out of obedience to and love for the friar, more than six thousand children between five and eighteen years of age went instead "to ask alms for the poor who were ashamed to beg." Luca Landucci noted in his diary: "Gifts were given without avarice; it appeared as though everyone wanted to give what he had, and the women gave most of all; it seemed that everyone wanted to make an offering to Christ and to his Mother." And he added: "I have written about these matters which are true, and I have seen them and felt such love; and some of my children were among those blessed and chaste groups."

On 17 February the children gathered on the steps of the Duomo and sang "sweet songs before the sermon . . . in such a way as to make everyone weep with tenderness, and the sanest minds among them wept the most, exclaiming, 'This is the work of the Lord.' "[15] These were the same terrible groups of children whom Savonarola sought to transform into instruments of "good living," re-educating them and sending them around the city "to overturn the baskets of Lenten cake, the card tables of the gamblers, and [to chastise] the licentious ways of the women." They were "the children of the friar," Landucci wrote. "These children," another contemporary witness observed,

met together and elected from their number officers, that is, gentlemen, counsellors and other officials who went about the land to put a stop to games and other vices. . . . They walked . . . about the city taking away playing cards and dice; and thus they also confiscated titillating books about love and cheap novels, and they threw everything into the fire. And again, while walking the streets, if they came upon some foppish young women, wearing indecent fashions, they greeted them politely, reproving them in a pleasant manner, saying, "Gentle lady, remember that you must one day die and leave behind all pomp and finery, all these vanities—"; and with other words appropriate to their work, if not for love at least for shame, one way or the other, the young people largely gave up their vanities. Thus, too, wicked and depraved men, for fear of being pointed to and exposed, abstained from doing many things. And the children went further still into the county, reaping great benefit, in such a way that matters came to a good end; and they gathered frequently in San Marco to take counsel.[16]

An Italian historian who was anything but opposed to the political dictatorships of his time and spoke without much sympathy of the "dictatorship of Girolamo Savonarola," pictured these bands of little rogues in very harsh terms, as "genuine inquisitors," violent and tough, inclined to wield the stick to obtain alms, and to take recourse to informing and espionage. He described them going through noble Florentine homes tearing paintings from the walls, books from the shelves, and jewels from the women's coffers; the friar, an astute politician, used all this to strengthen his own tyranny with the ingenuous and fiery enthusiasm of the young.[17] The honest Nardi, who had seen these events himself, speaks not of incited youth but of little rascals who had been abandoned to themselves, reduced by the friar to "such modesty that the spectators, and especially the foreigners, could not help but weep at such a miracle." This picture given by the old Florentine historian is certainly also exaggerated.

To judge the friar of San Marco one must abandon the common notion of a Florence entirely bathed in the brilliant light of a renaissance in full flower, then suddenly plunged into the dark shadow of a survivance of the Middle Ages. The age of Lorenzo concealed a profound economic and political crisis already in process; difficulties of every kind were increasing continuously. The problem of an ever more serious and menacing external situation was coupled with discontent with the Medicean "tyranny" inside the state, as well as with the estrangement of a displaced former ruling class, deprived of its possessions and bloodily defeated at the time of the Pazzi conspiracy.

When Lorenzo died, it was not Savonarola who refused him absolution, as maintained by a legend dear to nineteenth-century historians but which today has been entirely discredited. One of the old optimates, who had bitterly bewailed the consolidation of the power of the "new Falaris," noted in his diary, "Death of Lorenzo de' Medici, evil tyrant"; after giving a dour portrait of Lorenzo, the diary concluded: "For many years he has been most pernicious and cruel . . . to our city," consuming "an inestimable public treasure . . . solely for his own purposes . . . of no utility whatever for our republic." The one who wrote these words also manifested a great distrust in his co-citizens, by then "for the most part corrupt and degenerate from long servitude . . . who have lost the taste for liberty and good and honest living."[18]

Alamanno Rinuccini was an unsuspect witness. He was a man entirely in tune with the new times, close to the great humanists in the line of Bruni and Manetti, learned in Greek, and full of veneration for the knowledge of antiquity. He had fought vigorously to have the greatest of all Byzantine scholars, John Argyropulos, come to teach in Florence. He was a promoter and exponent of the reborn culture. But to him, a republican, tyranny was odious, and to him, a good Christian, the vitiated rhetoric of the court and the easy prostitution of too many intellectuals to the masters of the state were intolerable. Conscious of the grave crisis that afflicted Florence and Italy, he knew that what was needed was resolute and frank leadership; Florence no longer needed a subtle diplomatic game interspersed with such paltry tricks as the defrauding of two hundred thousand florins from the public funds in order to "corrupt and buy the consent of cardinals and the pope" to make Lorenzo's son, "in his boyhood," a cardinal.

This was the Florence to which Friar Girolamo Savonarola had come to work. He was close to men who remained among the most noble representatives of renaissance civilization. He was most dear to Giovanni Pico, who strived so hard to have him return to the city at a decisive moment in his life. He was learned in philosophy, but not a philosopher; he was certainly also versed in literature, but not devoted to the *studia humanitatis*. He had grown up in Ferrara where he attended the humanist school of Guarino Veronese, but he remained under the traditional influence of the austere physician Michele Savonarola, his grandfather.

Fra Girolamo entered the monastery in obeyance to an irresistible religious calling, although it was not a verse of the Scriptures but a poem of Virgil which rang an insistent inner bell and impelled him far out of his century. In a letter to his father on 25 April 1475, he declared in an especially lofty tone the reasons for his flight from the world: "the great misery . . . the iniquities of men, the violations, the adulteries, the robberies, the arrogance, the idolatry." And he laments: "Many times have I sung these woeful verses, *heu fuge crudeles terras, fuge litus avarum. . . .** I could not endure the great malice of the blind people of Italy."[19] But the monastery did not signify a retirement to pious contemplation. In his invective against human baseness he had before his eyes the corruption and moral misery of the clergy, high as well as low, and he was invoking the intervention of Christ:

Soccorri a la Romana
Tua Santa Chiesa, che il demonio atterra.†

In Florence he experienced his first real test, and he returned there in 1490 at the request of Pico. It was then that the great activity of the "preacher of the despairing," as he was sometimes called, began—in that Florence that was so profoundly troubled, so full of the malcontent and the desperate despite all her splendor; in that Italy so rent and so fragile, despite its rational equilibrium; in that church of Rome whose head was soon to be the infamous Borgia. According to one of his biographers, Savonarola did not at first have a large following: "He did not preach about especially unusual things which would be appreciated by the wise of the world, but about useful and devotional matters, to fructify the soul."[20] However, very soon the fervor of his rude eloquence and his prophecies of imminent calamities and upheavals stirred minds profoundly. In a sermon on the Genesis, delivered during Advent in 1492, he announced that the sword of God would smite the church, that one would come from

* "Flee this cruel earth, leave this sad land. . . ."

† Come to the aid of your Holy Roman Church,
Which the devil defames.

"beyond the mountains, as Cyrus, and the Lord will be his guide and leader, and no one will be able to resist him."

In 1492, the "arrogant, avaricious, and cruel tyranny" of Piero di Lorenzo de' Medici succeeded that of Lorenzo in Florence, observed a contemporary, "in order to exhaust and consume the blood of this miserable people." In Rome Alexander VI ascended to the chair of Saint Peter—in that Rome which, according to a writer of the time, "virgins were being abducted, matrons were selling themselves, sacred objects were being defiled, houses were being looted, people were being thrown here and there into the Tiber, murders were being committed day and night and going unpunished"; in that Rome in which "*monasteria quasi omnia facta erant lupanaria.*"[21] The morals of the pope, according to Guicciardini, were well in tune with all these "most obscene customs, no honesty, no shame, no truth, no faith, no religion, insatiable avarice, ambition, intemperance, a cruelty greater than the barbarians."[22]

In such a climate, at a time in which prophecy was a living experience and in which, anxious over the future, men wanted now a scientific answer of astrology, now a statement by an intellect directly enlightened by God, Savonarola never lost sight of the need for a specific and serious commitment to reform. The new Ferrarese Socrates[23]—as one follower called him—clearly perceived the new human society, the peaceful and holy city of men, and he worked to build it with great wisdom. The reform was to originate in Florence. Florence, in which the old republican liberties were to be reconstituted, was to be renewed politically; it would then renew politically "the blind people of Italy." San Marco, where the Dominicans had returned to former habits, was to initiate the spiritual renewal of the church.

The separation of San Marco in May 1493 from the Lombard Congregation, which was tied to the Pope, provided the necessary basis for Savonarola's future activity; it was an event of great importance.[24] The spiritual transformation of the Dominicans of the Florentine monastery and the growing moral prestige of the friar were to correspond with the most serious unrest in the city and with the tragic collapse of the Italian political situation. Charles VIII was invading; the sword of God was falling upon the sinners. "Not I, but God has predicted it to thee," the friar exclaimed on 1 November 1494. "And now he is come." And he continued, striking terror:

A voice calls: . . . O Italy, ye shall suffer for thy lust, for thine avarice, for thine arrogance, for thine ambitions, for thy robberies and extortions. . . . A voice calls . . . O Florence, O Florence, O Florence, ye shall suffer many hardships and misfortunes for thy sins, for thy tortures, for thine avarice, for thy vices, for thine ambitions. . . . O clergy, clergy, clergy . . . who art the main cause of these evils, for this storm is born of thine evil, many tribulations await thee for thy sins. Woe, woe I say unto he who has a tonsured head!

Thus the blame lay with the spiritual and temporal leaders; on them would descend the sword of God. But pardon and peace would be granted the repentant people: "I have wept for thee so many times, Florence, that it should suffice thee. . . . O Florence, I want to speak to thee this morning and to each one in particular and openly, for I can do no other. Still the voice calls . . . calls and cries out to thy Lord God. I turn to thee, my Lord, thou who hast died for our love and for our sins. . . . Pardon, pardon, Lord, this thy people, pardon, O Lord, the people of Florence who wish to be thine!"[25]

This was truly Savonarola's heroic moment. The moment at which Florence expelled Piero to the cry *popolo et libertà,* the friar was fighting on two fronts, using all his prestige and shrewdness in negotiation with the king of France in order to save the city from being sacked, and relying on the magic of his word to soothe hatreds and to prevent retaliations and massacres: "Peace, I say, peace, Florence! If thou willst make peace, thou willst be the friend of God, who wants nothing more than peace. And God in this way will guard thy city. . . , and if thou shouldst not make a true peace, hear what I say unto thee: this will be thy final destruction. Hence, peace, peace, I say."

The blood of citizens was not shed. Guicciardini wrote that there was "peace and unity." "How many statesmen," a historian asked recently,[26] "descend to their graves or mount the gallows with this admirable result, that they desired and realized, be it only momentarily, the union of souls and the harmony of citizens?" But Savonarola preferred a difficult path to easy popularity. From Florence he began to work for the regeneration of all Italy: "Hear Florence, . . . what I say unto thee; hear what God has imparted to me. . . ; from thee shall spring the reformation of all of Italy."

Thus was born the free state of the people of Florence. Savonarola was reactivating the civic inspiration of the old Florentine ruling class, but he intended to renew it, gathering to him the demands that the Medicean principate had augmented and that the internal crisis had accentuated.[27] His political venture was crushed between the opposition of those whose interests were threatened and the incomprehension of the people for whom he fought. And his religious reform was spent in face of the cynicism of a pontiff and a clergy ready to use any monk's quarrel in order to avoid confronting that problem which was soon to lead them to the spiritual division of Europe.

At a certain moment Savonarola desired martyrdom: "O Lord . . . let me die for thee, as thou hast for me." And to the people of Rome he hurled his true prophecy:

O Rome, Rome! Ye shall have so many tribulations that ye shall regret ever having been against this work. Thou sayest that thou art blessed, and we are the excommunicated, and *tamen* thou fight as damned and infidels . . . and there in Rome thou write that that friar who is in Florence, together with his people, wants to combat thee as Turks and pagans; and that we want to die and to be martyred; and that I have the great wish to be martyred by thee. O Lord, grant me this grace! Thou, Rome, hope to frighten me. I have no fear whatever.[28]

"His" people led him to the Piazza Signoria, to that gallows that seemed a cross, and then for centuries laid flowers at the spot of his martyrdom. He was an unusual man for his period. His political writings may be placed without too much difficulty between the generation of the great humanist chancellors and that of Machiavelli and Guicciardini, who yet esteemed him. He was a prophet in a time that believed in prophets; his severity was worthy of an ancient sage. He expressed an undeniable aspect of the sickness of an age deeply tormented; yet he so desired harmony and peace, that peace which for one moment he believed to have conquered for "his" Florence, as in the sweet verses of the "possessed" Marietta:

Un'arra di Paradiso
Questa città pareva;
Sendo ciascuno unito
*Gran pace si vedeva.**[29]

* A token of paradise
This city seemed;
With all united
Great peace was seen.

Not long after his tragic death on the stake and after Ficino, who had not hesitated to insult the poor dead friar, had also died, the Camaldolite Paolo Orlandini in a significant work placed together, in final peace, all the great figures that had met to dispute in the cloisters of San Marco, and he enjoyed picturing them still united in a noble castle in heaven:

Stava tra essi con magno decoro
El nostro degno prior Bernardino,
Johanni Pico in suo nobil tesoro;

Dipoi Messer Marsilio di Ficino,
Savonarola e Messer Olivieri
*Per loro ingegno savio e peregrino.**

Elsewhere, addressing himself directly "as a disciple and . . . son" to Savonarola, "good father, benign and merciful," he added:

Et or mi volgo a te, doctor perfecto,
O Ferrarese e gran Savonarola,
Savio e prudente, benché a noi despecto,

Da poi ch'io t'ho trovato in questa scuola,
Clara di luce provida e serena,
Che sopra gli altri com'aquila vola,

Non dirò adesso di cosa terrena
Qual di te parla ciaschedůna gente. . . .†[30]

* There were among them with great dignity,
Our worthy prior Bernardino,
Johanni Pico with his noble treasure;

Then Messer Marsilio di Ficino,
Savonarola and Messer Olivieri
For their wise and rare genius.

† And now I address myself to you, perfect doctor,
O Ferrarese and great Savonarola,
Wise and prudent, although defamed by us,

Since I have found you in this school,
Clear with serene and providential light,
Who flies above the others like an eagle,

I will not speak of earthly things
What all the people say of you. . . .

The verses of the friar from Camaldoli are not beautiful, but his testimony is not without value, since it was written so close to the time of Savonarola's execution in the Piazza Signoria. Nor is the concept unimportant of an ideal reconciliation of all the great spirits of Florence from the end of the Quattrocento, reunited beyond any struggle in a common work of human reconstruction.

Notes

1. See A. Panella, "Alla ricerca del vero Savonarola," *Pegaso* 3(1931): 655–67, and the article on Savonarola by Palmarocchi in the *Enciclopedia Italiana,* Vol. 30, 1936. Important information is contained in G. Spini, "Introduzione al Savonarola," *Belfagor* 3(1948): 414–28. Some penetrating and explicit observations are contained in L. Russo, *Machiavelli* (Bari, 1949), pp. 1–10, 201–09. I will refer frequently to a basic work by Roberto Ridolfi, *Vita di Girolamo Savonarola* (Rome, 1952). For the most recent biography since the nineteenth century, see M. Ferrara, *Savonarola* (Florence, 1952), Vol. 2, and a separate edition brought up to date, *Bibliografia savonaroliana* (Florence, 1958). Also see the eminently well-known P. Villari, *La Storia di Girolamo Savonarola e de' suoi tempi* (Florence, 1930), Vol. 2; and J. Schnitzer, *Savonarola,* Italian ed. (Milan, 1931), Vol. 2. (See the review of the Schnitzer work by D. Cantimori in *Annali di R. Scuola Normale Sup. di Pisa,* Ser. 2, 1(1932): 90–104.) Among the encyclopedia articles, see especially that of M. M. Gorce in *Dictionnaire de théologie catholique.* A. Gherardi, *Nuovi documenti e studi intorno a Girolamo Savonarola* (Florence, 1887), pp. 11–35, contains valuable bibliographical references.

2. For this passage, see Russo, *Machiavelli,* p. 2. On the nineteenth-century "piagnoni" in Florence, see G. Gentile, *Gino Capponi e la cultura toscana del sec. XIX* (Florence, 1922). I take this occasion to refer for its valuable information to the baccalaureate thesis of A. M. Pelleri, *Gli studi savonaroliani e la tradizione piagnona nell' 800,* which was presented at the Faculty of Letters and Philosophy of Florence in 1950, and which has not been published.

3. *Cedrus libani, ossia Vita di Fra Gerolamo Savonarola scritta da Fra Benedetto da Firenze l'anno 1510* (ed. V. Marchesa), in *Archivo Storico Italiano,* Vol. 7, App. 23, pp. 41–42. Two other works of Marchesa are also valuable: the *Lettere inedite di Fra Gerolamo Savonarola e documenti concernenti lo stesso,* in Vol. 8 of *Archivo Storico Italiano,* App. 25, pp. 8–71; and "Sunto storico del convento di San Marco," *Scritti vari* (Florence, 1860), Vol. 1.

4. See the introduction by G. Balsamo-Crivelli to the *Dell' Italia* (Turin, 1926), 1: 15. See also the review by Tommaseo of the 1864 edition (Florence: Guasti) of the *Canzona che fa uno Fiorentino a Carnasciale trovandolo fuggirsi con uno asinello charico di sua masseritie et col fardello in spalla et domandandol qual sia la chagione del suo partire risponde Carnasciale esserne suto causa lo sbandimento del fuoco allui facto dalla ciptà di Fiorenza. Et però fuggirsi per la Italia in Babylonia.* (It should be noted that Babylonia is Rome. Carnival says: "From whence, moved by pain, I came to Rome which believes in me.") The re-edition, with an introduction by Del Lungo and including the description of the burning by Girolamo Benivieni, has a different title

(*Canzona d'un Piagnone pel bruciamento delle vanità del Carnevale del 1489*). Tommaseo's comment appeared in *Rivista contemparanea nazionale Italiana* 38 (1864): 125–56.

5. Ugolini Verino, *Carmen de Christianae Religionis ac Vitae Monasticae foelicitate ad Hieronymum Ferrariensem, theologum Ordinis fratrum Praedicatorum insignem*. I use the edition included by Gherardi in *Nuovi documenti*, p. 295. Verino, who by then had become a Ficinian, discusses poetry and the Platonic interdiction in the introductory note to the *Carmen*, concluding: "Meritorious poets seek to benefit the reader by pregnant turns of phrase and, even more, to delight him by choosing elegant expressions; dull or licentious writers, however, should be shunned like the plague." It is not the fault of art but of those who abuse it. Verino invokes Pico's authority; see especially, in ms. Conv. D. 2, 502 of the National Library of Florence, a letter dated 30 September 1489, in which the stylistic form is compared to the key which opens the door to truth; to open it, it matters little whether the key is made of gold, *praestat omnino aperire lignea, quam aurea occludere*. See *Giornale Critico della Filos. Italiana* 31(1952): 523–24; the text is important because it demonstrates the groundlessness of the hypothesis of A. Ferriguto in *Almorò Barbaro* (Venice, 1922), p. 321, that Pico changed his position after 1485. For this hypothesis, see also Q. Breen, "Giovanni Pico della M. on the Conflict of Philosophy and Rhetoric," *Journal of the History of Ideas* 13(1952): 385. As is known, Savonarola answered Verino with the famous *Apologeticus de ratione poeticae artis* and with the well-known thesis: "I do not condemn the science of rhetoric or the art of poetry . . . nor the embellishment of language and the refinement of eloquence, but the very vain display of these in those poets who believe that they know everything, while they know nothing, nor do they possess any other knowledge except that of the pen, of the spondee and meters . . . and they boast of their knowledge of all the sciences, while they possess only the science of poetry" (edition Venice, 1952, p. 46; translated by Mattii, Siena, 1864, p. 49; see the ms. Magliab. 7: 1150, in which the *Apologeticus* follows the writings of Verino). In this Savonarola did not assume a position different from that of Pico in 1485 in the famous polemic with Barbaro. For the *Marciana academia*, see Petri Criniti, *de honesta disciplina* (Lugduni, 1543), 2: 44, and G. Uzielli, "Dialogo fra G. Savonarola etc.," *I Centenari del 1898*, periodical publication edited by P. Gori (Florence, 1898), pp. 46–48.

6. See Guicciardini, *Storia fiorentina del 1378 al 1509*, ed. Palmarocchi (Bari, 1931), p. 156; Guicciardini, *Dialogo del Reggimento di Firenze* (1932), p. 18; and, above all, his important *Estratti savonaroliani*, included by Palmorocchi in his *Scritti autobiografici e rari* (1936), p. 285. The observation quoted is in V. De Caprariis, *Francesco Guicciardini dalla politica alla storia* (Bari, 1950), p. 12. It should also be pointed out that the considerations of Bernardo del Nero in the *Dialogo del reggimento di Firenze* refers to concepts and at times to the same words of the *Trattato* of Savonarola (see especially 1: 3). They are also parallel to those which had been pointed out opportunely by Ridolfi (*Vita*, 2: 92–93) in his portrayal of the tryant. Ridolfi's accurate observation that Savonarola owed very little to the *De regimine principum* of Saint

Thomas could probably be elaborated. At any rate, Guicciardini's debts to Savonarola were many and very significant.

7. See Savonarola, *Discorsi*, 1: 2. Also with regard to Machiavelli, the essay by J. H. Whitfield, "Savonarola and the Purpose of *The Prince*," *The Modern Language Review* 44(1949): 44–59, seems entirely convincing; nor should the conclusions which could be drawn from it be ignored.

8. Luca Landucci, *Diario fiorentino dal 1450 al 1516*, ed. Iodoco Del Badia (Florence, 1883), pp. 92–93.

9. G. Savonarola, *Glosa super Apocalipsim de statu ecclesiae ab anno salutis presenti scilicet 1481 usque ad finem mundi* (Geona, 1480). The sermons are *ex Genua* 1480. On the "signs of the antichrist," besides the verses by Verino already quoted in the text, see the letter by Fonzio, *frati Simoni Cinozo ord. pr.* (ed. L. Juhász [Budapest, 1931], pp. 47–48). On the coming of the Antichrist in general, and for the preaching of the Dominicans on the subject, see Lynn Thorndike, *A History of Magic and Experimental Science* (New York, 1934), 4: 264, 5: 124. Very important for the connection established by Ficino between Savonarola and the Antichrist is the essay by A. Chastel, "L'Apocalypse en 1500. La Fresque de l'Antéchrist à la Chapelle Saint-Brice d'Orvieto," *Bibl. d'Humanisme et Renaissance*, Mélanges Renaudet 14(1952): 124–40. The problem of the identification of Savonarola with the Antichrist is also treated in the *Storia* by Tizio (see G. Rondoni, "Una relazione senese su Girolamo Savonarola," *Archivio Storico Italiano*, series 5, 2[1888]); Tizio, however, denies the identification (referring also to a text by Landino): "That antichrist, the main false prophet, is yet to come. He will arise in the first phase of the sign of Aries during the conjunction of a triple mutation. It is now beyond question that the conjunction we were talking about was a minor one in the sign of the Scorpion. Therefore, if we are to attach any significance to the stars at all, we might say that Girolamo Savonarola was but a minor prophet."

10. In Gherardi, *Nuovi documenti*, p. 301. On p. 295 of the same work, see the other very important poems:

> All in the world tumbles down like a brook in the mountains;
> nothing endures on earth, time flies irretrievably,
> nor does a day, once gone, return. All that are born grow old,
> whatever was raised falls down; the wild fig-tree strikes root in
> the cracks of marble,
> foreordained is the ruin of doomed cities;
> the massive stones with which lordly mansions are built
> will soon be used for other dwellings and other men become
> their masters.
> Whatever the fury of war may spare must perish through rot. . . .

11. Reviewing the *Vita* by Ridolfi in *Lo Spettatore Italiano* (1952), p. 395, A. Frugoni concluded: "This is the only 'medievalism' I recognize in Savonarola; it is an archaic way of expressing himself and of habit. . . . But

his personality is entirely open to the religious problem of the society of his time." And see Ridolfi, *Vita,* 2: 19. The question of prophecy (see also F. Tocco, "Il Savonarola e la profezia," in the volume *La vita italiana del Rinascimento* [Milan, 1893], pp. 351–96), is raised again in terms of his relations with Gioachino da Fiore by Spini, and challenged in very explicit terms by Cantimori in his review of Schnitzer, (*Annali,* pp. 98–100). The problem, which is highly complex, cannot be reduced in terms to an exact and conscious dependence of Savonarola on Gioachino's texts, which his friend Pico owned and studied, extracting from them some of the theses which he proposed in the Roman discussion. Savonarola felt his own prophetic calling, and spoke in an environment in which prophecy was an actual experience (Landucci, *Diario,* p. 72: "We do not believe the latter is a prophet; he does not deny this in his sermons, but he always says *on the part of the Lord*"). He belonged to an order which was completely permeated by preoccupations of this type, and whose theoreticians were involved in discussing the nature and sources, not of reality, but of prophecy. The treatises of the period are full of the problem: the most radical ones, being tied with Avicennism, see prediction in a natural and rational light. (See for example the physician Andrea Cattani, who was a professor at the hospital in Florence, in *opus de intellectu et de causis mirabilium effectuum* [Florence, 1505], and who accepts Avicenna's thesis.) Then there were some who tied foretelling to the stars, which they believed possessed prophetic capabilities, not only for making calculations (genuine astrology), but also for influencing nature. And, finally, there were those who maintained that prophecy was attributable to supernatural agents, which could be either diabolical or divine. Savonarola, who argued with the astrologers and urged Pico to write the great treatise that he later resummarized in Italian, hoped to safeguard the supernatural character of prophecy and combatted other naturalistic interpretations. The problem then became one of knowing whether predictions were attributable to God or to the devil. Ficino, in his anti-Savonarola tract, did not deny prophecies but considered them due to malign influences. In reality, however, he also believed in foretelling the future, just as he believed in the imminence of future events. It is interesting to study such texts as the *Oraculum de novo saeculo* by Nesi (1496), dedicated to the "piagnone" Giovan Francesco Pico, as well as the works of the same Giovan Francesco Pico which are truly basic, such as *De rerum praenotione,* or the brief *Operecta . . . in defensione di Pietro Bernardo da Firenze,* which was published by Cherubelli in 1943 in a small booklet for weddings: it was taken from the very important Magliab. 35: 116. For the tie between Savonarola and the "fraticelli," according to contemporaries, see *Nuovi documenti intorno a Fra G.S.,* published by C. Lupi in *Archivo Storico Italiani,* series 3, 3(1866): 44.

12. Benedetto, *Cedrus Libani,* p. 67. In *Compendio di Rivelazioni,* Savonarola wrote: "and Florence being in the center of Italy, as the heart is in the center of the body, it was deigned to elect this city, in which such things are foretold. . . ."

13. See P. Luotto, *Il vero Savonarola e il Savonarola di L. Pastor* (Florence, 1900), pp. 23–24; and see Ridolfi, *Vita*, 1: 224.

14. Iacopo Nardi, *Istorie di Firenze*, published and edited by A. Gelli (Florence, 1858), 1: 91–92. See the *Canzone* cited in which the Florentine asks the Carnival: "Where are your children?/the wooden beamed and stone houses/holidays, games and so much fun/with many other playthings?" And the Carnival answers: "The children are my death/They have taken away my glory/with another sweet story/they have chased me from their court,/they no longer remember me. . . ." Who were these children, of low condition, who enjoyed *mira . . . licentia* and who fed prostitution, often sold by their parents, as is evident from the acts and condemnations, such as are found in Chapter VII of the Council of Florence for 1517–18, which "acriter insurgit contra eos qui pueros prostituunt." On Savonarola and the children, see as a main source Schnitzer, *Savonarolas Erzieher und Savonarolas als Erzieher* (Berlin, 1913), and *Savonarola*, 1: 305.

15. L. Landucci, *Diario*, pp. 122–24.

16. *La vita di Giovanni da Empoli, da che nacque ache mori, scritta da Girolamo de Empoli, suo zio*, published in *Viola del Pensiero, Miscellanea di Letteratura e Morale* (Livorno, 1841), 3: 101–32, and reprinted in *Archivio Storico Italiano*, 3(1846): 22–23. Much could be said about the "children." See, in any event, the *Epistola di Bernardino de fanciulli della città di Firenze mandata a essi fanciulli el di di Sancto Bernaba apostolo, adì* XI *di giugno MCCCCLXXXXVII* (printed, it seems, almost immediately); *Epistola di Frate Domenico da Pescia mandata a' fanciulli fiorentini, Florentie, in Sancto Marco, die* III *septembris MCCCCLXXXXVII; Petrus Bernardus de Florentia inutilis et indignus servulus Jesu Christi et omnium puerorum bonae voluntatis* in the ms. Magliab. 35:116, c. 60*v*–72. With regard to Girolamo da Empoli's discussion of the gentleness of the "children," see in Landucci (*Diario*, p. 123), the information on frequent incidents: "and on the day of 7 February 1495, the children lifted a veil from the head of a girl and there ensued a scandal with her people in the via de' Martegli."

17. F. Ercole, "La dittatura di Gerolamo Savonarola," in *Civiltà Moderna* 2(1930): 205.

18. *Ricordi storici di Filippo di Cino Rinuccini dal 1282 al 1460 colla continuazione di Alamanno e Neri suoi figli fino al 1506 . . .*, ed. G. Aiazzi (Florence, 1840), p. 116. Lorenzo is called "a new Falaris" in the dialogue *De libertate*. But it is important to compare Rinuccini's reaction to the "tyrant" (that is, that of an exponent of the old oligarchy that had been overthrown by the Medici) with that of Savonarola and of so many of those who were under Savonarola's influence. For the "legend" of the relations between Lorenzo and Savonarola, see what Ridolfi says—and these are definitive passages. But I believe that a careful examination of the letter from Politian to Antiquario also reveals, subtly, the influence that Savonarola exercised until 1492 in Lorenzo's circle. It is not a coincidence that Lorenzo complained that "his" Pico was

not there, with Politian, at his bedside! Something had changed for everyone with the coming of the friar.

19. See Cp. Ridolfi, *Vita*, 1: 12, 2: 89 (and for the text of the famous letter, the edition of Ridolfi himself [Florence, 1933], p. XXXII sqq. and p. 1). The verse which Savonarola recited with tears is by Virgil, *Aeneid*, 3: 44.

20. The "sages of the world" enjoyed the sermons of fra' Mariano; see on this subject the unusual letter (of 1490) from the Urbinate Andrea Corneo (ms. Vat. Capp. 235, ff. 92*v*–96*v*).

21. The texts of Infessura and of Lippo Brandolino in G. Pepe, *La politica dei Borgia* (Naples, 1946), pp. 20–21. Pepe's just and sensible pages on Savonarola (pp. 108–12) are used here, as are many of Spini's observations.

22. The judgment of Guicciardini in book 1 of *Storia d'Italia* is mentioned by Ridolfi, *Vita*, 1: 81, 2: 110–11. (The following words are no less significant: "the most insistent rapacity to exalt in any way whatever the children, of whom there were many." Poor Savonarola! F. S. Nitti, in an article written in 1947 ("*Firenze di Savonarola,*" *La Patria*, Florence, 5 October 1947), compared him to Mussolini.

23. The likeness is in Nesi, *Oraculum*.

24. On this essential point of Savonarola's activity, see Ridolfi, *Vita*, 1: 94.

25. From the *Prediche sopra Aggeo* (Ridolfi, *Vita*, 1: 121–22, 2: 123.)

26. G. Pepe, *La politica*, p. 109.

27. See Spini, *Introduzione*, p. 427. On the "disperati" of *Cedrus Libani*, p. 75: "He was the refuge and great consolation/of the poor and disconsolate:/He nourished the famished poor. . . ."

28. From the *Prediche sopra l'Esodo* (Ridolfi, *Vita*, 1: 334. See also 2: 201).

29. *Stanze fatte da una donna la quale ha nome Marietta ch'era spiritata*, ms. Magliab. 35: 116 (see Cherubelli in "Memorie Dominicane," [1941], and M. Ferrara, *Contributo allo studio della poesia savonaroliana*, [Pisa, 1921]).

30. National Library of Florence, Ms. Conv. G, 4, 826 (cc. 74 and 81).

IX
Florentine Culture at the Time of Leonardo

In a famous lecture on Leonardo the philosopher at the "Leonardo da Vinci" Circle in Florence in April 1906, Benedetto Croce, "playing the devil's advocate" as he later admitted, argued energetically and persuasively that it would be difficult to call the artist a philosopher—that, if anything, he could be characterized as a "penetrating, rigorous, and tireless investigator of nature" and "certainly a constructor of scientific laws and technical contrivances."[1] These arguments are perhaps not entirely acceptable today. Nor is it probably admissible to claim unqualifiably that Leonardo had no knowledge of philosophical principles on whose bases he could evaluate the significance of the laws of nature and of the "engines" he was building.[2]

Croce stressed in his lecture that Leonardo's attitude was entirely "empirical" and that his preoccupations were purely scientific. But even Croce, aside from the argument imposed on him by the demands of pragmatic oratorical panegyrics, would have given, I believe, due importance to certain of the extant formulas that were properly speaking philosophical. For whoever examines these formulas carefully, compares them with Leonardo's other general conceptions, and resituates them in the cultural environment of his time will gather new and plentiful arguments about the specific limits of Leonardo the philosopher as well as Leonardo the scientist.

Confronted with the myth of Leonardo, which took hold rather late and is of little help in gaining a historical understanding of the man and of the period, it is useful to try to define as precisely as possible his true place in his century, keeping in mind his own rather ironic and perhaps somewhat melancholic evaluation in the *Codice Atlantico* (p. 119*v*):

Seeing that I cannot acquire material of great utility or reward, because men born before me have taken for themselves all the useful and necessary themes, I will do as the person who out of poverty comes last to the fair, and, being unable to provide himself with anything else, takes all the things that have already been seen by others and discarded as being of little value. I will accept this despised and rejected merchandise that remains after many buyers, add it to my modest burden, and with it I will go, not through great cities but poor villages, and distribute it, taking whatever recompense the thing given by me merits.[3]

The impressions conveyed by the passages of the famous Leonardo codex have been accentuated in resounding phrases: the strange and beautiful forms of plants, animals, new machines; the calculations that are alternated with sayings and riddles; the undertakings; the long lists of words, even fictitious words; the disconcerting sentences, thoughts repeated without pause until a clear, effective form is found. However, these describe traits, which, although remarkable, pertain to Leonardo the artist, the poet—the greatest if you like—rather than to Leonardo the scientist and philosopher. He could correct himself sternly, but always in order to achieve ever greater clarity and truth, not in order to pursue heedlessly the most beautiful image or the most fitting tone.

When the work of Leonardo strikes our eyes and fancies, we do not admire him most for his great logic and precise reasoning. For the historian and the critic dedicated to their professions and not bent merely on finding an occasion to eulogize the artist, many of Leonardo's celebrated texts will eventually appear more like notes jotted down during hasty readings than like carefully thought-out conclusions. Regarding validity, the scientific content is frequently confused and contradictory.[4] All one needs do is re-examine some of the principal themes of his thought—for example, that concerning force or impetus—and one will quickly realize what a strange mixture they are of diverse motives and sometimes of quite contrasting theories which come together but are not synthesized in these curious pages of notes.[5]

The person of artistic temperament and esthetic sensitivity will doubtless experience—as he is almost compelled to—emotion and overwhelming awe. But the historian of ideas will at times be unable not to feel dismay and discomfort; he will certainly recognize in Leonardo's work the unquenchable thirst for knowledge, together with an unusual wealth of expression, a rare insight, and an unexcelled capacity not only for visual observation but also for translating different moods into visual terms; yet he will also have to acknowledge a certain inability to schematize rational syntheses and to organize incisive experimental procedures. It is easy to praise reason, but it is difficult to reason well; it is easy to call upon experience, but it is difficult to organize experiences systematically. When Leonardo proclaimed, "Before making this case a general rule, prove it two or three times," he had not really established a solid law for experimental science; nor had he indicated appreciable methodological progress by comparison with a physicist such as Buridan, whose brilliant discussions of mechanics were usually concluded with the remark: "*ego hoc non sum expertus, ideo nescio si est verum.*"* [6]

It is commonly repeated that Leonardo was an innovator and a forerunner—that from the beginning, facing the authority dominant in the schools and confronting the wave of literary-rhetorical erudition of humanism based on the imitation of the ancients, Leonardo, *omo sanza lettere,* was the first, or nearly the first, to oppose concrete experience integrated with mathematics, thus asserting himself as the founder of a new science. In contradiction to his times—that is, to Aristotelian scholasticism in the field of philosophy and in the natural sciences, as well as to rhetorical humanism in the moral and historical disciplines—Leonardo is considered truly to have been the first of the new men, a sort of miraculous intellectual hero who emerged spontaneously to upset the existing order.

To confute this opinion is by now neither a difficult nor an uncommon task. It is enough to refer to a work which appeared at the end of the nineteenth century and which has unjustly been ignored. The *Storia del metodo sperimentale in Italia,* by Raffaello Caverni, contains the observation that schools in the late Middle Ages were already teaching many of the rudimentary principles from which Leonardo was to draw his conclusions about rational mechanics. Caverni stresses that a serious historian would be ashamed to attribute to Leonardo the origin of experimental science, and he concluded with the statement that it is not too difficult to discover in the scientific traditions prior to the Cinquecento the natural sources from which sprang the encyclopedic variety of doctrines professed by the great artist of the Renaissance.[7]

Nearly a decade later, and quite independently, the leading French

* "I have not experimented with it; therefore, I don't know if it's true."

historian and scientist Pierre Duhem, in his famous studies that would later be completed by Marcolongo, disclosed many of Leonardo's debts to his predecessors, primarily in the field of physics. This research is naturally not always satisfactory, due either to *lacunae* or to a certain obstinate tendency to overrate the importance of the Cusan's influence in the Italian culture of the Quattrocento. On the other hand, if Leonardo is finally resituated within his historical environment, the uncertainties of evaluation and the absence of an exact knowledge of the various aspects of this environment weigh negatively on the attempt to establish in a true perspective the real significance of the scientist and thinker. All this notwithstanding, the ambiguous image of Leonardo as a *omo sanza lettere* persists—the critic of scholasticism in the name of the Renaissance, of philological humanism in the name of science, and of the *evasive* Florentine Platonic idealism in the name of practical experience.[8]

Today a more exact historical placement of da Vinci within his time must unquestionably be remade on the basis of precise research into the background in which he was formed. The first thirty years of his life (and they are of great weight in the spiritual formation of any man) Leonardo spent in Florence; he remained in the city until 1482, precisely the year in which Ficino's *Theologia Platonica* was published. (Leonardo was probably acquainted with Ficino.)[9] He was later to go to Milan, Pavia, and Venice, culturally very different environments. However, he was to return to Florence many times. Hence it is impossible to comprehend his mind without understanding in depth the complex Florentine world, which certainly cannot be illuminated by the standard, euphuistic references to humanism, Neoplatonism, "an environment saturated with cultivated esthetes and idealistic dreamers." Florence in these years was the center of European culture; people came from Germany to learn the sciences and arts, and the "news" from Florence was awaited and read as the new gospel by professors at the Sorbonne.[10]

The central figure of philological humanism in Florence during the second half of the Quattrocento was Angelo Politian. Politian, who was two years younger than Leonardo, was neither a pedant, a dull imitator of antiquity, nor an effete grammarian. Reference should be made to him at the outset in defining the exact nature of philological humanism. He continued the great tradition of Valla. An expert in philosophy, a jurist and historian, a sensitive poet of religious and secular verse in Greek, Latin, and the vernacular, he exemplified the entire force of a great spiritual revolution in process. For him philology was the search for the meaning of the word in all its significance and its rediscovery within its own historical dimensions. Philology was criticism that led every form of theory back into a world of human activity—that relocated every document, every doctrine, every dogma, every authority in its own period. For only humanistic philology properly speaking (and this could not be repeated often enough) set in motion and justified at base the most objective criticism of every authority. Only philology could instill the mental habit of resituating, returning to the periods and environments in which they were created, the most ancient and venerable texts, including the Holy Scriptures of every religion.

To see with one's own eyes—that is, with the eyes of reason alone, free of any preconceived notions—this was the praise Erasmus gave Valla and which we could well apply also to Politian. Valla had subjected the New Testament and the Donation of Constantine to the boldest examination. Politian directed his attention to the Justinian *Corpus*. In this school the tables of every law underwent the most frank scrutiny. And it was precisely this school that taught one to study with an absolutely open mind the great book of the universe. The texts of Leonardo that are best known—his "repeaters" and "trumpets" and so many others based on the *auctoritates*—seem flat compared with the reawakening of logic affirmed by Valla in his *Dialettica*, a work which moreover was well known and widely disseminated in Italy! In this work Valla does not specifically take issue with Aristotle but seeks to locate his method historically, to present it not as a necessary law of human thought, but as an historical product, historically justified and historically superseded by the progress of knowledge. The *Elegantiae*, which had become a school text and was one of the greatest works of the century, is filled with a rare sense of the humanity of language, a profound taste for the word and for life, a sense of the importance and significance of conversational exchange.

If we examine those long lists of words in the Leonardo codices (possibly extracted from Perotti or Tortelli) and rediscover that taste, that anxious tenderness for the verbal term which translates in essence and fairly points in all its nuances the movement of the soul, we inevitably think not of an enemy of humanism but of a loving son or of a too passionate lover who in the end is disillusioned in finding that his beloved is only a woman.[11] For one of the most valid aspects of humanism was exactly this quest, whose goal was to encompass all thought and reveal it in its most hidden recesses, so that between the thought and word, between the soul and the body, there would be no dissimilarity; in the end the entire body, truly illuminated by the soul, would not appear to be its mask, or that barred prison, but a shining disclosure and complete revelation. Just as in Valla, so also in Politian—in his notes for his lectures at the Studio, even in the comments that we may read on the margins of his books—we always come upon this same impassioned reverence for the sacred character of the word—the miraculous sacrament of the word, as Valla said. The word—that unrepeatable word of the poet, of the historian, or of an unknown author who wrote it down in an ancient scroll or on a stone—speaks to us of a time, a life, a soul; it celebrates, beyond time and space, a truly holy communion.

Far from reacting against this theme of humanism, Leonardo da Vinci seemed at times even to have exasperated it and to have carried it to its extremes, especially in those disconcerting manuscripts in which he seeks with an ecstatic, almost sensuous, love the revelational possibilities of a word. His tendency is the same when, feeling the inadequacy of words, he passes to pictorial language in an intimately gained awareness of a profound convergence of painting and poetry: "Painting is mute poetry, and poetry is blind painting, and both imitate nature as much as is within their powers."

But, it is argued, humanism was the imitation of authors and not of nature, whereas Leonardo always preferred the referral to nature to the referral to authors. Certainly much could be said on one or the other point. But Politian clearly testified on what the humanists considered to be imitation in a celebrated polemic with Cortesi, the reverberations of which were not only profound in Italian culture but was widespread in Europe during the Cinquecento. Politian lucidly clarified what it signified to imitate Cicero or Seneca: It meant to acquire an awareness of oneself in a relationship with another; to return to oneself and to create in the same way in which others had created; to rediscover one's own nature; to rediscover nature. Using the ancient and perennially new Socratic image, Marsilio Ficino was to say that those masters prod us to what we ourselves produce; that to imitate is to create, to rediscover artful nature at its source.[12]

At the time Leonardo was studying in Florence, Politian was not yet teaching at the Studio. But beginning in 1456 Cristoforo Landino taught there. Landino was a good friend of Marsilio, an admirer of Alberti, and an enthusiastic Platonist, although at times rather naive and impetuous. A faithful and perhaps somewhat servile court devotee of the Medici, he was every bit a schoolmaster. (A half-hearted admirer once stated that Landino would have done better if he had held classes in Prato rather than in Florence.)[13] Leonardo owed a great deal to one of Landino's works, a translation—and not entirely a happy one—of Pliny's *Storia Naturale* which Leonardo used extensively.

Landino was associated with another, greater teacher, the Byzantine Argyropulos, who began his courses in the same academic year. Leonardo knew Argyropulos and had conversations with him, as we may gather from the scanty information contained in his notes. What the talks were about we may readily surmise from the letter of a student who wrote about them to a friend who had remained in the country. He describes a Sunday afternoon when students and friends went to the house of the professor. They found him reading one of Plato's dialogues. Argyropulos began to discuss the work with them and this led to a further discussion of Platonic thought and Greek philosophy. After a while they all left the house together and walked through the streets in the center of town, debating all the way to the Annunziata. In front of the church they were joined by a monk, some acquaintances met on the way, and a few curious onlookers, and they continued to argue quietly and amicably about philosophical problems.[14]

This letter is quoted because it is without artifice and was not intended for public perusal, as its inaccurate and hurried writing indicates. It would be easy, however, to multiply the examples, to refer to the descriptions of Crinito or, half a century earlier, those of Niccolò della Luna, as well as to the conversations in the cloisters of San Marco where men of very different tendencies and sentiments gathered. One should never lose sight of the extremely lively and rapid circulation of ideas within a basically limited circle in Quattrocento Florence, from which it radiated until all came to participate in a certain cultural climate. This climate ranged from the modest but sincere grammatical culture of Landino to the elevated philosophical thought of Argyropulos, a perspicacious scholar and outstanding commentator on Aristotle in Greek and (among other Aristotelian works) on the *Physics* in the light of Greek culture up to Philoponus. Philoponus is mentioned because with his thesis of a *χινητιχὴ δύναμις* and a *ενέογεια χινητιχή* he elaborated a theory not far removed from that of Buridan and Albertuccio on *impetus* which Leonardo studied assiduously.[15]

If Leonardo's mention of Argyropulos is significant, his recollection of Paolo Toscanelli, noted in the *Codice Atlantico,* is no less important. The great Paolo Fiorentino was a scientist of first rank, an astute investigator of physical, astronomical, and mathematical problems with a Europe-wide reputation, and a friend of the Cusan, whom he introduced to mathematics and astronomy. His influence—as a great German historian wrote—was to extend through Peurbach and Regiomontanus to Copernicus.[16] Landino has left us a rather fine portrait of Toscanelli as somewhat shy, withdrawn, lost in thought, and detached from the life of the city (which nonetheless was close to him and well-disposed toward him), studiously engaged in natural experiments, and a great mathematician. It was this same fruitful union of observation and mathematics which in Leon Battista Alberti was united with rare power as a writer and unusual depth as a philosopher.[17]

All these names appear in Leonardo's notes, and not by chance. They were men who could also meet, on a holiday afternoon, somewhere between the church of the Servi di Maria and the Piazza dei Signori, to converse around the steps of a well or in the cloisters of a monastery with some good friar or a young and promising artist. They discussed matters to do with experience and reason, light and shadow, knowledge and love. They also discussed a strange anatomical experiment ("since no one can be a qualified physician unless he is thoroughly familiar with the anatomy of the human body") carried out at the Faculty, whose laws of thrift authorized, besides the emaciated corpses of both sexes donated by the commune, the bodies of the executed—provided the students ran immediately to obtain them, "because the human corpse begins at once to stink and putrefy."[18]

Florence of the Quattrocento presents the image of a city completely enraptured by the music of lutes and enveloped in the fumes of incense from Neoplatonic rites, because the venerable Giorgius Gemistus had given the shrewd Cosimo the idea of diverting the civic-mindedness of the cultivated bourgeoisie to a contemplation of the unity of sources. The reality was somewhat different. At the Studio Argyropulos was teaching to a large following a modernized and refined Aristotelianism, which had become enriched during the learned Byzantine's studies in Padua with the whole problematics of the most advanced schools of logic and physics. The "English" logic—that is, the latest developments of the logical-methodological discussions of the nominalists, which at times bore a striking resemblance to the new methodology—had stimulated a continuing interest in Florence from the beginning of the century. To call this logical nominalism is expressing the need for a new method in the empiric sciences, which would incorporate the results of mathematical processes.[19] It was not coincidental that with regard to questions of logic the bold and weighty conclusions of Parisian physicists were being studied.

At the end of the fourteenth and the beginning of the fifteenth century, discussions of this kind were exceptionally lively on the banks of the Arno, where they seemed quite natural. As early as the Trecento the friar Bernardo d'Arezzo, who took his university degree in Florence and accentuated the phenomenism of Ockham, had met and clashed with that redoubtable logician, Nicolas d'Autrecourt, who fulminated during one of his lectures at the Sorbonne *contra Magistrum Bernardum de Aretia.*[20] The name of Nicolas d'Autrecourt suggests a model empiricist; he appears exemplary in this sense to modern scholars. The name of Ockham connotes the author of a theory of motion which, when once developed, could have disproved Aristotle's positions and has been placed for its refinement and acumen beyond the most astute physicists and logicians of the Quattrocento. Ockham, it should not be forgotten, upset something else than the Aristotelian theory of motion. At the end of the Trecento, Florentine scholars also sang his praise in verse, at a time when Biagio Pelacani—whom Leonardo was later to quote and study—was at his height amid the universal admiration that resounded in the pages of the *Paradiso degli Alberti.* From the registers of books lent by libraries one may see that, if not gentlewomen, certainly good friars were contending for the writings of Buridan.[21] Biagio was writing on perspective, on the speed of movements, on meteors, on the sphere, on all the usual arguments.

At the close of the Quattrocento many interests had undeniably changed in Florence. The official teaching of terminist logic, such as was done in Pavia, was unthinkable. But the logical-physical discussion on the one hand, and experimental research on the other, were the order of the day. There are traces of this everywhere. Curiously—but not too curiously—the interests of the humanists in verbal terms appeared at times to correspond with the achievements of the logicians. It is important to keep in mind that in the schools the teaching of logic was frequently entrusted to humanists and, since it is coupled with grammar and rhetoric, to the *sermocinales* disciplines. Politian, who taught logic and dialectics, was what we would call today a grammarian, a linguist, and a philologist. On the other hand there were physicians and physicists, experimentalists and anatomists. In Florence after 1470, they continued to polemize for reasons of prestige and salaries with jurists and grammarians. But men who passed from one discipline to the other were not uncommon nor were those who professed more than one discipline. Ficino was a physician, a philosopher, and a man of letters; Politian was also a jurist; Antonio Benivieni alternated between humanist studies and major research on pathological anatomy. Even after the Studio had moved to Pisa, the masters debated in Florence. Bernardo Torni, a physician, argued brilliantly with the great Marliano, whom Leonardo was to read and study at length in Milan.[22]

The famous Florence of the "idealistic dreamers"—in sum the atmosphere in which Leonardo da Vinci was formed and which later was to become the Italian and European high culture—was, viewed from one of its leading and most informed centers, in these years perhaps the most important, the most varied and complex. Thomism, with its considerable interest in concrete experiments after the great Giovanni Dominici and the holy bishop Antonino, was to find an extraordinary supporter in Savonarola; the friar was to give considerable space to extracts from the works on nature of Albertus Magnus in his handbook of philosophy for use in schools. I do not know how many among those who are accustomed to sing hymns of praise in admiration for Leonardo's "fables" have ever held in their hands the rude text that is the compendium of the friar of San Marco—which in fact contained nothing original and has been justifiably ignored. But whoever has would certainly have been struck by the similarity between Leonardo's notations and the texts of

Albertus Magnus, which were still circulating in preparatory schools —that is, with the medieval lapidaries and bestiaries.[23] Albertus and Thomas, the lapidaries and Pliny, are united in a note of the *Codice Atlantico* with Filelfo's letters, with the *Facezie* of Poggio, with the *de honesta voluptate* of Platina. (The latter, title notwithstanding, deals not with the joys of contemplation but with cooking recipes; it is, in short, a cookbook.) These were books that were commonly read, even by a friar of San Marco; in whose library, moreover, one finds everything, including Poggio and Platina.[24]

Undoubtedly, the Thomism in the line of Dominici, Saint Antonino, and Savonarola could also represent the extreme right of Florentine Quattrocento culture, although a scientist such as Benivieni—a famous physician, a rare interpreter of clinical cases, and an outstanding anatomical pathologist—at a certain moment came close to this right. But the nuances of philosophical and scientific Aristotelianism of these years in Florence were innumerable—from that liberal and objective Aristotelianism of Argyropulos, to that of the physician Niccolò Tignosi, which was scholasticizing and yet open to new problems, to that of Torni, which was subtly present in the most informed discussions on physics. Yet another strain was the moral and political Aristotelianism of Acciaiuoli's circle, which continued the tradition of Manetti; the pure Avicennism was espoused by some doctor at the hospital of Santa Maria Nuova.[25] There were then theoreticians of astronomy and astrology, and geographers; there were—and most important for understanding Leonardo—artisans who mixed alchemistic and magical formulas and incantations with recipes for the coloring of cloth and the working of metals, and who united the most ancient hermetic traditions with the most prosaic and material technical interests. There were great scientist-philosopher-artists like Alberti and pure scientists like Toscanelli.

Lastly, there was Marsilio Ficino, with his little Neoplatonic coterie. Much more should be said about Ficino: that he never abandoned the study of medicine, that he wrote about hygiene, that he was always interested in magic and in general in what were called "the experimental arts." He started by dealing with problems of physics, with perspective, and immediately confronted a field of enquiry that was to remain basic for him: light and vision.[26]

To affirm that Ficino's entire thought was centered about the two themes of light and love would not be far from the truth. Love, he said, is the very heartbeat of universal life: "Love is in all things and reaches out toward all things; . . . it is master and lord of all the arts. . . ." But if for Ficino love was the intimate force and soul of reality, the vestment of the universe was light. Reality was felt as love with love; it was understood as form through seeing. This convergence of seeing with loving, the generator of vital fruits, permeates Ficino's thought. The *Codice Trivulziano* contains a well-known passage by Leonardo: "The lover moves toward the object of his love as the subject embraces the form, as sense the sensible, and unites with it and makes it one and the same thing. . . . The work is the first thing born of this union." It is not difficult to see the similarity, even in the language, to Marsilio's *Convito*. The resemblance is even more pronounced in two other passages from the *Trivulziano:* "The senses are terrestrial, reason is outside them when it contemplates. . ."; "Our body is subjected to the heavens, and the heavens are subjected to the spirit." These were trite enough motifs in the Florentine culture of the time. This lapidary affirmation was not in fact original to Leonardo but had been made before him in more forceful and expressive language: *nihil magnum in terra praeter hominem, nihil magnum in homine praeter mentem et animum; huc si ascendis, coelum trascendis.** [27]

This leads us to a whole complex of precise investigations and discussions of astrology, astronomy, magic and necromancy, mathematics and experiment, of true causes and signs which Leonardo took up again and recapitulated, at times with remarkable imagery ("necromancy, . . . a floating banner, moved by the wind"). But we should not lose sight of the fact that Leonardo's speculative antecedents and philosophical background should also be sought, at least in part, in those Florentine cultural attitudes characteristic of the years in which the artist was being formed. His milieu abounded in fervid interests of every kind; at the same time Ficino was slowly perfecting his masterpiece, which is to some extent the *Summa* of a whole orientation: his *Theologia platonica,* which was begun in 1469 and published only in 1482. Light and problems of optics together with metaphorical references to light—the eye as the center of the universe (not the sensible eye but the mind), man the microcosm and

* "There is nothing greater on earth than man, nothing greater in man than his mind and his spirit; if you rise to their heights, you transcend the heavens."

man the artificer and poet, that is, man the creator—all this was Ficino in Florence between 1470 and 1480.

"The eye, the moment it is opened, observes all the stars of our hemisphere. . . . The mind leaps in one instant from East to West and its quickness makes it quite dissimilar to all other natural things. . . . The soul can never be corrupted by the corruption of the body, but it works in the body as the wind that makes the organ sound, so that if one pipe is out of order, the result is empty of effect." Thus Leonardo echoed Ficino in passages of the *Codice Trivulziano* and the *Codice Atlantico*. Force, that universal force that moves the soul and animates everything, is also defined with repeated insistence as spiritual:

> Force is a spiritual power, incorporeal and intangible. . . . Spiritual, I say, because there is invisible life in it, incorporeal and intangible . . . because the body in which it was born does not grow in form or weight. . . . Force is a spiritual essence. . . . Force is nothing else than a spiritual quality, an invisible power which is created and infused through accidental violence from sensible into insensible bodies, giving the latter the semblance of life; and this life is a miraculous evolution; embracing and mutating the place and form of all things created, it hastens toward its own disintegration and becomes diversified according to the causes.

Manuscript B of the Institut de France contains a similar passage: "I say that force is a spiritual, incorporeal, invisible power . . . ; I say spiritual, because it contains active incorporeal life; and I say invisible, because the body in which it is born does not grow, either in weight or form." Again, in the *Codice Atlantico:* "Force is entirely itself, and it is all in every part of itself."

Leonardo Olschki speaks in this regard of "the blurred vision of the most objective observer caused by the fumes of incense with which *die Florentiner Schwärmer sich die Atmosphäre bildeten.*"* I do not know how much of this trenchant observation may be conceded, but it seems to me that Olschki is right in his basic historical judgment.[28] The concept of spiritual force has very little to do with rational mechanics, while it has the closest affinity with the Ficinian-hermetic theme of life and universal animation. Whoever sets out to follow theme after theme would travel a long as well as profitable

* "the Florentine enthusiasts created their own climate."

road. But two of Leonardo's characteristic themes, which are also compulsory reading in Leonardian hagiography, should not be passed over in silence. The most important is his comment that *the Godliness of the painter's science* consists in the fact that "the mind of the painter is transformed into a likeness of the divine mind." This solemn affirmation should be combined with another well-known statement, that painting "is science and the legitimate daughter of nature, because painting is the offspring of nature," so that "we would rightly call it a grandchild of nature and a relative of God." With respect to this last passage, which is truly not extraordinary, the commentators, who are also not extraordinary, refer to Dante. But Leonardo's thesis on painting and nature here must be viewed within its larger framework.

Marsilio Ficino, in the fourth book of the *Theologia*—which deals with the causes and the infinite reasons that govern nature—observes:

If human art is none other than the imitation of nature, if this art of man produces its own works by the means of certain reasons (*per certas operum rationes*), nature operates in a similar way; and with a skill that is much more alive and knowing, as more living and beautiful are its works. And if finally the art that produces inanimate things operates by means of live reasons (*si ars vivas rationes habet*) . . . , how much more alive must be the reasons of nature, the creator of living beings and the producer of forms? . . . What is human art if not a nature that molds matter from without? And what is nature if not an art that intimately modifies matter; how would it be if the molder of wood should himself be of wood? But if human art, although fashioned from without, yet adheres to and is intrinsic to the work that it produces, to the point of achieving a synthesis between work and idea (*ut certa opera consummet certis ideis*), how much better does nature do this! It does not touch the surface of matter with alien instruments as the mind of the geometer when he delineates his figures on the ground, but it is like a geometrical mind that intimately forms imaginary matter (*ut geometrica mens materiam intrinsecus phantasticam*). In this fashion, in fact, the mind of the geometer, while it turns over the reasons for its own figures, inwardly gives expression to fantasy according to the various images, so in nature a divine wisdom molds and forms matter with supreme ease from within by means of those reasons with which the vital force and the motor joined to it are pervaded. What is a work of art if not the mind of the creator which penetrates isolated matter? What is the work of nature if not the mind of nature which is intrinsic to matter itself. . . . Would you then hesitate to grant that these are explicit reasons in nature? In that way human art, which operates from without, produces according to contingent reasons and molds contingent forms, while natural art, which generates and expresses essential forms from the bosom of matter, works by means of essential and perpetual reasons.[29]

The magic point of union between the science of the painter and the science of nature, for both of whom the mind of man "is transmuted into a likeness of the divine mind"—this ideal nexus which is the very soul of Leonardo's thought—has its roots precisely in Platonic-Ficinian philosophy. Because the painter, in order to be a true "creator," must discover the secret of "artful nature"—that is, reach from a superficial view to a profound vision, to the "reasons" of experience, to "necessity" which ties effects to causes—in order to become himself intrinsic to the cause. Painters then grasp with their creative "reason" the "reasons" of experiments, the mathematical necessities for contingent appearances: the forms, the dyes that the eye of the mind rediscovers in passing beyond the sensory eye. Leonardo writes admirably of himself:

> And drawn by my craving thirst, I roam about to observe the great mass of varied and strange forms produced by skillful nature. And moving about among shadowy rocks, I came to a great cave, at the entrance to which I remained, stupified and ignorant of such a thing. I leaned over, bracing my tired hand above my knee, and my right hand shaded my narrowed, lowered eyelids. And I bent down frequently to peer here and there in order to see if I could discern something. But this was denied me by the great blackness that was inside. And suddenly two feelings arose in me: fear and desire; fear because of the menacing and dark cavern, and desire to see if there were something miraculous within.

From Plato's *Timaeus* Leonardo was to take up again the whole geometric theory of the elements which is contained in Manuscript F of the Institut de France. In his commentary on the *Timaeus* Marsilio Ficino discusses at great length *quomodo Physica constent ex Mathematicis, Physica per Mathematica probaturus.** And he insists on the necessity of uniting empiric knowledge with mathematical knowledge, which is the path and the instrument of every science (*omnis eruditionis ingenuae vis*).[30] He then enumerates the examples of con-

* "how physics is founded on mathematics, how physics can be explained through mathematics."

temporaries, from Pier Leone da Spoleto, a physician, to Francesco Berlinghieri, a cosmographer, but he refers mainly to Leon Battista Alberti. Leonardo, in his turn, when propounding his famous principle that "no human research can be called true science unless it is subjected to mathematical proofs," rather than indicate an exact instrument of investigation in mathematics, restated the Platonic-Ficinian theme of applying empiric research to those mathematical foundations which constitute the absolute rational structures of everything. This then is the speculative implication of his insistence on the profound necessity which governs harmoniously the whole universe and which constitutes the true miracle of the world: "O miraculous, O marvellous necessity, with your law you compel effects to participate via the shortest route in their causes; these are miracles. . . ."

This was precisely the extent of Leonardo's experimentalism: in these mathematical "reasons," in a metaphysical presupposition rather than a logical instrument of research. He did certainly insist on experience, of which he declared he was a son, but when he encountered a barrier in the metaphysical assumption of an objective plan of ideal reasons, with immutable forms, his experimental investigations were fractionized into a series of individual observations, while his formulations of the so-called natural "laws" were vitiated by arbitrary metaphysical extensions. The ambiguous character of his mathematical reasons forced him to oscillate between an insufficiently probed philosophy and an unmethodically organized science. His experimentalism, as well as his technique and his absurd or faulty engines, gives the impression of comminuted research or whimsical chicanery, while his astonishing general formulations at times reveal gratuitous philosophical assumptions. The "Science of the Painter," which at a certain moment he intended to constitute as a total conception of being under the visible species, is spent in contemplative asceticism; the experiment is dissipated in a strange notation; the engine becomes a diverting plaything for the festivities of Lodovico il Moro.

In Leonardo we will always find an amazing artist and a sublime and disconcerting poet in his truly unique prose; but we will not find modern technique, nor the modern experimental science of a Bacon, nor the synthesis of a Galileo, and, lastly, not even Ficino's metaphysics. From Ficino Leonardo borrowed not only the central themes of his "philosophy" of light, but even the metaphors on the sun for that celebrated *Lalda del Sole,* in which he indicates that he was indebted to the natural hymns of Marullo but which is probably inferior to the moving poetry that dominates Marsilio's work. For example, in this treatise in praise of the sun, he imagines for one moment all light, even the stars, extinguished and the universe immobile, frozen into night. And again the sunrise, and the life it gives, and the prayer of thanksgiving of all living beings who hail the sun, the source of life and the true simulacrum of God, because the light, whose source and symbol it is, is the true life of bodies and minds. Leonardo notes in the *Codice Atlantico:* "Would the Lord, who is the light of all things, deign to enlighten me, the describer of light."[31] But Ficino, in many of his passages devoted to the sun, went further. He discounted at base the possibilities of geocentrism; he created the psychological atmosphere of heliocentrism; he stressed the necessity of the central position of the sun. Pico, more subtly and with greater scientific preparation, demonstrated the historical reasons for Ptolemy's system, showed how they were outdated and unsatisfactory, and, at the same time, referred back to the theory of the plurality of inhabited worlds.

So much emphasis on Ficino may appear useless and out of place. But it is done with the clear intent of opposing the commonly held opinion of the influence of the Cardinal of Cusa which from 1800 on has been unusually exaggerated as a factor in the formation of Italian culture. Duhem devoted a large part of the thick volume of the second series of his *Studies* to demonstrating the filiation of the Cusan and Leonardo. This demonstration was repeated later by Cassirer and commonly accepted as self-evident.[32] Today, not only are there no convincing proofs that da Vinci was familiar with the difficult philosophical writings of the Cusan, but it is certain that they were also very little known by Platonic scholars like Ficino and unavailable to Pico at whatever expense he could afford for codices. Certain doctrinal similarities, far from being conclusive, indicate, at most, common sources and are only a proof of great ingeniousness. An eminent historian, for example, finds the mark of the Cusan in a text by Leonardo because "Hermes the philosopher" is mentioned in it; this explanation ignores Ficino's translation of the hermetic books, which was published in 1471, had seven editions in about twenty years, and was one of the greatest successes of the time—so great in fact that it established a veritable fashion.[33]

In reality, Leonardo da Vinci, who lived in one of the most cultivated and accomplished milieux in Europe and who was introduced to the most developed and informed research of the time, encountered, in the circles of Pavia, Milan, and Venice and in the North in general, an even stronger accentuation of those logical and physical discussions which since the fourteenth century had been steeped in an antique image of the world. Though a remarkable artist and most original writer, Leonardo certainly did not create the experimental method, nor the synthesis between mathematics and experience, nor the new physics; but he may well be considered the symbol of the transition from a profound critical elaboration, whose results he epitomized, to the formulation of renewed concepts.

He came into contact with methodical processes and with the mechanical theories that by then had surpassed the old Aristotelianism, and he made in Florence and elsewhere the broadest contributions of clear observations. Yet, in the field of philosophy he did not attain a new vision of reality, but limited himself to repeating refined variations of current themes. In the scientific field, if he did not elaborate original theories, he probed deeply in more than one case into the fruitful theses that he found already formulated. An untiring observer, he set down his experiences with splendid eloquence, but he did not always go beyond an unsystematic pursuance of "magical" experiments. He felt, with the intuition of genius, the great value of technique, and he was certainly an extraordinary "engineer." But in more than one case he pursued fantastic visions without passing through the prosaic processes necessary to concrete achievements; and in this too he was at times more similar to Roger Bacon than to Galileo. He was, above all, the typical exponent of an epoch and of an exceptional city, of the restlessness of a changing world. But in this he was no more exceptional than many others of his time—receptive to every interest, conscious of the central position of man, who builds his own world with his own hands.

To lead Leonardo back to his time, to his concrete historical dimensions, to his human size beyond any myth, is perhaps the best way of honoring a man who at times had a sense of measure that could be called most pure and who, beside the apocalyptic unleashing of disordered forces, always dreamed of the immortal harmonies of forms as though they were enchanting feminine images.

Notes

1. B. Croce, *Leonardo filosofo, Conferenza,* an appendix to *Saggio sullo Hegel* (Bari, 1913), pp. 213–40. On Leonardo *non filosofo,* see especially pp. 217–18, 220–21 ("the spirit and the prose of Leonardo elevate us, no doubt; but for all that they do not elevate us to philosophy"), p. 226 ("unphilosophical as a naturalist, and antiphilosophical as an agnostic"), and p. 235 ("the little satisfaction which the treatise of Leonardo gives to whoever turns to it to look for a philosophy of art . . ."). See also the eloquent essay by Gentile (now in *Il pensiero italiano del Rinascimento,* [Florence, 1940], pp. 117–49) and his preliminary considerations ("in view of these considerations it may be said rightly that Leonardo does not belong to the history of philosophy"). See the important contemporary study of Luporini, *La mente di Leonardo* (Florence, 1953), for a very different position than the one taken here.

2. Croce himself stressed (*Leonardo,* p. 213 *n*), by way of putting us on guard, his polemic intention; this does not mean, however, that his observations are not in substance valid. On the limits of Leonardo's "logic," see the comments of F. Albèrgamo, *Storia della logica delle scienze empiriche* (Bari, 1952), p. 49.

3. Judicious limitations to the romantic myth of Leonardo are made with precise observations by A. Marinoni in his *Scritti letterari* (Milan, 1952). (On p. 21: "The excessive insistence on the presentient character, real or presumed, of certain . . . thoughts has diverted our attention more to the periphery than to the core of his personality.") G. Fumagalli is, however, excessive at times in his admiration in his *Leonardo "omo sanza lettere"* (Florence, 1938), although it is a valuable book, rich in doctrine, in fecund themes, and in incisive conclusions.

4. Solmi wrote in "Le fonti di Leonardo da Vinci," *Giornale storico della lett. ital.,* Suppl. 10–11(1908): 3: "The *Manoscritti,* which remains extant in the form of preliminary and disconnected notes, present us with the entire fruit of Leonardo's mind, that which is in itself a simple copy of his works which are now forgotten, but which were well known in the 15th and 16th centuries. . . ."

5. In order to realize the difficulty of organizing Leonardo's thoughts on the primary themes, it is sufficient to consult the texts on *impetus* as they have been reconstructed by Uccelli (*I libri della meccanica* [Milan, 1942], pp. 385–98). The difficulty is undoubtedly increased by the impossibility of dating with certainty all of the various fragments; the fact remains that the thoughts gathered by Uccelli derive from doctrines and theories which are diverse and not reconcilable with each other, and which require a more exact placement

in time. So far as the various forms which the theory on impetus takes, see among others the excellent studies of A. Maier, *Die Impetustheorie der Scholastik* (Leipzig-Vienna, 1940) and *Die Vorläufer Galileis im 14. Jahrhundert . . .* (Rome, 1949), pp. 132–54. And on motion, we should not overlook the very lucid theories of Ockham. (On the need to date the philosophical fragments, see the concise statement by G. Castelfranco, "Leonardo scrittore," *L'Arte*, October 1937, p. 263).

6. The text of Leonardo is contained in Codex A of the Library of the Institut de France, folio 47r (and in Fumagalli, *Leonardo "omo sanza lettere,"* p. 43). The text of Buridan is in *De coelo et mundo*, ed. E. A. Moody (Cambridge, Mass., 1942), and in A. Maier, *Die Vorläufer Galileis*, p. 137. L. Thorndike (*A History of Magic and Experimental Science*, [New York, 1941], 5: 16 exaggerates, and certainly excessively, the value of Leonardo's experimentalism, but it is undoubtedly true when he affirms (p. 19): "This representation of da Vinci as far in advance of his time and in touch with modern science reminds one of the similar picture drawn of Roger Bacon by his earlier modern admirers." An even stronger view of Leonardo's limitations is expressed in the article by J. H. Randall, Jr., "The Place of Leonardo da Vinci in the Emergence of Modern Science," *Journal of the History of Ideas* 14(1953): 191–202.

7. R. Caverni, *Storia del metodo sperimentale in Italia* (Florence, 1895), Vol. 4. (See P. Duhem, *Études sur Léonard de Vinci*, 2nd. series [Paris, 1909], pp. 361–63; and *Sur la mécanique de Léonard de Vinci et les recherches de Raffaello Caverni*). It was Marcolongo who called Duhem's attention to Caverni's work, since Duhem also stated in the first volume of his studies (1906, p. 123) that "the newest and most daring visions of Leonardo had been suggested and guided by medieval science." As is well known, R. Marcolongo completed and brought up to date Duhem's research (in *La Meccanica di Leonardo da Vinci, Atti R. Acc. delle Scienze Fisiche e Matematiche*, series 2, Vol. 19 [Naples, 1933]). A. Uccelli writes (*I libri*, p. 33): "R. M. deserves credit for having synthesized and brought up to date Duhem's work in line with our latest knowledge in Italy with regard to the Vinci codices."

8. In an analysis that contains many valid observations (*Geschichte der neusprachlichen wissenschaftlichen Literatur* [Heidelberg, 1919]), Leonardo Olschki maintains that Leonardo left Florence to flee the nebulous Neoplatonism; but all have correctly emphasized to what extent, for better or worse, Leonardo remained fundamentally in its debt, from Gentile to Cassirer (*Individuo e cosmo nella filosofia del Rinascimento*, Italian trans. [Florence, 1935]) to F. M. Bongioanni (*Leonardo pensatore* [Piacenza, 1935]), Fumagalli ("*omo,*" p. 44, no. 4), Marinoni (*Scritti*, pp. 11–12). It is useful to recall the frank praise which, after Ficino's death, the Neoplatonist and Ficinian Giovanni Nesi gave to Leonardo, who—Gentile reasserted in 1937—"possessed the inspiration and the manner of thinking of the head of the Florentine Academy."

9. The famous list of works and authors, written in red ink in the *Codice Atlantico*, folio 210r contains the title *de immortalità d'anima*, which

G. d'Adda (*Leonardo da Vinci e la sua libreria, Note di un bibliofilo* [Milan, 1873]) identified with the *De Immortalitate animae* by Ficino (see Richter, *The Literary Works of Leonardo da Vinci* [London, 1883], 2: 442, 444; and Marinoni, *Scritti*, p. 243). Solmi ("Le fonti," pp. 153–54), excludes this without valid reasons, indicating an improbable vulgarization of Filelfo's texts. The enormous impact everywhere in Italy and abroad of Ficino's work escapes Solmi.

10. R. Gaguin writes (Paris, September 1946), *Epistolae et orationes* (Paris, 1904), no. 76 (P. O. Kristeller, *Supplementum Ficinianum* [Florence, 1937], 2: 242): "Your scholarship and your wisdom, Ficino, are so well known at our Academy of Paris that at meetings of the greatest scholars as well as in the students' classrooms your name is mentioned with affection and reverence." This is one of many testimonies; one can easily point to Germano di Ganai, or Lefèvre d'Etaples, or Reuchlin, or many other very well-known witnesses.

11. On the study that Leonardo made of Perotti, see, in synthesis, Marinoni, *Scritti*, p. 227. De Robertis wrote ("La difficile arte di Leonardo," in *Studi*, [Florence, 1944], p. 79): "The notes were born in Leonardo after long labor. He was always in search of the maximum precision with the maximum brevity, to stimulate inventiveness. Entire pages are filled with masses of words; interminable enumerations, which in his mind must have been so many nuclei from which he expected to free his metaphorical language."

12. The Politian-Cortesi polemic on *imitazione* is reproduced in *Prosatori del Quattrocento* (Milan-Naples, 1952). On humanistic *imitazione*, the precise observations of L. Russo, *Problemi di metodo critico* (Bari, 1952), should be kept in mind. On the repercussions in Europe of certain concepts, see B. Weinberg, *Critical Prefaces of the French Renaissance* (Evanston, Ill., 1950).

13. The negative judgment of Landino is from Acciaiuoli (ms. Magliab. 8: 1390). On the very considerable use that Leonardo made of Landino's *Plinio*, see E. Solmi, "Le fonti," pp. 235–48. For a severe contemporary critical judgment of the translation of Pliny, see B. Croce, "Uno sconosciuto umanista quattrocentesco: Giovanni Brancati," *Quaderni della Critica* 10(1948): 20–21. A very explicit description of Landino's teaching is given by Marinoni, *Scritti*, p. 231, with regard to Leonardo's linguistic studies. Solmi's assertion that Leonardo was acquainted with Barbaro's *Castigationes plinianae* ("Le fonti," pp. 85–86) is, on the contrary, not convincing.

14. Ms. Magliab. 6: 166, cc. 108–109v. See *Codice Atlantico*, f. 12v; Solmi, *Leonardo* (1923), pp. 12–14.

15. See the introduction to Uccelli, *I libri di meccanica.*

16. Cassirer, *Individuo*, pp. 61–62.

17. On Alberti and Leonardo, see Solmi, "Le fonti," pp. 37–43; unfortunately Solmi, almost as though he feared that Leonardo would be diminished by the greatness of Alberti, arrives at very strange conclusions ("L.B.A. is a compiler . . . he manifests a distressing superficiality . . . he is a popularizer . . .

he courts knowledge in order then to make it of public use . . ."). On the other hand, Uccelli (p. 155) rightly insists on the need to broaden the investigation. I have attempted to prove elsewhere that the same "reasons" of Leonardo were present in Alberti.

18. *Statuti della Università e Studio Fiorentino* . . . (Florence, 1881), p. 74. With regard to the rather widespread use in Florence of autopsy, see L. Thorndike, *Science and Thought in the Fifteenth Century* (New York, 1929), pp. 123–32, 290–95 ("A Fifteenth Century Autopsy," carried out by Bernardo Torni). But it is enough to read again the *De abditis nonnulis ac mirandis morborum et sanationum causis* by Antonio Benivieni (published posthumously by Girolamo in 1506). On Benivieni, see the introduction by Luigi Belloni to the edition of *De regimine sanitatis* (Turin, 1951), and that of Renato Piattoli to the *Elogio di Cosimo* (Florence, 1949).

19. See L. Geymonat, *Caratteri e problemi della nuova metodologia,* taken from *Atti e Memorie della Colombaria* (Florence, 1952), p. 11; and J. R. Weinberg, *Nicolaus of Autrecourt. A Study in 14th Century Thought* (Princeton, 1948).

20. On friar Bernardo, see N. Papini, *Etruria francescana* (Siena, 1707), 1: 11; on his relations with Nicolaus of Autrecourt, see J. Lappe, *Nicolaus von Autrecourt, sein Leben, seine Philosophie, seine Schriften,* "Beitrag z. Gesch. d. Philos. des Mittelalt.," 6, 2(1908), and especially B. Nardi, *Il problema della verità ecc.* (Rome, 1951), pp. 46–53.

21. For Leonardo's use of quotations from Pelacani, see Solmi, "Le fonti," pp. 227–29. On Pelacani, see L. Thorndike, *A History of Magic,* 4: 65–79, and A. Maier, *Die Vorläufer Galileis,* pp. 279–99 (for his introduction to *Paradiso degli Alberti,* see the edition by Alexander Wesselofski [Bologna, 1867], 1: 132–42, 3: 18–19). Interesting information on the *letture* that took place in Florence at the end of the fourteenth century is contained in N. Brentano Keller, "Il libretto di spese e di ricordi di un monaco Vallombrosano per libri dati o avuti in prestito," *Bibliofilia,* Vol. 41, 4(1939): 136–58. Among the works most widely circulated are those of Buridan, Pelacani, Albert of Saxony, the English logicians, etc.

22. Interesting writings by Torni are contained in Riccardiano 930, including Marliano's discussion on problems of motion (c.26r). For the studies Leonardo made of Marliano, see Solmi, *Leonardo,* pp. 85–86; "Le fonti," pp. 207–09; Uccelli, *I libri,* pp. 153–54. But the picture of Florentine cultural life could be amplified: even a theologian like the conventual Gargano from Siena, who died in 1523, but who had been for many years, from the end of the Quattrocento, professor at the Studio, discussed questions of "physics" with men of science (see the ms. of the National Library of Florence, Conv. D. 2 502).

23. Savonarola, *Compendium totius philosophiae* (Venice, 1452), pp. 324 sqq. This does not mean, as Solmi believed he could conclude ("Le fonti," p. 47), that Leonardo had a broad knowledge of Albertus Magnus ("it could be concluded with certainty that Leonardo had read and reread the works of Albertus Magnus . . . but the ideas of Leonardo go way beyond Albertus in

depth and loftiness . . ."). As Uccelli observed, Leonardo quotes Albertus definitely and explicitly only once (*Codice Atlantico,* f. 210 r a), and not Albertuccio; and to what extent he drew directly from the great scholar, rather than from intermediaries or critics, has not been demonstrated either by the general comparisons of Solmi, or those of others.

24. This is the famous list in red ink of the *Codice Atlantico* (210 r a), which was studied thoroughly at the end of 1873 by Girolamo d'Adda. On the *Chiromantia* in particular, see the introduction by Frezza to the edition of the *Chiromantia* by G. Marzio (Naples, 1951).

25. For Leonardo's knowledge of Avicenna, see Solmi, "Le fonti," pp. 78–81. It should be kept in mind that Avicenna was a current text in university courses in medicine—as well as, at times, courses in philosophy. This is a specific reference to Andrea Cattaneo da Imola, of the hospital Santa Maria Nuova in Florence, under the gonfaloniere Pier Soderini, and a lecturer on philosophy at the Studio. Tignosi is well known as a physician and philosopher.

26. It is unnecessary to repeat here how much Ficino contributed to the philosophy of light. For his writings on perspective, see the *Vita* in Palat. 488 of the National Library of Florence—probably written by Caponsacchi, in which one may read: "He was also interested in mathematics and astronomy, and how much progress he made in these in a short time can easily be judged by many of his essays. He was also interested in perspective, and I have seen some of his written observations on vision along with others on plane and concave mirrors. . . ."

27. This is a very well-known text by Pico. Leonardo speaks of man as a microcosm in the *Codice Atlantico,* fol. 55v. In his *Oratio,* Pico called it *tritum in scholis.*

28. L. Olschki, *Geschichte,* 1: 260. The passage is also quoted by G. Castelfranco in his perspicacious essay "Il concetto di forza in Leonardo da Vinci," *Proporzioni* 3(1950): 121, which contains explicit affirmations on the spirituality of force, as it was understood by Leonardo. The Neoplatonic influence, in whatever way it might be evaluated, is integral to one of the essential theses of Leonardo's thought, although we should keep in mind, as I have tried to demonstrate elsewhere (*Scientia* Volume 46[1952]) the significance of "subtle and mobile matter" which is frequently to be attributed to the term "spirit."

29. Ficino, *Opera* (Basle, 1576), 1: 122–23.

30. Ficino, *Opera* 2: 1464r; see also, by Leonardo, Ms. *F.* fol. 27r–v (*I libri di meccanica,* pp. 1–3). On Plato as a source for Leonardo, see Solmi, "Le fonti," pp. 231–34 and *Studi sulla filosofia naturale di Leonardo da Vinci* (Modena, 1898), pp. 88–89. Solmi maintains in several cases that the derivation, rather than from the well-known *Timaeus,* was from Albertus Magnus. Solmi was always of the opinion, not in fact proven, that Leonardo had "read and reread" Albertus. But there is much more still to be said about some of Leonardo's "sources," as I have attempted to point out through several specific cases in a brief note for the *Colombaria* of Florence in 1953.

31. For Marullo, see M. Marulli, *Carmina,* ed. A. Perosa (Zürich, 1952), p. 136. (*Hymnorum* 3, I: Soli). The theory of vision would warrant a longer discussion (see Solmi, *Nuovi studi sulla filosofia naturale di Leonardo da Vinci* [Mantua, 1905], pp. 137–218). The influences of the *Prospettiva* of Peckham, of Vittelione (Alhazen), and of the *Prospettiva* of Bacon have been pointed out (See Solmi, "Le fonti," pp. 81–84, 226–27, 295–97). In other instances, it is a question of diffuse theories. See, for example, what is said in the *Codice Atlantico* (270v) about vision ("I say that visual capability extends through visual rays up to the surface of opaque bodies, and that the property of these bodies extends up to visual capacities . . ."). Ficino, in *Plotinum, De visione, Opera* (2: 1750), says: "Vision becomes possible mainly because either the visual ray proceeds from the eye to the visible object, or from the visible object, illuminated as it is, an image proceeds to the eye . . ."; which is then the theory of *Timaeus* (45 b), on which see Chalc. 257. Leonardo also said: "This soul of ours . . . keeps its spiritual members far distant from itself and one may see clearly in the lines of visual rays, which, having ended in an object, immediately transmit to their reason the character of the form of their breaking." Ficino, fol. 1751, says: "One [opinion] is that the [human] spirit reaches out by means of the rays of sight—which are not unlike hair or hands—in order to touch in this manner the sense-perceptible . . . ; the other [opinion] is that the spirit does not reach out by means of rays, but that they [of themselves] extend toward the object, like shoots, and that, from there, they are reflected to the spirit; the third [opinion] is that the light is shaped by the object and that, in this way, the shape is transmitted to the eye. . . ." This does not mean that Leonardo knew these passages in Ficino or Plotinus; it indicates the diffusion of certain discussions and also of certain images.

32. Cassirer, *Individuo e cosmo,* p. 85: "We know how close the actual relations between the Cusan and Leonardo were . . . how Leonardo took directly from the Cusan a great number of problems. . . . Leonardo traces back to the Cusan . . . and takes up his heritage. . . ." Solmi is on much more solid ground in "Nuovi contributi alle fonti dei mss. of Leonardo da Vinci," *Giornale Storico della Lett. Ital.* 58(1911): 304–05.

33. Duhem, *Études,* 2: 151.

Index

72 73 74 12 11 10 9 8 7 6 5 4 3 2 1